Jehovah God-like Mind is a Good Father-like Character

A 365-Day Devotional

Mizraiim Lapa-Pethe

Jehovah God-like Mind is a Good Father-like Character
A 365-Day Devotional

First published in Australia by Mizraiim Lapa-Pethe 2023.

Copyright © Mizraiim Lapa-Pethe 2023.
All Rights Reserved.

ISBN: 978-0-6485541-4-1 (pbk)
ISBN: 978-0-6485541-5-8 (ebk)

Typesetting and design by Publicious Book Publishing.
Published in collaboration with Publicious Book Publishing.
www.publicious.com.au

No part of this book may be reproduced in any form, by photocopying or by any electronic or mechanical means, including information storage or retrieval systems, without permission in writing from both the copyright owner and the publisher of this book.

DEDICATION

This book is dedicated to my newborn baby girl, my third-born, Christos, to the glory of the Father, Son and the Holy Spirit. Before I conceived her, God spoke into my heart and said I was going to have a child and name the child Christos (Christos meaning Christ, the bearer of Christ). Also during that time, God wanted me to write this book, *Jehovah God-like mind is a Good Father-like Character*, to show how Jesus Christ came and lived His name, which is His character that shows His love. His twelve common names are what I am writing about. Christos was to remind me of how God sent His Son, Jesus Christ, who carried His name and came to live the Father's name to show His love. All these encounters with God happened around September 2020. A year later I conceived, in September 2021, and during my pregnancy journey I started writing this book.

This is what God said through His Holy Spirit in my heart: I have an unborn baby within me who I love so much although I can't see her, and I am excited to meet her after she is fully developed in my image. This is also how we should love the Father. We can't see Him, so Jesus came and lived His name in flesh to show His love in living the Father's name. This is why the Father has given the name of Jesus power and authority over every other name.

Only in the name of Jesus Christ will every knee bow and confess He is Lord. Like how I love my unborn baby so much and am full of joy because my baby is alive in me and I will meet her soon, we too are to love God so much. We can't even see our heavenly Father, but we carry Jesus in us, and since He is alive in us we are to be always joyful and be excited that we will meet Him soon. I have to carry my unborn baby for NINE MONTHS for her to be fully developed in my image. We also need to carry Christ in living the NINE FRUIT of the Holy Spirit to be fully developed in the image of God. Jesus Christ came and lived our Father's character, His name. Now that we carry Christ in us, we have to live Christ's character, which is the nine fruit_of the Holy Spirit, so we can become that son and daughter who are called by our Father's name to inherit the twelve names of the Father, and live our Father's name in Jesus' name to the glory of the Father.

> *Bring my sons from afar and my daughters from the ends of the earth—everyone who is called by my name, whom I created for my glory, whom I formed and made (Isaiah 43:6-7, NIV).*

A special mention and thank you to Thomas Pethe for being a good father figure to Angelilly, Blessed and Christos. Without your support, caring, providence, understanding and love, this book would never be published. We have all fallen short of the glory of God, but God has never failed us in providing all we need through you. Also in memory of my dear papa Clark, I would like to crown our heavenly Father in heaven with thanks and praises, for always taking the form of my late papa, and appear in my dreams to show me answers to solve life's struggles and challenges of this world. This normally happen when I pray to the heavenly Father to give me solutions for my struggles. I am so blessed to still see and hear my papa Clark as that good spirit with the Creator of life.

> *….and the dust returns to the ground it came from, and the spirit returns to God who gave it. (Ecclesiastes 12:7, NIV).*

CONTENTS

Introduction	i
Why I wrote this book	iii
Special tribute: Sir Grand Chief Michael Somare.	vi
You should read this book	ix
To the partners of this book	x
What readers say about my previous books	xi
January: I AM Jehovah! Our Lord God!	1
February: Jehovah Nissi! I AM Your Banner!	44
March: Jehovah Adonai! I AM Your Master!	83
April: Jehovah Jireh! I AM Your Provider!	124
May: Jehovah Elohim! I AM Your Creator!	169
June: Jehovah Tsidkenu! I AM Your Righteousness!	214
July: Jehovah El Shaddai! I AM Your abundance of supply, all sufficient.	258
August: Jehovah M'Kaddesh! I AM Your Sanctifier.	304
September: Jehovah Shammah! I AM There for you! Your ever-present help!	345
October: Jehovah Rophe! I AM Your Healer!	392
November: Jehovah Rohi! I AM Your Shepherd!	442
December: Jehovah Shalom! I AM Your Peace!	483

INTRODUCTION

After publishing my first book in 2019, *Christ-like Mind is Child-like Character*, the Lord spoke instantly into my heart to write the book *Holy Ghost-like mind is a Good Mother-like Character*. Under the control of the Holy Spirit, I took that journey. It took me just a year to complete it. I have little ones to delay me, a one-year-old and five-year-old at that time, but because I was being used by the Holy Spirit everything was going at Spirit-speed.

I remember after publishing *Holy Ghost-like mind is a Good Mother-like Character* in 2020, God spoke into my heart to write a book about fathers, *Jehovah God-like Mind is a Good Father-like Character*. I told God it was impossible, as I only know some good characters of a father and my knowledge is limited in writing a 365 daily devotional, so for sure I would run out of words to write. However, what is impossible with man is possible for God. The seed God conceived in me that I said was impossible became possible as His Spirit rested upon me and raised me up to write this book.

The Revelation of the Father
This is how God revealed to me His love for us as a Father and that He is always at work for us. In the month of October, 2020, on a rainy day while I was driving, God showed me all the men working and doing different roles. He showed me builders and fathers who work in the office going into their work, and this is what He said, 'You see all these fathers are working so hard. The rain is pouring,

but look at the construction workers—they are still working. These men are fathers and are working to provide for their families. So am I. I too am working all the time to provide for my children. I am a Father full of love and compassion, and this is what you are going to write about. Jesus came and lived my name, my twelve common names. This is why I have given power and authority over to His name. His name lived my name and made it come alive so my children, who are co-heirs with Christ, can live in it.'

'Jesus mentioned that in John 5:17, He said, "My Father is at work and I too must work. I live my name and work by my name to provide. For example, I AM Jehovah Rophe, My name is healing and I work to heal you." And that is what Jesus did—He lived my name. You are going to write about my twelve names and how I, as a Father, work by my name, which is my Character. From January to December (twelve months), what you will write about is my twelve names. I introduced my name as "I AM" to Moses, and you are going to introduce again my twelve common names, which are my characters, in this book, *Jehovah God like-mind is a Good Father-like Character*.'

The insight He took me through in putting these writings into a book was amazing. As you go read, you will experience the anointing that was upon me to write it—all for the Father's glory.

Why I wrote this book

This book is written to show us that our heavenly Father is all loving and kind. Many people, especially in the past, thought He was an angry God who liked to punish anyone who sinned. We only reap what we sow, and yet we blame God whenever anything goes wrong in our life. Following are the twelve names of the Father that Jesus lived to show how loving and caring our Father is. We are now to live the Father's name in Jesus name to the glory of the Father.

His name is I AM! (Exodus 3:14)

1. I AM Jehovah - Our Lord God. (See Psalm 83:18, KJV).

2. I AM Jehovah Nissi - Our Lord God, our Banner! Moses built an altar and called its name, "The Lord is my Banner", to celebrate His victory over the amalekites. (See Exodus 17:15, NKJV).

   In Christ, our Father has raised us up like a banner in His Spirit to show our victory over sin and death to live His name, Jehovah Nissi in Jesus name.

3. I AM Jehovah Adonai - Our Lord God, our Master! He is the Master of our lives and no other thing must become master over our lives. We are to live like how our Master, Jesus, who lived the Father's name by taking the position of a servant, to serve and not to be served. (See Luke 9:38, KJV).

4. I AM Jehovah Jireh – Our Lord God, our Provider.! He provides in perfect timing when our need arises. We live our Father's name, Jehovah Jireh in Jesus name when we provide to others when they need us. (See Genesis 22:14, NIV).

5. I AM Jehovah Elohim - Our Lord God, our Creator! He creates in us a new heart and spirit when we renew our mind to have the mind of Christ. We are designed in the image of our Father to live His name and be creative to create new great things in our life in Jesus name. (See Genesis 1:1, NIV).

6. I AM Jehovah Tsidkenu - Our Lord God, our Righteousness! We are to live our Father's name by remaining in Christ who is the Father's righteousness. Everything will be given to us because we have seek first His kingdom and righteousness. (See Jeremiah 23:6, NKJV).

7. I AM Jehovah M'Kaddesh - Our Lord God, our Sanctifier! We are to live our Father's name by setting ourselves apart from the things of this world and be holy, because our Father is Holy. (See Leviticus 20:7-8, NIV).

8. I AM Jehovah El Shaddai - Our Lord God, our Abundance (Supplier)! He will supply abundantly even living standards of this world rise above us. (see Genesis 35:11, NIV).

9. I AM Jehovah Shammah - Our Lord God, who is there! The ever-present presence of the Father that will always go before and after us, wherever we want to go. We are to live our Father's name and be there to spend time in Word and prayer with Him on a daily basis. (Ezekiel 48:35, NIV).

10. I AM Jehovah Rophe - Our Lord God, our Healer! He heals us when we are sick or in any pain in life. To be healed and to be a healing to others. We are to live His name by remaining in His Word who is Jesus whom He sent to heal us. (Exodus 15:26, NIV).

11. I AM Jehovah Rohi - Our Lord God, our Shepherd! We are to live the Father's name as His shepherd to feed the lambs that Jesus asked us to. We will never be in want when we are led by our Shepherd through the voice of the Holy Spirit within us. (Psalm 23:1, NIV).

12. I AM Jehovah Shalom - Our Lord God, our Peace! He is our Peace when we feel alone and troubled in this world. We are to live our Father's name by producing the fruit of His Spirit, peace.

Jesus came and lived the Father's name to show us that our Father is LOVE. His name that Jesus lived is His character and that is who He is to show to us His love. The Father has given the name of Jesus power and authority over every other name. (Judges 6:24, KJV).

Mizraiim Lapa-Pethe

Special tribute in honour of the first Prime Minister of Papua New Guinea (PNG), Sir Grand Chief Michael Somare.

On September 14, 2019, I was on my way to PNG with my four-year-old daughter and six-month-old son. It was a divine meeting, I would say, as I bumped into our first Prime Minister at the Sydney International Airport. I say divine because I've been approached as the first Papua New Guinean to have written a daily devotional book. I stand humbled and corrected if I am wrong here, but as far as I have been told that is true, and to meet the first Prime Minister and sit down and chat with him was an honour.

I was on my way to PNG to launch the daily devotional book *Christ-like Mind is Child-like Character* and he was on his way to give a speech on the Independence Day celebration for PNG, coming up on September 16. He laughed with my kids and we spoke about many things. I mentioned to him one of his daughters, Emma Somare, who lives in Cairns. Emma is a godmother to my kids. When I mentioned about Emma, I saw his face light up with a smile, like any proud dad of their children. As he spoke to me about Emma, I could see a face looking back that was filled with good memories. He was not only a good father to his children, but a good father to our beautiful nation of PNG. He was the very one who stepped forward without fear and declared independence for PNG on September 16, 1975.

When Grand Chief Sir Michael Somare peacefully left earth to transcend on to another life, I led a forty-day prayer fasting for God to raise new leaders who would be good fathers in their homes so they can make great fathers to our nation, Papua New Guinea. One of the seeds, Sir Michael Somare, had gone down, and many would rise up from that.

Below is the devotional extract from December 7:

~ We have been set free to walk and live in peace ~

I will walk in freedom, for I have devoted myself to your commandments (Psalm 119:45, NLT).

April 25, 2021, was a beautiful Sunday morning, the last day of the forty-day prayer journey we took to give respect to the first Prime Minister of Papua New Guinea (PNG) who served his life very well to the nation. I asked the Lord to give me a Word to end this prayer journey.

I went to church that morning for a wonderful Anzac service where we celebrated the lives of the heroes who served Australia to defend freedom and peace. As I was looking at the front pulpit and thinking how nicely it was set up, and the sound system, the Holy Spirit gave me the word to end the forty-day journey: You see, there are some people who set up beautifully the front stage so you can come and enjoy the church service, with a lovely gifted music team. You don't have to do anything. It has been done already and you just came and enjoyed what was done. It was the same with the

Grand Chief, Sir Michael Somare. He has done everything already in bringing PNG into freedom by gaining independence, and so everyone born in PNG can live in freedom and peace. It's the same with Anzac Day—today, you remembered the lives of those who served Australia and laid down their lives so everyone born in Australia can enjoy the freedom of living in peace. And it is the same with the Son of God. He laid down His life so everyone who is born again in the kingdom of God can live in freedom and in peace. Jesus strongly stressed it Himself that He has given us peace to live in this world and be an overcomer.

Praise the Lord, whether we live in PNG, Australia or any part of the world. Jesus said, 'I come to serve and not to be served.' He laid down His life so everyone in this world we all live in who is born again can have freedom and live in peace.

So the message is this: Every day is the day that the Lord has made already for us to rejoice and be glad in it. The day has already been made new for us to enjoy that brand new 24 hours. We have a battle to face every day, but Jesus has given us peace to walk in victory and freedom.

You should read this book

This book is a must read to have a revelation of the Father. Once you have a personal encounter of who Your Father is and how great and powerful He is, you will never be asking Him for little things. I remember always asking Him for a million-dollar home along the beach—mortgage free. I always tell our Father, 'I know who you are and I ain't going to ask for little things.' And just like that, He struck the deal for me last year (2021). While I was struggling to save up for a $400,000 home loan deposit, he opened and parted the way and settled me in a suburb where a two-bedroom home starts from two million Australian dollars. As I write, I am humbled before the Father so He can lift me up and carry me more in His Almighty arms. For I do not know what the future holds, but I know our Father holds the future and He has great plans to give me hope and a successful future.

This book will help you to know who your Father is, and that as a child and an heir to His inheritance, you will inherit and live His name in Jesus' name. The devil will no longer trap you in living a limited life of struggle. In Jesus' name you will inherit our Father's name, and this is when you will find your name is called into high places where successful people are placed.

Mizraiim Lapa-Pethe

To the partners of this book

I would like to make a special mention to the awesome people who support me in the publication of this book. The gift offering seed you sow into this ministry to move our Father's kingdom will be measured back to you in hundredfold.

Anna and Johnson Lusin, Annell Ovia, Albertina Posa, Christina Adam, Debra Alim, Dorothy Yawinuai Hriefi, Elizabeth and Willie Edo, Emma Somare, Etty Fred Ruthana, Helen Teino, Jean and Ivan Molo, Joanne Kilip, Joanne Simons, Jennifer Gagau, Leah and Stanley Simons, Lucy Wani, Margaret and Gareth Rus, Maureen and Viliami Kalu, Nancy Kopyoto, Naomi Kuapaitam and Sarah and Fego Kiniafa..

Jehovah God-like Mind is a Good Father-like Character

What readers say about my previous books

Christ-like Mind is Child-like Character

I am speechless! Thank you Holy Spirit, thank you Abba Father ... your book is amazing, with powerful truths we need for our everyday lives. It was the Holy Spirit who gave you every word to write down. I am just crying reading your book. Most parts take me back to when my kids were babies, and as a mother I was raising them in the Word and principles of the Kingdom.

~Emma Somare~

In every beginning of my new day as I mother two toddlers, I find refreshing content and am overwhelmed by the outcome of the spiritual nourishment of this book. This serves me well with time spent with my children. It's an honour and a blessing to have had it hand-delivered to me here, in London, UK, by my inspiring and true friend, Mizraiim and her beloved daughter, Angelilly.

~Maggi Kawa~

Holy Ghost-like mind is a Good Mother-like Character

You know, beloved, I really appreciate that I AM reading this POWERFUL BOOK. So interesting, as I always wanted to really know the Holy Spirit and His role. Your knowledge, direct from the Holy Spirit, has opened my mind to really know who He is and his role. I came to know the Holy Spirit through reading one of Pastor Benny Hinn's books, 'Good Morning Holy Spirit'. Your book has really kept me busy on wanting to know the characters referring to a good mother. You quote the scriptures, then the inspiration of the quoted scripture. So powerful indeed.

~Cathy Tepa~

Hi Mizzy, I wanted to let you know that I have started reading your book and it is so beautiful and refreshing. It's like drinking a cool cup of water and hanging with the Holy Spirit. Much love and hugs to you and your precious family for Christmas. Thank you for being obedient to the Holy Spirit.

~Beth Byrnes~

Jehovah God-like Mind is a Good Father-like Character

JANUARY

I AM Jehovah! Our Lord God!

~ ALIVE in death ~

For none of us lives to himself, and none of us dies to himself. For if we live, we live to the Lord, and if we die, we die to the Lord. So then, whether we live or whether we die, we are the Lord's. For to this end Christ died and lived again, that he might be Lord both of the dead and of the living (Romans 14:7-9, ESV).

January 14, 2021, the Lord showed me how our life is like playing with a ball, and how you handle the ball to keep it going to win the game. As you play the ball on the field, you have your team members and supporters cheering you to take it home and put a score. So it is with your life, how you handle it and keep it going in running your race. Your faith teammates are the clouds of witnesses cheering you on to completion, to fight the good fight of faith and bring your life home, like how you take the ball home and put a score, you also take your life and bring it home, and this is how heaven gains a score.

I was pointed to this scripture (it's a gain to God when a saint dies):

In the sight of the Lord, the death of his faithful ones is valued (Psalm 116:15, ISV).

Years back, I knew of a good father who'd tell his family, 'Do not expect me to return home when I leave for work. Anything can happen to me. I can die or anything happens.'

He was preparing his family to accept the most fearful news no one would want to receive. He wanted his family to know in advance that God can take his life away at any time, so they must be prepared for that. Not only was he preparing himself to meet the Lord, but he was preparing his house to accept the day when he will be taken into glory to be with the Lord.

But, as it is written,

What no eye has seen, nor ear heard, nor the heart of man imagined, what God has prepared for those who love him (1 Corinthians 2:9, ESV).

God is our good, loving Father, Jehovah, our Lord God. He gave His own life to us in flesh through His only Son, Jesus Christ, who took it back home. Jesus has now given us the Holy Spirit, who lives inside us and is preparing us each day to bring our life home.

Each day of the month of January and every day, prepare yourself to live a life of love, joy and peace with yourself and others. Most of all, take into you the Word of God and let the Word in you prepare you to meet the Love of your life, Jesus.

January 1

~ Create your day in the goodness of the Father to overcome evil around you ~

You crown the year with Your goodness, And Your paths drip with abundance (Psalm 65:11, NKJV).

January 1, 2021, Angelilly, my six-year-old then, drew a beautiful picture for me. I loved her drawing and could see how happy she was for her creation of work. Then Blessed, my two-year-old, scribbled on it. She was so upset and hurt, and brought her work to me, complaining about what Blessed did.

This is what the Holy Spirit taught me: You see, God has blessed this new year with His goodness and gave you all the 365 days, made with love and filled with goodness. But because it falls into a fallen world, the enemy steals it by adding his version of evil onto it, just like that scribble which Blessed put onto Angelilly's good work. And this is why you go around being upset and complain about how your day was ruined. This is an evil world, but our Father has crowned it in His goodness. Use that goodness of the Father to create your day to overcome that evil.

I was reminded of the scripture in Psalm 65:11, 'You crown the year with Your goodness, And Your paths drip with abundance.'

> *Moreover, as for me, far be it from me that I should sin against the Lord in ceasing to pray for you; but I will teach you the good and the right way (1 Samuel 12:23, NKJV).*

Jesus came and lived His goodness each day, living our Father's name, Jehovah, our Lord God. Even on a Sabbath day, He was working, doing good things for people. He said, 'My Father is always at work and I too must be working' (see John 5:17). Evil increases when we good people stop doing good things. When we also stop praying, evil starts to rise up more.

Like how Blessed scribbled on Angelilly's good work of creation, we too must keep creating something good in our new day and stop the evil upon any good work happening to us or around us. When evil was scribbled upon the prophet Nehemiah doing a great work, He silenced those voices and said, 'Why must I stop the good work I am doing?' (see Nehemiah 6:3).

Every new day, live the Father's name, Jehovah, our Lord God of goodness, and rise up and pray against any evil that the enemy plans to work upon this new day. Stop and silence the voice of the enemy who would scribble on any good work that is going to happen for that day.

January 2

~ Let your heart always smell of the goodness of the Father ~

Our lives are a Christ-like fragrance rising up to God. But this fragrance is perceived differently by those who are being saved and by those who are perishing (2 Corinthians 2:15, NLT).

I explained to my two-and-half-year-old that Jesus lives in his heart, and I showed him his heart where Jesus is. Because of that, he would bring his heart to me and ask me to put perfume on Jesus in his heart. The morning of September 28, 2021, when I put on the perfume, he asked me to put it on Jesus in his heart. This is what the Holy Spirit taught me and opened my eyes to see: My son asked me to do this because as a child still in the spiritual realm, he can actually see that Jesus lives with us and is alive. Emmanuel is His name—God with us. He knows that perfume makes us smell nice and he wants Jesus to also smell nice.

We carry Him through the Holy Spirit we receive, and must make others smell this fragrance of Him. Before Jesus was to die, the woman with alabaster oil perfumed Him. Jesus regarded that as an act of worship to Him and said she was preparing His body for burial. We make Jesus smell nice in us when we die to self and walk in the Spirit. When we die to self we release a sweet fragrance of offering from us. To the enemy the smell is disgusting, just like how a dead person smells. This smell not only puts the devil off from coming closer to us, but also, how can he bother someone who is dead? You see, when someone is dead we can't talk to them or make them do anything, and this is how the devil views a body of Christ who is dead to sin.

> *For the death he died he died to sin, once for all, but the life he lives he lives to God. So you also must consider yourselves dead to sin and alive to God in Christ Jesus (Romans 6:10-11, ESV).*

Jesus lived our loving Father's name, Jehovah, and made a way for us back to the Father by showing us that the Father loves us so much and sent Him to connect us back to the Father. A good dad dies to self and makes sacrifices for his children so they can live the good life he desires for them. He sits in Word and prayer every day to lead him and show him the way to lead his children in that path. Jesus is the only way back to the Father.

Every day, we are to die to sin and become alive in Jesus, and become a sweet fragrance unto our loving Father in heaven.

January 3

~ Write a new story of God's love and live in it ~

> *...and have put on the new self, which is being renewed in knowledge in the image of its Creator (Colossians 3:10, NIV).*

This is the prayer of a good dad:

> *... for your love and kindness are better to me than life itself. How I praise you! I will bless you as long*

> *as I live, lifting up my hands to you in prayer. At last*
> *I shall be fully satisfied; I will praise you with great joy*
> *(Psalm 63:3-5, TLB).*

On September 27, 2021 on a beautiful warm Monday morning, I was at the beach taking beautiful photos of the kids. Because our place was close to the beach, most times I would just grab them and we'd head off to the beach, like that day, with messy hair but happy little humans—and that was what mattered. I got some lovely photos of them, and later worked on cropping out what I didn't like in the photos so I could make the images perfect. Whatever imperfection showing had to be cropped off.

This is what the Holy Spirit taught me: The kingdom of God is like this. You must crop out whatever is not of Christ in your old life so you can be the perfect image of the new life in Christ. The new life of Christ in you must be seen in your image.

The love of the Father is so perfect. Jesus showed us that love and lived the Father's name, Jehovah, our Almighty loving Father. We are to walk and live in love. Whatever is not of the nature of the Father's love has to be cropped out of our life. Some people may not be part of our new image of Christ, and so God will allow situations to cause us to crop them out. This is so they don't rub their bad habits on us and ruin our image and reputation.

Every day, walk in the power of love and crop out anything that comes in your path that is not of Christ's nature. When you write a new story to live, it should be a story with your 'old me' life images cropped out, leaving only the images of Christ's nature for people to read.

January 4

~ Your value is found in the throne room of God ~

He is before all things, and in him all things hold together (Colossians 1:17, NIV).

I was doing some home schooling with Angelilly, my six-year-old daughter, during the lockdown of winter, 2021. We were doing some place value of numbers. Because she was in year one, the activities were focused mostly on finding the values of 100s, 10s and ones. Sometimes there would be one exercise on 1000s. The numbers were placed according to their values under their correct context.

This is what the Holy Spirit reminded me: God places you right where you are because you have a value for that place. It doesn't matter what level of value you have, what matters is you have a value and a purpose to serve. You see, every number needs the place value of a Ones or Tens. They have a role to play, and without them the 'place values' of the bigger numbers will not be complete. So it is with you. Without you playing the role where God placed you, there will be incomplete functions.

As a body of Christ that houses the Holy Spirit, we have a value to serve right where we are. Each part of the body of Christ has a purpose to play, a role. You may think you are a just a little finger or toe, but without a toe or finger the body is incomplete and doesn't look good.

We may not like the country where we are, the marriage we feel stuck in, the house or the street we are at, BUT that doesn't matter if you are connected to the throne of God. The throne of God is where your value is found for you to serve from where you are at.

A good dad knows he is where God placed him. He has a value to play his role as a dad, husband and son. As long as he is a good son to His loving Father in heaven, he will be living and showing the Father's love in all the goodness he does. His value is in the goodness he displays in walking in the fruit of love.

Jesus lived our loving Father's name, Jehovah, and showed the value of how to live the Father's name. And it's in the fire that our values are polished more to become more valuable.

God places you right where you are, and He is right where He is, and He will always be where He is, on His throne. It doesn't matter where you are, as long as you are connected to Him your source of abundance will flow from the river of life where the throne of God is.

Connect yourself to the Word of God every day to get easy access to the throne room of God through His Holy Spirit.

January 5

~ Live the Father's name in Jesus' name to the glory of the Father ~

Therefore God exalted him to the highest place and gave him the name that is above every name, that at the name of Jesus every knee should bow, in heaven and on earth and under the earth, and every tongue acknowledge that Jesus Christ is Lord, to the glory of God the Father (Philippians 2:9-11, NIV).

On the morning of September 29, 2021, I was thinking of packing some of the stuff I wouldn't be using in a suitcase and labelling it with the name of what was in there. That way I could just look at the name on the suitcase and know what is in it.

This is what the Holy Spirit taught me: So is your name. It says who you are. When your name is mentioned, people who know you think right away of your identity, of who you are, what you do and where you live. Jesus lived our Father's name, and He wants us to know Him so we can know who our Father is, where He lives and what He does.

The name of our loving Father is His characters. Jesus lived in the name of the Father, and so the Father gave the name of Jesus power over everything. We are now to use our name in the name of Jesus to live the Father's name for His glory. Just like how the characters of the nine fruit of the Holy Spirit summarise the love of the Father, all the names of the Father are His character and it is summarised in the name of Jesus. This is because Jesus lives the Father's name. Jesus is the only way to the Father. He lives the Father's name, His nature, and He lives the nature of the Holy Spirit, which is the Spirit's nine fruit. Jesus, God the Son, flesh lived on earth to live the nature of God the Father and God the Spirit. There is power in the name of Jesus.

God, our loving Father, has a name, and His name is Jehovah. Jesus came and lived the Father's name, showing us who He is, where He lives and what He does. Jesus even said, 'How can we believe in Him the heavenly things if we cannot believe in Him the earthly things He is speaking of.' He was trying to connect earth to heaven so the Father's will in heaven can be done on earth.

> *But if you don't believe me when I tell you about earthly things, how can you possibly believe if I tell you about heavenly things? (John 3:12, NLT).*

Every new day is another day to look forward to connecting yourself to the Word of God, to connect your earth to heaven so the Father's will in heaven will be done on earth for you.

January 6

~ Let your body be an instrument to serve love ~

Do you not know that your bodies are temples of the Holy Spirit, who is in you, whom you have received from God? You are not your own; you were bought at a price. Therefore honour God with your bodies (1 Corinthians 6:19-20, NIV).

A good dad knows his body is not his own but has been bought at a high price. His body is the temple of the Holy Spirit and he is the body of Christ. The day he dies his name will no longer be mentioned to his lifeless body, rather, he will be named as 'the body'. To make his lifeless body 'the body' of Christ, he dies to Christ in his sinful nature while he is alive. So when he is dead, he only become alive in Christ. He knows His body which is dead is alive, because it is the body of Christ and Christ is alive. This gives him peace as he prepares his body to live for the glory of his loving Father in heaven.

Every day, he dies to his sinful nature in producing the fruit of righteousness. Being the body of Christ who has the mind of Christ (see 1 Corinthians 2:16). He has to meditate in Word and in prayer and renew his mind to have the mind of Christ.

Jesus came and lived our loving Father's name, Jehovah, so we can become sons who are like our Father, full of loving kindness to everyone around us. Our body lives in peace because our mind is set in peace.

Every day is another day to control our body with the fruit SELF-CONTROL to faithfully live and move as a body of Christ where the Holy Spirit lives. Let's be gentle and good to this gift of life we have. Do not let your body be an instrument to serve sin. You are the body of Christ where His Spirit lives.

January 7

~ *Glorify God with your mouth* ~

> *Let no corrupting talk come out of your mouths, but only such as is good for building up, as fits the occasion, that it may give grace to those who hear (Ephesians 4:29, ESV).*

A good dad watches over his body and takes care of it with gentleness because he knows his body is the temple where the Holy Spirit of His Father resides. He uses the fruit self-control to control what comes out of his mouth. Since the parts of the body action the content of the heart, he meditates daily in Word and prayer and renews his mind to say words that will build and not break. As the dad and husband he is the male figure that his children and wife look upon to build up their courage. He looks upon his loving Father in heaven, Jehovah, for His Word that comes out from His mouth and lives on His Word.

Jesus lived our Father's name, Jehovah, our Almighty Father, who is faithful in loving us. Jesus spoke with words of kindness to build our mind and heart. He is the spring of living water who speaks timely words of healing which is wisdom. Wisdom is timely words that give joy and peace to a weary soul.

> *Jesus answered, 'It is written: Man shall not live on bread alone, but on every word that comes from the mouth of God' (Matthew 4:4, NIV).*

The Word of our Father is food, and most of our words that come out of our mouths must be in line with what our Father thinks and says of us and others. Jehovah, our loving Father, says and thinks great things of us. Just like how we take food into our mouth and we become what we eat, we must also take into us the Word of God as the living bread to become alive in what the Word says of us.

The words we give out from our mouth become what we say. You see, if you eat unhealthy, fatty food your body will become what you eat. If you also give out unhealthy, negative words, you not only remain a lonely, broken person in life, but will also bring destruction to your connection.

Today, and every day, let's be kind, good and gentle with the words we release out of our mouths. Also, let's watch what we eat and have some self-control to only take into our mouth the right kind of food. Our body is the temple of the Holy Spirit. Let's watch what our mouth takes in and gives out. Just like how we take in food into our mouth for strength to live, we must also give out words that will build and strengthen someone. Let our mouth serve its purpose to the glory of the Father.

January 8

~ The Love from God only can pour out peace and joy over an anger strike moment ~

… and with your feet fitted with the readiness that comes from the gospel of peace (Ephesians 6:15, NIV).

A good dad is faithfully gentle and controls himself with his body actions when in a heated moment, just as he is watchful with his tongue to speak only life. He watches his feet to walk in peace.

His feet may stumble on whatever he walks through, but his shoe is custom made in peace for his feet. He lives Psalm 119:165 and makes it become his flesh always. Jesus did what our loving Father would do by washing the feet of the disciples so they could walk and live in peace. A good dad follows the footstep of Jesus so he can become like His Father in heaven.

> *Great peace have those who love your law, and nothing can make them stumble (Psalm 119:165, NIV).*

When someone is angry, they quickly walk off in a hurry, trying to find the person who has done them wrong. They do not want any delay; they want to quickly show up when the anger is fresh and release it out. When anger is fresh it comes out with so much force and can be hurtful to the receiver.

A good dad knows his body is the dwelling place of the Holy Spirit, and so he is gentle to himself and faithfully has self-control over any anger issue by using his feet to only walk in peace. Every day, he speaks life from his tongue into his feet to walk in peace and live in love with his family.

Our loving Father, Jehovah, is so full of love, and that love can pour out peace and joy to cool off any anger that rises in a boiling heat. Every day, let's live the peace of our Father and show off that peace by walking away from an anger strike situation.

January 9

~ *Glorify God with your tongue* ~

> *The tongue has the power of life and death, and those who love it will eat its fruit (Proverbs 18:21, NIV).*

A good dad knows his body is where the Holy Spirit, the Spirit of his loving Father, resides. He breathes inside of him, and in everything he does with his breath, he praises his loving Father, Jehovah.

He focuses and pays attention to the parts of his body and is careful in how he uses his body. He watches his tongue. Though the tongue is the smallest part of his body, it needs a lot of self-control to be gentle with the words it releases. It can build someone up or tear them apart. It's the entry of where life and death comes out.

The words his tongue speaks and releases builds his universe to live in. God spoke and declared His Word and the universe came into existence. A good dad also creates his own universe with his words. Every day he speaks life, he speaks joy and peace into his family. He controls his tongue with the fruit SELF-CONTROL to be GENTLE in declaring FAITHFULLY only words that will give life, light and love to himself and his family.

He renews his mind in the Word of life, light and love and allows his tongue to have a talk with the mind before it releases any words. He thinks before he speaks. He wants to declare words of life, just like his loving Father, Jehovah.

> *If you have been foolish enough to become proud and make plans against other people, stop and think about what you are doing (Proverbs 30:32, ERV).*

Jesus lived our Father's name, Jehovah, our loving Father. He spoke words of life, light and love. He is the life, light and love from the Father to show the world the love of the Father in action, not only in words. The Word who became flesh. There was healing in every word He declared upon all that needed healing. There was peace in

His Word to the troubled hearts, and there was eternal joy when He was raised from dead.

Jesus gave us this life, light and love to be at joy and peace all the time through the Holy Spirit who lives in us. And so, every day we have to pay attention to our tongue and speak words of life, light and love to ourselves and our contacts.

January 10

~ *Seeking God's wisdom to sow* ~

Unless the Lord builds the house, the builders labour in vain. Unless the Lord watches over the city, the guards stand watch in vain (Psalm 127:1, NIV).

A good dad knows His Father is a perfect gardener and will give him seed to plant for the harvest. He will not give him the wealth he desires but rather the seed, so he can ask him for wisdom to get wealth using that seed. He sows seed everywhere and remains in the Word and watches the seed prayerfully. Unless the Lord builds, the builder watches in vain. He not only prays but fasts as well. He fasts so he can make his flesh weak and his spirit strong to receive all the spiritual blessings in Christ in the spiritual realm. He invests his time in Word and prayer and actions his faith in sowing the seed so there will be abundance in store for his children and his children's children.

Jesus lived our loving Father's name, Jehovah, in showing His characters and principles of sowing and reaping. He is the very seed of the Father that the Father sowed into the world so He can reap many sons from His one and only Son. The only Son has not only all the treasures of the Father, but He is also the very wisdom of the Father.

> *The promises were spoken to Abraham and to his seed.*
> *Scripture does not say 'and to seeds,' meaning many people,*
> *but 'and to your seed,' meaning one person, who is Christ*
> *(Galatians 3:16, NIV).*

We are the harvest from the seed of Christ and we have to be fruitful in producing the fruit of the Holy Spirit every day.

January 11

~ *Everyone we come in contact with needs the fresh fruit of love from the Holy Spirit* ~

> *A new command I give you: Love one another.*
> *As I have loved you, so you must love one another*
> *(John 13:34, NIV).*

A good dad's goal is to make the fruit of the Holy Spirit productive in his house, so his rules and regulations to his children are to be kind, patient and good. He teaches his children to be faithful in doing it, and to have self-control to try not to do anything wrong. He also makes it clear to be careful and be gentle to life. Life is fragile. He teaches his children that no other relationship must steal the love, joy and peace they have found in their relationship with Jesus in the fruit of His Spirit. He watches his steps to follow in the footsteps of his loving Father in heaven, Jehovah. It is the faithful love of the Father that never fails, even when he goes out of step sometimes. And it is that same love that has the power to make him faithful, gentle and have self-control so he doesn't step out of living in the righteousness of Christ.

> *'I am Jehovah, the merciful and gracious God,' he said,*
> *'slow to anger and rich in steadfast love and truth.*
> *I, Jehovah, show this steadfast love to many thousands*

> *by forgiving their sins; or else* I refuse to clear the guilty, and require that a father's sins be punished in the sons and grandsons, and even later generations.'*
> *(Exodus 34:6-7, TLB).*

Jesus bears the love of the Father in carrying out and living His name. He carried all our pain, worries and suffering in that love. The love of the Father was greater than any sin and Jesus showed that love when He accepted the cup of suffering that the Father allowed, and He forgave freely the suffering that was poured upon Him on the cross.

Every day is a new day to carry out the new commandment to love one another the way Jesus loved us. Love is a fruit, and it's so refreshing to someone when we give them fresh love each day. They are renewed and filled with our love.

January 12

~ There is great reward for being faithful to God in your pains, struggles and shames ~

> *The Lord was with Joseph, so he succeeded in everything he did as he served in the home of his Egyptian master*
> *(Genesis 39:2, NLT).*

A good dad is always faithful in his relationship to his loving Father in heaven. The life of Job and Joseph speaks volumes to him, that faithfulness to Jehovah in the pains, struggles and shame brings around big success.

Job lost everything anyone could not even lose in a lifetime, yet he remained faithful to God with his breath, which was the only thing he had left. Let everything that has breath praise the Lord because you are alive. And Job did that.

This is what I read about Joseph:

Joseph shared one father, Jacob, with his siblings, while four different mothers gave birth to them. One was his aunt (his mother's sister) and two were his mother and aunt's servants. His father was known as a liar and cheater who cheated his own twin brother, Joseph's uncle. Joseph was hidden by his mother and ran away to Joseph's grandfather (the father of his mother, Rachael) only to harvest what he sowed. His father in-law also lied and cheated on him. It was too embarrassing and shameful to have a father like Jacob in society in those days. If that was not enough, Joseph's own brothers hated him and had him sold to traders to go through suffering for thirteen years. Joseph thought life was doing great because his boss favoured him, but then the wife of his boss accused him of an attempt of rape upon her and he ended up in prison.

This was more than enough to get mad at God, but Joseph remained faithful to God and trusted the process he was going through. He knew God and he knew what they meant for evil, God meant for good (see Genesis 50:20). And we know how successful this man became because of being faithful.

Not only have we entered a time of hardship with the pandemic that has cost our faith, but we have everyday battles personally that will make us remain faithful to God, or see us go out into the world to find a solution.

That's why the most important thing you can do is build, maintain and prioritise your relationship with God. Jesus suffered in pain and was humiliated and mocked in public, but He remained faithful and humbled Himself to the cross. And at the cross He forgave everyone who had caused Him hardship. This is how great and big the Father's love is, to which He lived His name, Jehovah.

January 13

~ Let your inner man who has Christ become alive ~

Put on then, as God's chosen ones, holy and beloved, compassionate hearts, kindness, humility, meekness and patience (Colossians 3:12, ESV).

One winter's evening, June 9, 2021, I was cooking chicken drumsticks. I decided to boil up the chicken then cut it into small bits to have it as chicken and vegetable soup. After removing the hot cooked chicken from the pot, I placed it on the plate. Then I thought *it's easier and faster if I just let the cold water run through it so it will be cold for me to hold and cut into smaller bits.* After I did that, it was cold enough for me to start removing bits from it into smaller pieces. As I started peeling it, I felt how hot it was from the inside. The hot inner part of the chicken was the actual state of its condition.

This is what I heard the Holy Spirit say: Whatever the state of our condition, it will remain as it is from the inside. We may try to put something into our outer appearance to make us look cool, and that we are good in the eyes of others, but who we are will still remain the same. Our inner state of character is the real us.

If someone is always angry, they may pretend to be a good, loving person, but the more you rub around them, you will discover the hot tempered person they are.

A good dad faithfully controls his SELF with the fruit self-control so he doesn't do something that will grieve the Holy Spirit when his human nature is attacked by surprise.

Jesus came and lived our loving Father's name, Jehovah. He had all the inner qualities of our good loving Father. There was nothing good about His appearance, but the more His disciples and those who knew Him rubbed onto Him and stuck with Him, they discovered all the goodness, compassion, mercy and kindness that flowed out from Him in abundance.

January 14

~ Being slow to anger is having patience in your anger ~

Love is patient (1 Corinthians 13:4, NIV).

A good dad doesn't complain aggressively from his home. When dogs bark aggressively from their home, no one will go near that home. So it is with the dad. If he gets easily offended and gets angry all the time, he cannot be good company and no one will want to be where he is. Most of all, the Holy Spirit won't be able to produce His joy in his life, for the Holy Spirit cannot live in a home that is full of anger.

Any dad can run out of love, joy and peace if he is full of anger. And this is why a good dad sits daily in Word and prayer and asks His Father in heaven to fill him with His love that is able to flush out any anger and resentment. Every day he sits in the Word and in prayer to empty out any anger kept inside of him towards anything and fill himself with peace and joy. He prays and asks forgiveness of what made him angry until he feels that peace and joy. Whenever that anger tries to come back, he is gentle, patient and kind to himself by applying self-control to control himself from being angry. The more he faithfully removes anger, the more he finds peace within himself.

> *The Lord is gracious and compassionate, slow to anger and rich in love (Psalm 145:8, NIV).*

Jesus lived our Father's name, Jehovah. Our Almighty loving Father is slow to anger. This is patience in anger. Jesus was patient with His anger many times and filled it with peace. He was peace Himself and has to be at His place of peace always.

Every day we are to live in love and live our Father's name. He is love, and love is patience in everything, even in anger.

January 15

~ *Slow down when you are about to collide into anger* ~

> *A hot-tempered person stirs up strife, but the slow to anger calms a dispute (Proverbs 15:18, NASB).*

Just like a car that goes with force when it's in motion, but you control it within its speed limit so no accidents take place, a good dad understands that is how anger also moves. It moves with strong force to knock him out because the dark forces are behind it. He has to control his SELF to be gentle, just like how a car is controlled when driven in its speed limit. It's alright for him to get angry so he can express what he is not happy about, but he has to be slow in his anger by being patient, gentle and kind in how he deals with his anger.

Road signs will also say to slow down! This is to avoid colliding with what is ahead, and so it is with us when it comes to dealing with anger. We have to slow down. Our loving Father in heaven is slow in anger and is patient with our rebelliousness.

Jesus lived our Father's name, Jehovah, our loving Father. He never allowed what people said to upset Him about His relationship with His Father. He just let His actions speak the love of the Father. He nailed perfectly what the Father's love is when He was nailed on the cross.

Every day lets nail away and crucify our rebellious self that wants to hurry off and get angry. Let's be gentle and kind in how we use our tongue, even if we are angry.

January 16

~ We are paid with love and we owe God love ~

For I will be merciful toward their iniquities, and I will remember their sins no more (Hebrews 8:12, ESV).

One winter's night, August 29, 2021, my two-year-old child got my six-year-old child's piece of craft work and played with it. While playing, it got torn. I told him to collect the rubbish and put it in the bin before his sister saw it or he would be in trouble with her. His sister, who was outside, heard it and ran quickly into the house. She asked me, 'What did my brother do?' And I said, 'Oh well, you have to ask him yourself.' So she went to him and asked him. Her little brother took her to the trash bin and showed her what he'd done, then began hugging her as a way to show her he was sorry. Instead of being upset, his sister was moved by his gestures and hugged him back with forgiveness.

Our Father, Jehovah, is so loving and full of compassion. His love is so full of patience and faithfulness that He is waiting for us to go and show him the damages we have done and go into His loving, open arms of forgiveness. We must own up to Him our sins and not hide them away. His love is greater than any sin, more peaceful than any broken and troubled heart, and His joy is stronger than any pains in our lives. Little children display the characters of the kingdom of God and my two-year-old toddler was showing that.

> *Yes, now I see it all—it was good for me to undergo this bitterness, for you have lovingly delivered me from death; you have forgiven all my sins (Isaiah 38:17, TLB).*

Jesus came and bought our sins and wrong doings with His precious blood. The value and worth of our life was so high it cost His life, position and title, just so He could bring us back to our loving Father, Jehovah. We are fully paid for with love and we owe God love, to love Him with all our heart, soul and body.

January 17

~ We need God to survive ~

> *The faithful love of the Lord never ends! His mercies never cease. Great is his faithfulness; his mercies begin afresh each morning (Lamentation 3:22-23-NLT).*

A sign on a church notice board read, 'Try God Week'. The idea was simple enough: if you try Him for a week and don't like the results, you can go back to your old life. A fish doesn't try water; it needs water to survive. A plant doesn't try soil; it needs soil to grow. Likewise, we don't try God, we need God. For us to grow and root into Him we need to produce the fruit of LOVE.

Fish get lost easily in the water because this is where they freely survive. We also are to get lost easily in the temple of God because that is where we survive freely. Jesus was lost in the temple.

Any dad can be loyal to their family, but a good dad is not only loyal to his family but is faithful to his wife as well. As long as he remains committed and faithful to his loving Father in heaven by walking in obedience to His instructions, he remains a faithful partner to his wife and dad to his children. That is his place of happiness and this is where he finds his happiness.

The love of our Father, Jehovah, is faithful. As a loving Father, He is faithful and committed to loving us. Our happiness and growing well in our Father's love comes from making someone happy in serving them. Let's be faithful in our relationship with Jesus and produce the fruit of love that the Holy Spirit produces in us. Let that be our place of happiness.

January 18

~ Renew your mind to think more of the Word and less of you ~

Humble yourselves before the Lord, and he will lift you up in honour (James 4:10, NLT).

A good dad walks in humility. That doesn't make him a door mat for people to walk on, but rather, he leaves behind every ego on a doormat and acknowledges God as his loving Father who is the source of what he has. He gives all credit to God.

Humility is not thinking less of yourself, but thinking of yourself less. John 3:30 comes to work. Jesus becomes great and you become less. You think of yourself less and think of Jesus more. What would He do if He was walking in your shoes? To know Him and what He would do, you have to have a daily relationship with Him in Word and prayer.

Jesus walked in humility until death. He thought of Himself less and of the Father more. You ask why or how—because He is God. You see, He was God the Son, and He was sent by the Father so He had to live by what God, the Father, assigned Him to do. He was living the Father's name more than His own to show the Father's love. This is why the Father exalts His name above all names and gave Him power. The name of Jesus has lived the name of the Father perfectly.

> But Jesus replied, 'My Father is always working, and so am I.' (John 5:17, NLT).

We are now to live our Father's name, Jehovah, in Jesus' name, in everything we do. Jesus becomes great and we become less. Our loving Father, Jehovah, is always at work. We too must be at work in whatever we do, knowing that we do it in Jesus' name for the Father's glory.

January 19

~ Follow the steps of Jesus and walk in peace ~

> Be imitators of me, as I am of Christ
> (1 Corinthians 11:1, ESV).

July 29, 2021, while doing home schooling one morning, I noticed that Angelilly was beginning to write well. In fact, her writing was beginning to be like mine because she was following me. Most times when we were home schooling I would be writing research or the discussion we'd do, and after that she would write it out herself.

Our loving Father is Love and wants us to love unconditionally. This is why He came in our form through the God Son. The more we follow Him in the way He walked, we will begin to walk like Him. You see, Angelilly was following me in how I wrote, and she began to write like me when her writing was improving. We too will begin to walk in love like Jesus when we start spending time in His Word and walking in obedience to the Word. Our life will also improve and become like Jesus'.

A good dad wants to be like his good Father in heaven, to love like Him all the time, and so he follows His Word and actions what His Word says. He talks to the Father in prayers to prayerfully prepare the way of his lifestyle to live only in what the Word says. He hears and sees with compassion through the lens of love.

> *Follow God's example, therefore, as dearly loved children and walk in the way of love, just as Christ loved us and gave himself up for us as a fragrant offering and sacrifice to God (Ephesians 5:1-2, NIV).*

Jesus was the love of the Father, Jehovah, and lived His name. He washed the feet of His disciples to demonstrate that our feet are to walk in peace and bring love to people. We are to walk like Jesus, who is the peace from the Father.

Every day there is a war going on inside of us to choose good over evil, and we are to walk like Jesus and be at peace with ourselves. He has made peace between our old rebellious self and our new life (see Ephesians 2:15).

January 20

~ Jesus took the uncomfortable position at the cross so we can have a comfortable position in the Holy Spirit, our Comforter~

> *Now let your unfailing love comfort me, just as you promised me, your servant (Psalm 119:76, NLT).*

July 28, 2021, Angelilly was not wearing a shoe when riding her scooter, hurt her big toe and made it bleed. I put some ointment on it and got a Band-aid to cover it. I thought it was alright without a Band-aid as it was not something big requiring me to over-nurse it, but I went ahead and put one on, only to realise there was no point at all as it could not be positioned well where the cut was on her toe. She then got up and told me she, '… do not feel comfortable with that Band-aid.' I told her, 'I knew this was going to happen and I shouldn't have put the Band-aid on, but I just went ahead and did.'

Jesus already knew the uncomfortable position at the cross. He knew, and didn't like the pain He was to suffer, but because of the Father's love and for us to receive forgiveness, He stepped into the uncomfortable, painful position so we can have access to our rightful, comfortable position to rule and reign with Him, and also to receive the comforter, the Holy Spirit.

> *What a wonderful God we have—he is the Father of our Lord Jesus Christ, the source of every mercy, and the one who so wonderfully comforts and strengthens us in our hardships and trials. And why does he do this? So that when others are troubled, needing our sympathy and*

> *encouragement, we can pass on to them this same help and comfort God has given us (2 Corinthians 1:3-4, TLB).*

Our Father, Jehovah is His name, and He is love. Jesus lived our Father's name and we are to live that name too. We may never be able to love someone who betrays our trust and puts us in an uncomfortable position, but we can love them with our Father's love by taking them to our Father and asking Him to forgive them because they do not know what they are doing. Jesus did that to the ones who beat and crucified Him to death.

So when you find it hard to love easily when your love is betrayed, listen—Judas betrayed Jesus, and that was the moment the great love of God was exposed. It is at such moments that you are to show that you have your Father's perfect love.

January 21

~ God is love ~

> *For God so loved the world that he gave his one and only Son, that whoever believes in him shall not perish but have eternal life (John 3:16, NIV).*

On the morning of July 20, 2021, I was doing home schooling with Angelilly. We would do the research, then I would write it in my handwriting. Then she would write again with her handwriting in her workbook. The story and work is hers and it's in her handwriting, which shows that it belongs to her.

Our loving Father wants our own writing that His Word belongs to us. And this is why He had to be in the form of flesh through the

Son, so we can have access to our own writing. The Word becomes flesh. Jesus lived what was written about Him. Jesus showed us everything about the Father and to know that He is all loving and wants us to live the life like the Son.

Jesus wrote the story of love again for the woman caught in adultery. (See John 7: 53- 8:11). When we feel we belong, we feel loved. There is a law placed to stone the woman for her sinful act, but with the fruit of the Spirit there is now no law (see Galatians 5:22-23). Love covers all sin (see 1 Peter 4:8).

We are to write in our own writing what Jesus wrote for us in love, and we must live that life of love.

> *Dear friends, let us love one another, for love comes from God. Everyone who loves has been born of God and knows God. Whoever does not love does not know God, because God is love (1 John 4:7-8, NIV).*

Love makes you look at someone with compassion and not judgement. A good dad looks with compassion without judging. He focuses on supporting his house to grow in love, to feel belonging so they can live the story of love. He focuses to see and love through the perfect love of our loving good Father, because his own love is limited.

Jesus lived and showed us that our Father is so loving. He lived our Father's name, Jehovah. Our Father is love. He is our love and will always be our love. Jesus dined with sinners and spoke to them because they are the very reason the Father sent Him, so they can rewrite their story of love of how they are accepted and how they feel belonging.

January 22

~ God is love, love is patient. Patience is a living person (the fruit of the Spirit becomes a person when we action it) Flesh become word ~

Love is patient (1 Corinthians 13:4, NIV).

A good dad wakes each day and takes his time to patiently wait upon His Father in heaven to teach him His Word to be patient for the day. As a dad to his children, and as a husband, he has to be patient. His wife blooms in love when he is patient with her. His children seek him more to teach them when he is patient with them. The love of the Father from patience takes time and effort to grow in him so he can be that good dad.

Whatever he is wearing for the day, he reminds himself that he is wrapped with love and clothed in patience.

If you have a fruit tree in your home that produces a lot of fruit, you and your family will share with your neighbours and friends. So it is with us. We are a home to the Holy Spirit who has the fruit from the Tree of Life—Jesus. Our Father is the gardener and His name is Jehovah El Shaddai, our Almighty Father, He is our Abundance. He is producing the fruit of the Spirit in abundance, because He is always at work (see John 5:17). Jesus came and lived the love of our Father, Jehovah, to show us that His loving kindness is patiently waiting for us with open hands to return home.

The Lord is not slow in keeping his promise, as some understand slowness. Instead he is patient with you, not wanting anyone to perish, but everyone to come to repentance (2 Peter 3:9, NIV).

Today, let's share the fruit of patience with our family, friends, neighbours and wherever we are engaged to live and work. Let's action love through patience every day.

January 23

~ God is committed in loving us ~

Hope never makes us ashamed because the love of God has come into our hearts through the Holy Spirit Who was given to us (Romans 5:5, NLV).

One winter's day, July 11, 2021, I was thinking of the commitment I had and was trying to attend to it (posting some things to a friend). This is what the Holy Spirit taught me: Your Father in heaven is also committed in loving you. God loves us so much and sent His only Son into the world to save us. The love that loves us when we are in the world is for our FLESH. We receive His love and have the relationship with His Son in the Word (the Word who has become flesh). And then He gives us His Holy Spirit. Our Father is still committed to loving us by pouring His love through the Holy Spirit (see Romans 5:5).

This is a specific love for us believers who are committed in remaining in the Word, the love for our SOUL, the eternal being, through the eternal Word of the Father. Then finally comes the LOVE that the Holy Spirit produces in us (see Galatians 5:22-23). This is the LOVE for our SPIRIT which our flesh has to action and produce. This is the love that shows our Father's love, that we receive Jesus and we have a relationship with the Father in the Word. This is the perfect love of the Father where we live and walk—the love that can make us love our enemies.

> *But the fruit of the Spirit is love, joy, peace,
> patience, kindness, goodness, faithfulness, gentleness,
> self-control; against such things there is no law
> (Galatians 5:22-23, ESV).*

Our loving Father, Jehovah El Shaddai, our Almighty Father is our Abundance. His Love is in abundance and has filled the earth. Regardless of us failing Him, our Father's love for us never fails. He is committed to loving us.

January 24

~ The real you is your inner being, how you pour out yourself to behave ~

> *He is the image of the invisible God, the firstborn of all creation. For by him all things were created, in heaven and on earth, visible and invisible, whether thrones or dominions or rulers or authorities—all things were created through him and for him (Colossians 1:15-16, ESV).*

On the night of July 4, 2021, I was watching a show on television, 'Farmer Wants a Wife', where forty beautiful ladies were competing to win the hearts of five farmers. As the farmers made their way into the room, the ladies would start commenting and saying how 'these guys look so good!' in their actual presence, more than the image they saw online. This is what I heard the Holy Spirit say: You see, people may try to make themselves look how good-hearted and caring they are in the electronic world, but the actual who they are is what they do in their real life every day. The ladies saw the images of the farmers just to give them the insight of who they were, but when the farmers appeared to them, they saw who they actually were and they even commented on how good looking the farmers appeared in person.

All the prophets of God were talking about the day Jesus would come and show the Father's loving kindness and His goodness in saving mankind from the nature of sin and evil. Many of those heroes of faith who are now cloud of witnesses (see Hebrews 12) saw it only from a distance. The eyes of faith. All of them have longed to be in the times of A.D.

Jesus came and made His appearance for us to taste and see that our Father is good. What the prophets spoke of Him was not received well by people, but when He appeared Himself, everyone was in awe of the great things He did to glorify the Father. Even the prophetess, Anna, said she could now die because the day she had been waiting for, for Jesus to come, had arrived and she had seen the salvation of mankind (see Luke 2:36-38).

> *The Word became flesh and made his dwelling among us. We have seen his glory, the glory of the one and only Son, who came from the Father, full of grace and truth (John 1:14, NIV).*

Every new day is another opportunity to show in appearance the love of our Father, Jehovah, so He can get the glory He originally designed in us.

January 25

~ The love of the Father has set us free ~

> *… and you will know the truth, and the truth will set you free (John 8:32, ESV).*

One cold morning, July 26, 2022, I looked out the window and could see the black clouds hanging around closely. There was a tree outside the house which the clouds covered. All I could see was the shape of the tree in the dark clouds. It was already 6 am, but the place was still dark. After a while, the clouds cleared and I saw that beautiful tree with its original colour of green. This is what I heard the Holy Spirit say: This is how the dark forces surround and cover us to keep us blind and hide our original design of who we are. They can also use us to attack other flesh and blood. This is why we have to get into the Word, for it is the light to remove this darkness.

You see, our Father Jehovah, our Lord God, loves us so much and wants to restore us back to our original image of who we are in Christ, and so He sent Jesus Christ to us.

Jesus lived our Father's name, Jehovah, our Lord God, and came to us as a shepherd. He had to leave the ninety-nine righteous and look for that one lost sheep. The other ninety-nine were well fed and had shelter already. He was concerned about that one lost sheep that was stolen to be killed and destroyed by the enemy.

Like me, seeing the dark clouds over the beautiful tree, hiding its original beauty, we too were trapped somewhere, blind and with no sight to come back home to the Father. We were cold, hungry and without shelter and life.

> *The thief comes only to steal and kill and destroy.*
> *I came that they may have life and have it*
> *abundantly (John 10:10, ESV).*

That lost sheep was stolen by the enemy to be killed and destroyed. Trapped and blind, it could not find its way home and was dying slowly without the truth. You and I are that lost sheep Jesus rescued, but He had to pay the price to set us free. Our Father loved us so much that He gave Jesus to us to pay the price with His life.

Every day is a new day to celebrate the freedom of being alive in Christ. The first breath that you wake up to is to praise the Lord. Let everything that has breath praise the Lord (see Psalm 150:6).

January 26

~ *The Holy Spirit is the proof that you are already being bought with the blood of Jesus* ~

> *In him you also, when you heard the word of truth, the gospel of your salvation, and believed in him, were sealed with the promised Holy Spirit, who is the guarantee of our inheritance until we acquire possession of it, to the praise of his glory (Ephesians 1:13-14, ESV).*

Just like how you make a deposit so an item can be put aside for you until you return with the complete payment, the Father has deposited the Holy Spirit into us as the payment from what Jesus has done. The finished work will be done when Jesus returns Himself and takes us into Him to share the Father's glory.

> *And I am certain that God, who began the good work within you, will continue his work until it is finally finished on the day when Christ Jesus returns (Philippians 1:6, NLT).*

There was a caravan that cost $6,000 that I wanted so badly. I made a deposit of $300 to claim ownership and said, 'Give me some time to prepare a place for that caravan and I will come back and complete the rest of the payment.'

So it was with the Holy Spirit when Jesus died. He made the payment with His blood, and by faith when we believed in Him, our Father deposited into us the Holy Spirit and set us aside for Him. Jesus has returned to the Father to prepare a place for us (see John 14:2-3). Once He prepares a place for us in the Father's house, He will come back for us and complete Himself as the head to our body. The head and the body have to become one to live in the Father's house, but for our body to fit the head of Christ, it has to house the Holy Spirit.

The Holy Spirit is the perfect love of Christ in our body to make our body perfectly fit Him as the head. Only when we become that body for the Holy Spirit and make Him feel at home, then we will be that perfect body to the head of Christ to live forever in the Father's house.

Jehovah, our loving Father, loves us so much He did everything possible for us so we can live with Him forever in heaven. The enemy doesn't like this and is doing everything he can to steal, kill and destroy us so we won't have the freedom to live but will be chained and trapped in our self-centred life.

Every new day comes with new opportunities to help us grow perfectly in the Father's love by continuing to give love to those who cause us wrong.

January 27

~ Make space in you to receive new beginnings from the Father ~

In the same way, let your light shine before others, that they may see your good deeds and glorify your Father in heaven (Matthew 5:16, NIV).

June 24, 2021, I was typing on my phone, making space to paste the writing I had extracted from another source, when the Holy Spirit opened my eyes to see in a vision a vacant land. The land was cleared and ready for planting to take place. You see, the kingdom of God is like this. When you want to do something new, you must make space for those new things. Some things need to be cleared out or removed for the new beginnings. Your Father in heaven is so loving and good that when He wants to bring something good in your life, He will burden you to give away what you have so you can make space to receive something new from Him.

When the rich man wanted to follow Jesus, He told him to give his riches to the poor. Jesus was asking him to let go of what he had to make space for the eternal riches that he would receive in following Him (see Matthew 19:21).

A good dad strives each day to be like His loving good Father in heaven, and so he sits in the counsel of His Word. There may be some directions in life that the Father directs Him towards and he may not like it, but as long as it's the Father's leading, he will follow the lead of the Father.

> *You are good and do only good; make me follow your lead (Psalm 119:68, TLB).*

Jesus came to live and show us that our Father, Jehovah, is all loving and only wants good in our life. People of the past thought Jehovah was always angry, and that whenever anything bad happened in their lives it was Him punishing them. Our Father in heaven is not a bad Father; it's the bad things we do that we reap the harvest of.

Every day is another opportunity to plant a seed of a good deed so anyone who sees that will praise our Father in heaven. The enemy is now attacking us to show how good we are at doing something and then displaying it on social media. Pride can slowly creep in when we think how good we are over someone and focus on getting praises from people for our own gain.

January 28

~ God's love is goodness ~

If you, then, though you are evil, know how to give good gifts to your children, how much more will your Father in heaven give good gifts to those who ask him! (Matthew 7:11, NIV).

January 28, 2021, I was having lunch with Angelilly. She kept moving and moving. I realised her feet were going into a shopping bag I'd brought back from one of my visits to Papua New Guinea (PNG). I was upset and quickly asked her to remove her feet, because it wasn't just a shopping bag. The bag, brought all the way from PNG, had a beautiful picture of the PNG bird of paradise.

This is what I heard the Holy Spirit say: The kingdom of God is like this. A dad is not just a dad. He is a good dad on earth when he sits in the counsel of the teachings of His Father in heaven. Just like that bag you brought all the way from PNG, his life is all the way from the eternal life of Jesus, the good life of abundance that Jesus gave for us all to enjoy.

Our Father in heaven is loving and His Spirit produces His love in the fruit of goodness inside of us. This fruit of goodness from the Holy Spirit is the gift of life Jesus gave. Jesus lived a good life in overcoming evil when He laid His life down. There is life and death, and there is good and evil. The goodness of Jesus' life gives us eternal life and the evilness of being disobedient to that life brings eternal death.

Every day is a new good day that arrives into this fallen, evil world. We are to make it become better by living in the loving kindness of our Father's love, in giving that love by being good all the time.

January 29

~ God's Word will always accomplish His purposes ~

... so is my word that goes out from my mouth: it will not return to me empty, but will accomplish what I desire and achieve the purpose for which I sent it (Isaiah 55:11, NIV).

It was March 20, 2021, when a friend sent me a message about delivering food to the needy. I got involved with some lovely friends who were delivering food to anyone in the community who was going through struggles. My friend explained to me that as soon as the food comes to them, they deliver it right away as it can be used while it's fresh. The food ranges from bakery items to vegetables, frozen goods, fruits and canned food. I really don't know how fresh this food is, but as soon as it comes to my friend it is delivered to our contact list.

This is what I heard the Holy Spirit say: The kingdom of God is like this. When you receive the teaching of the Word of God from someone, you do not know how fresh it is from that person who delivers it to you, but the Word of God still achieves the purpose it is designed for, just like the food you give out. You do not know how fresh it is, but it still does its purpose and satisfies a hungry person. So it is with the Word of God that goes forth; it accomplishes its purpose.

It is good to receive your spiritual food through someone, but it is even better when you receive it fresh from God Himself, in His Revelation, because then you will know how fresh it is. And when you serve that revelation of the Word right away to someone, they will taste the delicacy of its freshness. The timely Word for the season makes them taste and see that the Lord is good (see Psalm 34:8). The Word of God is food. Good food to make us grow stronger, and healthier, in our relationship to God, others and ourselves.

A good dad always longs for His Father in heaven, He is always hungry and thirsty for His righteous Word, and so His Father feeds Him right out of His mouth every time he seeks Him in His Word. Just like any good dad that works hard to feed and satisfy the hunger of his family, our loving Father in heaven feeds us instantly when we seek Him in hunger. The fresh revelations of Himself from His Spirit inside us is the fresh spiritual food to our spirit. Physical food is taken from outside of us, into us, to sustain and give strength to our body. Spiritual food is taken from inside of us from the Word we received to give us strength to become an overcomer.

Jesus is the Word of God who has become alive in us. Man cannot live by bread alone, but by every Word that comes from the mouth of God. Jesus showed us our Loving Father, Jehovah, our Lord God, by becoming His living bread, the living manna from heaven. He is the very Word of the Father that comes out of His mouth.

January 30

~ God's love is joy ~

I will praise you each day and always honour your name (Psalm 145:2, CEV).

I have noticed that almost every morning, Blessed (my almost two-year-old) will wake up and run with excitement when he sees either me or his dad. February 17, 2021, I remember him doing it again. A naturally happy boy since birth, as I was watching him getting so excited to see us I heard the Holy Spirit say: The kingdom of God is like this. A good dad will always be a child to His Father in heaven. Every new day, when his loving Father calls him to wake up to it, he runs into His Father's lap with gratefulness that he is able to see Him. He understands that seeing a brand-new day is seeing Him, because He made that day for him to live again. And it's a JOY to be alive. It's that joy of the Lord that gives him strength to work and provide for his house.

This is the day that the Lord has made; let us rejoice and be glad in it (Psalm 118:24, CEV).

Our loving Father, Jehovah, our Lord God, desires for us to inherit His Joy. It's a joy to Him when He sees us alive in Jesus. Jesus gave us the Holy Spirit so we can produce His fruit of Joy every day when we wake up to a new day. This is the day that the Lord has made. We will rejoice and be glad in it.

January 31

~ Love is the greatest force that drives you to give ~

The point is this: whoever sows sparingly will also reap sparingly, and whoever sows bountifully will also reap

> *bountifully. Each one must give as he has decided in his heart, not reluctantly or under compulsion, for God loves a cheerful giver (2 Corinthians 9:6-7, ESV).*

Love is giving. A good dad gives his giving as seed, sowing into his garden of love. He knows the power of love can do anything because His loving Father in heaven loves a cheerful giver. A good dad abides in love, and that is where his seed of giving brings forth the harvest, because it is love that drives Him to give. He knows the power of love can do anything. He is always grateful that he has a seed to sow. Jehovah, our loving Father, loves to see His children give just like Himself.

> *For you have been born again, not of perishable seed, but of imperishable, through the living and enduring word of God (1 Peter 1:23, NIV).*

Jesus lives our Father's name, Jehovah, and gave Himself to us. He walked in obedience even to death (see Philippians 2:8). We are His seed from the imperishable Word in the new life. Everything about our new life is all about giving. This is how we are designed. We find joy and happiness in abundance when our heart and hands work together in giving. With each day comes new opportunities to look around and give whatever we can with what we have. God loves a Cheerful giver. This is our seed to sow for a greater harvest.

FEBRUARY

Jehovah Nissi! I AM Your Banner!

WE ARE THE BANNER OF GOD IN CHRIST!

~ We are the temple that Jesus built in three days, and the Holy Spirit raised up in three days ~

Moses built an altar there and named it Yahweh-Nissi (which means 'the Lord is my banner') (Exodus 17:15, NLT).

Jesus came and lived our Father's name, Jehovah Nissi, our Almighty Father is our Banner. He is the head who came to build us, His body to be the banner.

Every night I would watch bedtime stories with my kids to put them to sleep. One summer's night, January 2, 2022, we watched a bedtime story of a king who banned every toy in his kingdom because one day, he was walking in his kingdom and tripped over a piece of toy and had a bad fall. He was so frustrated, that all the toy factories were shut down and anyone found with toys was severely punished. Toys were even snatched from little children's hands.

When king Herod heard about the birth of Jesus, that on that day in Bethlehem a king was born, he tried to kill every baby boy born around the time of Jesus' birth. Jesus' mission was to die and save His people, but at the appointed time, not to have a miscarried death. The king in the bedtime story trampled over a toy and he banned toys. When Jesus, the King of kings and the eternal life was born, death knew it was going to lose its power and would no longer hold people in its dark valley.

Jesus' appearance was so He could destroy the work and power of the devil, that is sin and death upon our body. He was going to make a way for His Spirit to have access and live and rest in our bodies so we can rise up in the Seven Spirits of the Father as a banner. Our Father rested on the seventh day after His work of creation. Jesus rested and finished the work the Father purposed for Him by laying His life down for us on the cross. The work of the Holy Spirit can be finished too and He rest in us when we put to rest our "old life' by dying to sin each day.

> *And the Spirit of the Lord shall rest upon him, the Spirit of wisdom and understanding, the Spirit of counsel and might, the Spirit of knowledge and the fear of the Lord (Isaiah 11:2, ESV).*

Each day of the month of February, and every day, remember that your body is the temple and altar that Jesus built so His Spirit can find rest and live. Therefore, every day we are to die to sin and rise up like a banner in the Spirit of the Lord, the Spirit of wisdom and understanding, the Spirit of counsel and might, the Spirit of knowledge and the fear of the Lord. We can do this by connecting daily in Word and prayer with our loving heavenly Father, Jehovah Nissi.

February 1

~ *Rise up thoughts in your mind like a banner in the mind of Christ* ~

> *Though I am like a wineskin in the smoke, I do not forget your decrees (Psalm 119:83, NIV).*

A good dad may come from a background of addiction, poverty, depression, abuse and low self-esteem, but this is not something he will rise up with to live his life. He renews his mind to not dwell on what his mind is aware of, but in the mind of Christ and what his loving Father thinks and plans for him. He fixes his thoughts in the Word.

This is his prayer: Though I am like a wineskin in the smoke, I do not forget your laws (Psalm 119:83).

In Biblical times, animal skins were made into wine containers. At first they were flexible and easy to work with, but over time they grew rigid and lost their ability to expand. That's why Jesus said, 'No one pours new wine into old wineskins. [It] would ... burst the old skins ... New wine must be put into new wineskins,' (see Matthew 9:17). For God to also give you new insights, you have to have a renewed mind with a new heart and spirit. Throw out your old wineskins! God won't infuse a fossilised mind with fresh ideas, but He will change your life when you line up your thinking with His.

Jesus came as the banner of our loving Father. He lived our Father's name, Jehovah Nissi, our Almighty Father is our Banner so we can rise up in our thoughts like a banner in what we think and have the mind of Christ. Only when we have a renewed mindset, we get new insights and fresh revelations from our Father in heaven. The fresh new insights from Him go into a renewed mind.

Every day, renew your mind in the Word and rise up like a banner, in the mind of Christ, to receive fresh new revelations.

February 2

~ Rise up like a banner in the characters of Christ and live your story ~

The Lord of heaven's Armies has sworn this oath: 'It will all happen as I have planned. It will be as I have decided.'
(Isaiah 14:24, NLT).

On August 10, 2021, while home schooling with my six-year-old, we were doing book reading and had to involve the characters of the story, where it took place, what was the problem in the story, and how the problem was solved. This is what the Holy Spirit taught me: The kingdom of God is like this. Every one of us has a story written for us before we were born and we are to live that story. We are the character of the story. We are to live the characters of Jesus in the story that was written by our loving Father in heaven. Where the story took place is right where we are, as this is where our Father placed us, and He is the gardener. He is working in us. Every time we have a problem, as soon as one finishes, one comes up, because we are living a story written for us. We have to know how to find the solution to that story.

The story we were reading was about two children who had no money to buy a gift for their mum on her birthday, so their dad helped them to pick some apples from their garden and sell them. Their problem was they had no money, but they solved that problem by selling apples and buying the gift for their mum.

The problems in life will keep coming. You don't need to stress yourself, just look for a solution. If you can't find a solution, then pray and cast it over to God and rest in Christ. The devil is interested to steal your moment of joy and peace and he will use the problems as his opportunity. Our Father is so loving He asked us to ask Him for wisdom, because only with wisdom we will know the solution to how to solve our problems. We may gain educational knowledge, but that is to help us know about something, work and earn our living, it can't give us the right direction on how to go about solving our life's problems—that's the job of wisdom. God said to give wisdom to anyone who asks, whether you are a saint or a sinner (see James 1:5).

> *I have refined you, but not as silver is refined. Rather, I have refined you in the furnace of suffering (Isaiah 48:10, NLT).*

Jesus lived our Father's name, Jehovah Nissi, our Almighty Father is our Banner, He has lived perfectly the story that the Father wrote for Him. He rose up like a banner as the wisdom of our loving Father for us to live in. Every day, we are to live the Father's name in Jesus' name and rise up like a banner and live that love story. Jehovah Nissi, our Almighty Father is our Banner and He is love.

February 3

~ Rise the banner of your new life of abundance ~

I have come that they may have life, and that they may have it more abundantly (John 10:10, NKJV).

I remember, one winter's day, August 23, 2020, looking at an image of me and my toddler in a frame. And the Holy Spirit taught me this: It's hard to see yourself in the picture when the photo was taken with you in it. But you can see yourself in the photo after the photo is taken. There's a world outside of you; you must get outside of yourself and see it through the eyes of others. To meet people's needs, you must first find out how they think. That calls for humility, getting over your personal agenda, and trying to understand the other person's point of view. The Bible puts it this way:

Let each of you look out not only for his own interests, but also for the interests of others (Philippians 2:4 NKJV).

Every day we have to live our Father's name, Jehovah Nissi, our Almighty Father is our Banner. We have to come out of our old 'me it is' life and rise up in our new life in Christ, the life of abundance.

Jesus came into the world as the Word who became flesh. The Holy Spirit raised up His body as the banner for all to see that He is the resurrection of life. Jesus had to come out from the life, He laid down and gave His life for us to live. Each day is another opportunity to come out from our old life of SELF and rise up like a banner in the new life of abundance for others to see Christ in us.

February 4

~ Rise up in the Word and exercise your faith ~

And nations shall come to your light, and kings to the brightness of your rising (Isaiah 60:3, ESV).

June 24, 2021, I was cleaning the fridge and removing the old stuff we never used. There were also some fruits and vegetables not being used and they all gave bad odour. This is what I heard the Holy Spirit say: There are some Christians who never produce the fruit of the Spirit and their actions sting and smell towards others. The fruit of the Spirit within us is meant to be used up to exercise our faith. But when we do nothing about it, we become a toxic Christian who affects everyone we have a relationship with or come in contact with.

A good dad renews his mind in the Word by receiving into him the Word. Then he thinks about how he is going to rise up in the Word in his actions to his loved ones, and all whom he comes in touch with. He talks to his loving Father in prayer to use the fruit of the Holy Spirit in all the seasons of his life when it is needed. The fruit of the Spirit he actions in all seasons not only attracts the favour of the Father but also man.

Jesus, the very Word of the Father, lived our Father's name Jehovah Nissi, our Almighty Father is our Banner, by raising up His life like a banner by the power of the Holy Spirit. He was the Word and the Holy Spirit is only attracted to work on the Word. The Holy Spirit's power rose up the Word of the Father like a banner for us to use the Word to overcome death, curse and grave matters.

> *May we shout for joy when we hear of your victory and raise a victory banner in the name of our God. May the Lord answer all your prayers (Psalm 20:5, NLT).*

Banners are raised up to celebrate special occasions. Every day, let's rise up and live our Father's name, Jehovah Nissi, and rise up to action and exercise our faith from hearing the Word. We are to celebrate the life of Jesus that He raised up.

February 5

~ Remain clean by renewing your mind ~

You are already clean because of the word I have spoken to you (John 15:3, NIV).

August 20, 2021, I was preparing breakfast and used avocado and tomato. I had to remove the skin of the avocado and the tomatoes needed to be washed. The Holy Spirit pointed out to me that some of the fruits you have to just wash them and eat them, like apples. And others, you have to remove the skin and eat it right away because the actual part to eat is hidden underneath the skin. Oranges are one of those. You don't need to wash the orange.

Jesus said, 'You are clean because of the Word I say to you.' Even Peter asked him to wash his head and hands, and He told Peter he was already clean (see John 13:9-10). We are already clean from inside because of the Word we receive into us, and when we remain in the Word, JESUS, we remain clean. Like the orange, where the inside is already clean so we remove the skin to eat it, so are we. We are already clean; we just have to remove our flesh desires by renewing our mind in the Word that remains present in us, and allow the fruit of the Holy Spirit inside of us to be enjoyed by whoever God puts in our path that needs it. I don't feed my children when they are full, only when they are hungry. It's those who are hungry and empty, with no patience, no kindness and no goodness, who are in greater need of us to feed them with the fruit of the Spirit.

A good dad remains and abides in the Word, and just like he needs to wash and clean himself every day, he also needs to be in the Word every day to remain clean and fresh so he can live the Father's name, Jehovah Nissi, our Almighty Father is our Banner. And so, he rises up in the fruit of love like a banner to welcome anyone into the love of the Father.

> *Remain in me, as I also remain in you. No branch can bear fruit by itself; it must remain in the vine. Neither can you bear fruit unless you remain in me (John 15:4, NIV).*

Our Father gave us Jesus to live His name, Jehovah Nissi, and Jesus has now given us the Father's Holy Spirit for us to live the Father's name and bring glory to His name.

Every day, let's go into our world and give the love of Jesus with our patience, kindness and goodness. But to do that, we have to be fruitful first.

February 6

~ *Feeding on the Father's love messages* ~

> *For it was I, the Lord your God, who rescued you from the land of Egypt. Open your mouth wide, and I will fill it with good things (Psalm 81:10, NLT).*

When feeding my toddler, she gets distracted by anything she sees. From time to time, she would go and do whatever she wanted, then come back to eat. And there I am, just waiting for her to come back and get fed. Because I love her, I want her to eat something so she can have strength. The Holy Spirit reminded me of how our loving heavenly Father waits patiently for us to go to Him to be fed by His Word. We are so distracted by what life throws to us that we run around trying to catch the wind. At times, we go for a five or ten minute snack with Him, then hurry off again because of our busy schedule.

Let's be reminded that God loves us so much, He wants to feed us from His mouth. He knows the taste of His Word from His mouth will strengthen and nourishes us thoroughly. Psalm 34:8 says, 'Taste and see that the Lord is good. We know that man does not live on bread alone but by every Word that comes out from the mouth of God (see Matthew 4:4).

> *The Lord is gracious and compassionate, slow to anger and rich in love (Psalm 145:8, NIV).*

Jesus lived our Father's name, Jehovah Nissi, our Almighty Father is our Banner. He is the love of the Father to the world and the love found in the Holy Spirit who produces the nine fruit of love for us to rise from within as victors.

A good dad has patience in everything he does to his household. He lives His Father in heaven's name, Jehovah Nissi, our Almighty Father is our Banner. And when anger rises up in him, he rises up the banner of the Father's love and shows patience. It is love that saved him and it will be that love that he will rise up like a banner to show his victory.

Every day we are winners and we have to live our Father's name and rise up the banner of love. We are loved to live and move in love, and nothing in all creation can separate us from our Father's love (see Romans 8:38-39).

February 7

~ Rising up within you the banner of peace ~

His flesh shall be fresher than a child's: he shall return to the days of his youth (Job 33:25, KJV).

It is in your battles and storms that God wants to build His new strength in you. So, if your health is failing, He will clothe you in His strength, that you will come out from your health battle with your flesh stronger and more youthful. Let's keep practising patience, kindness and goodness in our battlefields.

When you buy a product from a manufacturer, under the warranty, you have the right to take it back to them to have it fixed for you and make it work again if it is not working in the way it was designed for its purpose. So are we. We are designed by our Creator to carry out His purpose He planned for us. Those battles and storms are part of our life so we can go back to Him to work on us, in creating new strength, so we can continue to live and reach new levels in our lives.

A good dad appreciates and is grateful for storms because they come to bring him to a new level of his potential. He is growing from glory to glory for the Father's glory, and from strength to strength from the Father's strength. For him to be strong for his family, he commits himself daily to draw out the strength of His loving Father in heaven from His Word.

Blessed are the peacemakers, for they will be called children of God (Matthew 5:9, NIV).

Jesus was the peace from our Father and the Prince of Peace, and He wants us to raise Him up as that banner of peace in our battlefields. He lived our Father's name, Jehovah Nissi, our Almighty Father is our Banner. He made peace in His death and was raised by the Holy Spirit to show the world that He is the peace. Through Him, we can now live our Father's name, Jehovah Nissi, and rise up our banner of peace in our storms.

Every day, when we wake up to sail in our journey, there will be storms coming from nowhere. We just have to be prepared to rise up our banner of peace.

February 8

~ Rise up your prayer life like a banner ~

Then they will come to their senses and escape from the devil's trap. For they have been held captive by him to do whatever he wants (2 Timothy 2:26, NLT).

August 7, 2021, I was watching this beautiful story with Blessed, my two-year-old then, of a whale and a snail who were best friends. There were some traps that humans used to try and trap the whale so they could catch her. This is what the Holy Spirit taught me: This is what the devil does also. He tries to trap us by coming in the exact form of what we would like. From the way we live, he knows what we want in life. Just like how you go and surf the net for something you want, the next minute you will start seeing advertisements in social media—everything related to what you are interested in. The devil also uses the information from your actions to set a trap and catch you to be his victim.

We are in the end times, and in these challenging times we are not to be lazy and slumber. It is time to rise up from our sleep and get our eyes open in the Word of Jehovah. A good dad is watchful over his family in prayer. Like His Father in heaven, he doesn't slumber in his faith life but rises like a banner to show everyone, including his enemies, that He is awake and ready to celebrate each day, the resurrection life of Christ in him. The enemy cannot trap him while he is celebrating his new sight. He can see clearly every move the enemy makes towards His life. Our Father's name is Jehovah Nissi, our Almighty Father who is our Banner. A good dad rises up in his new sight like a banner and celebrates his victory.

> *… and he said to them, 'Why are you sleeping? Rise and pray that you may not enter into temptation.'*
> *(Luke 22:46, ESV).*

Jesus lived our Father's name by watching and praying. He never slumbered. He even rebuked his sleepy disciples. He lived our Father's name, Jehovah Nissi, and rose up like a banner in prayer. We have to live like Him by rising up our prayer life like a banner so we do not become a victim to be trapped and caught by the devil.

February 9

~ *God is love and love is kind. God made mankind to be kind* ~

> *Let your speech always be gracious, seasoned with salt, so that you may know how you ought to answer each person*
> *(Colossians 4:6, ESV).*

A good dad always thinks and speaks positively and sends good wishes, not only into the lives of his household, but to all that come into contact with him. When his mouth opens, it is to build up someone's life or to speak an act of kindness. His ears listen and respond kindly to his household.

When someone is in darkness, his eyes are the light to help them see the way to becoming a better person. He receives insight from seeing into the light of the Word and raises it up like a banner for the world to see that light. He lives our Father's name, Jehovah Nissi, our Almighty Father is our Banner. He constantly builds himself up in the light of the Word from his loving Father in heaven so that he can easily shine it out for others to see and build their life.

> *Therefore encourage one another and build each other up, just as in fact you are doing (1 Thessalonians 5:11, NIV).*

Jesus lived our Father's name by raising His voice of Word, which is the light, like a banner for the world to see the good news of the Father's love. He has now given us the Holy Spirit. The Holy Spirit raises His voice like a banner within us so we can see and hear the voice from the mouth of our Father. When He talks to us, it is a feast of celebration, that joy of hearing the Holy Spirit is indescribable.

> *At that time, Jesus, full of joy through the Holy Spirit, said, 'I praise you, Father, Lord of heaven and earth, because you have hidden these things from the wise and learned, and revealed them to little children. Yes, Father, for this is what you were pleased to do. All things have been committed to me by my Father. No one knows who the Son is except the Father, and no one knows who the Father is except the Son and those to whom the Son chooses to reveal him' (Luke 10:21-22, NIV).*

You know you have inherited the light from the kingdom of the Father when you receive the joy of the Holy Spirit by hearing

His voice revealing who Jesus is in your life. The joy you receive brings into your life eternal peace. Each day, live the Father's name, Jehovah Nissi, and raise your voice like a banner joyfully for everyone to see.

February 10

~ Walk by faith and not by sight ~

For we live by faith, not by sight
(2 Corinthians 5:7, NIV).

On the morning of July 26, 2021, I woke up and did my normal daily devotional of word and prayer. I thought of how I was really putting my energy and effort into praying, but I was not seeing or receiving anything I was asking for. The Spirit of truth started revealing this truth to me: That is what faith is all about; you are seeing the promises of God, but not with your physical eyes. Walk by faith and not by sight.

A good dad walks by faith. He hears and hears what His Father in heaven says in His Word, and He goes by it. He doesn't focus on what he sees, as that will bring disappointment to him because it is not of eternal value. He knows what His Father is preparing for him no eyes have seen and no ears have heard. All he does is he pray for the Father to prepare him to be in a position to be able to receive it.

However, as it is written:

'What no eye has seen, what no ear has heard,
and what no human mind has conceived' the things
God has prepared for those who love him
(1 Corinthians 2:9, NIV).

Jesus lived a life that rose up like a banner to show us that He is the Word who became flesh. He lived our heavenly Father's name on earth. Jehovah Nissi, our Almighty Father is our Banner.

What the Father is preparing for us through Jesus is within Him and cannot be seen. This is the gift of the Holy Spirit who has come and lives inside of us through the life of Jesus that He has laid down. No ears can hear and no eyes can see what the Father is preparing for us in the Holy Spirit within us.

Each day, we are to live our Father's name to raise up our faith like a banner. Even that mustard seed of faith has to rise up from within us as a banner for the world to see that we have victory over everything and we can move the mountains.

February 11

~ Rise up the banner of the light from the life of Christ in you ~

I am the light of the world. Whoever follows me will never walk in darkness, but will have the light of life (John 8:12, NIV).

One night, July 22, 2021, as I was trying to fall asleep I realised how tired I felt. I was just about to doze off to sleep and rest when I heard the Holy Spirit say: The burdens of this world, the struggling, labouring and worries need to be put to rest and sleep. This is what makes one so tired. Jesus said for us to receive His burden, which is light. When you receive the light, you will see clearly that these burdens are of the world, and not yours. They belong to the old life and have to be put to rest with your old life that you have put to rest. You have to rise up like a banner, the light of Jesus, so the world can see the light of Jesus. Jehovah Nissi is our Father's name, our Almighty Father is our Banner. Jesus lived the name of the Father and raised up His life as the light for the world to see on the third day.

A good dad puts his old self to rest and lives His Father's name, Jehovah Nissi, and rises up like a banner in the light from the new life from Christ. He knows his good loving Father in heaven is in control, and he should never worry or try to figure out anything of this life.

Jesus was the light of the world. The light entered the darkness and took away all the burdens, worries and fears of death. The Father was glorified when Jesus rose up like a banner, this new life of light for the world to see that death was conquered.

> *Then Jesus said: 'Come to Me, all of you who are weary and carry heavy burdens, and I will give you rest. Take My yoke upon you. Let Me teach you, because I am humble and gentle at heart, and you will find rest for your souls. For My yoke is easy to bear, and the burden I give you is light.' (Matthew 11:28–30 NLT).*

Each day is another day to put to rest the burdens of today in Jesus and rise up like a banner, the light in Jesus, and live without worries.

February 12

~ Rise up the banner of love with kindness ~

Love is kindness (1 Corinthians 13:4, NIV).

A good dad knows that for him to grow up to be what his heavenly Father designed him to be, He has to be kind. Our

Father created manKIND to be KIND, just like how He created woman for the man. Man is created to be kind. God has created everything of its own kind to be kind to each other. Man is kind and God is Love, and that's how love between man and God connects them into one.

The Love of God can only be shown when kindness is shown in WORD and accompanied by ACTION. The Word has become flesh. The Word we speak in kindness must be actioned by flesh.

Jesus was the Word who became flesh. He lived our Father's name, Jehovah Nissi, our Almighty Father is our Banner. Wherever He went, He raised up the Love of God as a banner through His acts of kindness. He was so busy, yet He had time for everyone.

> *Little children, let us stop just saying we love people;*
> *let us really love them, and show it by our actions*
> *(1 John 3:18, TLB).*

We are to live our Father's name, Jehovah Nissi, in raising up our new self in kindness and being a mankind that was designed with love to be kind to all man. We have to fast with kindness in our rebellious OLD SELF so it can live to action kindness. When we fast with kindness upon our OLD SELF we are implying that our old self is going to live for kindness. It's just like how we fast with water by allowing ourselves to drink water only.

Live a purposeful life each day by looking out to serve someone with kindness. Only the fire of kindness can burn away the fats of greed. Live the Father's name, Jehovah Nissi, and rise up the banner of love with kindness.

February 13

~ Rise up the banner of love with peace ~

Blessed are the peacemakers, for they will be called children of God (Matthew 5:9, NIV).

While having breakfast with my kids one winter's morning, July 21, 2021, as always, Blessed (two years old then) wanted to follow everything his sister did. Whatever she was eating, he wanted to eat that as well. He just wanted to be like her in everything. This is what the Holy Spirit taught me: The kingdom of God is like this. When you are born again in the kingdom of light you become a son and you will start to do things to be like Jesus, who is the firstborn of all the creation. Whatever you want to do, you want to be like him.

I will confirm that it is true, as I have experienced that in my journey of growing in my relationship with Christ. I am so conscious of every little thing I do and whether I am producing the fruit of the Spirit, which is the character of Christ. I never did that when I was a new Christian, but after a while, having spent more time in Word and prayer, it feels different. I am aware of my every little movement.

For to us a child is born, to us a son is given, and the government will be on his shoulders. And he will be called Wonderful Counsellor, Mighty God, Everlasting Father, Prince of Peace (Isaiah 9:6, NIV).

A good dad wants to be good like his heavenly Father, and so he follows in the footsteps of Christ by walking in peace. Jesus washed the feet of His disciples for them to walk in peace, since it's anger that rushes the feet to cause a war. Every good deed of the Father, Jesus exposed it. He came down as the Prince of Peace and is now the King of all kings. Ruling as the King of peace, He is the peacemaker, and His blessings are upon the children of God who are the peacemakers.

Jesus lived our Father's name, Jehovah Nissi, our Almighty Father is our Banner. He is the Prince of Peace who was raised up like a banner for all to witness Him as peace made for the world. The Holy Spirit who produces the fruit of peace raised Him up from the power of death.

The Holy Spirit now resides in us and produces peace all the time. Every morning is another opportunity to live the name of our Father, Jehovah Nissi, by rising up the banner of love with peace from the Holy Spirit.

February 14

~ Our life is an instrument for the Father to use for His glory ~

But you are the ones chosen by God, chosen for the high calling of priestly work, chosen to be a holy people, God's instruments to do his work and speak out for him, to tell others of the night-and-day difference he made for you – from nothing to something, from rejected to accepted (2 Peter 2:9-10, MSG).

I am not a pilot, but I know that flight instructors will normally train new flight trainees to focus on how to use the instruments rather than focusing on what is outside when flying. What is important is how to use the instrument and not what the pilot sees outside. When a storm hits, a pilot may not be able to see what is outside, but as long as he knows how to use the instruments inside with him, he will make it through the storm. This is what a good dad does. He equips himself with the Word of his loving Father in heaven so he can be that instrument to be used for any good work the Father has for him. He can make it through any storms in his life because he focuses on himself, and all that he is to be, to be used as an instrument for the Father's glory. He uses the Word as an instrument.

Jesus was the very instrument of the Father. He lived the Father's name of Jehovah Nissi, our Almighty Father is our Banner. The Holy Spirit who lives inside us is the same Spirit who raised Him up like a banner to show the world that our Father loves us so much that He sent His only Son to come into the world and die for us, only to take His life up for us to live.

> *No one can take my life from me. I sacrifice it voluntarily. For I have the authority to lay it down when I want to and also to take it up again. For this is what my Father has commanded (John 10:18, NLT).*

Every day, we are to live our Father's name, Jehovah Nissi, our Almighty Father is our Banner, and raise up our new life as an instrument for the Father to use for His glory.

February 15

~ Rise up the banner of the Living Stone that covers all sin ~

> *Above all, keep loving one another earnestly, since love covers a multitude of sins (1 Peter 4:8, ESV).*

Most of the winter days of 2021 I was doing home schooling with Angelilly, who was in year one then. One day, July 26, 2021, I was thinking of how Angelilly used to bring my handwriting to me to explain to her when she didn't understand it. Whenever we are doing home schooling I will write something down, then explain, and she will follow it.

This is what I heard the Holy Spirit say: The kingdom of God is like this. Jesus had to come and explain also the handwriting of the Father, His Word. Jesus is the Word of the Father who has become flesh. Our Father in heaven is so loving and the laws He gave to Moses were not to punish us harshly. The laws are to guide us in doing the right thing. When the adulterous woman was caught in the act, the religious leaders wanted to stone her to death. They brought her to Jesus to test Him and even quoted the law of Moses, which God had given. Jesus bent down and wrote on the ground. What He wrote is a mystery, but we know He explained to everyone after He wrote on the ground. He said, '… if you have never sinned then you can raise the first stone on her.' He raised up love. The fruit of the Holy Spirit is love and there is no law against the fruit of the Spirit (see Galatians 5:22-23).

Jesus was the only one in the position to raise the stone on her because He had never sinned. Instead, the living stone raised Himself up and forgave her. Jesus lived our Father's name, Jehovah Nissi, our Almighty Father is our Banner. He rose up as the Living Stone not to hurt, but to love the sinners.

A good dad depends on his loving Father in heaven to explain the writing of his story written in His Word. His desire is to rise up and live the Father's name, Jehovah Nissi, to rise up the banner of the Living Stone, Jesus, not to hurt, but to love with the eyes of compassion.

February 16

~ *Raise up your hands in prayer like a banner; victory is yours* ~

> *The Lord will fight for you while you [only need to] keep silent and remain calm (Exodus 14:14, AMP).*

A good dad holds up his peace in walking daily with his loving Father in heaven in His Word and raises his hands in the joy of victory as a banner of prayer. He knows His Father's name is Jehovah Nissi, our Almighty Father is our Banner. He only has to be still and know that His Father is fighting for him to remain in victory. As long as his hands are raised like a banner in prayer, His Father is at work on his behalf.

Jesus lived our Father's name, Jehovah Nissi, our Almighty Father is our Banner. He is the very peace of the Father for us to hold onto so we can find rest, knowing that our life is victorious over anything the fallen world is failing at. Even though He was God in man-form, He always rises up in prayer. If God can rise up in prayer, then we, mankind, have to commit daily to rising up in prayer.

> *And rising very early in the morning, while it was still dark, he departed and went out to a desolate place, and there he prayed (Mark 1:35, ESV).*

Every day, we have to rise up and hold up our peace and joy as the banner of our victory from the peace that Jesus gave to us. We have to also declare that Joy Jesus gave us through the Holy Spirit. We have to declare them all as the banner of love so the enemy can see we are still celebrating victory.

February 17

~ Rise up the banner of love ~

The Lord is gracious and compassionate, slow to anger and rich in love (Psalm 145:8, NIV).

A good dad knows he will still get upset and angry over something he has no control over. Every time the anger rises up within him, he also rises up the banner of love from his heavenly Father to remind him that His Father's love can conquer everything. He applies patience and self-control from the love of the Father to slow the movement of anger out from him, and the anger slows down and fades away.

It's just like turning the volume of loud music down. The music is on, but its volume is down. Our anger also goes down instead of coming up and out from us, when we slow it down. Our loving Father is slow to anger. It is our goal to become like our Father and be slow to anger.

Our Father's name is Jehovah Nissi, our Almighty Father is our Banner. We are to live our Father's name and raise up the banner of love, who is Jesus, to reign in every area of our life. Jesus is the banner of love from the Father who was risen by the Holy Spirit to show victory over death.

And if the Spirit of him who raised Jesus from the dead is living in you, he who raised Christ from the dead will also give life to your mortal bodies because of his Spirit who lives in you (Romans 8:11, NIV).

Every day, rise up in your new day and live our Father's name, Jehovah Nissi. The same Spirit who has risen Jesus as the Father's banner of love now lives in us, to raise us up in His fruit of love to show we have victory in life.

February 18

~ Rise up as a banner the fruit of the Holy Spirit ~

You will not have to fight this battle. Take up your positions; stand firm and see the deliverance the Lord will give you (2 Chronicles 20:17, NIV).

A good dad knows his rightful position in Christ and he takes up that position in the Word. Like Job, even Satan the devil respects his position, that he has to get permission from his heavenly Father before he enters his property and all in his care. To occupy that rightful position, a good dad makes sure he is on the right path to eternity by walking with the Holy Spirit in producing the fruit of righteousness. Every day, he rises up in the fruit of righteousness that is in him and gives it to all who need it. He is a threat to the kingdom of darkness because of the eternal life that is found in the fruit of the Spirit. He lives the name of our Father in heaven, Jehovah Nissi, our Almighty Father is our Banner by raising the fruit of the Father's Spirit.

May we shout for joy over your victory and lift up our banners in the name of our God. May the Lord grant all your requests (Psalm 20:5, NIV).

Jesus is the very banner of our loving Father in heaven. He lived the fruit of righteousness in His everyday living. The Holy Spirit raised up His life as the banner of the Father's love so we can also be raised up in this new life of righteousness. We are the righteousness of Christ in the Father. The power of the devil through death and sin is being conquered and destroyed.

Every day we are to live our Father's name and rise up in the fruit of righteousness of the Holy Spirit as the banner of the Father's love.

February 19

~ Rise up and remind the devil that his work has been destroyed ~

Jesus replied, 'Very truly I tell you, no one can see the kingdom of God unless they are born again' (John 3:3, NIV).

July 7, 2021, was a school holiday winter's day, so we all decided to put on the heater and watch a movie in our big room. Blessed then did a poo in his diaper. Because the door was closed to keep the room warm from the heater, the smell filled the, whole room. I took him to the bathroom and gave him a wash, but the smell was still there after we returned to the room. To remove the smell, I had to open the door and the windows. I even sprayed freshener to make the room smell nice.

This is what I heard the Holy Spirit say: When sin entered the world through disobedience, it remained and is still there. Everyone who is born into this world is born into sin and must be born again to be born out of sin. The first man sinned and he is gone, but the sin he committed remains. It is just like how you took Blessed and cleaned him already, but the smell still remains in the room. You had to open the door for new, fresh air to come in and remove the smell of the poo. This is what your loving Father in heaven also did. He had to send Jesus down into the world to remove the sin. However, our sin can only be removed if we open our hearts to Jesus and receive Him in to remove the sin and cleanse us with the work of His blood.

A good dad refreshes himself in the fragrance of his loving Father in heaven to be a good dad to his household. He rises up in his spirit and connects to the Holy Spirit to open up the doors of his path where the light of Jesus needs to travel through. He gives directions to his contacts that Jesus is knocking on the door of their heart.

> *Here I am! I stand at the door and knock. If anyone hears my voice and opens the door, I will come in and eat with that person, and they with me (Revelation 3:20, NIV).*

Jesus did the work on the cross to pay for our life and cleanse us from any unrighteousness. Jesus lived our Father's name, Jehovah Nissi, our Almighty Father is our Banner. He is the banner of the Father who has been risen on the third day. The demons tremble in fear and flee because they know anyone who believes the work of the cross can also rise up like a banner and destroy their work. Jesus is now standing at the door of our heart and knocking for us to invite Him to come and live in us so we can rise up like a banner in His new life and remind the devil that his work has been destroyed.

February 20

~ Rise up in the image of the Father everywhere you go ~

Be perfect, therefore, as your heavenly Father is perfect (Matthew 5:48, NIV).

A good dad renews his mind to keep it attached to what his heavenly Father's promises are for him. He may not be the best, most perfect dad to his children, but he knows he has a perfect Father in heaven, whose love is perfect, to work on his imperfect love. He is the cheerleader who draws out the best in his children, not the critic who points out failures. He raises up the banner of knowledge of goodness, self-control, patience, godliness, kindness and love towards his family. He does whatever it takes to bring out the best in his children.

> *Because you have these blessings, do all you can to add to your life these things: to your faith add goodness; to your goodness add knowledge; to your knowledge add self-control; to your self-control add patience; to your patience add devotion to God; to your devotion add kindness toward your brothers and sisters in Christ, and to this kindness add love (2 Peter 1:5-7, ERV).*

A child can become so successful in his career path when he has a father figure who believes in him. A single mother who plays both roles of mother and father raises successful children when she believes in and cheers for them in life. Even our Father in heaven believes in His one and only Son and sent Him to earth. Jesus successfully walked the path of life. He lived our Father's name, Jehovah Nissi, our Almighty Father is our Banner. Everywhere He went, He raised the image of the Father for everyone to have that godly knowledge of the Father. Jesus' self-control, patience, His devotion to the Father, His kindness and the perfect love of the Father was raised as a banner for all to see.

Every day is another great opportunity for us to rise up and live our Father's name, Jehovah Nissi. We carry His image to raise it up in love and live in it so others can see and give glory to our Father.

February 21

~ *Rising up as a banner of holiness* ~

> *For you are a people holy to the Lord your God. The Lord your God has chosen you out of all the peoples on the face of the earth to be his people, his treasured possession (Deuteronomy 7:6, NIV).*

On the morning of June 10, 2021, while I was doing cornrow on Angelilly's hair, I accidentally missed a little piece of her hair and did not include it with the others I was doing braids on. This is what the Holy Spirit pointed out to me: You see, that day is coming, and it is coming now, where many people are missing out on the calling of the Father. You do not want to miss out. You missed out on picking that hair out because you couldn't see it. It's the same here; many will miss out because they can't see the signs of the end time. They are blind. Just like all those hairs you were collecting and putting aside together to do a beautiful braid, the Father is also hand-picking and putting aside whoever is holy to sanctify them for His purpose.

A good dad puts aside his life to serve and be devoted to the holiness of His Father in heaven. He raises his life up to honour and glorify the Father in all that his hands find to do.

> … *who has saved us and called us with a holy calling, not according to our works, but according to His own purpose and grace which was granted us in Christ Jesus from all eternity (2 Timothy 1:9, NASB).*

Jesus lived our Father's name, Jehovah Nissi, our Lord God, our Banner, by living a life of holiness among the unholy people. He came to show us that we can set aside our life to serve in holiness while living among unholy people. He died and rose again, His life as a banner of holiness. His Spirit who is Holy is the Spirit of truth, and when we walk in the truth, we are walking on a holy path.

Every day, we have to set aside our life that is risen in Christ to serve and glorify the Father in His holiness. We are the holiness of Christ in the Holy Spirit. Our life has to rise up as a banner of holiness and be set apart especially for the kingdom of the Father.

February 22

~ Rise up within you like a banner, your new fresh victorious life which is in Christ ~

What delight comes to the one who follows God's ways! He won't walk in step with the wicked, nor share the sinner's way, nor be found sitting in the scorner's seat. His passion is to remain true to the Word of "I AM," meditating day and night on the true revelation of light. He will be standing firm like a flourishing tree planted by God's design, deeply rooted by the brooks of bliss, bearing fruit in every season of life. He is never dry, never fainting, ever blessed, ever prosperous (Psalm 1:1-3, TPT: The Passion Translation).

On the morning of December 22, 2022, my son Blessed turned three years and ten months old. I was thinking of how amazing the date was, 22.12.22., when I saw a tree in my phone that someone sent. The tree caught my attention because of its uniqueness. It was an old, dead tree, but inside of it another new, strong fresh one grew. The Lord opened my eyes to see the beauty of our new life in Christ. When our new life is in Christ, it starts to grow more beautiful when we feed daily from the Word of God. The old self in us starts to die, and our new self in the image of Christ starts growing fresh from within us because it abides in Jesus and the Holy Spirit lives in us. You see, just like how I was thinking about how unique the date was, this is also how people will see how unique our new life in Christ is.

The Holy Spirit is the resurrecting power of God who raised Jesus from the dead. He is the same Spirit with the same power who lives in us now (see Romans 8:11), and He will rise up our new life in

Christ to be fresh, new, prosperous and ever-blessed. Jesus lived our Father's name, Jehovah Nissi, our Lord God is our Banner, and rose from the grave His life by the resurrecting power of the Holy Spirit. He then rose in His glorious body into heaven, so He can give us the Holy Spirit to raise our new life in Him.

> *But I will bless those who trust me, the Lord. They will be like trees growing beside a stream— trees with roots that reach down to the water, and with leaves that are always green. They bear fruit every year and are never worried by a lack of rain. (Jeremiah 17:7-8, CEV).*

Every day, we are to live our Father's name, Jehovah Nissi, our Almighty Father is our Banner, and keep planting ourselves like a tree in the Word of God so the Holy Spirit will breathe in the Word stored in us, and raise us up like a banner where everyone will find the comfort to rest in our presence, just like how someone longs to rest under the cool of a big shady tree after a long, hard walk in the heat.

February 23

~ *Love was raised like a banner to cover all sin* ~

Above all, love each other deeply, because love covers over a multitude of sins (1 Peter 4:8, NIV).

On the morning of June 26, 2021, while catching the sunshine, my two-year-old son and his sister were playing with their toys. Angelilly flew a plastic aeroplane while her brother brought me a plastic toy of a little milk container that had its lid on. He wanted me to open it, but I couldn't, no one could because it was factory sealed to be like that.

This is what I heard the Holy Spirit say: The kingdom of God is like this. There are many things in your life that must not be open for people to see and have access into. Jesus did many good things of the kingdom of our Father, but He doesn't want it to be known. He wants it to be done secretly. We are in a fallen, broken world. People are falling all the time and have fallen short of the glory of God. The good things you do for your Father's kingdom can be ruined because not everyone has the mindset of Christ. The enemy can easily access the fallen people and use them to destroy the great work of the Father that you do. Not everything is to be known. There are some things that need to be kept secret.

A good dad lives in the shelter of the unconditional love of his loving Father, and whenever he opens up his life to his loved ones and all who surround him, it opens in love. All people see is love, and love covers all sin that no sinner can destroy it. The power of sin has been destroyed by love. But whatever good things he does, or has in progress, he keeps it hidden until he births it out.

> *He is not here; he has risen! Remember how he told you, while he was still with you in Galilee: 'The Son of Man must be delivered over to the hands of sinners, be crucified and on the third day be raised again.' Then they remembered his words (Luke 24:6-8, NIV).*

Our Father's love was shown in the divine life of Jesus on earth. He lived our Father's name, Jehovah. While doing the good things, He wasn't showing off as it was not for His personal gain, it was for the Father's glory. And as long as the Father knows the connection of His heart to Him, it's all good. This was why He didn't want the public to know. There is a time for everything and the public will know when it's time has come. On the day of His death, the

Father's unconditional love was officially accessible as curtains were torn apart. There was now access into the most holiest place of the Father. A new life was birthed and risen. Jesus lived our Father's name, Jehovah Nissi, our Lord God, our Banner. Love was raised like a banner to cover all sin.

Every day, we are to raise our life in Christ up in love like a banner in living our Father's name, Jehovah Nissi, so everyone can see nothing but the life of love dwelling in us in the Holy Spirit.

February 24

~ As long as you are alive in flesh, you will be aware of the work of flesh around you ~

Therefore, if anyone is in Christ, the new creation has come: The old has gone, the new is here!
(2 Corinthians 5:17, NIV).

On the eve of the new year, I was praying, and asked for a word from the Lord for the old year falling into the new year. This is what I received at around 1:37 am on December 31, 2022.

This is what the Holy Spirit pointed out to me: It is just like you staying away from social media. You didn't log out or deactivate your Facebook account, and so you still have the Facebook app running on your phone. What happens is you will still get notifications popping up on your phone, but because you made up your mind to stay away from social media, you will not check your notifications to see what it is. The same is with your old life — it is still there, as long as you are alive in your flesh, and so this is how you are going to be still aware of the happenings of the flesh. Now that you have a new life in Christ, you are not going to respond to the attacks of the flesh happening to you. You will just let them come through without doing anything, because you want to stay away from that. Just like how I was reminded of what happens if I stay away from social media, I would still get notifications coming through because I have the app running.

> *I love God's law with all my heart. But there is another power within me that is at war with my mind. This power makes me a slave to the sin that is still within me (Romans 7:22-23, NLT).*

Jesus came and lived our Father's name, Jehovah Nissi, our Lord God is our Banner. God the Father had to sacrifice and sent God the Son to come in flesh. Jesus laid down His flesh so we can now live in our flesh and be adopted by God as a son. As long as we live in our flesh, we will still be aware of the desires of the flesh around us, and in us. This is why Jesus was called, Son of man and Son of God.

Every day, we are to live our Father's name, Jehovah Nissi, in Jesus' name, and rise up in our flesh, like a banner, the new life in Christ, whenever our new life receives signals of the work of the old life trying to become alive.

The year 2022 is going to go, and 2023 will come in the next day. You have lived through all the days of the year 2022, and whatever you were doing in 2022 will appear again in the year 2023. Let it be and come through, and do not accept anything that will drag you back. Allow and receive into you only things that add value to your new life in the new year (2023). May this note be applied to all the new years you will walk into.

February 25

~ Lay down your old life and raise up your new life as a banner ~

I appeal to you therefore, brothers, by the mercies of God, to present your bodies as a living sacrifice, holy and acceptable to God, which is your spiritual worship (Romans 12:1, ESV).

A good dad lives by sacrificing his life for his family to give them the very best. He offers himself as a living sacrifice to his heavenly Father. Only when he knows how to offer himself as a living sacrifice by laying to rest his old life, and raising up his new life as a living offering to the heavenly Father, can he then offer sacrifice of whatever he does for his family without being worn out. He is renewed and refreshed every time he is grateful for his new life that is raised in Christ.

When we were baptized, we died and were buried with Christ. We were baptized, so that we would live a new life, as Christ was raised to life by the glory of God the Father (Romans 6:4, CEV).

Jesus, the very kingdom of our Father, has come and brought His will from heaven to live on earth. The new life that Jesus raised from the dead is the kingdom of God to live. He lives the Father's name, Jehovah Nissi, our Almighty Father is our Banner, by sacrificing His life and raising it up again like a banner so we too can have His selfless life. More of Jesus and less of us (see John 3:30).

Each day, we are to live our Father's name, Jehovah Nissi, in rising and holding up our selfless life of the kingdom of our loving Father. Be a living sacrifice to our Father in the finished work of Jesus.

February 26

~ Raising up the voice of the Word like a banner ~

Our people defeated Satan because of the blood of the Lamb and the message of God. They were willing to give up their lives (Revelation 12:11, CEV).

A good dad's desire is to silence any voices, so when he raises his voice it can be heard. And so he stays connected in Word and prayer with his heavenly Father, the Father of Truth, so the father of all lies, and his lies, will not deceive him to fall and get trapped in his lies. One of the ways he silences the voice of Satan is by producing the fruit of self-control to defend himself. He may fail at times, but his aim is not to be living by self, because the enemy has access through the SELF, the 'ME IT IS LIFESTYLE'.

Jesus was the very voice of our Father in heaven. He is the Word, the breath and voice of God who has become flesh. He lived the name Jehovah Nissi, our Lord God, our Banner, when He was raised up from the grave. The Voice of the Word was raised. We now have to raise that voice of the Word as a banner so the father of lies can see that we are victors over death and we cannot be deceived by his lies. If we do not know the truth in God's Word, the devil can easily make us believe his lies.

A person without self-control is like a city with broken-down walls (Proverbs 25:28, NLT).

Every day, rule over your own spirit with self-control. Whoever has no rule over his own spirit is like a city broken down, without walls. Your failure to maintain self-control is like opening the city gates and issuing an invitation to the devil to attack you.

February 27

~ Rise up the Kingdom lifestyle of righteousness as a banner ~

Now God has not only raised the Lord, but will also raise us up through His power (1 Corinthians 6:14, NASB).

On the morning of December 27, 2021, after returning home from the shop with groceries, I asked Angelilly to put the orange juice in the refrigerator so it would be cold. Now the orange juice was the refrigerated one, already cold. As she picked it out of the shopping bag to put it into the fridge, she said, 'Mom, it's already cold. Why should I put it in the fridge?' To which I responded, 'So it remains cold.' This is what I heard the Holy Spirit say: The kingdom of God is like this. When Jesus saved you and gave you His new life of righteousness, you had to continue to remain in Him to live a righteous life and produce His fruit of righteousness. The kingdom of God is not about eating and drinking but of righteousness, peace and joy in the Holy Spirit (see Romans 14:17).

A good dad rises up with each new day, knowing that to live His Father in heaven's name, Jehovah Nissi, our Almighty Father is our Banner, he has to rise up in his new kingdom life of righteousness as a banner. He does it by renewing his mind in the Word and with prayers. Isaiah 60:1 is his focus for the day.

Arise, Jerusalem! Let your light shine for all to see. For the glory of the Lord rises to shine on you (Isaiah 60:1, NLT).

Jesus lived our Father's name, Jehovah Nissi, our Lord God, our Banner. He is the kingdom of God; His kingdom of righteousness will never come to an end. And so, even death couldn't hold Him back. He is Life and Light that even death and darkness cannot remain in His presence.

Every day, we are to live our Father's name, Jehovah Nissi, and rise up the kingdom lifestyle of righteousness as a banner. Jesus Christ's risen victorious life is our banner that we are to raise to show that our King of kings and Lord of lords is alive and lives forever. And because He lives, we too live.

February 28

~ Raising your voice as a banner to give and build life ~

> *But we Christians have no veil over our faces; we can be mirrors that brightly reflect the glory of the Lord. And as the Spirit of the Lord works within us, we become more and more like him (2 Corinthians 3:18, TLB).*

January 4, 2020, a friend took a beautiful picture at our local beach and shared it with me. I was looking at this image of a person putting both her hands on the sand and her feet up in the air. She balanced herself so well, making the image more beautiful. With the reflection from the sun, her shadow was showing also on the sand.

This is what I heard the Holy Spirit say: No one but yourself can pull you up and out from where you are. If you can't balance the goodness within you from the evil around and maintain your position in Christ, then you will keep stumbling. For you to gain that kind of energy you want, use that kind of energy on others. For example, if you want kindness to be done, you must go around spreading kindness. You reap what you sow.

> *True, God made everything beautiful in itself and in its time (Ecclesiastes 3:11, MSG).*

Life is an echo and reflection of what you did yesterday. Make sure you use your today to create a memory that will become a beautiful yesterday to put a smile on your face when you look back—a beautiful picture that will reflect the beauty of you today, and a beautiful voice that will root you deeper to love.

A good dad is always that good voice to his children. He raises his voice like a banner to his children to reflect back to him. To be that good dad, he spends time daily in Word and prayer to hear the voice of His Father in heaven so he can be that good voice to his children.

Our lovely Father in heaven is Jehovah Nissi and that is His name. Our Almighty Father is our Banner. Jesus lived our Father's name and carried it out when He raised His voice out loud and called Lazarus out of the grave. Jesus did it to give glory to the Father. We also are to raise our voices into situations of our life that are dead and restore them back to life for our Father's glory.

MARCH

Jehovah Adonai! I AM Your Master!

Mizraiim Lapa-Pethe

OUR LORD GOD IS OUR MASTER.

~ Serve your Master faithfully, even in your broken moments ~

We are pressed on every side by troubles, but we are not crushed. We are perplexed, but not driven to despair. We are hunted down, but never abandoned by God. We get knocked down, but we are not destroyed (2 Corinthians 4:8-9, NLT).

I have this kettle that has a broken lid, but it still functions and boils water quickly. I have used other good kettles, but they do not boil water faster than this one. We have another good one which is perfect and not broken. Tom keeps telling me to throw it away and use the unbroken one, but I keep saying that even though the kettle has a broken lid, it still functions well, and it even does a better job. I am not going to throw it away, but will let it stay until it fully serves its lifespan. It makes me feel good and proud to keep that kettle, because even though that kettle is old and broken, it keeps serving its purpose to me.

One spring day of October 9, 2020, the Lord spoke to me: See that broken lid of the kettle. It also makes me so proud when someone keeps serving me the purpose I created them for, even though they are broken. When you are in your broken state with pain and scars, but you continue to serve me, I feel so proud of keeping you in my presence. These broken moments are the times I get closer to you to save you. I am close to the broken heart.

The Lord is close to the brokenhearted and saves those who are crushed in spirit (Psalm 34:18, NIV).

You see, that kettle will one day completely stop functioning and its lifespan will end. For you and me, even as we grow old and wrinkle and our bodies can no longer function well, God will keep us well by giving us new strength as promised by His Word in Isaiah 40:31 if we keep putting our hope in Him.

> ... but those who hope in the Lord will renew their strength. They will soar on wings like eagles; they will run and not grow weary, they will walk and not be faint (Isaiah 40:31, NIV).

And even when our life ends and we die, we will receive a new eternal life. So keep serving God. The best times to serve Him are when you are in a broken condition or when you are in the storms, fires and waters.

We are called in Christ to serve our Master, our loving Father in heaven and live His name. Jesus lived our Father's name, Jehovah Adonai, our Almighty Father is our Master. He faithfully served Him on the cross with His broken flesh dying in pain and suffering.

Each day of the month of March, and every day, we have to remind ourselves that the pain and suffering we go through is nothing compared to what Jesus suffered for us so we can enjoy and share in His glory (see 1 Peter 4:13). In everything, we are to remain faithful to our Master.

March 1

~ *Be knowledgeable of our heavenly Father in His Word* ~

> *I pray that the God of our Lord Jesus Christ, the Father of glory, will give you a spirit of wisdom and revelation that*

> *makes God known to you. I pray that the eyes of your heart will have enough light to see what is the hope of God's call, what is the richness of God's glorious inheritance among believers (Ephesians 1:17-18, CEB).*

A good dad knows that the knowledge he gained from his education is to be acted upon and be put into use and achieve its purpose. This is where he works for his family and provides. With his faith life also, he has to sit with God daily and learn from His Word to gain knowledge to act upon His Faith.

God gives wisdom to whosoever that ask, but knowledge is gained from seeking God in His Word so one can understand how faith from the Word works.

A good dad seeks God for wisdom, knowledge and understanding so he can use the Word and make it become a reality in his life and his house that he masters.

> *Righteous Father, even the world didn't know you, but I've known you, and these believers know that you sent me. I've made your name known to them and will continue to make it known so that your love for me will be in them, and I myself will be in them (John 17:25-26, CEB).*

Our Father in heaven, Jehovah Adonai, our Almighty God, our Master, is all loving. Jesus, whom the Father sent to us, is the wisdom, knowledge and understanding of the Father. We will only be able to master our life well when Jesus becomes the Lord and Master of our life. He is the wisdom and knowledge of God that will enable us to understand our Father. He came from our Father and understands Him, and He lives with us so He understands everything we go through in this world. He wants us to have that understanding so we can understand and love people the way the Father loves them. Because He walked through what we walk, He understands.

Every new day, ask the Father for the wisdom in which He created that day, and seek Him in His Word to gain knowledge so you can understand His loving kindness and extend it to someone.

March 2

~ Live the mastership that Jesus gave over to us ~

Your own ears will hear him. Right behind you a voice will say, 'This is the way you should go,' whether to the right or to the left (Isaiah 30:21, NLT).

One summer's day, January 16, 2021, we were walking at Pearl Beach, one of the beautiful suburbs of New South Wales, Australia. I told Tom, 'Let's take the path so that the cars will drive towards us. We know it's a safe traffic rule to walk towards the coming traffic so you can see the oncoming car. Sometimes when you give your back to the car you don't hear the approaching sound. This is what I heard the Holy Spirit say: The kingdom of God is like this. Jesus said, 'You have to have ears to hear and eyes to see. This is so whatever path you take, you will be safe. Even if you are going forward there will be something coming from your back to distract or slow you down, just like oncoming traffic that would slow you and make you stop, or delay you from keeping on going while on the road. But if your eyes and ears are open, you will see and hear where it is coming from and where it is going.'

Hear this, you foolish and senseless people, who have eyes but do not see, who have ears but do not hear (Jeremiah 5:21, NIV).

A good dad knows that as the master of his house, his voice must be heard so his household can see what he is talking about. To be the voice, to be heard and be given insight, he listens to the voice of his heavenly Father in His Word and he knows that God listens to the prayers of the godly.

Jehovah Adonai, our Lord God, our Master, is the voice that all creation listens to. He is the Lord and Master over all creation, He gave that role to the first man who let Him down through disobedience. The last man, Jesus Christ, lived the Father's name and became the Master of all creation when He glorified our Father by being obedient even to death.

The first man disobeyed God and lost his master-ship over the creation. When we disobey God, we lose our master-ship role because we have serve the wrong master. The last man, Jesus, obeyed God and gave the master-ship over to us again. Every day, we are to live our Father's name and have good master-ship over what He has entrusted us with.

March 3

~ Whoever master we serve on earth is to give glory to our Master in heaven ~

Tears may flow in the night, but joy comes in the morning (Psalm 30:5, GNT).

The tears flowing in the night are in your dark days, where you go through the pain, but joy is waiting for you when the light of a new day comes out from your darkness.

Fathers don't show their emotions in public, even when they are at breaking point. They have to be the strong master for their house. They want a strong household, and so they want to be that strong person. A good dad sees that regardless of who he is, to his heavenly

Father, he will always be a boy who cries to Him whenever things crush him. Just like King David, he may be the king and master of his household, but to His Father in heaven, he is a broken boy crying to His Father. He knows His Father collects his tears and records it, then turns those tears into joy. The one who turns water into wine turns tears into joy.

> *Slaves, obey your masters in all things. Do not obey just when they are watching you, to gain their favour, but serve them honestly, because you respect the Lord. In all the work you are doing, work the best you can. Work as if you were doing it for the Lord, not for people (Colossians 3:22-23, NCV).*

At the wedding, the master of the ceremony was told that the wine had run out. The Master of the universe was there and turned the water into wine. (See John 2:1-11). Jesus lived our heavenly Father's name, Jehovah Adonai, our Almighty God is our Master, by being there for any master who needed Him. He is the King of kings, Lord of lords and Master of masters. Whatever masters we serve in life it is to give glory to our King, Lord and Master, Jesus Christ.

Every new day is another gift of life to be alive and serve our day faithfully in whatever we do for our Master and Father, Jehovah Adonai, in Jesus' name.

March 4

~ Live in the life of your Master and Lord, Jesus Christ ~

> *Then the Lord said to Satan, 'Have you considered my servant Job? There is no one on earth like him; he is blameless and upright, a man who fears God and shuns evil' (Job 1:8, NIV).*

A good dad lives his life like Job. And like Job, as the master of his house, a good dad brings his house to His Father in heaven every day. He abides in Joshua 24:15, and tells his heavenly Father, 'as for me and my house, we will serve the Lord.' He knows the devil is roaming around looking for an opportunity for him to come out of Christ so he can attack him, and so he abides in Christ even in his trials, tests and temptations.

When God asked Satan what he was doing, he said roaming around the earth. He was roaming around waiting for Job to come out of God so he could attack him. But since Job never came out of the presence of God, Satan Lucifer entered the presence of God to have His approval to attack Job. He asked God's permission to put him through a storm so Job could come out of God and not abide in Him, but still Job never did. This is the story of one of the good dads who was faithful in serving His Master, Jehovah Adonai.

> *One day the angels came to present themselves before the Lord, and Satan also came with them. The Lord said to Satan, 'Where have you come from?' Satan answered the Lord, 'From roaming throughout the earth, going back and forth on it' (Job 1:6-7, NIV).*

Jesus Christ is the Master and Lord over our life. He lived our Father's name, Jehovah Adonai, our Lord God, our Master by laying down His life for us so we can receive and remain in it. As long as we remain in His life, the enemy, Satan, sees himself as being defeated.

Every day, remain in your new life in Christ so the devil can see that Jesus is the Lord and Master of your life.

March 5

~ Quit playing the blame game and take the responsibility of your life ~

For we are each responsible for our own conduct
(Galatians 6:5, NLT).

February 10, 2021, a summer's morning, I needed to fill up Angelilly's water bottle for her to take to school and noticed it was not there. I asked her, and she started blaming her two-year-old brother, saying, 'Oh, Blessed took it out from my bag.' She continued blaming him, and I said, 'Stop, no more putting blame on your brother. It is your water bottle and you are responsible for it.'

This is when the Holy Spirit opened the eyes of my heart and taught me this: The kingdom of God is like this. You must take responsibility and not play the blame game. You are responsible for your own life and are not to blame the enemy when you do something not right. The first man blamed the first woman and she blamed the serpent.

A good dad doesn't play the blame game in his household. He takes responsibility. As the master to his house, it is his responsibility to respond to every situation in a calm and gentle manner, and so he looks for ways to fix a problem. He holds to the Master of his life, his heavenly Father in heaven, to hold his hands and give him direction.

The man said, 'The woman you put here with me,
she gave me some fruit from the tree, and I ate it.'
(Genesis 3:12, NIV).

Jehovah Adonai, our Lord God, our Master, is always at work for our good. Jesus lived our Father's name, and as the Master of our life, He took the responsibility. And at the right time, He came down in flesh and took the blame upon his flesh and nailed it to the cross once and for all.

Every new day make Jesus Christ the Master and Lord over your life and do what He would do. Jesus already took the blame upon Himself so we can be responsible for our new life in Him and master it well.

March 6

~ Master your life in a humble and gentle way ~

He leads the humble in what is right, and teaches the humble his way (Psalm 25:9, ESV).

A good dad is meek, not weak, every day of the week, just like his loving Father in heaven. His strength, from the Word of God and prayer, is invested into his life to have a quiet and gentle heart so he can produce the fruit of gentleness from the Holy Spirit and be that good master of his household. A quiet and gentle heart is the most powerful heart, that serves the loving kindness of the Father with compassion.

Take my yoke upon you, and learn from me, for I am gentle and lowly in heart, and you will find rest for your souls (Matthew 11:29, ESV).

The love of our heavenly Father was actioned by Jesus, a quiet and gentle heart who sought to serve and not to be served. This is the heart of the Master: To lead with gentleness. He is a gentleman and the fruit of His Spirit is gentleness.

He lived well the name of our Father, Jehovah Adonai, our Almighty Father is our Master, by serving Him faithfully, as our Master, even to His final breath.

Every new day is another opportunity to live our Father in heaven's name, Jehovah Adonai, and run and lead our race in a humble lifestyle. This is how a master serves and lives down their life for others.

March 7

~ Be strong in the Lord ~

Finally, be strong in the Lord and in his mighty power (Ephesians 6:10, NIV).

January 26, 2021, I remember Angelilly brought me a pen that was hard to open. As I was struggling to open it, this is what I heard the Holy Spirit say: God designed man to be strong in flesh. This is so they can be strong to protect, provide and pray. This also puts a man or father in a position where they are strong enough to open up emotionally to their heavenly Father in heaven. Some of their hearts can be hardened to opening easily or being poured out in public, just like how you struggle to open up the pen and use it, they too struggle to open up to God. Women were approached mostly to spread and release openly the good news of Jesus Christ, such as the woman at the well, the women at the tomb of Jesus and many others.

A good dad uses his strength to be more strengthened in the Word of God so he can be a good master to his household to protect, provide and pray for their needs. He opens up to being obedient to His Father in heaven so he can be that dad that his children can obey. The energy of openness and obedience that he releases creates an atmosphere of freedom for his household to operate freely.

> *In his kindness God called you to share in his eternal glory by means of Christ Jesus. So after you have suffered a little while, he will restore, support and strengthen you, and he will place you on a firm foundation (1 Peter 5:10, NLT).*

Our loving Father in heaven is so strong, His name is Jehovah Adonai, our Almighty Father is our Master. Jesus lived our Father's name, Jehovah Adonai, and as the Master of our life, He was strong for us, even when He didn't want to drink from the cup of suffering. He is now working in our life through His Spirit to make us strong and be more like Him. He allows trials, temptation and tests that we face in life, so He can use them to have His way in us to become that strong person He designed us to be.

March 8

~ Our Master provides peace and protection for His house ~

> *I run in the path of your commands, for you have broadened my understanding (Psalm 119:32, NIV).*

On the evening of January 9, 2022, after preparing dinner, I was watching a program about animals. It focused on snakes and how they would attack the eggs of other animals and eat them. While I watched, the Holy Spirit begin teaching me this: The kingdom of God is like this. Once you have a new life, do not try to expose yourself, try to hide yourself by having daily relationship with Jesus in Word and prayer. When you don't, you are exposed and left in the open for the enemy to attack and end the life you are just trying to start. You see, it's just like the eggs that were left in the open and exposed for the enemy to attack.

A good dad is always around his family to protect them. To be that provider of protection and that good security to his household, he sits in the shadow of His Father in heaven to protect him so he can protect his house. Jesus lived our Father's name, Jehovah Adonai, our Almighty Father is our Master. He showed His Lord and Mastership in being that good shepherd who is always there to protect His sheep from the enemy's harm.

> *In peace I will lie down and sleep, for you alone, O Lord, will keep me safe (Psalm 4:8, NLT).*

Every day we are to sleep in peace and security, and wake up in joy and strength, because we have Jesus as the Master and Lord over our house.

March 9

~ *Pray in the will of God* ~

> *This is the confidence we have in approaching God: that if we ask anything according to his will, he hears us. And if we know that he hears us—whatever we ask—we know that we have what we asked of him (1 John 5:14-15, NIV).*

One summer evening, December 22, 2020, Blessed, my twenty-two-month old, thought he was helping out, but instead gave me extra work. I got his towel to give him a wash, but instead he went and grabbed another towel and brought it to me. I had to take that towel and go put it back at the place he took it from. I had the towel he was using, but he went for another which was not his.

This is what the Holy Spirit taught me: Sometimes God is fixing up all our mess we make, before he starts working on His will He has for us. Also, that is what happens when we don't pray in the will of God. When we pray in the will of God, He does what we ask of Him because He is ready to do that for us.

To be a good master to his house, a good dad always prays for the will of his heavenly Father to have its way in his household. To know more of the Father's will, he spends quality time in Word and prayer. Everything he prays is in line with what the Father instructs. All his other prayer needs are summarised with this word of prayer, 'Let your will be done on earth as it is in heaven'. And so the will of the heavenly Father, as the Master, is done through him on earth.

Jehovah Adonai, our Almighty Father is our Master is His name, and His will in our life is to look at us and see the image of Christ. Jesus Christ came on earth and served as a Master by washing his disciples' feet. And our Father in heaven wants us to do that too, to wash the feet of people He brings into our life. When we wash their feet we are taking the lead and responsibility as a master of our house. The Spirit of God takes the lead and responsibility when we house Him inside of us. This is the will of the Father because Jesus said, 'Follow the example I am doing.'

March 10

~ Controlling the move of anger ~

The Lord is gracious and compassionate, slow to anger and rich in love (Psalm 145:8, NIV).

One summer's day, December 21, 2020, a friend sent me scriptures of anger management and this is the revelation I received: A good dad is slow to anger. He may be angry and frustrated over many matters of his household as a master, but he is slow to anger. He doesn't direct his energy on the mistake done; he directs it on making anger leave him, slowly, from inside to outside of him. He understands that for anger to lose its energy and purpose it must flow slowly from within. This is how he doesn't have the energy of anger to direct towards his household. He looks for the solution of what made him angry.

God was the Master of the Garden of Eden and He left it in the care of Adam and Eve. They disobeyed Him and ate the forbidden fruit. God, our loving Father and Master of our life., didn't shout angrily at them instantly, rather, He met up with them as usual, later in the evening. He clothed their nakedness and sent them out of His beautiful garden. The tree of life was in the garden of Eden. Now that they knew evil and good, they might reach out and eat the tree of life and live forever. Evil cannot live forever, and so God had to make them leave the garden.

> *And the Lord God said, 'The man has now become like one of us, knowing good and evil. He must not be allowed to reach out his hand and take also from the tree of life and eat, and live forever.' (Genesis 3:22, NIV).*

Jesus came and lived the Father's name, Jehovah Adonai, our Almighty Father is our Master. He showed us that our Father is not angry with us. As our Master, He wants to bring us back home to be with Him forever. He loves us so much He sent Him to come and die for us so we can live with Him for eternity. Our loving Father is now clothing us in the righteousness of Christ.

Every day, we are to remain in the righteous life of Jesus Christ and serve Him as our Master in whatever we do.

March 11

~ Enjoy your Christ-like life before you meet Him ~

Our life is like a flower that grows quickly and then dies away. Our life is like a shadow that is here for a short time and then is gone (Job 14:2, ERV).

I received a loyalty card for being a faithful customer, offering 50% off on a limit of ten items. The expiry date to enjoying this gift was December 3, 2022, which was the next day. I had received this gift a month earlier, but never got around to using it until I realised on December 2 that tomorrow was the expiry date.

Even though I didn't need to buy something, I just had to use it up well. The Holy Spirit spoke in my heart and reminded me of how our life is like that, living now and gone tomorrow, and we have to make use of every day with this gift of life.

Hear this: I had to enjoy this gift of a 50% discount or the time would be up and I would lose the privilege I had been given. The reason I had that privilege was because I signed up with that store as a faithful customer. So it is with the life we have — it is a precious gift, but for that life to be alive and full of love, light and life, we need Jesus to be our Master by receiving Him into our hearts and making Him Lord and Master over our life.

Jesus came and lived our heavenly Father's name, Jehovah Adonai, our Almighty Father is our Master. Our Father loves us so much and gave Jesus, who is the Love, Light and Life. He laid down His life to give us that life as a free gift to enjoy all the treasure found in Him.

Jesus is now standing at the door of our hearts, for us to invite Him into our life and make Him the Master and Lord of our life so we can enjoy every day with what His gift of life offers before our time on earth expires (see Revelation 3:20).

If you have already made Jesus the Lord and Master of your life, then enjoy your every day in Christ, living a life of love, peace and joy, because you do not know when your time will be over in this life.

> *Your word, LORD, is eternal; it stands firm in the heavens. Your faithfulness continues through all generations; you established the earth, and it endures. Your laws endure to this day, for all things serve you (Psalm 119:89-91, NIV).*

Every day, dip your temporary life into the truth of God's Word to continue to receive His Master-ship, because everything has a limit, except the Word of God.

March 12

~ *Think big in the greatness of God* ~

> *If then you have been raised with Christ, seek the things that are above, where Christ is, seated at the right hand of God. Set your minds on things that are above, not on things that are on earth (Colossians 3:1-2, ESV).*

There is a flowering plant called Lobelia Cambridge Blue that normally grows wild and spreads. One summer's day, December 12, 2020, I placed the flower in a bottle and it grew only to the size of the bottle. This is what the Holy Spirit taught me: Your mind is like that flowering plant. It can grow big and further out, but it depends on how you think. The greater you think, the greater you become, but if you are limited to a thinking storage like this bottle that holds the flower, your thoughts will be limited. And you can't give birth to great things because you can't think big.

A good dad understands that as the master of his household he has many responsibilities, and so he renews his mind in the Word of God that has no ending, to expand his mind in thinking thoughts of heavenly nature where His Father lives.

He must become greater; I must become less (John 3:30, NIV).

Jehovah Adonai, our Lord God, our Master and our heavenly Father, has seated on His right-hand Jesus, and we, as His sons through adoption, are to rule and reign with Christ in that position. Jesus came down and lived the Father's name, Jehovah Adonai, by serving and not to be served. He is the Master of our life, serving us by interceding on our behalf to the Father. In Him is all the treasure and wealth of God, which rightfully belongs to those who live in the righteousness of Christ. We just have to think John 3:30, Christ becomes great and we become less in our lives.

Each new day is an opportunity to live our Father's name, Jehovah Adonai, in the name of Jesus to the glory of the Father, to serve our earthly master like we serve our heavenly Master, Jesus.

March 13

~ Looking ahead in the light of God's Word ~

To You, Lord, I lift up my soul (Psalm 25:1, NASB).

One late summer's night, January 2, 2022, Tom was driving and decided to put the headlights on high beam to show the road ahead.

We could see even the furthest distance that was dark, but whenever oncoming cars came he would put the headlight's high beam off, as we knew it could blind the driver coming our way.

This is what the Holy Spirit taught me: The kingdom of God is like this. The more and deeper you get into the Word of God, which is the light, the more you can see the path you are taking in this eternal journey to joy. The headlight is put on you when Christ becomes the head of your body. The power of eternal light is upon you, and it can blind whoever that come against you. Just like how our headlight can blind the oncoming cars to us.

A good dad knows that to be a good master to his household he has to lead a prayerful life in his house and remain daily in the Word of God. To remain a good father on earth, he prays to his heavenly Father, 'To you, Lord, I lift up my soul.' It's his prayer that reveals to him to take one step forward at a time when he can't see a way forward. But the more he sits in the counsel of the Word every day, the more he can see where His Father in heaven is leading him to.

Jesus was the light of the world, the Master Chief light, and lived our Father's name, Jehovah Adonai, our Almighty Father in heaven is our Master. Our Father loves us so much, He sent Jesus to come open our eyes to see Him as the light to lead us back to our loving Father.

> *When Jesus spoke again to the people, he said, 'I am the light of the world. Whoever follows me will never walk in darkness, but will have the light of life.' (John 8:12, NIV).*

Every day is another opportunity to get more into the living Word, which is the light unto the path, so we can see ahead how to walk successfully in the right path to our destiny. Let the Word of God always have mastership over your life.

March 14

~ No longer a servant but a friend to Jesus ~

I no longer call you servants, because a servant does not know his master's business. Instead, I have called you friends, for everything that I learned from my Father I have made known to you (John 15:15, NIV).

We have a rich dad who took the form of flesh to be like us and became poor so we can become rich. He is the Master and He wants us to take mastership over the riches of the earth and not have those things be master over our lives and control us. You can have money, have mastership and control over it, but do not have such love for money that it becomes your master. Do not serve money, but let money serve you in serving others if you can help in little ways the needs of others. Money can deceive you and lead you astray from loving the Lord your God, Jehovah Adonai.

A good dad loves the Lord God with all his heart, soul and flesh, so that God becomes the priority over what he masters in his household. This is how he becomes rich with love so he can provide that love to his family. His family needs his unconditional love in spending quality time with him more than the money.

God is love and we are commanded to love Him with all our heart, soul and body, because when we do this, His love takes mastership over us. We are controlled by love, and so we begin to do things with love towards others.

Greater love has no one than this, that someone lay down his life for his friends (John 15:13, ESV).

Jesus was the love of God who lived our Father's name, Jehovah Adonai, the greatest master of our life who laid His own life down for us. No earthly master can do such a sacrifice for a servant. Jesus sees us as a friend. Only a loyal, faithful friend can lay down their life and make sacrifices for their friends.

Every day, we have to sacrifice our time, committing to remain in Word and prayer so the connection of the friendship with our Master can become stronger.

March 15

~ Preparing ourselves for the coming of the Master ~

And a servant who knows what the master wants, but isn't prepared and doesn't carry out those instructions, will be severely punished (Luke 12:47, NLT).

One March day, of the year 2021, I was working on making the house look tidy, neat and presentable for the landlord, who is the master of the house. The Holy Spirit began to teach me that Jesus is the master of your house. Every day I am to make my house, His temple and body, more presentable, clean and tidy it well for Him, because any hour of any day the master is returning.

A good dad understands that as the body of Christ and temple of the Holy Spirit, he was bought with the precious blood of Jesus. He ensures that he is clean and washes every day with the blood of Jesus so he remains spotless and clean, well prepared to meet the Master on that glorious day.

Jesus lived our heavenly Father's name, Jehovah Adonai, our Almighty Father is our Master. As the Master and head of us, He wants to connect us back to the Father. Therefore, He laid down His life for us so we can then live His life to reconnect back to the Father.

> *And if I go and prepare a place for you, I will come back and take you to be with me that you also may be where I am (John 14:3, NIV).*

Every day we have to prepare ourselves to meet the Master of our life who is preparing a place for us to live with Him forever.

March 16

~ Communicate in the language of the Spirit to confuse the enemies of the dark spiritual realms ~

> *For if you have the ability to speak in tongues, you will be talking only to God, since people won't be able to understand you. You will be speaking by the power of the Spirit, but it will all be mysterious (1 Corinthians 14:2, NLT).*

December 10, 2022, I was raking the dry brown leaves outside our house. Since the house is right under big rainforest trees, the dry leaves constantly fall. I was trying to call out to my families to do something, and then I thought, *if our family can speak one same language, then our neighbours will not know what I am trying to tell them if I speak to them in that particular language. If I raise my voice over to my families to tell them something, my neighbours will know, because I am outside the house where they can see me clearly.*

This is what the Holy Spirit taught me: You see, this is what speaking in tongues is all about. When you speak in tongue, your spirit being is expressing and calling out in the language that the dark forces in the spiritual realm won't understand. The enemy is confused and doesn't know what you are saying. It's a spiritual language from your spirit being, as a child of God, to the Spirit of God. Even the Holy Spirit expresses Himself in that way to the Father (see Romans 8:26).

This is the best way to communicate with the Holy Spirit to release the spiritual blessings that your heart desires, as this confuses the devil in his efforts to stop you from receiving what you are crying out for. Blessings and breakthroughs will start to manifest in the physical realm when your spirit speaks in tongues, the language of heaven. The will of heaven is done on earth. The Holy Spirit brought this sign of language on His arrival (see Acts 2:1-4).

There is something the Lord revealed to me some years back in Psalm 8:2: The words from babies and infants that we can't understand are like speaking in tongues and confuses and silences the enemies in the spiritual dark realms. Now, because of this, the plan of the enemy is confused and is on hold or delayed. This is one reason why the devil works extremely hard for babies to be miscarried or aborted before coming into full-term of life.

> *Out of the mouth of babes and nursing infants You have ordained strength, Because of Your enemies, That You may silence the enemy and the avenger (Psalm 8:2, NKJV).*

Jesus lived our Father's name, Jehovah Adonai, our Almighty Father is our Master. He is the Master of our life and wants to communicate with us so we can know what His movement in our lives will be. When we become one with Him as the head, and we as the body, we become one with His Spirit too. (See 1 Corinthians

6:17). Our spirit can speak in tongues of heavenly languages and confuse the enemy of what our moves are in Christ.

Every day, live the Father's name, Jehovah Adonai, our Almighty Father is our Master. Communicate with your Master, Jesus, for Him to show what His move for the day is, to destroy the work of the enemy for that day. Move around and speak the language of the Spirit whenever the Spirit leads.

March 17

~ Each day teaches us lessons to be prepared for the test in life ~

> *There are many rooms in my Father's house. I would not tell you this if it were not true. I am going there to prepare a place for you. After I go and prepare a place for you, I will come back. Then I will take you with me, so that you can be where I am (John 14:2-3, ERV).*

On the first Monday of the school holiday, December 19, 2022, I thought *I will have to prepare some educational things and teach Angelilly, who will be going to year 3 in 2023.*

This is what the Holy Spirit taught me: Every day, God prepares the day to teach us lessons to live that good, kind and patient life. If you didn't do well today in being patient in the situation you faced, it is to teach you a lesson to do it better the next day, should you face that situation again.

Jesus came and lived our Father's name, Jehovah Adonai, our Almighty Father is our Master. Jesus is our Master, the Word who has become flesh. His Word is there to prepare our flesh to become an overcomer. As the Master of our life, He knows what challenges and struggles we face daily and He will not allow anything that is beyond our ability to enter our life.

> *No temptation has overtaken you except what is common to mankind. And God is faithful; he will not let you be tempted beyond what you can bear. But when you are tempted, he will also provide a way out so that you can endure it (1 Corinthians 10:13, NIV).*

As a master to his household, a good dad will always make it his priority to prepare himself every day to be equipped with the fruit of the Holy Spirit so he can serve his house when they are in need of his patience, kindness, goodness, gentleness and compassion.

Every day, we are to live our Father's name, Jehovah Adonai, in Jesus' name, and be a good master over our new life in Christ. We are to prepare that life to produce the fruit of the Holy Spirit daily. Jesus has gone to prepare a place, and will return to receive this life which He has Mastership and Lordship over.

March 18

~ As a son we have mastership over all creation ~

> *The Lord had said to Abram, 'Go from your country, your people and your father's household to the land I will show you. I will make you into a great nation, and I will bless you; I will make your name great, and you will be a blessing. I will bless those who bless you, and whoever curses you I will curse; and all peoples on earth will be blessed through you.' (Genesis 12:1-3, NIV).*

A good dad is aware that wherever he is and whatever he is doing is God's calling upon him, and this is where His Father wants him to be. He just has to be that good master to that land where he is building up his household. As long as he does everything in Jesus' name to the glory of the Father, the name of his family will be blessed to be a blessing to all the nations and not just the community he resides in.

> *I will proclaim the Lord's decree: He said to me, 'You are my son; today I have become your father. Ask me, and I will make the nations your inheritance, the ends of the earth your possession (Psalm 2:7-8, NIV).*

He is Jehovah Adonai. He is not only the Master over everything, but is a loving Father who wants the best for His children. Today, right now at this very moment of this hour, He wants us to ask Him anything. We have inherited His name in the name of Jesus and have become a son to inherit nations and kingdoms. Jesus has lived the Father's name, Jehovah Adonai. As a son through Jesus, we are to live the Father's name in Jesus' name and take over the mastership of the Father's creation so His glory can be reflected again through all creation.

Every day, remember that your real identity is in your name that you inherited through the name of Jesus. You are designed and destined in that name of Jesus for greater and bigger things.

March 19

~ *On a journey for the Master* ~

> *Praise be to the Lord, the God of my master Abraham, who has not abandoned his kindness and faithfulness to my master. As for me, the Lord has led me on the journey to the house of my master's relatives (Genesis 24:27, NIV).*

A good dad is aware of the journey he is on. He strengthens himself faithfully in the Word so he is not led astray from accomplishing his mission. As a master to his house, he leads them with kindness and faithfulness.

> *The Lord is good! His love and faithfulness will last forever (Psalm 100:5, CEV).*

As a loving Father, He sent Jesus on a mission and Jesus Himself lived our Father's name, Jehovah Adonai. He was the Master Himself, God in the form of flesh, a sacrifice He made. He knew what the journey was going to be like, but He took it because He wanted to connect us in our flesh back to the Father. The flesh had taken over our spirit being and we were dead in spirit. For the flesh to be dead and the spirit to become alive again, Jesus, God in flesh, took this death journey on earth. Because our Master took that death journey on earth, we can now take a journey full of life, light and love towards heaven.

Every day, we must be aware that we are on a journey for our Master to show the kindness and the faithfulness of His love. Have mastery over your new day by being kind to yourself. Fill yourself with kindness before you serve kindness, and do it faithfully.

March 20

~ Store up the Word of God and declare it over your life ~

> *I have stored up your word in my heart, that I might not sin against you (Psalm 119:11, ESV).*

One summer's morning, December 27, 2021, I was trying to store some things in the garage so I packed them into a box. After,

I looked again to see what I had placed in the box, just so I could put a label on the box to tell me what was in it. While I was doing that, I heard the Holy Spirit say: The kingdom of God is like this. You have to store into you and your house the Word of God, then start labelling yourself and declaring over, the Word of God that you stored into you. You have a Master over your life and His Word is what He has spoken over and made you. That is what you should contain and store.

Jesus is the Word who became flesh, the Word who was with the Father in the beginning to create whatever the Father spoke and declared. He lived our Father's name, Jehovah Adonai, our Almighty Father is our Master. Not only did He become the flesh, but the Master over the Word. Whatever the Word of God that we receive and declare into our life, the enemy, the devil, cannot steal it because we have a Master over us who has defeated his power of sin and death.

You have been set free from sin and have become slaves to righteousness (Romans 6:18, NIV).

Every new day, receive into you and declare every Word that God says of you and let the Word of God master your life in every decision you make. Be a slave to righteousness.

March 21

~ Fill yourself to your heart's content with the Father's love so you can serve others ~

I am the Lord your God, who brought you up out of Egypt. Open wide your mouth and I will fill it (Psalm 81:10, NIV).

On the morning of November 21, 2022, I looked at the powdered milk bottle which was almost empty. Then I thought about how I feel so satisfied and happy when the bottle is full, and that I knew I had enough to keep me going. You see, the Lord too is happy when He sees us full of Him to serve in Him the purposes we were created for. Just like how I see the powdered milk bottle full to serve me its purpose, this is also what our loving Father wants to see in us. He wants to see that we are full of His love to serve others. Every day, we have to wake up and fill ourselves up with the love of the Father to serve Him.

> *As you serve the Lord, work hard and don't be lazy. Be excited about serving him! Be happy because of the hope you have. Be patient when you have troubles. Pray all the time (Romans 12:11-12, ERV).*

Jesus came and lived our Father's name, Jehovah Adonai, our Almighty Father is our Master. He came to serve and not to be served. But for Him to serve, He has to go and spend time alone after emptying Himself out. We can't serve from an empty vessel.

A good dad refills himself in the Word every morning before he rises up to live his day in serving his households. He declares Joshua 24:15 is his declaration, *'But as for me and my household, we will serve the Lord.'*

Every day, we are to live our Father's name, Jehovah Adonai, our Almighty Father is our Master in Jesus' name. We have to wake up and fill ourselves up in Word and in prayer to serve our Master, Jesus, by serving whoever we are serving. We are to spend time in the Father's presence for Him to fill us up to serve His purpose He designed us for. He knows what we will face for the day, and

He will feed us the daily bread to give us the strength we need for the day to serve our purpose.

March 22

~ The Master feeds us in every season, even in the drought season ~

And the Lord said, 'Who then is the faithful and wise manager, whom his master will set over his household, to give them their portion of food at the proper time? Blessed is that servant whom his master will find so doing when he comes. Truly, I say to you, he will set him over all his possessions (Luke 12:42-44, ESV).

Jesus has lived our heavenly Father's name, Jehovah Adonai, our Almighty Father is our Master. And so the Father has set the name of Jesus above all other names and gave power and authority over the name of Jesus. Every knee shall bow in heaven and on earth and under the earth at the name of Jesus (see Philippians 2:10).

A good dad is faithful and a wise manager to his household. Just like Abraham, He knows His Father in heaven like a friend and trusts Him completely as the Master of His house who will always provide His household portions of food at the proper time.

All creatures look to you to give them their food at the proper time (Psalm 104:27, NIV).

As the Master to our household, our heavenly Father will always give us food at the proper time according to the seasons of time we go through. He also feeds us through the storms so we have the strength to go through that storm and come out stronger.

March 23

~ *From slaves of sin to slaves of righteousness* ~

Teach slaves to be subject to their masters in everything, to try to please them, not to talk back to them, and not to steal from them, but to show that they can be fully trusted, so that in every way they will make the teaching about God our Saviour attractive (Titus 2: 9-10, NIV).

A good dad makes the teaching of God attractive in the way he teaches everyone under his control. He is subject to his heavenly Father, Jehovah Adonai, the Master of the universe, and only lives to please Him with his faith. Faith comes by hearing and hearing the Word, and this is what He does.

> *Don't you realize that you become the slave of whatever you choose to obey? You can be a slave to sin, which leads to death, or you can choose to obey God, which leads to righteous living (Romans 6:16, NLT).*

Jesus lived our Father's name, Jehovah Adonai, our Almighty Father is our Master. He became the slave of righteousness in serving our Father on earth so He could set us free, as we were slaves to sin. Even the cup of suffering was too much for him and He couldn't take it with His human capabilities, but He pleased the Father in saying, 'Your will be done.'

> *You have been set free from sin and have become slaves to righteousness (Romans 6:18, NIV).*

We are now set free from being slaves of sin to slaves of righteousness to serve our Master, Jesus Christ, who has purchased us with His sinless blood. Every day, we are to serve the fruit of righteousness of the Holy Spirit as slaves of righteousness.

March 24

~ Be good stewards of your life ~

The man who had received five bags of gold brought the other five. 'Master,' he said, 'you entrusted me with five bags of gold. See, I have gained five more.' His master replied, 'Well done, good and faithful servant! You have been faithful with a few things; I will put you in charge of many things. Come and share your master's happiness!' (Matthew 25:20-21, NIV).

We gave an old phone to our two-year-old son to use. It was old, but in good functioning condition. He would watch his favourite YouTube cartoon characters. However, whenever he had the chance, he always liked to reach out and grab his dad's phone, which was more advanced and of good quality. Then, out of curiosity, he would open the cover and try to explore the phone, which can cause the phone to get damaged. One morning, January 17, 2022, he asked if he could use my phone. I said, 'No, I am not giving you my phone. You remember how you normally try to rip phones apart? You might do the same to mine.' But I told him that once he is big and knows how to look after it well, I will give him a big phone. He was happy with what I said.

You see, Jesus lived our Father's name, Jehovah Adonai, our Almighty Father is our Master. Our Father trusted Him and counted on Him that He would use His life to bring all lives lost in the world back to the Father. At such a time that was right for the Son to be born, He sent Him into the world. Jesus laid down His life so we could do away with our old lives and live His new life of abundance. I told my two-year-old son that when he is matured he will have a big phone like mine. So it is with us: When we are matured enough, we will inherit the Love of God, which is full of joy, peace and righteousness in the kingdom of God.

God allows immature, difficult people who constantly cause us hardship and aches in our life to make us mature in Christ. When we are faithful in giving them the life we have in Christ, God will allow great battles and challenges, because we will always know how to remain in peace and celebrate in joy in every battle that catches us by surprise. We have inherited and matured in God's love, the love that covers all sin (see 1 Peter 4:8). Also, when we inherit the love of God, we are able to love the world like our Father in heaven, even when the world brings us more aches, pains and sufferings.

Every day, be a good master with what little you have with your life in Christ and the Father will put you in charge of many things. Jesus lived the Father's name, Jehovah Adonai, and was faithful until His death. Therefore, the Father has given authority and power to the name of Jesus.

March 25

~ Our Lord, Jesus Christ our Master, became a servant to serve and led us in the Father's will ~

Who do people think is the greatest, a person who is served or one who serves? Isn't it the one who is served? But I have been with you as a servant (Luke 22:27, CEV).

June 10, 2022, I was working on this book and it was so cold! I got the little portable heater and directed it so the heat came straight towards me. This is what the Holy Spirit taught me: We too must get the Word of God and allow it to target that part of our life that needs fixing.

A master gives specific instructions to his servants. A good dad gives specific instructions to his household members. Being the master, he has to serve and lead his house on what he wants his household to do. He sits in the guidance of God's Word every day so he can lead his house in the truth.

Jesus came and lived our Father's name, Jehovah Adonai, our Almighty God is our Master. As the Master of our life, He came to serve and not to be served. He served and led His followers by showing them what the Father wanted. Even though Jesus was the Master, He said, 'I no longer call you servants, but friends.' He washed the feet of His disciples like a friend would do. Like my heater I targeted directly on myself, Jesus targeted directly the needs of a servant. Servants are always serving and they need a friend to serve them. Jesus became that friend and served them. He was the Master, yet He took the position of a servant and said, "I came to serve and not to be served."

> *I no longer call you servants, because a servant does not know his master's business. Instead, I have called you friends, for everything that I learned from my Father I have made known to you (John 15:15, NIV).*

Every day comes with a new challenge to live our Father's name, Jehovah Adonai, in Jesus' name, and be a good master to our household. Like our Chief Master, Jesus Christ, we are to take the position of a servant to serve and lead them in the truth of God's Word and what our Father desires of us.

March 26

~ Serve your earthly master like you're serving your heavenly Master ~

> *Masters, treat your bondservants justly and fairly,*
> *knowing that you also have a Master in heaven*
> *(Colossians 4:1, ESV).*

The life of every hero written in the bible was to teach us to learn from them. Most of them were men greatly used by God even though they showed many weaknesses and failures throughout their lives. A good dad lives the life and example of Joseph. He serves his earthly master like he is serving his heavenly Master.

He makes Colossians 4:1 become his flesh by treating his slaves justly and fairly, knowing that He has a Master in heaven who is the master of his life. Joseph was sold as a slave by his brothers and lived most of his young life serving as a slave. When he thought life was good for him, he was accused again for the evil he never did towards his master's wife, and was thrown into prison again. He knew what the life of a slave was like. God turned everything around for him in his favour, which would otherwise have cost him decades of years to work for. And just like that, from being a prisoner, he became the Prime Minister. He had the opportunity to make his brothers slaves forever for what they had done to him, but he knew that he had a good Master of his life who turned evil into good. This is the life of a good dad.

> *You intended to harm me, but God intended it for good*
> *to accomplish what is now being done, the saving of many*
> *lives (Genesis 50:20, NIV).*

Jesus our Master has shown us His life, which the enemy meant to be bad for us by having Him crucified and dead on the cross, turned out to be for our good. He saved our lives from sin and death, which is the power of the devil.

March 27

~ We are called to live for our Master ~

*We always carry around in our body the death of Jesus,
so that the life of Jesus may also be revealed in our body
(2 Corinthians 4:10, NIV).*

One summer's day, January 20, 2022, I was into my fourth month of pregnancy and was thinking of how I had been so careful with myself. Every time I wanted to do something, I took into consideration and was aware of the life I carried inside of me. There was an unborn baby in me and I didn't want to do anything that might harm her growth.

The Holy Spirit spoke into my heart and said: You also have to be careful because you carry the resurrected life of Christ inside you. Just like being careful and aware of everything you do, you also have to be careful in how you carry the life of Christ in you. Never do anything that will deform the image of Christ. As you wait for the NINE MONTHS to pass to bring your image into the world, you also have to develop and be matured in the NINE FRUIT of the Spirit to give birth to the image of Christ. When you die to sin by producing the fruit of the Spirit, you carry the death of Jesus so the life of Jesus is revealed in your body.

Jesus lived our Father in heaven's name, Jehovah Adonai, our Almighty Father is our Master. He is our Master who became flesh to not only live with us, but to live in us through the death and resurrection of His life. We now carry our Master in us and we do not want to do anything that will ruin the image of our Master. We are citizens of heaven who are ambassadors on earth.

> *But we are citizens of heaven, where the Lord Jesus Christ lives. And we are eagerly waiting for him to return as our Saviour (Philippians 3:20, NLT).*

Every morning we wake up to a new day because we are called to live for our Master, who has lived for us by laying down His life for us. Because He lives, we too live.

March 28

~ Live and action the Word in your home, then share to others ~

> *This is how one should regard us, as servants of Christ and stewards of the mysteries of God. Moreover, it is required of stewards that they be found faithful (1 Corinthians 4:1-2, ESV).*

January 20, 2022, I was appreciating the social media platform and how I use it to spread the love of God with my daily devotional books. I was thinking out loud that without it, who would I be reaching out to in sharing God's Word? This is what I heard the Holy Spirit say: You have your household members there to share daily the love of God and His Word constantly with them.

This really hit me hard, because even though we pray and I share and remind my house every day of the goodness of God, I have never seen them as people I have to preach to. I think within me that as long as they are with me, it's other people I need to reach out to, not them, that this is not what I was supposed to do.

As a master to what God has entrusted with me, what I preach to others should be actioned to members of my household.

Jesus lived our heavenly Father's name, Jehovah Adonai, our Almighty Father is our Master. He is the Word who has become flesh. Being our Master on earth, He actioned the Word of God that was preached and prophesied by the Prophet Isaiah (see Isaiah 61:1).

> ….and the scroll of the prophet Isaiah was handed to him. Unrolling it, he found the place where it is written: 'The Spirit of the Lord is on me, because he has anointed me to proclaim good news to the poor. He has sent me to proclaim freedom for the prisoners and recovery of sight for the blind, to set the oppressed free, to proclaim the year of the Lord's favour.' (Luke 4:17-19, NIV).

Each and every day, we are to live our Father's name, Jehovah Adonai, and be a good master in faithfully actioning the Word of God that shows the Father's love to members of our household.

March 29

~ Moving everywhere in the Master ~

> Have I not commanded you? Be strong and courageous. Do not be afraid; do not be discouraged, for the Lord your God will be with you wherever you go (Joshua 1:9, NIV).

One morning, January 14, 2022, I was looking at my young kids and thought, *everywhere I go, they will be with me, because they are part of the family*. So are we; wherever God moves us to we will move with Him when we become part of His family. He will always be where we are. This is because we move and have our being in Him (see Acts 17:28).

Jesus actually said, 'I no longer call you servants, but friends.' A servant won't know about the moves of the master, but a friend does. David saw this when he said he'd rather be a doorkeeper at the Lord's temple. You see, a doorkeeper knows the movement of the master, when he will leave and when he is going to return.

> *I would rather be a doorkeeper in the house of my God than dwell in the tents of the wicked (Psalm 84:10, NIV).*

Jesus lived our Father's name, Jehovah Adonai, our Almighty Father is our Master. Him being the Master to our house, we not only can contain Him, but also can know Him better in our lives, His every move through every season and time in our lives, what He is about to do and what He is doing.

As master to his house, a good dad knows every move of his household. He stays connected to His Father in heaven, Jehovah Adonai, every day in Word and prayer. This is how he can be wise and know what is happening in his household. As long as he knows the Master of the universe, a good dad will know how things in the universe move for his household.

Each and every day, we are to abide in Christ in His Word so we can know every move our Master is going to make in His house which is us.

March 30

~ *Prepare the way for your children to walk by serving them* ~

> *Ye call me Master and Lord: and ye say well; for so I am. If I then, your Lord and Master, have washed your feet; ye also ought to wash one another's feet. For I have given you an example, that ye should do as I have done to you (John 13:13-15, KJV).*

Children will not pay full attention to what the parents say, but will follow every action they do. Many times I catch my toddler doing things that I normally do every day. I find him climbing up to the sink on his little stool to do the dishes, or even taking his rubbish to the trash bin. I have also realised he says things that I say. Some things may not be a good example. Many times in my speech, I say, 'Later, I will do that.' Now when I ask him to have a shower, he says, 'Later.' Procrastination is not a good thing. As masters to what our Father in heaven has entrusted to us, we have to be careful and ask God for wisdom every day to be a good leader in our house.

Children serve by doing what services they see their parents serve in the house. Jesus lived our heavenly Father's name, Jehovah Adonai, our Almighty Father is our Master. Everything that our loving Father was doing invisibly in our lives, Jesus did visibly. Jesus points out His position as the Master by doing what a servant would do for his master, and not what masters would do for their servants. He did this to show that in the kingdom of God, being a master, one has to serve and not to be served, because in everything we do we are serving Jehovah Adonai, not men.

> *No one has ever seen God. But the unique One, who is himself God, is near to the Father's heart. He has revealed God to us (John 1:18, NLT).*

Every day, keep serving your children in your house what you, as the master, would like them to do in life. Jesus wanted us to wash the feet of others as He washed the feet of His disciples. This is how we are to prepare the way for others to walk in cleanliness. John the Baptist was the voice that prepared the way for Jesus to come and walk. And Jesus prepared the way for the Holy Spirit to come and live in us by washing our feet. So we can walk and be led by the Spirit to serve His fruit of love.

March 31

~ Fill up your cup in the Living water so you can master your days well ~

You anoint my head with oil, my cup overflows
(Psalm 23:5, NIV).

After returning from a morning walk on January 18, 2022, Angelilly finished her water which she'd taken out from the fridge. I asked her to refill and put it back in the fridge. This is what I heard the Holy Spirit say: Always refill yourself, every day, when you first wake up in the morning, with God's Word of goodness, because this is a fallen, evil world and has lots of evil activities that can drain your good energy. When you fill your cup, you have something to pour out from, and when you continue to sit in Word and prayer more, your cup starts to overflow.

Jesus lived our Father's name, Jehovah Adonai, our Almighty Father is our Master. He drank from the cup of suffering just so we can live a good life. We will always feel empty without Him because He paid for our life and He is the only one who can fill that empty space. We are the house of which He is the Master. We are to abide in Him and fill our cup from our Master. He is the living water who will spring out from us if we house Him and seek Him with all our heart, soul and strength.

Whoever believes in me, as Scripture has said, rivers of
living water will flow from within them (John 7:38, NIV).

Before you walk into your everyday schedule, fill your cup from the springs of living water within you. Our Master is waiting for us, His households, so He can play His Master role in our lives.

APRIL

Jehovah Jireh! I AM The Provider!

OUR LORD GOD, OUR PROVIDER.

~ Jesus provided His flesh to heal our body, so our body can become His body where His Spirit will reside ~

'Man shall not live by bread alone, but by every word that proceeds from the mouth of God.'"
(Matthew 4:4, NKJV).

On the morning of December 29, 2022, I wanted to have my quiet time in Word and prayer, but realised I had to attend to my seven-month-old who was hungry and hadn't eaten yet. I didn't spend time in Word and prayer, but instead went on to feeding my baby.

The Holy Spirit taught me this: Jesus' ministry was about attending to the physical needs of the flesh before He got into the spiritual. He was meeting that physical need to show and point out where the spiritual need was. The body carries the spirit being, so Jesus had to meet and heal that physical need, and once the receiver's eyes are open, they can also see and understand the spiritual manifestation of their spirit needs. For Jesus to reap His spiritual work in us, He has to first sow into the physical state of us. We now can also sow in our physical realm to reap our spiritual blessings and have them manifested for us in the physical world.

Jesus lived our Father's name, Jehovah Jireh, our Almighty Father who provides, by not only providing healing for our physical needs, but He also provided His own life so we can remain healed and receive all His great, glorious riches that His life provides. He sowed

His life so He can reap many lives, who will become His body where His Spirit can reside. The Holy Spirit sowed His power of resurrection by resurrecting the body of Christ back to life, so He can reap our body to become the body of Christ where He can come and live in us.

> *Jesus answered, "Everyone who drinks this water will be thirsty again, but whoever drinks the water I give them will never thirst. Indeed, the water I give them will become in them a spring of water welling up to eternal life." The woman said to him, "Sir, give me this water so that I won't get thirsty and have to keep coming here to draw water." (John 4:13-15, NIV).*

Every day, and each day of the month of April, we are to live our Father's name, Jehovah Jireh, and provide what we can to meet the physical need of someone, to help them see better their spiritual need that relates to their physical need. Jesus showed us by meeting the physical thirst of the Samaritan woman at the well, showing her that He is the living water who can satisfy her thirst for a relationship. He raised up Lazarus' dead body to show that He is the resurrection and life. He opened the eyes of the blind man to show that He came to give us sight to see.

Every new day is an opportunity to look out for someone. If you are like me, with younger kids, we are to provide for their daily physical needs and teach them, with our examples, the good fruit of the Holy Spirit. We will not be perfect in raising our children, but as long as we remain in the perfect love of God to be forgiving, good, kind and patient, we are raising them in the righteousness of God.

April 1

~ Move in the strength of God towards the coming dark forces ~

Finally, be strong in the Lord and in the strength of his might (Ephesians 6:10, ESV).

One wintery Saturday morning, June 19, 2021, while waiting for Angelilly at her swimming lesson parking area, I took off my seat belt because the car was not moving.

This is what I heard the Holy Spirit say: when the car is moving, you really need to put that seat belt on. It is your protection gear to keep you safe if you happen to have a crash when you are in a moving car. So is the word of God. It tells you to put on the armour of God when you are moving in your life. Your enemies are not flesh and blood but the principalities of the darkness. They are in the dark and are of the dark nature. You cannot see them. You see only the flesh that the dark forces have access through and attack you with.

> *Put on the whole armour of God, that you may be able to stand against the schemes of the devil. For we do not wrestle against flesh and blood, but against the rulers, against the authorities, against the cosmic powers over this present darkness, against the spiritual forces of evil in the heavenly places (Ephesians 6:11-12, ESV).*

A good dad always avoids any oncoming crashes in his life, or any crashes that are coming for his loved ones. The more he crashes himself daily in Word and prayer into His Father's love, the more he is equipped to stay out of sudden accidents in his life or his loved one's lives.

His flesh is living the Father's name, Jehovah Jireh, our Lord God, our Provider, by being the provider to his household. His spirit is always praying for each one of them.

> *Stand therefore, having fastened on the belt of truth, and having put on the breastplate of righteousness, and, as shoes for your feet, having put on the readiness given by the gospel of peace. In all circumstances take up the shield of faith, with which you can extinguish all the flaming darts of the evil one; and take the helmet of salvation, and the sword of the Spirit, which is the word of God, praying at all times in the Spirit, with all prayer and supplication. To that end, keep alert with all perseverance, making supplication for all the saints (Ephesians 6:14-18, ESV).*

Jesus lived our Father's name, Jehovah Jireh, our Lord God, our Provider, and provided His flesh. His flesh is the Word from the Father. His flesh is a double-edged sword which our flesh needs to receive to be able to escape and be sustained in any crash with flesh and blood that the dark forces use against us. Just like how we put the car's brakes on suddenly with our feet to avoid an accident that is right in front of us, our feet also need the peace of God to stand upon. When we walk in peace, we have fully walked away and escaped the enemy's attack. Jesus provided the peace to us through the Holy Spirit in us.

Every day, we have to live our Father's name and provide to others by providing our flesh to live and serve in love whoever we come in contact with. We are the provider of peace, joy and righteousness in the Holy Spirit within us (see Romans 14:17). Our enemies are not flesh and blood. We have to provide the light of Jesus to them to expose the dark forces using them.

April 2

~ We have the DNA of Jesus from His blood ~

*He spat on the ground and made clay with the saliva;
and He anointed the eyes of the blind man with the clay
(John 9:6 NKJV).*

Every morning, and not every night, but some, when I stay awake for long, my eyes feel as if they are burning. It just hit my mind to get my saliva to rub it on my eyes. It's been going on for years now. In the morning, my day is so awesome and glorious when I put my saliva on both my eyes. Most times I cannot think or see properly when I don't put saliva on my eyes. If you have been reading the devotional books I wrote you, will notice many daily revelations I have written.

I would start seeing the revelation of Jesus in His Word, and the joy filling me and the peace is just fulfilling. I didn't know what was going on in the divine spiritual realm. One morning, June 20, 2021, the Holy Spirit directed me to study this whole saliva thing. The DNA in our saliva comes from the blood. As a matter of fact, Jesus healed the blind man with His blood. He spat on the ground, then rubbed it on the blind man and healed him. Jesus showed how He has healed us from being born blind from what sin has caused.

The first man created by God from the ground was blind when he was deceived by the devil. Jesus, God in the flesh, made us see again by His saliva which has His DNA from His blood. For what Jesus has done, we can now see again from being born blind.

Dr. Samuel Rodriguez, president of the National Hispanic Christian Leadership Conference, points out that your DNA is in your saliva, so when Jesus spat, the blind man received a divine DNA transfer. The fact of the matter is that sin is in our DNA, and that's why Jesus goes back to the root of our problem!

Understand this: God doesn't merely treat your symptoms. He goes back to the source of your problem in order to set you free from it. To change the fruit, He changes the root. This man never had the ability to see as he was born blind and needed a creative miracle—and that's exactly what he got. Physical miracle and spiritual miracle—a total transformation.

In the physical realm, his parents were questioned because of this physical miracle and whether or not he had their DNA. In the spiritual realm, they questioned the blind man about Jesus because the DNA of Jesus was in him, there was a spiritual miracle, and he could now see.

It doesn't matter whether your parents contributed to your problem or you simply made bad choices in life, Jesus can set you free, make you whole and give you a new life. Jesus didn't blame this man or his parents. That's because God has no desire for your condemnation; His desire is for your transformation so He can be glorified through you. The Father is glorified when our eyes are open and we see Jesus revealing Himself in His Word.

> *The Spirit of the Lord God is upon me, because the Lord has anointed me to bring good news to the suffering and afflicted. He has sent me to comfort the brokenhearted, to announce liberty to captives, and to open the eyes of the blind (Isaiah 61:1, TLB).*

Jesus lived our Father's name, Jehovah Jireh, by providing His DNA from His blood that He purchased us from. A good dad always seeks His loving heavenly Father's face in His Word and prayer to reveal His ways more to Him. He uses the blood of Jesus daily from His DNA and declares cleansing upon his house.

We are now to live our Father's name, Jehovah Jireh, and provide the DNA from the blood of Jesus by declaring cleansing in our homes and for whoever needs it. Every day, we can rise up and say, 'As for me and my house, we will serve the Lord.'

April 3

~ Jesus has provided the cross for us to put to death our rebellious 'self' ~

God is spirit, and his worshipers must worship in the Spirit and in truth (John 4:24, NIV).

Jesus provided Himself as an altar place and offered Himself to the Father. He was the real demonstration of the true worshipper to worship the Father in Spirit and in truth. He is the way, the truth and life to the Father who has given us the Spirit of truth, to now worship the Father in Spirit, and in truth.

> *If we disobeyed the Lord and built our own altar to burn sacrifices on or to use for grain offerings or fellowship offerings, let the Lord himself punish us (Joshua 22:23, GNT).*

A good dad demolishes any altar in his life here on earth, that robs the rightful place of worship to His Father in heaven. The altars of self-interest, self-promotion, self-exaltation, self-preservation and self-righteousness. Every day he denies himself, takes up his cross and crucifies that self and follows Jesus in His Word. The cross has one purpose, and that is for the self to die upon.

Jesus Christ, the One and only Son, has lived the Father's name, Jehovah Jireh, our Lord God, our Provider. Jesus has provided that cross where we too can go to crucify the rebellious nature of our self.

> *For if you live according to the flesh you will die, but if by the Spirit you put to death the deeds of the body, you will live (Romans 8:13, ESV).*

We have a loving Father, Jehovah Jireh, our Lord God, our Provider. He provided Jesus to us, who has gone back to the Father and has provided to us the Holy Spirit so everyday we can live our Father's name, Jehovah Jireh, and provide ourselves as a living sacrifice to the Father, worshipping Him in our spirit in the Holy Spirit and through the truth in Jesus, who is the way, the truth, and the life.

April 4

~ *God blesses the hands that give* ~

It is more blessed to give than to receive (Acts 20:35, NIV).

A good dad knows His Father is a provider and it is His will to always provide for his children as a loving Father. Since he too wants to provide the best for his children, a good dad is always willing to live in His Father's will. This good dad is willing to be a giver and invest in the work of the kingdom of the Father. He willingly gives now because he trusts His Father to provide for all his present and future needs. He sows generously and watches his faith grow in the process.

He sows in a system that cannot fail. As a result, he experiences the peace and joy of knowing the Father will back him up in all his needs and bless him with whatever his hands find to do, because his hands are willing to give.

> *Give, and it will be given to you. A good measure, pressed down, shaken together and running over, will be poured into your lap. For with the measure you use, it will be measured to you (Luke 6:38, NIV).*

Jesus lived our Father's name, Jehovah Jireh, our Lord God, our Provider. He provided the best financial advice to a certain group of people who were worried about their finances. In Matthew 6, Jesus was giving the people assurance that God would provide for their needs, and they should seek after the kingdom of God, for then all those things would be given to them. All our spiritual blessings that will meet our physical needs are in the kingdom of God. We have to seek the kingdom of righteousness to receive them.

April 5

~ As peacemakers, provide peace ~

Those who love your laws have great peace of heart and mind and do not stumble (Psalm 119:165, TLB).

One cold winter's morning, June 13, 2021, I was trying to put a jumper on Blessed, aged two years, three months. He was holding onto one of his soft toys, which I removed from him so I could easily put his hands only in, but he kept grabbing his toy to hold. I couldn't put his hands and toy in together as the place his hands needed to go fit only his hands.

This is what the Holy Spirit taught me: so it is with your life. You are meant to only live your life before you die, and walk in life, not carry any other unnecessary stuff. The path to life is narrow, designed for you to not hold onto life's issues and problems. Whatever the burdens of others that get in your way, it is for you to pray, pray, pray until the peace of God lightens you up to walk in peace.

A good dad lives a life of peace, because when he dies he wants to die in peace. Before one dies, one has to live. He lives in the unconditional love of His Father in heaven and draws out the peace from that love by always receiving into him the Word, Who is Jesus, the peace from God.

> *Blessed are the peacemakers, for they will be called children of God (Matthew 5:9, NIV).*

The name of Jesus is the name above all names and has the power of authority. The name that lives the Father's name, Jehovah Jireh, our Lord God, our Provider, Jesus came and lived the Father's name by not only being the Provider of Peace, but He is the Peacemaker, and He tells us that the children of God are the peacemakers. He gave us the Holy Spirit with His fruit of righteousness, peace and joy (see Romans 14:17) so we can also make peace, and provide that peace to every chaotic situation we encounter.

Every day is the day the Father has given to us to show others we are His children by living His name, Jehovah Jireh, and provide peace. We have to live in peace so we can die in peace to meet the Prince of Peace, Jesus Christ.

April 6

~ Our Father has already provided for the seasons we will be journeying through ~

> *To every thing there is a season, and a time to every purpose under the heaven: (Ecclesiastes 3:1, NKJV).*

Jehovah God-like Mind is a Good Father-like Character

One summer's day, January 5, 2023, began with a cold morning. After giving my seven-month-old baby a wash, I was trying to put her in a jumpsuit because of the weather and I realised she was already growing too big for it. I decided that day would be the last time she wore it, even though it was her first time to wear it.

This is what the Holy Spirit taught me: there will be some people who come into your life once, to connect and give you the support you need. They meet your needs in that season, just like how that jumpsuit will meet your baby's need to be clothed for that weather only once because she is growing too big to be in it.

Hear this: we must never worry, because our Father in Heaven will always bring someone to our path in the season we walk through, to provide for what we need, even if it is only once. They may not come again in your picture because they were meant for that path you were walking on, in that season, and when you grow to another level, they can't be there for you anymore. They have their own limit to not expand with you. But always appreciate and be grateful for their life they have shared with you in that season.

> *So don't worry about tomorrow. Each day has enough trouble of its own. Tomorrow will have its own worries (Matthew 6:34, ERV).*

Our Father's name is Jehovah Jireh, our Almighty Father who provides. Jesus lived our Father's name here on earth to teach us not to worry. We mean so much to our Father, and He will provide everything we need for today. Therefore, we must not even worry about tomorrow.

God allows every happening in our life to teach us the meaning of life. Be grateful for the good things, and also for the bad things, for not only do they teach us to avoid such mistakes again, but in all things, God works for our good.

We know that in everything God works for the good of those who love him. These are the people God chose, because that was his plan (Romans 8:28, ERV).

Every day, we have to wake up and be grateful for everyone who is part of our lives. Some have supported us, while others have abused our goodness. They have all taught us lessons — that our Father will always provide for our needs and we must never worry about tomorrow's needs.

April 7

~ Our Father in heaven has provided to us the Spirit of wisdom, knowledge and understanding to be skilful ~

See, I have chosen Bezalel, son of Uri, the son of Hur, of the tribe of Judah, and I have filled him with the Spirit of God, with wisdom, with understanding, with knowledge and with all kinds of skills (Exodus 31:2-3, NIV).

A good dad knows he has a loving Father in heaven who calls him by name. He lives His Father's name, Jehovah Jireh, our Lord God, our Provider, by providing his skills to do work in what God has called and purposed for him in life. To be skilful, he pays attention to what His Father commands in His Word and does exactly as instructed. Like Bezalel, he may just be a son raised by his parents in a certain tribe, but when His Father in heaven calls His name to serve Him, He calls him a son and fills him with His Spirit of wisdom, understanding and knowledge in all manner so he can be more skilful in his career.

The Spirit of the Lord will rest on him—the Spirit of wisdom and of understanding, the Spirit of counsel and of

> *might, the Spirit of the knowledge and fear of the Lord—and he will delight in the fear of the Lord. He will not judge by what he sees with his eyes, or decide by what he hears with his ears (Isaiah 11:2-3, NIV).*

Jesus lived our Father's name, Jehovah Jireh, our Lord God, our Provider, and provided His life to serve everyone with workmanship. He was everything. He never went to any school, yet He was the best lawyer in town who made every law operate in love and compassion. Even though He was in the right position of a judge, He never judged anyone. He was all wisdom and knowledge of God, and He understands everyone because of the Father's love. He is the wisdom, knowledge and understanding in the Holy Spirit, who is now inside of us so we can always be filled with the Holy Spirit's wisdom, knowledge and understanding and be skilful in our calling to life.

Every day is another opportunity to stay connected to our loving Father in the Holy Spirit and allow Him to fill us with wisdom, knowledge and understanding so we can provide skilfully where God positions us to be.

April 8

~ Your provision through giving reaps greatness ~

> *A gift opens the way and ushers the giver into the presence of the great (Proverbs 18:16, NIV).*

One autumn day, May 30, 2021, I realised I had to remove some of Blessed's clothes as there were too many in the cupboard and the drawer could not close properly. After I removed some, the drawer closed easily because I had put the right amount in it.

This is what I heard the Holy Spirit say: our Father in heaven provides the right size of providence to meet our needs. We may want more and more, but if we are not in a position to be a giver, we cannot receive. Those God gives in an overflowing portion and in abundance are people who are givers. Because they give, they receive. You see, if they receive more from the Father and do not give, they will be like my cupboard drawer that could not close well. Their life will not go well with others. Each one of us will give an account of our life and what we have done with this gift of life.

> *Yes, you will be enriched in every way so that you can always be generous. And when we take your gifts to those who need them, they will thank God (2 Corinthians 9:11, NLT).*

A good dad lives a selfless life. He takes a position of giving. Being the provider to his household, he connects all the time to his loving Father who is the source and provider of everything life needs. He is the channel through which the blessings from the Father of the lights in heaven travel through to earth to reach those who are in need.

Jesus lived our Father's name, Jehovah Jireh, our Lord God, our Provider. He provided an abundance of life by being good and kind. He was kind in giving healing, giving food to the hungry, rescuing the condemned and many more. Needs were met instantly where He was. Whatever was stored within Him flowed out. He never ran out of anything to give to those He ran into who needed it.

Today, the store house of heaven who provides our daily bread is inside us to sustain us physically and spiritually. We just have to remain in Him, and in Jesus' name, live our Father's name, Jehovah Jireh, and provide to whoever we can that the Spirit leads.

April 9

~ As a house of prayer, always provide a prayer for someone ~

This, then, is how you should pray: Our Father in heaven, hallowed be your name, your kingdom come, your will be done, on earth as it is in heaven. Give us today our daily bread. And forgive us our debts, as we also have forgiven our debtors. And lead us not into temptation, but deliver us from the evil one (Matthew 6:9-13, NIV).

A good dad's lifeline is prayer. Being the head of the family, he has to steer and direct his family in the right path in life. It's not a spare wheel he pulls out weekly or when trouble approaches—it is his steering wheel that directs him in the right path throughout life. He connects himself to his heavenly Father in heaven and remain in Jesus, the Word who has become flesh.

Jesus was God in human form, yet prayed all His life. He lived our Father's name, Jehovah Jireh, our Lord God, our Provider. He provided ways of how to pray to our Father, and He even prayed for us to our Father before He went back to the Father (see John 17).

Our Father is in heaven, where heaven is His throne, and we are on earth, where it is His stool. The Father loves it when we are at His stool to pray and talk to Him. The earth, His stool, is where our Father's feet are and He loves for His children to come to His feet and talk to Him in prayer. This is the place to pour out all the concerns of life, and the place where we can remain humbled and be lifted up. Remember, there is no one higher from where our heavenly Father is, and when He lifts us up, no one can bring us down because there is no one higher than Him.

Human, the Lord has told you what goodness is. This is what he wants from you: Be fair to other people. Love kindness and loyalty, and humbly obey your God (Micah 6:8, ERV).

Every day, remain at the feet of Jesus and talk to Him. He is praying and interceding for us. He gave us the Holy Spirit to live inside of us so we can talk with Him, anywhere at any time. If God in the form of flesh is praying all the time, then we who are born into this world as sinners should pray even more.

April 10

~ Our Father provides the best taste of His Word through the flesh of Jesus ~

How sweet are your words to my taste, sweeter than honey to my mouth! (Psalm 119:103, NIV).

April 29, 2021, I was talking with a friend about where the best quality pies were sold in our area. We mentioned a certain place where we enjoyed their pies, but then we tasted a pie that was way better than we were used to, so we shifted over to that pie.

This is what I heard the Holy Spirit say: The kingdom of God is like this. You may taste and hear Jesus from someone, but when you have a personal relationship with Him and hear Him through the Holy Spirit, you will taste and see that the Lord is good. This is the good deal that will make you more hungry for the Word. And so, you will begin to spend more time in the Word to taste more of the goodness of the Word. God's Word is like honey and tastes so sweet to the soul and spirit.

A good dad works to provide food for his family. In order to always provide, he connects his inner being, his umbilical cord, to His Father in heaven and receives from Him to provide for his family, just like how an umbilical cord is the connection from an unborn baby to the mother to receive food and sustain life. A baby's eyes are closed and in the darkness of the womb, where they are sustained only by what they taste from the mother. A good dad may not see well in this dark world, but he remains connected and receives directly from his good, loving Father to be sustained.

> *I led them with cords of human kindness, with ropes of love. I lifted the yoke from their neck and bent down and fed them (Hoses 11:4, NCV).*

Jehovah Jireh is His name and He provides the umbilical cord, His Word, in the form of flesh to sustain and give life to us. Man cannot live by bread alone, but by every word that comes out of the mouth of God (see Matthew 4:4). Jesus lives the Father's name, Jehovah Jireh, and provided Himself as the eternal food for us to eat and live forever. He is the living manna from heaven for us to feed on to be able to live in heaven on that day.

> *Whoever eats my flesh and drinks my blood remains in me, and I in them (John 6:56, NIV).*

Every day, feed more on the Word of the Father, which Jesus has provided to us in His flesh. The Word who has become flesh. Once you start having this daily relationship with Him, you will taste and see the goodness of Him. He is the best quality deal one can ever find. To taste and see that the Lord is good is for you, you must do it yourself. No one can do it for you, it's a personal experience.

April 11

~ Be a provider of the light of Jesus ~

When Jesus spoke again to the people, he said, 'I am the light of the world. Whoever follows me will never walk in darkness, but will have the light of life.' (John 8:12, NIV).

I have a little Christmas tree-shaped light. When I put the light on, the whole tree lamp lights up in the shape it is.

This is what the Holy Spirit taught me: The Word who is the light has become flesh, and when you remain and walk in obedience to the voice of the Word your whole being lights up. The first man and woman realised they were naked because the light was removed from them and darkness appeared. This is why every one of us is born blind and in darkness.

A good dad is a light to his family. For him to be the provider of light for his family's life, he remains in the light of his loving Father in heaven who is the source and provider of light and life. His house is never in darkness as long as he commits to Word and prayer daily. He provides the light that shows the path of life and his house follows. This is his declaration: As for me and my house, we will serve the Lord (Joshua 24:15).

Jesus lived our father's name, Jehovah Jireh, our Lord God, our Provider, by providing the light. He not only provided the light, but He is the Father's light and life to us. He came into the World to provide us the light to save us from being blind and living in the kingdom of darkness. The light is now inside of us in the Holy Spirit. Our flesh and appearance becomes light in the image of Christ when Jesus comes to LIFE within us through the Holy Spirit in us.

For you were once darkness, but now you are light in the Lord. Live as children of light (Ephesians 5:8, NIV).

Every day, remind yourself that you are to live your Father's name, Jehovah Jireh, and provide light to the world you are in. You are placed wherever you are to help people see better in this world, because you carry the Holy Spirit who is the light and life. You live in darkness when you don't connect to the Word which is the light.

April 12

~ Provide goodness to defeat evil ~

Taste and see that the Lord is good; blessed is the one who takes refuge in him (Psalm 34:8, NIV).

I received a promotional email from a business wanting to sell me their products. They offered to me a thirty-day 'test and trial' to taste their products to see if they were good for me. I honestly have no interest in such things, unless recommended by someone I trust who I see is doing well because they are using the said products. Anyway, they were things which one can live without.

This is what the Holy Spirit taught me: The kingdom of God is like this. You are originally designed and a brand product of God. He handmade you in such a special and unique way. He allows you to go through the tests and trials of life, so the original you that you were created for will come out. The pains and struggles that you go through in the tests and trials are for you to taste and see that the Lord is good and His love is faithful. When you come out of your tests and trials, you will see the goodness of the Lord that has strengthened you to make it through and come out in the original design you were created for. The test and trials may not taste good, but because you have a good loving Father, you will see His goodness in it. In all things God works for our good (see Romans 8:28).

> *Consider it pure joy, my brothers and sisters, whenever you face trials of many kinds, because you know that the testing of your faith produces perseverance. Let perseverance finish its work so that you may be mature and complete, not lacking anything (James 1:2-4, NIV).*

In his tests and trials, a good dad remains in the loving goodness of His Father in heaven. There are days he is silent in the test he goes through as he rests in the peace of Jesus. Remember, students are silent in a test. It's in the testing room that the voice of the enemy is yelling that time is running out and you are never going to do better in life. Silence the voice of the enemy while you are in a test.

Jesus lived our Father's name, Jehovah Jireh, our Lord God, our Provider. He provided our Father's goodness and mercy and glorified His name in doing all the good work while on earth. The Father and the Son are always at work in providing goodness through the Holy Spirit with His fruit of goodness.

Every day can be a test and trial day for you. Taste and see the goodness of the Father in your day and live His name, Jehovah Jireh, and provide that goodness to someone to taste it too.

April 13

~ Provide a refuge for someone to take shelter in ~

> *My salvation and my honour depend on God; he is my mighty rock, my refuge. Trust in him at all times, you people; pour out your hearts to him, for God is our refuge (Psalm 62:7-8 NIV).*

To be that refuge where his family can seek shelter, a good dad remains in the refuge of his loving Father in heaven. He shelters himself in Word and prayer and moves in obedience to the Word. Our Father in heaven is our Mighty Rock. He is Jehovah Jireh, our Lord God, our Provider. He provided the Living Stone and Rock for us to be founded upon so nothing can shake and move us when the storms hit us.

> *Therefore everyone who hears these words of mine and puts them into practice is like a wise man who built his house on the rock. The rain came down, the streams rose, and the winds blew and beat against that house; yet it did not fall, because it had its foundation on the rock (Matthew 7:24-25, NIV).*

Jesus lived the Father's name, Jehovah Jireh, and provided Himself as the Mighty Rock, a place of shelter where we can dwell to be safe. Jesus wants us now to build upon Him so we can be that home that will never be shaken. He provides the Holy Spirit to live inside of us. When the Holy Spirit comes and fully lives in us, and we house Him, we can never be moved or be afraid of anything that would destroy our body. For greater is He that is in us than he that is in the world.

> *Do not be afraid of those who kill the body but cannot kill the soul. Rather, be afraid of the One who can destroy both soul and body in hell (Matthew 10:28, NIV).*

Every day, provide yourself as a place of refuge and shelter for anyone who is shaken by fears of this world. Be the rock to build up people with the Word so they can become a strong, solid house upon the Word of God. Jesus is the Living Stone and Rock and He wants us to use His Word and build people up.

April 14

~ Take one step into the unknown with faith, and Jehovah Jireh will provide for the journey ~

"Go in peace," the priest replied. "For the Lord is watching over your journey." (Judges 18:6, NLT).

As a daily devotional writer, God puts one small idea in me to write, but the moment I start writing He puts through everything He has for me to write. He provides what I need to write the moment I become obedient and step into what He asks of me. God makes every provision for all we need when we walk by faith into what He has called us to do. Jesus came and lived our Father's name, Jehovah Jireh, our Almighty Father who Provides. He called a couple of fishermen to use their profession to fish for souls. He provided them everything they needed when they obediently responded to His call. They did the fishing, and Jesus does the cleaning. If you have a medical profession, you care for the wound, and let Jesus do the healing. Whatever your profession, God is calling to qualify you to use your profession to sow into the kingdom of God. Do not be afraid. Jehovah Jireh, our Lord God who Provides, will always provide for the journey you are going to walk into.

Don't be afraid, for I am with you. Don't be discouraged, for I am your God. I will strengthen you and help you. I will hold you up with my victorious right hand (Isaiah 41:10, NLT).

Even Lazarus, who was dead, heard Jesus calling his name and walked out of the tomb. We all have a great seed of potential lying dead inside of us, and the enemy is blinding us to seeing that. Jesus came and provided His life to make us see and to resurrect every dead potential in our life. Our eyes will begin to open and see all this potential within us once we start living the life Jesus called us to live.

> *We can make our plans, but the Lord determines our steps (Proverbs 16:9, NLT).*

Each day of every day, you are able to wake up because Jesus called your name to rise up. If He can provide this new day to you, He will provide all you need for that day as well. Trust and obey is all we have to do, and walk by faith into what He has called us to be.

April 15

~ *Jesus has provided righteousness for us to live in* ~

> *My son, listen to your father when he corrects you, and don't ignore what your mother teaches you. What you learn from your parents will bring you honour and respect, like a crown or a gold medal (Proverbs 1:8-9, ERV).*

One cold autumn morning, April 15, 2021, Blessed put on the portable heater, then after a while he left. I checked the heater, thinking he wouldn't have turned it off, only to realise he had. Then it dawned on me that he normally heard me telling his sister to turn the heater off when she was not using it. I had repeated myself many times because she never did the right thing. Blessed did the right thing because he learnt from the mistakes of his sister.

This is what I heard the Holy Spirit say: The people recorded in the bible who did the wrong things in the sight of Jehovah did so for us to learn from and not to do what they did. This is so we can grow in the perfect, righteous love of God.

A good dad knows he is imperfect, and so he stays attached to the love and teaching of his perfect loving Father in heaven. The Father provides everything for him in all areas of life for his growth and development in His perfect love, so he can love the Father with all his heart, soul and strength. He walks in the righteousness of the Father provided by Jesus so he can do all the right things Jesus did through Christ Himself, who strengthened him.

> *But if we walk in the light, as he is in the light, we have fellowship with one another, and the blood of Jesus his Son cleanses us from all sin (1 John 1:7, ESV).*

Jesus lived our Father's name, Jehovah Jireh, our Lord God, our Provider. He provided the righteousness of God in flesh, so we flesh beings, can become the righteousness of God in Him by doing all the right things Jesus did for the Father. Jesus did nothing wrong that caused Him to be given a death penalty. He died willingly so He can be the provider of righteousness.

Every day, we have to remind ourselves that Jesus has provided the Father's righteousness for us to live and do the right things. The wrong things that we did were made righteous in the righteous, sinless blood of Jesus that He provided for us.

April 16

~ Provide your children the Word of God so they know the truth ~

Teach a child to choose the right path, and when he is older, he will remain upon it (Proverbs 22:6, TLB).

Many Christians, godly parents, have kids who have gone astray from the presence and dwelling place of God. I have asked the Lord to show me why this happens when they have very committed, God-fearing parents who raised them well in the teaching of God. The Lord made it clear to me: We can raise children in the Word of God, and even when they go astray, the light from God's Word within them will lead them back to the right path.

April 16, 2021, this question was answered. A beautiful morning, I was having tea with one of my favourite tea biscuits. Angelilly came to me and asked, 'Can I have one?' I said, 'This is my favourite biscuit and I am not giving it to you. You can go for something else. There are many biscuits in the cupboard.' She said, 'But please, I haven't tried this biscuit yet.' So, I gave some of the biscuit to her.

This is what I heard the Holy Spirit say: Angelilly tells you she has not tried the biscuit yet. Any child will still go astray and want to try the life of the world. Like Angelilly, not having tried the biscuit yet she wants to try it out and have a taste of it. So it is with children raised in godly homes—they will still go astray and want to try and taste the life of the world. You can never feel, taste and know something unless you go into it and they get into you. Therefore, they need to try out the things of the world, and the desires of the world have to go into them, in order for them to feel and taste what the evil world is like.

You may raise your children in the principles of God's Word and righteousness. They know about it, but because they have not tried what life is like in the world, and what everyone around them is doing, they will go into the world and do what the world requires of them. The good news is they have tasted and seen that the Lord is good because of the godly life they have been raised in, and so, they will return home.

The story of the prodigal son tells of a good father who raised his sons in righteousness. The younger son spent his inheritance from the father in the evil world. He tasted and tried out the evil world before returning to the goodness of his father. A good dad prayerfully waits patiently and looks forward to receiving his son back home. Because he raised him in the light of God's Word, he knows the Word of God will bring him back home safely (see Luke 15:11-32).

Change your life, not just your clothes. Come back to God, your God. And here's why: God is kind and merciful. He takes a deep breath, puts up with a lot, this most patient God, extravagant in love, always ready to cancel catastrophe (Joel 2:13, MSG).

Jesus lived our Father's name, Jehovah Jireh, our Lord God, our Provider. Our Father in heaven loves us, so much and sent Jesus to save us from the grip of this evil world where we are lost and bound for eternal death. Jesus came into the world and provided His life to us, so we can change our life to His life and enjoy the joy and peace in His life in this chaotic world. All the provision of a great hope and future for our life is found in the new life in Christ.

As the provider for our children every day, we can also provide the fullness of God's goodness in raising our children, that even when they go astray to the evilness of this world, they will conquer it with the goodness of God's Word within them.

April 17

~ Provide kindness and goodness everywhere you go ~

For everything there is a season, a time for every activity under heaven.

A time to scatter stones and a time to gather stones (Ecclesiastes 3:1,5, NLT).

One beautiful autumn morning, April 29, 2021, I saw lots of my garden stones scattered around and thought I would ask my little ones to collect them and place them in the right place. If I did it, it would just take a lot of time. This is what the Holy Spirit taught me: Do not collect and collect the riches of this world. You will use up all your time doing it, only to realise that everything you have collected will be left behind in the life you leave as you transcend out of this world. There is a time to collect and scatter. Sow and scatter into what is of eternal life, so you will collect only what is of eternal value in this life and the life after.

A good dad scatters and sows seeds of kindness and goodness. He inherits his loving Father's richness of kindness and goodness. He knows His Father is Jehovah Jireh, our Lord God, our Provider, who provides kindness and goodness. The goodness and kindness he scatters everywhere he goes, is a gain in his eternal life.

> *He is so rich in kindness and grace that he purchased our freedom with the blood of his Son and forgave our sins. He has showered his kindness on us, along with all wisdom and understanding (Ephesians 1:7-8, NLT).*

Our loving Father has made a provision of His kindness and goodness in the life of Jesus. Jesus lived the name of the Father, Jehovah Jireh, in providing kindness and goodness to everyone He crossed paths with. He always had time to treat everyone with kindness and goodness in His busy schedule. Even when dying on the cross, He was kind and good to those who put Him there. He has now provided to us the Father's kindness and goodness in the Holy Spirit that was given to us.

Each day is another good day made by our good, loving Father to live His name, Jehovah Jireh, and provide kindness to all the unkind people around us.

April 18

~ Ask the Father for wisdom so you can be a wisdom provider to whoever needs it ~

So also faith by itself, if it does not have works, is dead (James 2:17, ESV).

A good dad studies the Word of his loving Father in heaven and prays to bring it to action. He not only seeks to find knowledge and understand the Word, but to action the Word where necessary. He applies the Word in its time because there is a time for everything. A timely Word is wisdom.

He knows that sitting in the Father's presence, and absorbing His Word to gain knowledge and understanding of Him, without putting it into practice, is like going into a good restaurant to sit and just absorb and digest the writings of the menu, without placing an order to eat what's on the menu.

Jesus lived the Father's name, Jehovah Jireh, our Lord God, our Provider. He provided the knowledge, understanding and wisdom of God with how He lived His life. He was the wisdom of God. He knows the Father and so wants us to understand our Father's love for us that He sent Him to us. Jesus has now provided the knowledge, understanding and wisdom of the Father in the Holy Spirit. He gave us the Holy Spirit, who is the Spirit of knowledge, understanding and wisdom, so we can understand and be compassionate towards others before judging why they are doing what they are doing.

The Spirit of the Lord will rest on him—the Spirit of wisdom and of understanding, the Spirit of counsel and of

> *might, the Spirit of the knowledge and fear of the Lord—and he will delight in the fear of the Lord. He will not judge by what he sees with his eyes, or decide by what he hears with his ears (Isaiah 11:2-3, NIV).*

Every day comes with new opportunities to gain knowledge and understanding in the Word of our loving Father so we can provide timely Word, which is wisdom as a kind gesture to someone.

April 19

~ *The 'will' of the Father was provided to us to inherit when Jesus died~*

> *Now if we are children, then we are heirs—heirs of God and co-heirs with Christ, if indeed we share in his sufferings in order that we may also share in his glory (Romans 8:17, NIV).*

There's a story about a man bitten by a dog, and when he learned the dog had rabies he began a list. The doctor said, 'There's no need for you to make a will—you'll be fine.'

'Oh, I'm not making a will,' he said. 'I'm making a list of all the people I want to bite.'

Our will is where we state what we leave behind for our heirs when we die. Our loving Father in heaven has a great will for us, His original plan and what He hopes for our future. He is Jehovah Jireh, our Lord God, our Provider. He has to come in the human form to die so His 'will' can be provided to us to inherit eternal life of love, joy and peace. A good dad dies to his self in his everyday living so he can inherit the will of the Father that was provided through the death of Jesus. Only when he dies to the flesh is he able to inherit the abundance of love, joy and peace in the eternal life that our Father in heaven desires for us to inherit.

> *...but in these last days he has spoken to us by his Son, whom he appointed the heir of all things, through whom also he created the world (Hebrews 1:2, ESV).*

Jesus lives our Father's name, Jehovah Jireh, our Lord God, our Provider. He provided the Father's Will to us with His death. We are now co-heirs with Him. We are dead in Christ from the fleshly desires of sin and now rule and reign with Him in His new resurrected life. The Will of the Father that He provided for us from the death of Christ is to become like Christ by producing the fruit of the Spirit every day in the new resurrected life that the Holy Spirit has risen.

April 20

~ Provide the love of the Father to your daily contacts ~

> *... and you belong to Christ, and Christ belongs to God (1 Corinthians 3:23, NLT).*

A good dad is a good dad because he belongs to his loving Father in heaven. To belong is to be loved. People may reject him if he doesn't please them enough, but the love of the Father in heaven is always open and ready to accept him all the time. He sits daily in the teaching and learning of the knowledge of the Word of the Father and feels belonging by obeying what the Word says.

> *Christ redeemed us from the curse of the law by becoming a curse for us, for it is written: 'Cursed is everyone who is hung on a pole.' (Galatians 3:13, NIV).*

Jesus, the Word who became flesh and provided that love with His two arms stretched out and nailed onto the cross. It was love that caused Jesus to take the curse upon Him and nail it to the tree to have it removed. He would have died while on His way to the cross, but it was the Father's love that gave Him the strength to reach the cross. Jesus lived our Father's name, Jehovah Jireh, our Lord God, our Provider. He was the Father's love in action. The Father's name belongs to Him and He lived the name of the Father so we can live that name too. All things are possible in Jesus, and He has made it possible for us to be a provider of the Father's love by serving everyone whosoever in our daily contact with the fruit of the Holy Spirit. The Holy Spirit is the love of Christ in action through the fruit of righteousness.

Every new day, rise up and live the Father's name, Jehovah Jireh, and provide love where there is evil and hatred. Make someone feel loved and that they belong to the kingdom of God.

April 21

~ Provide mercy and kindness to all who needs it ~

He cancelled the record of the charges against us and took it away by nailing it to the cross (Colossians 2:14, NLT).

A good dad forgives and forgets whoever that owes him. He is merciful like his loving Father in heaven. Rich in mercy and kindness, the Father has not only made complete provision for the past, but for the future as well, 'having cancelled the written code, with its regulations, that was against us and that stood opposed to us; he took it away, nailing it to the cross'. Jehovah Jireh, our Lord God, our Provider. He provides His mercy, which is new every morning and fresh as the heavenly dew. A good dad renews himself in the richness of the Father's new mercy every morning, which overflows loving kindness in his life.

Jesus lived the Father's name, Jehovah Jireh. He provided Himself to the Father to use His sinless divine being. The Father took away all the list of sin from us; sickness, poverty, lack, unworthiness, death, and nailed it to the cross upon Jesus. The name of Jesus has power to clean us from all unrighteousness and keep us holy for the Father's use. Jesus has provided Himself to fully live the Father's will and calling and has returned back to Him. He has now made a way so we too can provide ourselves to the Father to be used by Him all the time. Jesus Christ is the only way, the truth and life to the Father.

> *Truly, truly, I say to you, whoever believes in me will also do the works that I do; and greater works than these will he do, because I am going to the Father (John 14:12, ESV).*

Every day is a new beginning to be available and provide ourselves to our Father to use us to produce the fruit of the Holy Spirit to everyone around us who needs it.

April 22

~ Provide peace and joy from the Father's love to remove fears ~

> *But cheer up! Not one of us will lose our lives, even though the ship will go down (Acts 27:22, TLB).*

A good dad is always of good cheer. Even in the midst of the storm, he puts on his jumpers of peace and clothes himself in gratitude. Like Paul, even when his life is sinking and he is drowning with bills, his heart jumps with joy. His loving Father in heaven will always provide a way to come out of it. Jehovah Jireh is His name, our Lord God, our Provider. His loving kindness provides the peace and joy to keep him cheerful in the storms and that is what matters. Faith comes by hearing and hearing the Word, and the more He is connected to the Father in His Word daily, the more he has faith over fears.

> *There is no fear in love. But perfect love drives out fear, because fear has to do with punishment. The one who fears is not made perfect in love (1 John 4:18, NIV).*

Jesus lived our Father's name, Jehovah Jireh, and provided peace and joy. Jesus is the provider of the peace and joy that the Father plans for us to have that will give us hope and future. The peace He provided to us and went to heaven is here with us in the Holy Spirit, who can come to us only if Jesus goes back to the Father. Jesus said, 'He will see us again and we will rejoice,' (see John 16:22). Jesus has seen us again through the Holy Spirit and no one, not even the devil, will take that joy away. That Joy is from the Holy Spirit every time He reveals to us Jesus in the Word of our Father.

> *So with you: Now is your time of grief, but I will see you again and you will rejoice, and no one will take away your joy (John 16:22, NIV).*

Every day, be of good cheer, because Jesus has provided the peace and joy from the Father's love to drive fear away from us. We are to live the Father's name, Jehovah Jireh, and provide that peace and joy from the Father's love to our household members so they will not have fear of what is happening in this world.

April 23

~ The Holy Spirit breathing inside of you in the life of Christ makes you clean inside ~

You are already clean because of the word I have spoken to you (John 15:3, NIV).

April 30, 2021, I remember Tom washed my car, but never got to vacuuming the inside. I was driving the car when I noticed. This is what I heard the Holy Spirit say: The real you drives and enjoys the car from your position inside. When it is dirty, you will never enjoy what the car can provide for your journey. Just like the car, the outside may look clean, and people can see from outside that the car is clean, but not the inside, which you are using for your trip. People can't see that. So it is with your life. You can make it so good and glamorous in how you carry it around to make yourself look better in the eyes of men, while the real you is not in order and needs a good vacuuming from within. Only someone who lives with you and does things with you will know the real you and know of your true character. This is why Jesus has to come and provide His clean, righteous life so we can live and remain in it. He has done it, we don't need to do anything but to confess it with our mouth. We just have to say the Word that Jesus said for us—we are clean.

When you make something, you are actually not inside that thing, but you stay outside and make it. When God made the first man, Adam, He made him from outside and breathed into him His breath of Spirit and he became a living being. Then man disobeyed and sinned and was separated from having a relationship with the Creator.

Our Almighty Father is Jehovah Jireh. He is our Lord God, our Provider. He is our loving Father and He can't just leave us separated from Him. He provided a way for us and sent His Son, Jesus, to make it possible for us so He can now live inside of us. The Holy Spirit who conceived Jesus inside the womb of a virgin is the same Spirit who resurrected Him from the womb of the tomb. He is now inside of us so we can enjoy the new resurrected life of Jesus.

Jesus lived the Father's name, Jehovah Jireh, and provided the Holy Spirit by coming into this world and dying for our sin and going back to the Father. It is the will of the Father that instead of breathing His Spirit into man to become alive, like what He did to the first man, He will now live inside a man and breathe inside of Him so he can remain alive in Christ. So in that way, nothing can ever separate us from His love.

> *For I am convinced that nothing can ever separate us from his love. Death can't, and life can't. The angels won't, and all the powers of hell itself cannot keep God's love away. Our fears for today, our worries about tomorrow, or where we are—high above the sky, or in the deepest ocean— nothing will ever be able to separate us from the love of God demonstrated by our Lord Jesus Christ when he died for us (Romans 8:38-39, TLB).*

Each day is a day to celebrate the victory of being alive in Jesus and that nothing can ever separate us from the love of God. Jesus said we are clean from inside because of the words He has spoken to us.

April 24

~ Each day provides what we need in Christ ~

> *For as the earth brings forth its sprouts, and as a garden causes what is sown in it to sprout up, so the Lord God will cause righteousness and praise to sprout up before all the nations (Isaiah 61:11, ESV).*

A good dad loves sowing. Like his heavenly Father, he joyfully gives whenever he can where there is an opportunity. He knows that when he sows and names his seed, he is making a provision of what he desires to receive in the name of the Father, Jehovah Jireh, our Lord God, our Provider. Our Father is a gardener, and like our Father, he gardens and remains planted in Christ. Apart from Christ, he cannot be fruitful and multiply from where he is planted.

> *I am the true vine, and my Father is the gardener. He cuts off every branch in me that bears no fruit, while every branch that does bear fruit he prunes so that it will be even more fruitful (John 15:1-2, NIV).*

Jesus has lived our Father's name and has given glory to His name. He is the glorious riches of the Father who can provide all that we need. Because of His living life that He provides to us, the name of the Father is alive and living in the name of Jesus. In the name of Jesus, we can now have access and remain in Jesus to be fruitful and multiply in abundance.

Our Loving Father provides each day, and in each day is a provision of what He has in store for us in Christ. We are not to worry but to just go with the flow of each day.

April 25

~ Change yourself to a position where God can provide to you to be a provider ~

> *... and to put on the new self, created after the likeness of God in true righteousness and holiness (Ephesians 4:24, ESV)*

January 11, 2021, while changing the pillow cases, I noticed the pillows were old and I needed to buy new ones. But then I thought, *oh well, it's still doing ok for me, and after I put freshly washed pillow cases on it is just nice and looks good.*

This is what the Holy Spirit taught me: You see, there are things that need changing in your life, but just because you think you are doing okay, you don't change them. To grow, there has to be some changes made. You are new in Christ and you are designed to change from glory to glory for the Father's glory. Let go of some old things and take a step forward into doing something new.

A good dad changes his way of living in providing for his family if that will bring him to another level up. His name, his identity, is who he is as a provider for his household. Just like Jesus, a good dad lives his name to bring glory to our Father in heaven. And so he makes any new changes in Jesus' name to the glory of the Father.

Jehovah Jireh, our Almighty Father, is our Provider. That is His name and Jesus lived our Father's name by providing everything in His name. We just have to live and call upon the name of Jesus that has in store all the provision of our needs. God will meet all our needs according to the riches of His glory in Christ Jesus (see Philippians 4:19).

> *Remember not the former things, nor consider the things of old. Behold, I am doing a new thing; now it springs forth, do you not perceive it? I will make a way in the wilderness and rivers in the desert (Isaiah 43:18-19, ESV).*

Our Father provides to us every new day with a new date. He places us in a position to change from each day's glory to the new day's glory to give all the glory back to Him.

April 26

~ Move, work and live your being in Christ while you have time ~

You should enjoy every day of your life, no matter how long you live. But remember that you will die, and you will be dead much longer than you were alive. And after you are dead, you cannot do anything (Ecclesiastes 11:8, ERV).

On the morning of December 18, 2022, while sitting at church I looked at my watch and noticed it was not working. The time was not moving at all because the battery was dead. This is what I heard the Holy Spirit say: When we die, we too won't move and we will stop working. God's name is His character and He is always working and moving in our life according to His character, His name.

But the time is coming—indeed it's here now—when true worshipers will worship the Father in spirit and in truth. The Father is looking for those who will worship him that way (John 4:23, NLT).

Jesus came and lived the Father's name. He is the time and is always working and moving. Jesus said in John 4 that 'a time is coming and the time is here'. He was the time and He is here. We move and have our being in Jesus. Jesus is actually the time from God to which we work, move and have our being. This explains why everyone goes by what the time is. We move and work by time. In order to work, we have to move.

For in him we live and move and exist (Acts 17:28, NLT).

When our time is up, the breath of God will be taken from us and we will die. We will no longer move or work, like the battery of my watch that was dead, so my watch was no longer working and the time was not moving.

> *But Jesus replied, "My Father is always working, and so am I." (John 5:17, NLT).*

Jehovah Jireh, our Almighty Father who is our Provider is His name, and Jesus lived our Father's name by providing time. He is the time who is always working and moving through His Spirit who lives in us. We are like the watch or clock and Jesus is the time. Jesus (the time) have to be alive in us (watch or clock) for us to move and work in Him. We can receive Jesus into our life, but we have to make Him alive by living in His Word. We have to be watchful of our time and not live a wasteful life. You see, the time was not moving because my watch was not working. The time will only move on my watch if it is working. Jesus is always at work, so is the Father too. Jesus is the time who is working and moving in the Holy Spirit.

Every day, we work, move and have our being in Christ who is the time. Live the Father's name each day by providing your time to someone, by showing the Father's love, by being good, kind and patient with them.

April 27

~ Always provide a seed to sow whenever there is an opportunity ~

And Isaac sowed in that land and reaped in the same year a hundredfold. The Lord blessed him (Genesis 26:12, ESV).

I have always wanted to own a credit card, and this what the Holy Spirit taught me: You are designed to lend and not borrow. You are to sow seeds, to give and not to borrow. When you own a credit card you work to repay what you owe. Your Father in heaven is always at work to provide for you. He is Jehovah Jireh, our Almighty Father is our Provider. Be content with what you are able to spend.

A good dad connects his transaction to His Father in heaven's love wallet. This is his connection of love, HE LET GOD BE IN IT. Instead of owning a credit card and working and repaying it, he is the seed of Abraham, and like Abraham's Son, Isaac, whatever he has in his hands is his love offering of seed that he sows into opportunities to receive back in one hundredfold.

He is always out there in the field looking for fertile soil to sow his seed of time, finances and skills. Whatever His Father gives him as a seed and directs him to sow is where he invests.

Jesus came down to show that our Father is the Provider. He Himself is the sacrifice that the Father provided once and for all. Jesus is now our Provider. He was provided by God to provide for us. Our Father wants someone to be in our nature and likeness to provide for us, and Jesus has taken that position. He is the very Word of God, the glory of our Father who became flesh.

> *He is the radiance of the glory of God and the exact imprint of his nature, and he upholds the universe by the word of his power. After making purification for sins, he sat down at the right hand of the Majesty on high (Hebrews 1:3, ESV).*

Every day we are to live our Father's name, Jehovah Jireh, and provide a seed of love into any fertile soil we find. There is a saying, another day, another dollar. And yet, it's another day and another opportunity to sow where our Father leads as He provides into our hands.

April 28

~ Always be there to provide prayers for someone ~

Do not be anxious about anything, but in everything by prayer and supplication with thanksgiving let your requests be made known to God. And the peace of God, which surpasses all understanding, will guard your hearts and your minds in Christ Jesus (Philippians 4:6-7, ESV).

A good dad never worries about the overwhelming stress of life. He knows he has a Father in heaven that he is connected to from earth. And so, all his earthly needs are met always on the hour of his needs. Jehovah Jireh, our Lord God, our Provider is His name, and He is always at work to provide to the household of His children. A good dad lives in the name of his heavenly Father in Jesus' name and offers prayers of thanksgiving at all times. He knows His Father has already made a provision for his needs to be met at the time of his needs.

But if anyone does not provide for his relatives, and especially for members of his household, he has denied the faith and is worse than an unbeliever (1 Timothy 5:8, ESV).

Jesus has lived our Father's name, Jehovah Jireh. He provides whenever there is a need. When the wine ran out at the wedding, He provided the wine with what was there. In Jesus' name we can do this too. We don't need to turn water into wine, but we can turn their worries into prayers to our loving Father who is our Provider.

Each day there will be someone we meet, or in our household, who has a need for which we can provide. It is an opportunity to live the Father's name, Jehovah Jireh, and provide for them.

April 29

~ Sow your seed from your cup; the harvest will continue to overflow ~

You provide delicious food for me in the presence of my enemies. You have welcomed me as your guest; blessings overflow! Your goodness and unfailing kindness shall be with me all of my life, and afterwards I will live with you forever in your home (Psalm 23:5-6, TLB).

One autumn day, April 29, 2021, I noticed that the kids' toy bucket was overflowing. I thought all those overflowing ones would have to be given away so there would be just enough to keep the place in order and neat.

This is what the Holy Spirit taught me: The kingdom of heaven is like this. You are designed to overflow and sow out the overflowing of what you have. You just need enough to enjoy and be content. Jesus is enough. Happiness comes from giving and seeing the receiver happy. This is how you were designed by the Creator. With nothing, you came into this world, and with nothing you will leave. When Jesus was ascended into heaven He never took anything with Him. The perishable things of the world can never last in heaven.

A good dad loves giving. He trusts His Father in heaven, the giver of every good and perfect thing. He sits in the perfect Word of His Father to lead him to find more fertile soil to sow along the path he walks. Jehovah Jireh, our Lord God, our Provider is His name, and He provides for his cup to overflow and runneth down so he can sow more. As long as he is sowing from his cup from the Father, a good dad is never in want.

Whoever has will be given more, and they will have an abundance. Whoever does not have, even what they have will be taken from them (Matthew 13:12, NIV).

Jesus lived our Father's name, Jehovah Jireh, and provided Himself as the living seed of life to come into this world and die for us. They buried Him in the tomb without knowing that He was the living seed of life and resurrected to life. How can one bury a seed, for it will always die into the soil to produce its fruit. The world was the soil that our Father provided for His living seed, Jesus, so we can harvest the overflowing fruit of the Holy Spirit in the abundant life of Jesus that He provides. And, also, the Father can have many seeds through Jesus.

Every day, be a provider of love, joy and peace and go out and sow into someone the fruit of the Holy Spirit. There is an overflowing and abundance of kindness, goodness and patience that you can sow into someone today to store up treasure in heaven.

April 30

~ Don't disfigure your original design ~

In their case, the god of this world has blinded the minds of the unbelievers, to keep them from seeing the light of the gospel of the glory of Christ, who is the image of God (2 Corinthians 4:4, ESV).

One autumn day, April 30, 2021, the Lord showed me a brand-new car, but then the car had a big crash on the front. The face of it was crushed. And the Holy Spirit spoke into my heart and said: Anyone who owns that car will never like it and will be upset because it's a nice, brand-new car and it just got crushed. This is not something nice that any owners will want to see. The owner will want to restore and bring it back to its original brand-new look.

You see, it's the same with you, when you become a newborn you have a brand-new life in Christ, but the devil is there also to crash your life and destroy it. So the brand-new image of Christ is now looking like a disaster in appearance. But don't allow yourself to remain in that appearance. Renew your mind and repent and get back into the righteousness of God in the eternal life of Jesus.

Our loving Father in heaven loves us so much that He doesn't want us to be in a state of brokenness. He is Jehovah Jireh, our Almighty God, our Provider. He not only provides to us a Saviour, but His righteousness and holiness as well, so we can remain in that to become a perfect image of His love. Our Father's goal is for His love to be made perfect in us, so when He looks at us He sees the brand-new image of the eternal life.

Every day, we are to remain in the Word to renew our mind so we don't lose our original design. We can then easily live our Father's name, Jehovah Jireh, and provide to others the holy and righteous life of our Saviour.

MAY

Jehovah Elohim! I AM the Creator!

OUR LORD GOD IS OUR CREATOR.

I have told you this so that my joy may be in you and that your joy may be complete (John 15:11, GNT).

One cold morning of July 25, 2022, I was looking at my kids and had the happy thought that I had created something like myself to keep me company. Watching my three-year-old talking and keeping me company made my joy complete. This is what I heard the Holy Spirit say: So it is with your Father in heaven. He wants to see someone like Himself. That is why He made you in His image: Someone in His image, created for His glory.

You see, the image of the glory of the Father created in us was stripped off when the first man disobeyed God. Our Father loved us so much, and wanted to restore us back to the likeness He originally designed for us in Christ for good works. And so, Jesus Christ came down to us and lived our Father's name, Jehovah Elohim, our Almighty Father is our Creator.

Jesus has created in Himself a new life for us to live for. He is the head and we are the body to this life. When our body becomes the house for the Holy Spirit to dwell, then the head who is Christ becomes one to us. The image of the Father that was originally designed has been restored and the Father gets all the glory in whatever we do. The joy of the Holy Spirit in us is complete.

But we have the mind of Christ
(1 Corinthians 2:16, ESV).

Each day of the month of May, and every day, live the Father's name, Jehovah Elohim, and create your new life by renewing your mind to have the mind of Christ. Your body becomes the temple of the Holy Spirit and Jesus becomes the head of your body because you have the mind of Christ.

May 1

~ Create more hope, faith and joy towards God's promises ~

Therefore I tell you, whatever you ask for in prayer, believe that you have received it, and it will be yours (Mark 11:24, NIV).

On the first day of the month of May, 2021, I told Blessed that his dad had just arrived home and was in the garage. Without even seeing whether his dad was there, he was so excited and joyfully ran out of the house saying, 'Daddy! Daddy!'

This is what the Holy Spirit taught me: The kingdom of God is like that of a child—they believe everything you tell them. They have a belief of no doubt, and so the prayers of a child are always answered. Blessed believed your words even when he didn't see his dad and was so excited he ran out to greet his father. Like Blessed, you have to start joyfully and excitedly believing in every promise your Father in heaven says, even when you don't see it. The heroes of faith are great faith believers. They cheer and praise God for His promises even when they don't see it coming. They die as heroes of faith because they keep believing in what God says He is going to do. Hebrews 11 and 12 speak of the heroes of faith who are the clouds of witnesses cheering for us to run our race.

A good dad believes in his loving Father in heaven and that He will do what He promises. He connects to the Father every day in Word and prayer to receive His promises. To be a super hero dad for his family and meet their physical needs he has to be a hero of faith.

Jesus is our hero of faith. He lived our loving Father's name, Jehovah Elohim, our Lord God, our Creator. He actions the love of the Father and creates hope for us to have an eternal future. We now have to receive it by faith. We have to believe like a child and with joy receive it. Blessed believed me without seeing his dad, and with joy he was running towards the garage to receive his dad. We may not see the promises of God, but we have to run to our loving Father with joy and seek Him to receive what He promised us. Living a grateful life to our Father for the promises He promised us should be our lifestyle. Always give thanks to God for His Word towards us.

> *For no matter how many promises God has made, they are 'Yes' in Christ. And so through him the 'Amen' is spoken by us to the glory of God (2 Corinthians 1:20, NIV).*

Every day is another day to live our Father's name, Jehovah Elohim, by creating hope and more faith in our life and looking forward with joy to receive all the promises of our loving Father in His Word, who is Jesus. The greatest promise the Father has given us is the Holy Spirit, and because He lives in us, we cannot see Him. It is by faith in Christ we receive Him, and so our joy is complete. This is our hope in Christ.

May 2

~ Your new being that Jesus created is highly valued ~

> *Anyone who belongs to Christ is a new person. The past is forgotten, and everything is new (2 Corinthians 5:17 CEV).*

One cold winter's day, June 23, 2021, I dropped into a thrift shop. I love to just pop in from time-to-time as you get good bargains. My main reason was I might see things from my country in there. I was thinking of how the prices are higher with the new stuff which has the original price tag on, while others have lower prices.

This is what the Holy Spirit taught me: Jesus paid a very high price for you so you can be created into a new being in His likeness. Your new being in Christ is highly valued. Many will never afford your presence and will lose you, while others who can afford you will follow you to do favours for you. Just like how you see the things with their higher price tags in a shop known for selling recycled and donated goods, not brand-new, so it is with your life. Your new life created in the likeness of Christ is new, but is in the fallen world called earth. That is alright, as long as you keep your price tag of your new being, then you will remain new and valued. You are worth much more than what is in the world because you have been purchased by the sinless blood of Jesus.

> *But he paid for you with the precious lifeblood of Christ, the sinless, spotless Lamb of God (1 Peter 1:19, TLB).*

A good dad knows how he makes sacrifices so his family can have new things. He understands that His Father in heaven is so loving that He sacrificed His Son in the flesh form so He could give him a life that is new and worth more in value.

Jesus lived our Father's name, Jehovah Elohim, our Lord God, our Creator. He not only created a life from His life for us, but He put a new price tag and stamp on us by giving us the Holy Spirit to live in us. He paid for us and completed the transaction. We are now to remain new with the price tag of the Holy Spirit inside of us in this fallen world. The price tag from the Holy Spirit tells us of how we are created new in the life of Christ and that we are of great value.

> *And you also became God's people when you heard the true message, the Good News that brought you salvation. You believed in Christ, and God put his stamp of ownership on you by giving you the Holy Spirit he had promised (Ephesians 1:13, GNT).*

Every day comes out new for us to also remain new by showing our price tag which is of the Holy Spirit. When we allow ourselves to be led by the Holy Spirit, we show we are new in Christ, because our Father has put a stamp of ownership by giving us the Holy Spirit.

May 3

~ Create love from God's perfect love ~

> *For I am convinced that nothing can ever separate us from his love. Death can't, and life can't. The angels won't, and all the powers of hell itself cannot keep God's love away. Our fears for today, our worries about tomorrow, or where we are—high above the sky, or in the deepest ocean— nothing will ever be able to separate us from the love of God demonstrated by our Lord Jesus Christ when he died for us (Romans 8:38-39, TLB).*

On the morning of May 3, 2021, I asked the Lord to reveal to me the Father's love. He gave me the word "separated" and said: You see, on social media people put their status as 'separated' in a relationship. Well, this is what sin has done to your relationship with the Father. It has separated you from the Father. But because of His love, nothing can ever separate you, not even death or life, demons or angels or whatever. Nothing, and nothing in all creation, can separate you from the Father's love because of what Jesus has done.

A good dad will never allow anything to come in the way to separate his love for his family. To be committed to that love, he has to remain committed to receiving and abiding in his heavenly Father's unconditional, perfect love. His love is imperfect, but not the Father's love. He remains in Jesus, the Word who is the love of the Father in flesh.

> *I have loved you even as the Father has loved me. Live within my love. When you obey me you are living in my love, just as I obey my Father and live in his love (John 15:9-10, TLB).*

Our Father is love. He is Jehovah Elohim, our Lord God, our Creator. He created love in flesh, who is Jesus. Jesus lived the Father's name, Jehovah Elohim, and created and showed love in everything He did. There is no greater love than to lay down your life for a friend, and Jesus did that. He did it for us, for we are His friends (see John 15:13-14). Our Father showed us how much He loved us so much in the life Jesus lived. Because death cannot even separate us from our Father's love, Jesus rose and defeated death to be with us forever.

Each new day, let's commit our day to remain in and live the Father's name, Jehovah Elohim, in the name of Jesus, and create love, joy and peace and share that with whomever we come in contact with.

May 4

~ *Create beautiful things in your life with wisdom in your struggles* ~

> *Wisdom gives: a long, good life, riches, honour, pleasure, peace (Proverbs 3:16-17, TLB).*

On June 4, 2021, Tom used a chainsaw to remove a beautiful trunk from a huge tree. The trunk was so heavy he couldn't even move it. I helped him, but it was so difficult! I paused a bit, prayed and talked kindly to the tree trunk. I told her that we wanted to make her into a beautiful coffee table and would love and treasure it. After saying that, the tree trunk was easy to move. I believe that every living thing from nature has a spirit to which you must speak kindly and with respect if you want to get something out from them. In the beginning of creation, God placed man to be in charge of nature with the responsibility of taking care of it. Nature is aware of man's lordship over them.

The tree trunk was so beautiful that people who passed by stopped to compliment its beauty. Finally, we moved it until we got it into our big van. This is what the Holy Spirit taught me: This is a very beautiful tree trunk that you want to create something beautiful out of, but you had to struggle a lot to bring it to the van. You have to know that beautiful things in life are created from the many struggles you go through. This is why you need wisdom over money.

> *The man who knows right from wrong and has good judgment and common sense is happier than the man who is immensely rich! For such wisdom is far more valuable than precious jewels. Nothing else compares with it (Proverbs 3:13-15, TLB).*

A good dad's focus is on obtaining wisdom over money. He understands that even if you have money, there are many things in life you will struggle with that money can't buy. He sits in the Word of the Father to receive more wisdom from Him, so he can be knowledgeable of Him and understand how to create a beautiful life with wisdom.

Jesus lived our Father's name, Jehovah Elohim, our Lord God, our Creator. He is the wisdom of God who created wisdom for us by giving us His life, which is our Father's wisdom. We can now receive this gift of life into our life and remain in the Word, who is Jesus, the wisdom of God, and create beautiful things in our life even in our struggles.

May 5

~ New creation in Christ ~

Therefore, if anyone is in Christ, the new creation has come: The old has gone, the new is here! (2 Corinthians 5:17, NIV).

A good dad only makes good things, regardless of the bad things in his way. Living the name of his loving Father in heaven, Jehovah Elohim, our Lord God, our Creator, he is creative in making his own new construction from the bad blocks that have been thrown onto him. He builds a strong foundation of his home on all those bricks of life's hardships. As long as he knows how to worship God in spirit and truth, he is able to take hold of all those thoughts and make them obedient to Christ (see 2 Corinthians 10:5). He renews his mind to have the mind of Christ, so he can build his new image of the new creation of him in Christ Jesus.

For, 'Who has known the mind of the Lord so as to instruct him?' But we have the mind of Christ (1 Corinthians 2:16, NIV).

Jesus lived our Father's name, Jehovah Elohim, our Lord God, our Creator. Everything was created for Him and through Him through the breath of the Father which is His Spirit. Jesus is now breathing in us through the Holy Spirit He gave us so we can live our Father's name, Jehovah Elohim, and create a new way of living from the new life in Him. The Holy Spirit breathes new life into our life. He gives us a new heart and a new spirit so we can live that new life. We just have to renew our mind all the time to live in that new life. All we have to do is breathe into ourselves (Psalm 51:10).

> *Create in me a pure heart, O God, and renew a steadfast spirit within me (Psalm 51:10, NIV).*

Every new day is a new opportunity to live our Father's name, Jehovah Elohim, and be renewed in the Word again, to create and develop the image of Christ within us.

May 6

~ Create mercy from the mercy of God that is new all the time ~

> *Surely your goodness and love will follow me all the days of my life, and I will dwell in the house of the Lord forever (Psalm 23:6, NIV).*

On May 6, 2021, Angelilly brought to me a Mother's Day gift. It was a beautiful coffee/tea travel mug. She got the right colour and exactly what I love because she knows my taste of colour. She kept asking if I liked her gift. I said yes, but she kept asking and asking, so I said, 'I have to put something into the cup and have a drink and tell you then.' This is what the Holy Spirit taught me: So is the gift of life Jesus gave. Some situations have to go into your new life for you to taste and see that the Lord is good.

Jehovah Elohim is His name, our Lord God, our Creator. He gave us the greatest gift, Jesus, who is life and light. He came down and tasted the evil we all taste and overcame it with the goodness of the Father. He lived the Father's name, Jehovah Elohim, our Lord God, our Creator, and created goodness and mercy. He saw things through compassion and had mercy on everyone and created goodness. Even on the cross, he repaid the evil upon Him with His goodness.

A good dad is full of compassion and has mercy on his household, and so every new day he lets himself get renewed in the mercy of our loving Father in heaven so he can create a new mercy.

This is His prayer:

> *Create in me a pure heart, O God, and renew a steadfast spirit within me. Do not cast me from your presence or take your Holy Spirit from me. Restore to me the joy of your salvation and grant me a willing spirit, to sustain me. Then I will teach transgressors your ways, so that sinners will turn back to you (Psalm 51:10-13, NIV).*

Every day is created for us to live our loving Father's name, Jehovah Elohim, and create His goodness to overcome the evilness entering our day. Everyone around us will see the love of our Father that surrounds us by tasting the goodness we created from the fruit of goodness of the Holy Spirit. This is the gift of life to live.

May 7

~ Create a righteous life in the righteousness of Christ ~

> *For those God foreknew he also predestined to be conformed to the image of his Son, that he might be the firstborn among many brothers and sisters (Romans 8:29, NIV).*

On May 7, 2021, Blessed, my then two-year-old, brought a little chair stool that normally belonged to Angelilly, her six-year-old sister. I was sorting Angelilly out for school and told her, 'Blessed seems to use and claim ownership over everything that used to belong to you.' This is what I heard the Holy Spirit say: When God adopts you into His family, everything that was created for Jesus and belongs to Him is now yours. You are co-heirs and you rule and reign with Him on the right hand of the Father. Jesus is the firstborn of all creation and what is His is now rightfully yours in His righteousness.

> *Yes, Adam's one sin brings condemnation for everyone, but Christ's one act of righteousness brings a right relationship with God and new life for everyone. Because one person disobeyed God, many became sinners. But because one other person obeyed God, many will be made righteous (Romans 5:18-19, NLT).*

A good dad seeks first the kingdom of his loving Father and delights in His Word that declares all the wonderful promises which are yes and amen in Jesus. He knows the Father, He is Jehovah Elohim, our Lord God, our Creator. Like His Father, he creates righteousness and always does the right thing, even when no one notices.

Jesus lives the Father's name, Jehovah Elohim, our Lord God, our Creator. The Father created us in His image, to which we lost our identity through the disobedience of the first man. But then Jesus came and restored this and created us in His new image by being obedient to the Father. He is the righteousness of God. Like Blessed, who is born into our family and has the rights and ownership of what Angelilly, the firstborn, has. When we become born again, we too have the rights to owning also what Jesus, the firstborn of the Father's creations, own.

Every day is a new day that gives us the opportunity to create in our life all the right things we want to do and live by, whether it is eating habits, exercises or forgiving those who do us wrong.

May 8

~ Create God's love within you to love the difficult people around you ~

You must be perfect—just as your Father in heaven is perfect (Matthew 5:48, GNT).

It was June 22, 2021. Thomas' car rego payment was due and he had to take the car in for inspection for his registration. However, it was the inside of the van he was mainly concerned about. Even if it looked nice outside, he was making sure everything inside was working fine. The van had to function properly with no fault within as it would be tested by an authority before he received the okay for the van to serve its purpose.

While I was watching him working on the van, this is what I heard the Holy Spirit say: You see, you may think you are looking fine outside, but what matters is your inner being, and this is where your loving Father tests you to make you come out pure. His love is perfect and pure and He tests you with that love. This is why you go through some situations where you find people you are close to becoming so difficult and hard to forgive. The Father's goal is achieved when His love is made perfect in you (see 1 John 4:12). Only when His love is made perfect in you, it has served its purpose.

A good dad's goal is to achieve the perfect love of God in his life. For him to be successful, he is creative with his love towards his wife.

He creates many things to show his love and loves her unconditionally, just like how Christ loves the church. He knows that the love of the Father serves its purpose when he loves his wife unconditionally. His wife is a gift from the Father and he has to love that gift the Father has given to him. When a wife is loved, she naturally blooms like a beautiful garden where all her family enjoys her presence.

Jesus lived our Father's name, Jehovah Elohim, our Lord God, our Creator, and also wants us to live that name. He created the Father's love from His life by laying it down for us. We can now create that love, and love from the place of where Jesus is seated with the Father. We can't love someone who hurts us with our human love, but we can create a love from where we rule and reign with Christ on the right hand of the Father and love them through the perfect love of the Father.

> *And this hope will not lead to disappointment. For we know how dearly God loves us, because he has given us the Holy Spirit to fill our hearts with his love (Romans 5:5, NLT).*

Every day is created new for us with this new command to love one another as the Father loves us. We have the Holy Spirit residing in us with the Love of the Father poured into His Spirit. From that love within us through the Holy Spirit, we can live our Father's name, Jehovah Elohim, and create more love so our Father can achieve His goal in our life.

May 9

~ Create more time to spend daily with the Father ~

> *Seek the Lord and his strength; seek his presence continually! (1 Chronicles 16:11, ESV).*

A reading app is provided by the school my six-year-old attends. The children are asked to read one book a night, then to fill in their reading card, and by the end of the term they are rewarded. June 2, 2021, I asked Angelilly to read four books when she was only supposed to read one. Now the reason I did that was because I know her potential and capabilities. She was good at her reading. Even with four books to read she would finish within 15 to 20 minutes, and could do it without supervision. I had a meeting with her teacher and was told she was very good at reading, and she even got some awards for it.

While I was asking her to read the four books, I heard the Holy Spirit say: You see, the kingdom of God is like this. Our Father gives us tests according to our potential and capabilities of how Word rooted and knowledgeable we are of Him. He allows temptation and trial into our life to the limit of our capabilities. You allowed Angelilly to read four books because she is able to do it. God also allows tests that may come in four directions of your life because He knows you are strong and able. He gave that kind of test to Job and allowed the enemy to walk into Job's life and cause destruction because He knew Job was able to sit through and pass those tests and trials.

A good dad always sits in the Word of his heavenly Father to be knowledgeable of Him and His richness in mercy, love and kindness. For him to be capable and live the potential of life, he has to create and make more time to spend on a daily basis with the Father.

> *Walk in wisdom toward outsiders, making the best use of the time (Colossians 4:5, ESV).*

Jesus lived our Father's name, Jehovah Elohim, our Lord God, our Creator, and created and made time for everyone who needed Him. Even when He was stopped and interrupted in His busy schedule,

He always had time. If our loving Father can create and give 24 hours every day to us, we too must create out of that 24 hours quality time to spend with Him. We have to live our Father's name in Jesus' name and start creating time to spend with Him, so we can be more knowledgeable of Him.

May 10

~ Creating a life of hope ~

This is the day the Lord has made. We will rejoice and be glad in it (Psalm 118:24, NLT).

March 8, 2021. I got a rental car, and so I thought I had to make use of it every day and enjoy this blessing. Every day, I woke up saying, 'Ok, I have to enjoy this blessing because very soon I will return it.' This is what the Holy Spirit taught me: The kingdom of God is like this. You will return that life back to where it's source is, so enjoy living in it while you have it in flesh on earth. In the grave, you will not be able to do anything.

A good dad wants to enjoy his everyday life with his loved ones. Before he gets started in his day, he sits in Word and prayer, seeking His Father in heaven for the strength, wisdom and anointing for the day so he can carry his life with those he loves, and make it successful in creating happiness from it. For him to create a life of joy and peace, he has to seek the one who creates joy and peace.

May the God of hope fill you with all joy and peace as you trust in him, so that you may overflow with hope by the power of the Holy Spirit (Romans 15:13, NIV).

Jehovah Elohim, our Lord God, our Creator, gives us the creative, inventive power to create. Jesus lived our Father's name by creating light and life in this dark, dead world that our life revolves in. When we receive Jesus into our life and believe in the power of His name that heals and saves, we receive His creating power and create that peace He gave us. We can also create joy from the Holy Spirit, through which God pours out His love.

May 11

*~ Create your value more in the Word of God.
You are valuable ~*

And endurance builds character, which gives us a hope that will never disappoint us. All of this happens because God has given us the Holy Spirit, who fills our hearts with his love (Romans 5:4-5, CEV).

Therefore, if anyone is in Christ, he is a new creation. The old has passed away; behold, the new has come (2 Corinthians 5:17, ESV).

One Sunday, March 28, 2021, I stopped by at our end of the month Sunday market where our community take whatever items they no longer use to sell. Similar to a garage sale, except that it is called a 'car boot sale' because most things are displayed from the boot of the car.

Most things were used items or clothes and you paid a dollar or two, but I noticed someone selling their old stuff for a high price. They were selling at hundreds of dollars, and beside the items they put descriptions. This is what I heard the Holy Spirit say: Its price is so high and it has a note besides it to explain its value and the high price put to it. You see, so are you. You were bought with heaven's highest price. The Word has become flesh and bought you with His blood. Only when you know who you are and what the Word says of you, then you will know your great value. The Word describes you, how the one who made you speaks of your worth and value, just like how the notes beside those items describe them and their value.

> *For you know that God paid a ransom to save you from the empty life you inherited from your ancestors. And it was not paid with mere gold or silver, which lose their value. It was the precious blood of Christ, the sinless, spotless Lamb of God (1 Peter 1:18-19, NLT).*

A good dad knows his worth and value from His Father in heaven. As a father who wants to be a good dad, he declares and says what his loving Father says of him. He creates his new life in the perfect love of the Father and His Word.

Jehovah Elohim is His name that all creation knows, our Lord God, our Creator. Jesus came and lived our Father's name. He died for us and gave us a new life of love, His perfect life from the Father. We are to live the name of our Father in heaven to create that new life in Christ in the Word, so the enemy too can know that we know who we are in Christ.

Each day is a new beginning of living our Father's name, Jehovah Elohim, in creating that new life we have in Christ so we can know the value and worth of our life and live in it. We will never lose our value because the blood of Jesus which has bought us is more precious and valuable at all times.

May 12

~ Create everything in and through Jesus ~

> *You are already clean because of the word I have spoken to you (John 15:3, NIV).*

A good dad knows that Jesus came and lived the way our Father in heaven wants. So for him to be that good father, like his heavenly Father, he has to create and program his nature to obey His Father's Word in much the same way a calculator is programmed to compute numbers. Jesus obeyed the Father, and that is what he is to do too. A calculator will give you only the right answer. It will never cheat. It is programmed in such a way that it will give you the correct output from the information you put in it. When you feed your new nature with God's Word, it is designed to give you the right response. That's why Satan tries to keep you so busy doing other things, so you don't spend time reading your bible. His goal is to keep you weak and ineffective.

> *For by him all things were created, in heaven and on earth, visible and invisible, whether thrones or dominions or rulers or authorities—all things were created through him and for him (Colossians 1:16, ESV).*

Jehovah Elohim, our Lord God, our Creator, is the Creator and source of life and light. Everything He created was through and in Jesus. Jesus came and lived so we would be able to create in Him and through Him. Every day is another new day and opportunity to create what we want to be in Christ in His Word.

May 13

~ *We can create a new heart by renewing our mind in the Word* ~

> *But if, when you arrive in the land the Lord will give you, there are any among you who are poor, you must not shut your heart or hand against them; you must lend them as much as they need (Deuteronomy 15:7-8, TLB).*

A good dad's focus is to live his life like his loving Father in heaven by giving. When he started walking with the Father in Word and prayer, the Father taught him how to open wide his hands to give. The more giving becomes his nature, the better his attitude becomes. Our Father in heaven is the giver and source of everything we have. The giver, source and Creator of life gave us life, so we can create within us a new life to live and give to others.

Jesus is the life that the Father gave to us because He loves us so much. The love from a heart is shown through the giving made by the hands. Jesus lived our Father's name, Jehovah Elohim, our Lord God, our Creator, by dying on the cross so He can create a new life for us from the life of sin we were born into.

> *...to put off your old self, which belongs to your former manner of life and is corrupt through deceitful desires, and to be renewed in the spirit of your minds, and to put on the new self, created after the likeness of God in true righteousness and holiness (Ephesians 4:22-24, ESV).*

His hands were open wide, showing how wide and deep his love was for us. We are now to live the Father's name, Jehovah Elohim, by creating a new life from our old self-centred life. The greed of that self-centred life can easily leave us when we learn to make giving our nature.

The Psalmist says create in me a new heart. By living Our Father's name, Jehovah Elohim, we can now create that new heart of giving because the Holy Spirit lives in our heart and makes us new every time we renew our mind in the Word to have Christ-like mind.

May 14

~ You can create your own beautiful weather where you are ~

A man without self-control is like a city broken into and left without walls (Proverbs 25:28, ESV).

When winter is arriving and the place starts getting cold, I normally put the heater on in the bathroom to warm the room before getting my kids in to shower or bath. On the morning of May 22, 2021, as I did so, the Holy Spirit taught me this: You see, the outside of this room is cold, but not in the bathroom because you decided to make it warm. It doesn't matter what is going on around you. You decide your weather and temperature level by how you feel about something. You can control what you need to do to become what you want with your life, but you can't control what's happening around you, just like how you can't control the winter's cold temperatures, but you can control the temperature inside and prevent yourself from feeling cold.

A good dad uses the fruit of the Holy Spirit, self-control, to control himself not to be affected by what is happening around him. He surrounds himself with the love of his loving Father to produce the fruit of self-control, to control himself to be obedient and submit to the Word of the Father. All the fruit of the Spirit flows out of the fruit LOVE. GOD IS LOVE.

Our Father is Jehovah Elohim, our Lord God, our Creator, and has given us a creative power to create something and adapt to changes and happenings in accordance with His Word. Jesus lived our Father's name by creating love where hate was manifesting.

He was making changes so we can adapt to these changes. When the woman was caught in an adulterous act, He created love out of the scene. He said whosoever that has not sinned cast the first stone upon her (see John 8:3-11).

Jesus Himself was the one who was supposed to stone her, because He has never sinned. But He was love, and this is what our loving Father is. He is love.

> *A new command I give you: Love one another. As I have loved you, so you must love one another (John 13:34, NIV).*

We can love all over again and again with each new day. Jesus said, 'I give you a new command to love one another.' A new day created for us to live our Father's name, Jehovah Elohim, and create love and walk in the new command. We can also create self-control to love where we can't love.

May 15

~ Create a house for the Holy Spirit ~

> *You didn't choose me! I chose you! I appointed you to go and produce lovely fruit always, so that no matter what you ask for from the Father, using my name, he will give it to you (John 15:16, TLB).*

Winter of 2021, on June 13, our little family was walking along rocks on the beach and I saw a little branch with so many little branches spreading out. And even though it was dead, it still looked strong. Because of its beauty, I had a plan in my mind of what I wanted to do with it, so among the other sticks and branches, I chose it and picked it up. I told my six-year-old to hold it for me.

She asked me what I was going to do with it, and I said, 'I have a plan to do something with it so we are taking it home.'

This is what I heard the Holy Spirit say: You see, the kingdom of God is like this. Your loving Father loves you and He chose you. He knows where He has placed you and He has chosen you in Christ because He has great plans and hope for you. In just the same way you chose that branch and have plans for it, your Father too has chosen you because He has plans for you.

A good dad knows that his loving Father is the Creator and source of life. He stays focused and connected to the Word which is the source of life. It is not a mistake he is a dad. He was chosen to be one because the Father has plans that will give him hope to bring hope to his household. It doesn't matter where he is, he is chosen in Jesus Christ to house the Holy Spirit so he can feel at home and produce the goodness from the fruit of the Spirit, just like how I got that branch because I had plans at home for it. Our Father's many great plans will come to pass when we house the Holy Spirit and feel at home with Him.

> *For we are God's handiwork, created in Christ Jesus to do good works, which God prepared in advance for us to do (Ephesians 2:10, NIV).*

Jesus lived our Father's name, Jehovah Elohim, our Lord God, our Creator, by creating a home for us here on earth. He made it possible by laying down His life so we can have access to His life. The Holy Spirit is the home of the life of Jesus. When we receive Jesus, we become the body of Christ who houses His Spirit.

Every day, we are to live our Father's name, Jehovah Elohim. We have to create love for someone who needs it to make them feel at home. Home is where you feel at peace, secure and comfortable. You feel belonging. Love makes you feel that you belong.

May 16

~ Ask the Holy Spirit to help you to create your new Christ-like life ~

...and have put on the new self, which is being renewed in knowledge after the image of its creator (Colossians 3:10, ESV).

Our loving Father created us in His image to be a creative being. This nature was corrupted by the fruit of the knowledge of good and evil that we inherit through the first man who disobeyed God. Jesus came to us in the fullness of love, life and light and created a new life in Himself, but we have the choice to receive it or not.

A good dad chooses every day to live the Father's name, Jehovah Elohim, our Lord God, our Creator, to create love, life and light in the gift of life he received from Jesus. It's the Word and prayer that he acts upon daily that is on his mind, and makes him creative to create more goodness in the days of evil around him.

In their case the god of this world has blinded the minds of the unbelievers, to keep them from seeing the light of the gospel of the glory of Christ, who is the image of God (2 Corinthians 4:4, ESV).

Jesus gave all the glory back to the Father by living in the image of the Father that He created Him for. Everything is created for and through Christ for the Father's glory (see Colossians 1:16). When the Father looks at you and sees the image of His Son in you, He is glorified. He has only one Son and He is interested in only that one person, whom He can see, the image of His Son in and through that person. This is why the heavens rejoice over one soul that receives the life of Christ.

Social media is confusing and leading us astray, because Jesus is coming back soon. Instead of us focusing on creating ourselves to be in the image of Christ, we are now focusing on showing our own image for people to praise it on social media. God looks at the heart and the motives of everything and He alone will judge us accordingly. He can see whether He is glorified in what you do.

Every day we are to live the Father's name, Jehovah Elohim, and create the image of Christ in us from His life He gave us. The Holy Spirit inside us will help us to be that image where the Father can see the Son and be glorified.

May 17

~ Create the new you in Christ ~

The Word became flesh and made his dwelling among us. We have seen his glory, the glory of the one and only Son, who came from the Father, full of grace and truth (John 1:14, NIV).

June 27, 2021, I was looking at a beautiful image of a bride in her white wedding gown and a white dove flying above her shoulder with the scripture of Revelation 22:17, '... let the Spirit and the bride say come'. As I was looking and thinking of how beautiful the image was, the Holy Spirit taught me this: The words match the image and reflect it perfectly. This is also what your heavenly

Father wants to see in you. He wants to see His Word reflecting well in your image, because when it does, He gets the glory. You are showing His image. When you have the mind of Christ, His Word is on your mind. As a man thinketh, so is He (Proverbs 23:7). And when you action the Word, you are moving and having your being in the Father.

> *For in him we live and move and are! As one of your own poets says it, 'We are the sons of God.' (Acts 17:28, TLB).*

A good dad moves and has his being in the Word who has become flesh. His hands carry out the love stored in his heart. He stays connected to the Word each day and prays about every move he will make in the day.

Jesus is the very image of the Father's Word who has become flesh. In every move He made, the goodness and love of the Father was moving hearts and meeting needs. He came down for us to see that image, then He died to create one person from which we can create ourselves to become that image of the Father. Jesus lived our Father's name, Jehovah Elohim, our Lord God, our Creator. He created a new life for us in the image of the Father, from which we can create and live to bring glory to the Father.

> *… by abolishing the law of commandments expressed in ordinances, that he might create in himself one new man in place of the two, so making peace (Ephesians 2:15, ESV).*

Each day, we are to live our Father's name, Jehovah Elohim, and create within us that one new man who is the image of Christ. This is how we create peace to live and move in.

May 18

~ Creating kindness ~

He must become greater; I must become less (John 3:30, NIV).

A good dad knows that he may not be able to do great things, but he can do small things in a great way with his mustard seed of faith. For him to become less and Christ become great, he plants himself in the love of his heavenly Father and sows kindness wherever he can. His Father is rich in kindness and he has inherited that kindness. He creates that kindness wherever there is unkindness.

> *For the creation waits with eager longing for the revealing of the sons of God. For the creation was subjected to futility, not willingly, but because of him who subjected it, in hope that the creation itself will be set free from its bondage to corruption and obtain the freedom of the glory of the children of God (Romans 8:19-21, ESV).*

Jesus lived the Father's name, Jehovah Elohim, our Lord God, our Creator. It was through Him and for Him our good Father created everything. And so, while He lived on earth He created kindness by showing the Father's unconditional love. The earth's creations are in bondage and are waiting for the sons to be revealed to them and become kind to them. The Father showed His loving kindness in sending His only Son so He can have many sons to live His name, Jehovah Elohim, and create kindness to every living creation on earth.

> *… in order that in the coming ages he might show the incomparable riches of his grace, expressed in his kindness to us in Christ Jesus (Ephesians 2:7, NIV).*

Every new day is created for us. Our Father wakes us by calling us to see the new day so we can be kind to everyone we are connected to or come in contact with. Our Father is rich in mercy and kindness and that is what we have inherited from Him in Jesus Christ.

May 19

~ Creating a new life after the fall ~

For God so loved the world that he gave his one and only Son, that whoever believes in him shall not perish but have eternal life (John 3:16, NIV).

May19, 2021. My jewellery hanger has a figure of a woman with her hat, and realising the hat had fallen off, I started searching for it. I knew if the wind had blown it off it wouldn't have gone too far, but would be close to where I'd left the jewellery hanger. This is what I heard the Holy Spirit say: You see, you too fell into this world and are lost. God came closer to you to save you and live in you. And so, He had to come in the flesh form, through the Son, into the world where you are to find you.

If you want to know a person, you have to draw out the goodness and potential of what is inside them. But you have to approach that person first. The real being of that person is not what you see in their appearance, but what is within them. Your Father in heaven had to approach you in flesh form in the fallen world that you are in to get you back to Him, because He wants to live in you and work through you to bring back to life every seed of potential within you. He came in the flesh form to meet your fleshy desire and put it to an end, so He can bring you back to your original spiritual being by living inside of you through His Spirit. The fleshly nature has to be put to rest first, then your spirit nature will be at work.

> *And if the Spirit of him who raised Jesus from the dead is living in you, he who raised Christ from the dead will also give life to your mortal bodies because of his Spirit who lives in you (Romans 8:11, NIV).*

Jesus lived our Father's name, Jehovah Elohim, our Lord God, our Creator. He lay down His life and rose again, and created a new life for us to live in that life and overcome everything in this world. The power of the same Spirit that resurrected Jesus to life is in us to create a new life of abundance. We live in this World, but we are not of this world. We are of the Word who has become flesh (see John 1:14).

Every day is created for us by our, Father, Jehovah Elohim, to create and to make our new life respond to the Christ-like life in the Word who has become flesh, and not the World that is killing our spirit.

May 20

~ Creating time to pray and have breakthroughs ~

> *By the seventh day God had finished the work he had been doing; so on the seventh day he rested from all his work. Then God blessed the seventh day and made it holy, because on it he rested from all the work of creating that he had done (Genesis 2:2-3, NIV).*

May 20, 2021. I remember that day well. I was quickly trying to turn into a lane. There was another car coming so fast towards me that if its brakes didn't function I was in the way; he could easily have bumped into me. This is what I heard the Holy Spirit say: You see, if your brakes don't work and his don't, then an accident can happen. In any relationship, both partners must have their brakes. When one spouse is rushing through, one has to put on the brakes so they do not collapse.

A good dad makes sure he puts on the brakes by taking a break. He goes into his man cave and reflects on the happenings of life. He creates time to listen more to His Father in heaven and talk to Him about everything in prayer. He uses this opportunity to rest, alone in the Father's amazing love, so he can be that amazing dad and husband. He lives the Father's name, Jehovah Elohim, our Almighty Father, is our Creator in Jesus' name, to create time. Where he can, he must pause and put a brake on so he can see breakthroughs in the life of his family. If Jehovah, our loving Father and Creator can take a break from His work, then it's a must. We must always take a break and rest.

> *After He had sent the crowds away, He went up on the mountain by Himself to pray; and when it was evening, He was there alone (Matthew 14:23, NASB).*

Jesus lived our Father's name, Jehovah Elohim, our Lord God, our Creator, and always created time to take a break from everyone and pray. He was always showing the Father's kindness and goodness in whatever he did for anyone, but for Him to be strengthened and more energised, He had to create time out with the Father and pray.

Each day in our busy, mad life we can live our Father's name, Jehovah Elohim, and create time by putting a brake on what we are doing, taking a break and resting in our Father's amazing love by listening to Him in His Word and talking to Him in prayer.

May 21

~ Create a new life in you from your old, withering life ~

> *… and said, 'Therefore a man shall leave his father and his mother and hold fast to his wife, and the two shall become*

> *one flesh. So they are no longer two but one flesh. What therefore God has joined together, let not man separate.'*
> *(Matthew 19:5-6, ESV).*

A rainy morning, May 21, 2021, I was sorting out the clothes to fold and realised I was missing one from a pair of socks. Knowing where I kept the other piece to it, I thought of putting it together. This is what the Holy Spirit taught me: This is what happens when you get married and are committed to your spouse. You are meant to be together. When one is by itself it cannot be put to serve its purpose, you see, you cannot wear that sole sock because another part of it is missing.

A good dad is a good husband. Even he goes through the hardest part of transition in becoming one with his wife. He is never going to shift blame in a relationship but take the responsibility of the leader and solve the problem. He will never run away from his problems but will run to his loving Father to receive counselling from Him. One has to sacrifice, to lay down his or her life, to become one in marriage. A good dad is willing to take that path as long as the Word of Jehovah, our loving Father, is the lamp unto his path.

> *When you send your Spirit, they are created, and you renew the face of the ground (Psalm 104:30, NIV).*

Jesus lived our Father's name, Jehovah Elohim, our Lord God, our Creator, by sacrificing Himself to create one eternal life from His life. Because of what He has done, we are all one in the Father. We are in Christ and Christ is in the Father. Not only that, but Jesus has given us His Spirit who creates life in us.

> *But whoever is united with the Lord is one with him in spirit (1 Corinthians 6:17, NIV).*

Every new day we have the opportunity to create a new life from this withering life that is fading away in the fears, troubles and problems of this world.

May 22

~ Create a space and distance yourself from anything that steals your time to grow in the Word ~

Instead, speaking the truth in love, we will grow to become in every respect the mature body of him who is the head, that is, Christ (Ephesians 4:15, NIV).

May 22, 2021, I potted the flower plant and gave it more space in the pot so it could grow. This is what the Holy Spirit taught me: The kingdom of God is like this. You have to give space in a relationship so it can grow. In marriage, each partner has to come to a certain time where they give each other space to reflect and grow. A time of silence. There may be time where you feel like the Father is not hearing your prayers or He is not showing up in your problems. It's your space he is giving for you to grow stronger. He is there, but not making it known. The strength you have grown into is His strength upon you.

A good dad understands his relationship as a father and husband. He gives space to his wife to refill herself. While she has her space, he also has his space, a time where he is growing more in His Father's love by producing and putting into action the fruit of the Spirit towards his loved ones. He fills every empty space in his life with the Father's love and gives Him all the glory in what he does. All he says to the Father is, 'Your love is better than life.'

> *Because your love is better than life, my lips will glorify you. I will praise you as long as I live, and in your name I will lift up my hands (Psalm 63:3-4, NIV).*

At the cross, the Father spaced Himself away from Jesus that He cried out and said, 'Why have you forsaken me?' There was silence. That was the moment that Jesus grew into the strength that took him into the valley of death and out into the dew of eternal life to which we all can have access to now.

> *The Lord will fight for you, and you have only to be silent (Exodus 14:14, ESV).*

Every new day gives us the opportunity to live our Father's name, Jehovah Elohim, our Lord God, our Creator, and create a space towards certain things and become silent so we can hear clearly the Father's voice which will give us the strength to continue and wait on the coming of the Lord Jesus. If it means to create space and be silent towards something that sucks our time, then we must do it.

May 23

~ Create your new life and close every access of unrighteousness to it ~

> *The reason the Son of God appeared was to destroy the works of the devil (1 John 3:8, ESV).*

I opened a cupboard drawer to get something out. I remember that day, it was March 22, 2021. After that I didn't close the cupboard properly. Then I thought, *this is why Blessed (my two year old then) gets everything out and messes it up, because the opened cupboard gives him easy access.*

This is what the Holy Spirit taught me: When you leave open some areas of your life that the enemy can access, he will walk right in and mess up what he can find, just like how Blessed has access to what he can find and mess it all up. Always close and seal up your life with the blood of Jesus. The life you are living is no longer yours but Christ's, and you need the blood of Jesus for His Life that you are living.

> *For the life of the flesh is in the blood, and I have given it for you on the altar to make atonement for your souls, for it is the blood that makes atonement by the life (Leviticus 17:11, ESV).*

A good dad opens his life only to Jesus, who is the Creator of his new life to live. He listens to the one who is Jehovah Elohim, our Lord God, our Creator, and opens the door of His life so the living bread can come in and nourish him more. Jesus has lived our Father's name, Jehovah Elohim. He created a new life and in Him we can find our way to the Father. The blood of Jesus has purchased us and the devil cannot mess with our life anymore. It is no longer us, but Christ who lives in us, and it is Christ who has conquered the devil and his work.

> *Behold, I stand at the door and knock. If anyone hears my voice and opens the door, I will come in to him and eat with him, and he with me (Revelation 3:20, ESV).*

Each day, use your power and authority in the blood of Jesus and keep destroying whatever work the devil plans to carry.

May 24

~ Create the 'tree of life' and feed on it ~

I am the true vine, and my Father is the gardener. He cuts off every branch in me that bears no fruit, while every

> *branch that does bear fruit he prunes so that it will be even more fruitful (John 15:1-2, NIV).*

May 24, 2021, I was removing the dry little branches of the flowers that had died and this is what the Holy Spirit taught me: The kingdom of God is like this. When you receive Christ into your life, everything of your old life in this world will die. You have to remove them in your life, just like you are removing those dying vines of the plants. The new image of you in Christ has to grow, and so you have to create space by removing anything of the 'old self' attached to you.

A good dad knows that his loving Father in heaven is the gardener and Jesus is the vine. He plants his life in the Word of the Father and offers himself as a garden where His Father, the gardener, can work on him. He remains in the Word, Who is Christ, and allows himself to remain in the waters of His life that cleanse him through all seasons so he can remain fruitful.

> *You are already clean because of the word I have spoken to you. Remain in me, as I also remain in you. No branch can bear fruit by itself; it must remain in the vine. Neither can you bear fruit unless you remain in me (John 15:3-4, NIV).*

Jesus lived our Father's name, Jehovah Elohim, our Lord God, our Creator. He created out of His death the eternal life, 'Tree of Life', which we must remain in to bear the fruit of the Holy Spirit, who is the gift from His life we have in us.

We are the lost garden of Eden that Christ has come to save and restore for our Loving Father to do His work as a gardener to us. Jesus' gift to us is His life, as the tree of life, to be in the garden of Eden. Our life is the garden of Eden and we must have the tree of life, Jesus, so the Father, who is the gardener, can prune us to experience His amazing love and be fruitful in the fruit of the Spirit.

Every new day gives us brand new opportunities to create our garden more beautifully by choosing only to eat from the tree of life and not from the tree of the knowledge of good and evil.

May 25

~ Create an image frame of Christ on your image ~

I have hidden your word in my heart, that I might not sin against you (Psalm 119:11, NLT).

May 25, 2021, while tidying up the room, I noticed the wallpaper was tearing off. There was a little peeling done by my two-year-old when he was around one. I thought I'd put some framed photos of us over to hide it.

This is what I heard the Holy Spirit say: You see, the kingdom of God is like this. Your identity is sin. You were seen as a sinner. You are righteous now because of what Jesus did. When you keep remaining in the Word and take into you the Word, you are no longer who you are as unrighteous and sinner. You stand blameless. Just like how you want to use a photo image of yourself to hide that torn wallpaper, you need to get the Word of God, which is the image of Christ, and hide it in your heart so you cannot sin. Jesus said you are clean by His Word, so keep getting His Word into you to remain clean. When you hide yourself in the Word, it hides you.

But put on the Lord Jesus Christ, and make no provision for the flesh, to fulfill its lusts (Romans 13:14, NKJV).

A good dad hides himself in his loving Father's image, His Word. He walks in obedience in the Word that when people see him, they see the Father's love working in his life.

> *For he himself is our peace, who has made the two groups one and has destroyed the barrier, the dividing wall of hostility, by setting aside in his flesh the law with its commands and regulations. His purpose was to create in himself one new humanity out of the two, thus making peace, and in one body to reconcile both of them to God through the cross, by which he put to death their hostility (Ephesians 2:14-16, NIV).*

Jesus lived the Father's name, Jehovah Elohim, our Lord God, our Creator, and created from Himself one new man. He created peace. This is what Jesus created for us to live in so we can also create it for others to live in.

With every new day given to us comes new opportunities to live our Father's name, Jehovah Elohim, and create the image of Christ by walking in obedience to the Word. This is so our weary, unrighteous ways can no longer be seen, but only the righteousness of Christ can be seen, His new image which we have framed into our image to do away with our old ways.

May 26

~ Create a new love for those who are difficult towards you ~

> *A new command I give you: Love one another. As I have loved you, so you must love one another (John 13:34, NIV).*

I have been asking the Lord to reveal to me more of His amazing love. I know I have not really comprehended this perfect love of God. His love is too deep and too high, yet is reachable and possible because Jesus brought it to us. This is what the Holy Spirit showed me through a promotional email I received. May 6, 2021, I received an email saying 'redeem your gift of $50 in store'. I thought *wow*, so I clicked on the link to see what I had to do to receive the gift. It said I had to spend $120 to redeem the gift of $50.

This is what the Holy Spirit taught me: The love of God that He sent through Jesus to save you has no terms and conditions. You don't need to do anything, but only to believe and confess with your mouth that you are a sinner and need Jesus to redeem and save you. Even while you were a sinner, Christ died for you and everyone in the world. God didn't wait for you to be or do some right things first so you could be saved. This is what the devil does—he puts into people's mind that once they get rid of some of their bad little habits then they can fully receive Jesus in their heart as their redeemer and saviour. But no, God is so full of love, and that love is so perfect that it doesn't need you to come to Him as perfect. That love is there to perfect you, so come as you are with your imperfection.

A good dad knows how imperfect he is and cannot love people with his human love, so he depends entirely on his heavenly Father so he can love through the Father's love that is perfect. The difficult people he encounters all around him are an opportunity to love them. He has to live the Father's name, Jehovah Elohim, our Lord God, our Creator. He creates new love from his new image of Christ.

> *… and have put on the new self, which is being renewed in knowledge in the image of its Creator (Colossians 3:10, NIV).*

Jesus lived the Father's name, Jehovah Elohim, our Almighty Father is our Creator, and created in Himself one new man when he resurrected from life. (See Ephesians 2:15). That new image of Christ is love. We are to create that image as well, as that is how people will see Jesus in us. Others see Jesus in us when we show love where it's impossible, because with men it is impossible, but with God it is possible.

Each new day is created brand new to remind us always of the new commandment to love. We can live our Father's name, Jehovah Elohim, by creating new love towards people who make it impossible for us. The way we see our children and love them in a new, fresh way is how God sees and loves us all the time. He is forever faithful in loving us.

May 27

~ Create a new life of peace because you are your Father's child ~

For God so loved the world that he gave his one and only Son, that whoever believes in him shall not perish but have eternal life (John 3:16, NIV).

A good dad may not be born rich, but he knows the way to becoming rich. He loves giving because this is the way of getting rid of the spirit of poverty. He is blessed to be a blessing because it is blessed to give than to receive (see Acts 20:35). Blessings are attracted to you in your giving not receiving. To be like his loving Father in heaven, he gives. God loves the world so much that He gave His only son. Love is all about giving. You can say you love someone with your mouth, but it is dead when you don't show it in your actions. Faith without action is dead.

The story about the old poor woman who gave the only money she had is like how God gave His only Son because He loves the world so much. From that one and only Son, many sons are created from His life. Jehovah Elohim, our Lord God, our Creator, is so full of love to create new breeds of loving sons and daughters. According to its kind, God will create from what you place in His powerful hands.

> *Peace I leave with you; my peace I give you. I do not give to you as the world gives. Do not let your hearts be troubled and do not be afraid (John 14:27, NIV).*

Jesus lived our Father's name by laying down His life and creating a new life of peace. Every day is a new opportunity to live our Father's name, Jehovah Elohim, in Jesus' name, and create that new life of peace. We show we are God's children because we become peacemakers (see Matthew 5:9).

May 28

~ *Create peace in this chaotic world* ~

> *Blessed are the peacemakers, for they will be called children of God (Matthew 5:9, NIV).*

A beautiful evening, May 28, 2021, I was thinking of teaching Angelilly to make my tea the way I like it. I wanted to teach her so she could learn how to do it herself for me. This is what I heard the Holy Spirit say: You see, the kingdom of God is like this. Every day, your heavenly Father is teaching you a lesson so you can learn to be able to get through life. That storm and test He allows into your life is to make you stronger to be able to live the life He designed for you to live. Just like how you would like to teach Angelilly to make your tea so you can just rest and relax, so it is with your Father in heaven. When He see that you are now able to do something in life and fight through that storm victoriously, He will be at rest in you because you can now rise up from Him and always win, victoriously. This is where you feel at peace in your battles and storms.

A good dad is always at peace, regardless of whatever storms through his door, because he has opened the door of his heart to hearing the Word and receiving it. The Word, Jesus Christ who is our Peace, has become flesh of his heart. And so, he can easily create peace in every life-threatening battle he faces.

Jesus lived our Father's name, Jehovah Elohim, our Lord God, our Creator, and created peace. He battled death and brought back to us life from death so we can never fear death. He created peace and lived in peace while on earth, and He left peace with us when He went back to the Father.

> *For in him all things were created: things in heaven and on earth, visible and invisible, whether thrones or powers or rulers or authorities; all things have been created through him and for him (Colossians 1:16, NIV).*

Every day is created for and through Christ, who is our Peace to create peace and live in peace among ourselves, for this is how God's children live. We are to live our Father's name, Jehovah Elohim, and create peace in this chaotic world we live in.

May 29

~ Create your universe in the Word and live in it ~

> *Do not be deceived: God cannot be mocked. A man reaps what he sows. Whoever sows to please their flesh, from the flesh will reap destruction; whoever sows to please the Spirit, from the Spirit will reap eternal life (Galatians 6:7-8, NIV).*

Just like the law of gravity, the law of sowing and reaping is there. Whatever you sow in that direction, that you will reap. Whatever you throw in the air in that direction, to that direction it will fall.

A good dad understands that if he sows his time into his family they will always be there for him and have time for him. To be time rich so he can have more time on his hands to use, he spends time with His Father in heaven. From the 24 hours a day His Father gives, he gives one-tenth back to Him, which is 2.4 hours.

Our Father, Jehovah Elohim, the Lord God, our Creator is His name, and He creates time for us to also create or make time for Him. He not only creates Himself to become flesh, but also made time to come down and live with us so He can go through what we go through all the time. Jesus is the Word who became flesh (see John 1:14). It was the Word who created and sustained life. We can now also use the Word to create our universe to live and sustain our life. God used His Word to create His universe for us to use. He loves us so much and has given us the Word to also create our own universe to live. In the beginning, God created the heavens and the earth (see Genesis 1:1, NIV).

> *The Word became flesh and made his dwelling among us. We have seen his glory, the glory of the one and only Son, who came from the Father, full of grace and truth. (John 1:14, NIV).*

Every day, rise up and live the Father's name, Jehovah Elohim, in Jesus' name, and create your universe with the Word and live the Word.

May 30

~ Use the creating power God gave to attract what you want in life ~

For indeed, the kingdom of God is within you
(Luke 17:21, NKJV).

A beautiful day, January 30, 2021, I was sitting at the playground and watching the kids. I was looking at the flowers and how they were attracting beautiful butterflies. What would the Lord teach me today about this beautiful scenery? This is what I heard the Holy Spirit say: The butterflies are attracted to the flowers. They are around because of the flowers. God gave you the creating power to be able to make what you want to attract in life. God created the first man, Adam, in His image. Then man disobeyed God. All human race has sinned and gone astray away from God and created themselves. A homosexual creates himself to be a homosexual. That was not what God created us to be.

A good dad creates himself to become Christ-like by renewing himself in the knowledge of Jesus Christ so he can have a God-like mind. He wants LIFE, and so he creates eternal life by losing his old selfish life. Just like how the butterflies are attracted by the flowers, when he renews himself in the knowledge of Jesus Christ, he attracts the new eternal life. A life of abundance.

Our loving Father in heaven is Jehovah Elohim, our Lord God, our Creator, and that is His name. Jesus lived our Father's name by rising up from death and creating a new eternal life that we may receive to live a life of abundance. He has given us power to trample over Satan and create the person God created and designed us to be. We have the creative power from our Father to live His name,

Jehovah Elohim, in Jesus' name every day and create that strong, wisdom-filled person to glorify and honour God.

May 31

~ Create your new life in Christ in the truth of God's Word by the Spirit of truth ~

...and have put on the new self, which is being renewed in knowledge in the image of its Creator. (Colossians 3:10, NIV).

December 6, 2022, I was working on the edited manuscript and started thinking about the many parts of our house that needed work to be done. Then I thought how it was much easier when I was living in a rental property. I had nothing much to do around the house to improve it and make it the way I wanted it to be, because the house didn't belong to me. It was more relaxing for me, as there was not much to do.

The Holy Spirit opened my eyes to see how it is the same when we lose 'our self', our old life, and find our true new life in Him. He is the Spirit of truth and our true life is found in Him. When we find our true life and identity, we will need to work more on our self to become that new person we are in Christ. A lot of work has to be done to put on the new self which is to be renewed in the knowledge of the Creator. To have the knowledge of who we are in Christ, we have to spend quality time in the Word and in prayer on a daily routine.

...and to put on the new self, created to be like God in true righteousness and holiness (Ephesians 4:24, NIV).

We house the Holy Spirit and we have to work more on our house which is our body, soul and spirit. Just like how I now have my own house and have to work on it more to improve and maintain it because it belongs to me, so it is when we find our true life and identity in Christ. We will work on it and maintain our relationship by communicating with our Father every day in Word and in prayer.

Jesus lived our Father's name, Jehovah Elohim, our Lord God, our Creator. He created a new life of truth by the resurrecting power of the Spirit of truth who raised Him up. We will have that life in us when we receive Christ into us.

Every day, we are to live our Father's name, Jehovah Elohim, and create our new life in the knowledge of the Word who is Christ so the Holy Spirit can powerfully raise us up in the house we provide for Him to live.

JUNE

Jehovah Tsidkenu! I AM Your Righteousness!

OUR LORD GOD IS OUR RIGHTEOUSNESS.

~ Sow the fruit of righteousness everywhere you go ~

But the fruit of the Spirit is love, joy, peace, patience, kindness, goodness, faithfulness, gentleness, self-control; against such things there is no law (Galatians 5:22:23, ESV).

Angelilly's school provided an app called PM, where they have all their reading books. You can click on the app and read the stories from the books available. The app also has an audio recording of each book, so if your child doesn't know certain words and gets stuck, they can play the audio to hear the words. Angelilly normally uses the audio to play the words for her when she comes across a new word or words that are difficult for her. One autumn morning, March 26, 2021, I was reading a book to her and told her I would read each page first, then she could read the page after me, just like the audio does in the app. With me, it was different. I grew impatient and started getting upset after I read a page and she still got stuck reading certain words.

The Holy Spirit taught me this: You have to learn to be patient. If she was doing her reading with the audio she would never struggle because she would overcome difficult parts by playing the audio. The audio will not be impatient and upset. The audio was programmed to do what its being called, designed and purposed to do. In your new life with Christ, you have been designed and called to sow the fruit of the Holy Spirit so you can reap righteousness. You have to program your mind to have the mind of Christ. In that way, you will always be patient and not get upset when reading the book again to her and she gets stuck.

A good dad knows that each day is another day to sow the fruit of the Holy Spirit into any difficult issues he is having in his home. In human nature it's hard, so he stays attached to the Father to help him get through. He knows the name of the Father, Jehovah Tsidkenu, our Lord God is our Righteousness. To be like His Father, he must stand up for the truth and the right things, even if he is standing alone. He may be standing alone on earth, but in heaven, the throne room of God's residence is standing with him.

> *And because of him you are in Christ Jesus, who became to us wisdom from God, righteousness and sanctification and redemption (1 Corinthians 1:30, ESV).*

Jesus is the very righteousness of our loving Father in heaven who showed us how to live the right way to bring glory to the Father. He went back to the Father so the Spirit of righteousness can come and live in us to produce His fruit of righteousness.

Each day of the month of June and every new day is a new opportunity to sow into someone the fruit of righteousness, to reap righteousness, because we are the righteousness of God in Christ.

June 1

~ *Use your gift in the right way to serve and worship God* ~

> *Whatever you do, whether in word or deed, do it all in the name of the Lord Jesus, giving thanks to God the Father through Him (Colossians 3:17 NIV).*

A good dad knows that he is the righteousness of God in Christ and whatever he does, he does it and uses it in the right way as an obedience to His Father in heaven. No matter what tool he uses in his trade—a hammer, keyboard, mop, football, spreadsheet, an espresso machine—he uses it as an act of obedience. It's the mechanism whereby he worships His Father in heaven by using it the right way to serve with a cheerful grateful heart.

> *And being found in appearance as a man, he humbled himself by becoming obedient to death—even death on a cross! (Philippians 2:8, NIV).*

Jesus lived our Father's name, Jehovah Tsidkenu, our Lord God, our Righteousness. He was the righteousness of the Father and He did everything right in the right way, which He learnt from our heavenly Father. This is also what He wants us to learn from Him and also do. He lived a life of obedience even to death, because dying was the only right way for the righteousness of the Father to live within us in the Holy Spirit.

Whatever you are using every day is your tool of righteousness to use in the right way and live the Father's name, Jehovah Tsidkenu. Every day, clothe yourself in the righteousness of God and walk in obedience, even if it is you alone who stands for righteousness.

June 2

~ Remain always in the righteous finished work of Jesus ~

> *My little children, I am telling you this so that you will stay away from sin. But if you sin, there is someone to plead for you before the Father. His name is Jesus Christ, the one who is all that is good and who pleases God completely. He is the one who took God's wrath against our sins upon himself and brought us into fellowship with God; and he is the forgiveness for our sins, and not only ours but all the world's (1 John 2:1-2, TLB).*

We normally book the roadside kerb collections of rubbish with our city council for big household items like furniture. I piled mine out on my kerb, but since I hadn't made the necessary bookings, it remained there. I remember March 29, 2021, while I was looking at that pile of rubbish, the Holy Spirit begin to teach me about the kingdom of God: To live in the kingdom of God, you have to ask God to continue to remove any kinds of sin that you have lodged in your house. Like your rubbish that has not been removed, your sins too can remain if you don't ask the one who is supposed to remove it to do so. Only Jesus can remove your sin and make you righteous, because He is the one who paid for your sin.

A good dad remains in the righteousness of Christ because he knows that he is already clean because of Jesus who is the Word.

> *Already you are clean because of the word that I have spoken to you. Abide in me, and I in you. As the branch cannot bear fruit by itself, unless it abides in the vine, neither can you, unless you abide in me (John 15:3–4 ESV).*

In Jesus' name we are righteous, for He has lived our Father's name, Jehovah Tsidkenu, our Lord God, our Righteousness. We are now living our Father's name in the righteousness of Christ in Jesus' name.

Every day we are called by our new name, the righteousness of Christ. All we have to do is serve and live that name so everyone can see and praise our Father in heaven.

June 3

~ Every day is the right day to live in the righteous name of Jesus ~

Seven times a day I praise you for your righteous laws (Psalm 119:164, NIV).

April 2, 2021, was a beautiful morning. I looked at my collection of necklaces and I thought *I am so spoilt with choices*. While I was thinking, the Holy Spirit instantly spoke into my thoughts: Of course you are, and of course you are spoilt with God's great promises too. Just like how you look at your jewellery and think how spoilt you are with choosing which to wear, you must also look at God's promises and see how spoilt you are with which one to clothe yourself and use it every day.

Fathers have the right to their household. A good dad always chooses righteousness, even if he has many other choices. He remains in the righteousness of Christ in the Word to live his heavenly Father's name, Jehovah Tsidkenu, our Lord God, our Righteousness.

> *I, the LORD, speak righteousness, I declare things that are right (Isaiah 45:19, NKJV).*

Every promise of God is righteous and when we use them, it makes us stand right with God. Jesus is the very righteous Word of the Father who lived our Father's name, Jehovah Tsidkenu.

Each day is made just right for us to live our Father's name, Jehovah Tsidkenu, in Jesus' righteous name.

June 4

~ Even in the battlefield, keep remaining in the righteousness of God ~

But we have the mind of Christ (1 Corinthians 2:16, NIV).

One cold winter's morning, June 6, 2021, I was battling to lift the bedding and put it onto the clothes line. I was struggling for a while, then realised I would need Tom's height. So I called out to him to get the bedding and put it up on the laundry line. This is what I heard the Holy Spirit say: You see, your loving Father in heaven also allows you to go through some battles in life so He can use what you experience for His glory. After experiencing the struggle that I couldn't put the bedding on the line, I reached out for Tom's help because he had the height to do it easily. Our Father in heaven also wants us to go through the struggles and challenges and have an experience, then to reach out for His help so we can taste and see His goodness.

A good dad sees all his battlefield as a place where he is to glorify God. This is where his status as a dad comes out, reflecting that he is the son of the Almighty Creator of the universe. He is a good dad, like his good Father in heaven. It is in his battles that he remains in the righteousness of God in producing the fruit of the Holy Spirit to fight the good faith. His connection every day with the Father in His Word puts him in the right position to win any battles.

> *You will not need to fight in this battle. Stand firm, hold your position, and see the salvation of the Lord on your behalf, O Judah and Jerusalem. Do not be afraid and do not be dismayed. Tomorrow go out against them, and the Lord will be with you (2 Chronicles 20:17, ESV).*

Jesus is the righteousness of God who lived the Father's name, Jehovah Tsidkenu, our Lord God, our Righteousness. Our mind is the battlefield of our life. We are the righteousness of God in Christ for we have the mind of Christ. Each day, we have to learn to capture every thought and make it obedient to Christ. We are to make every thought right to what the Word says. This is how we win, because we begin to walk in obedience to what our Father desires for us in our life.

June 5

~ Inheriting and living the life of righteousness ~

*I have said what I would do, and I will do it
(Isaiah 46:11, NLT).*

June 12, 2021, I was driving and thinking about how I normally send money through Western Union. What happens is the money goes by my instruction according to the details of the receiver. Certain countries allow the money I send to go directly into their bank account, while in others, the receiver has to go with their identification to the location of the agent for pick up. This is what I heard the Holy Spirit say: You see, God also sent His Word to the receivers. His Word was Jesus, who He sent for us to receive. Everything our loving Father planned to equip us to do, every good work is in Jesus, the Word who has become flesh. We have to have faith by receiving the Word. Faith comes by hearing and hearing the Word. Our identity of being a son and receiving the inheritance of the Father is from our faith in hearing the Word and actioning the Word. When we action our faith, we live a life of righteousness.

I send the money and it sits in the account of the receiver for the receiver to draw it out and use it, so is the Word I receive into me also sits inside of me. I have to draw it out from within me to use it. And just like how the receiver will have to go to an agent to show their identification to receive the funds sent to them, I too have to have within me the Holy Spirit and house Him. He is my identification in Christ. And so, I will receive all the promises of the Father, that is yes and amen in Christ, when I ask Him.

Who can tell you what is going to happen? All I say will come to pass, for I do whatever I wish (Isaiah 46:10, TLB).

A good dad receives into him the Word of his loving Father on a daily basis and has it stored within him. The Holy Spirit works upon the Word inside of him, which enables him to produce the fruit of righteousness. He lives a life of joy and peace which he inherited from the Father, so he can become more and more like his loving Father in heaven.

> *For the kingdom of God is not a matter of eating and drinking but of righteousness and peace and joy in the Holy Spirit (Romans 14:17, ESV).*

Jesus lived our Father's name, Jehovah Tsidkenu, our Lord God, our Righteousness. He identified Himself as the peace from the Father and gave us peace before He went back to the Father. He also promises us that unless He goes, the Holy Spirit will come to us. Jesus identifies the Holy Spirit as the joy. Our Joy will be complete when He goes back to the Father and the Holy Spirit comes to us. The Holy Spirit is the joy from the Father for us to inherit.

Receive into you every day the Word and draw out the peace of Jesus and the joy of the Holy Spirit to use. This is living life in the righteousness of the kingdom of the Father's love.

June 6

~ Even when you go off-track, always return back to the righteousness of God ~

> *I was born to do wrong, a sinner before I left my mother's womb (Psalm 51:5, ERV).*

It was getting dark as Tom drove through the hospital road one winter's eve, June 6, 2021. It usually gets dark at around 5 pm in the winter season. We were trying to turn right when I realised he didn't put on the car signal to indicate he was turning right. I pointed that out to him and he said, 'Oh well, there is no car at the back of us.' I said, 'It's not about whether there is a car—it's all about doing the right thing all the time.' Because it was a Sunday evening, the place was quite empty with no signs of life, and that obviously led him to do what he did.

This is what the Holy Spirit taught me: It's all about your relationship with Christ in always doing the right thing—all the time. Jesus is the righteousness of God. When you start doing the right thing you become the righteousness of God in Him. You can easily go off the track in doing the wrong thing because it is your nature, but always remember to get back on the right track when you realise you did the wrong thing. The mercy and grace of God is always there to renew and put you back on track.

A good dad may go off the path of righteousness, but as long as he spends time with His Father in heaven on a daily basis, he will always get back on track to do the right things. He carries the identity and name of His Father, Jehovah Tsidkenu, our Lord God, our Righteousness.

Jesus lived our Father's name, Jehovah Tsidkenu. He did the right thing to solve the problems of everyone who did the wrong thing. He did the right thing to the woman caught in the adulterous act and there was peace (see John 8:1-11). He told the truth of righteousness to the woman at the well who was practising the wrong lifestyle. He even became a guest in the home of the cheating tax collector, who then started doing the right thing. In the midst of all our wrong acts, Jesus is there, knocking on the door to come in so He can eat and drink with us and make things right for us to live His life of righteousness.

> *Look! I have been standing at the door, and I am constantly knocking. If anyone hears me calling him and opens the door, I will come in and fellowship with him and he with me (Revelation 3:20, TLB).*

Every day is a new day with new opportunities to live our loving Father's name, Jehovah Tsidkenu, in Jesus' name, by doing the right thing in everything we find that is wrong.

June 7

~ Your position in Christ is to remain in His righteousness ~

> *...that he worked in Christ when he raised him from the dead and seated him at his right hand in the heavenly places, far above all rule and authority and power and dominion, and above every name that is named, not only in this age but also in the one to come (Ephesians 1:20-21, ESV).*

June 6, 2021, while driving by a suburb called Toukley, I saw a billboard that said 'position available', and this is what I heard the Holy Spirit say: You see, the sign says position available, because in this particular building there is a vacancy for someone who is able to perform that role. When you don't take your rightful position in the righteousness of Christ, the enemy will have access and use it to do what he wants. Your rightful position is your birthright that you inherit when you receive Christ. But you have to use that birthright. It's your place of authority. Jesus defeated the power of Satan, which is sin and death. You not only have power, but also authority. The devil will try to find ways to have access into you to have power over you, but he will still never have authority. Jesus has given you authority over him to overcome all his power (see Luke 10:19).

If you remain in the righteousness of Christ, Satan can only go to God and ask Him for permission to have power over you, but he is limited to where God allows him to go (he did that to Job). Your position in Christ is to remain in His righteousness. When you don't occupy that position, you give easy access to the enemy to do whatever he wants to do to your life.

A good dad remains in the righteousness of his righteous Father. He makes sure each day that he takes his position of authority so he can command the devil to be removed from remaining in anything that is of his concern and connection. He lives the name of the Father, Jehovah Tsidkenu, our Lord God, our Righteousness, just like Jesus.

> *Little children, let no one deceive you. Whoever practices righteousness is righteous, as he is righteous (1 John 3:7, ESV).*

Jesus lived our Father's name, Jehovah Tsidkenu, by living the right way the Father asked of Him to live. He is the righteousness of God, and He came down and lived the Father's name so we can also live our Father's name when we are born into His Family. We become the righteousness of God in Christ to remain in Him and produce the fruit of righteousness.

Each day, before we walk into our day, let's make sure we occupy our position of righteousness and live our Father's name, Jehovah Tsidkenu. Let's not live a vacant space in our life where the devil can access to occupy and cause problems for us.

June 8

~ Silence the enemy with the righteous blood of Jesus all the time ~

For the accuser of our brothers and sisters, who accuses them before our God, day and night, has been hurled down. They triumphed over him by the blood of the Lamb and by the word of their testimony; they did not love their lives so much as to shrink from death (Revelation 12:10–11, NIV).

This is how Satan works: He puts into your mind about this certain person hating you, and he also puts into that person's mind that you hate him. And so, you begin to feel that each of you doesn't feel comfortable in the other's company.

A good dad is aware of how Satan moves around because he remains connected to His Father in heaven in Word and prayer and he only moves in the commands of His Father. To avoid the clever, evil tricks of Satan, a good dad produces the fruit of righteousness all the time to feed his thoughts. He also stretches out his hand in kindness, which is one of the fruit of righteousness from the Holy Spirit.

For our sake he made him to be sin who knew no sin, so that in him we might become the righteousness of God (2 Corinthians 5:21, ESV).

Jesus lived the Father's name, Jehovah Tsidkenu, our Almighty Father is our Righteousness, by purchasing us with His righteous blood so we can use it and silence Satan every time he whispers thoughts of hatred towards someone into our mind. Every time Satan puts an evil negative thought of someone into your mind, pray blessings of good health and prosperity over that person. Whatever the enemy meant for bad, you can create goodness over it. Silence him with the blood of Jesus.

Guide your each day with love by thinking righteous good thoughts. (see Philippians 4:8). So you can live the name of the Father, Jehovah Tsidkenu, and do the right thing.

June 9

~ Train yourself to live in the righteousness of God ~

For the Lord your God is he who goes with you to fight for you against your enemies, to give you the victory (Deuteronomy 20:4, ESV).

June 9, 2021, on a winter's night of the 'State of Origin' series, I asked the Holy Spirit to teach me something as I was watching the game. After some minutes, I heard the Holy Spirit say: You see, those guys can run around and not get exhausted. They have been trained and trained to come out and play in the field without getting exhausted. Their coach/trainer gives them instruction on how to train, but they have to physically do it with their flesh to be able to be fit. So it is with your faith. The Word of God can tell you to do all the right things. Even Jesus lived the righteousness of God so you can become the righteousness of God in Him. But only when you learn to train yourself every day to action the fruit of righteousness of the Holy Spirit within you, then you won't be weary, worn out and worrying about how you'll survive in this fallen, evil world. You know you are always going to have victory over your rivals, who are not flesh and blood. Since your rivals are not flesh and blood, you don't even need to prove to anyone how good you are—just live your life the way God designed you to live and enjoy.

> *The Lord God is my strength; he will give me the speed of a deer and bring me safely over the mountains (Habakkuk 3:19, TLB).*

A good dad trains himself to live the right way of how his loving Father would love for him to live. All the goodness and loving kindness of the Father was lived by Jesus in everything He did.

Jesus lived the Father's name, Jehovah Tsidkenu, our Lord God, our Righteousness. He was the peace. He left peace with us and told us He had to go back to the Father, so the Helper, the Holy Spirit who is the joy, can come to us and complete our joy. Our joy comes from the nine fruit of the Holy Spirit, which is love, and when we action those fruit of righteousness of the Holy Spirit we action the love of the Father.

Each day is a great new day to live our Father's name, Jehovah Tsidkenu, as we are to live in righteousness by producing the fruit of the Holy Spirit to everyone we come across who needs it.

June 10

~ *The sweet fragrance of God rises out from the righteousness of God in Christ within us* ~

Taste and see that the Lord is good; blessed is the one who takes refuge in him (Psalm 34:8, NIV).

One wintry morning, June 10, 2021, while watching the morning cartoon and having breakfast with Angelilly, the Holy Spirit pointed out to me this: When someone is cooking a nice meal in their home, one can smell it when they walk past the home. So it is with you. When you carry the presence of God within you, it is a sweet-smelling aroma that leaks out from you and others can sense it when you walk past them. This is why you find people giving you a smile or a nice gesture of kindness. It is the flavour from the favour of the Lord that gives out that sweet smell, just like the right flavours one uses in cooking that give out a delicious aroma.

A good dad speaks with kindness in his voice of authority. The more he listens to His Father in His Word, the more he prays to His Father regarding the Word so the Word can become his Flesh. For him to be that walking Bible, with that sweet aroma of delicacy, he is to be the chef of the kingdom of God. Being that chef of the Word, he not only makes the Word smell nice with the flavours of kindness and grace, but he makes sure whoever tastes it will taste and see that the Lord is good.

> *Because of Christ, we give off a sweet scent rising to God, which is recognized by those on the way of salvation—an aroma redolent with life (2 Corinthians 2:15, MSG).*

John the Baptist was preparing the way for Jesus to come and live. Jesus came and lived our Father's name, Jehovah Tsidkenu, He is the righteousness of God and came to prepare the way for the Holy Spirit to come and live inside of us so we can become the righteousness of God. We are the house of the Holy Spirit, who is inside of us and producing His fruit of righteousness. When we produce that fruit of righteousness of the kingdom of the Father and live in His name, it releases the sweet, fresh aroma that attracts the attention of whoever we meet or stay connected to.

Every day, live in the Father's name, Jehovah Tsidkenu, In Jesus' name, and release from within you, where the Holy Spirit is lodged, the fruit of His righteousness, which is a sweet aroma from heaven.

June 11

~ *Putting into action the Word of righteousness* ~

I put on righteousness, and it clothed me (Job 29:14, ESV).

One cold morning, June 10, 2021, I was watching a cartoon with my six-year-old, and she told me she could spell the word 'later'. She spelt it as latre! I said no, and corrected her, telling her she'd mixed the letters. This is what the Holy Spirit pointed out to me: You see, the devil does that. He deceives us with the truth by twisting only one word or rearranging it, just like how Angelilly did. The devil has clever tricks, as the scripture says. Just like how we can easily trick children, he can trick us easily if we are not matured in the Word of God.

A good dad wants to be matured in the love of His Father. He puts that love into action with every Word he takes into him. He wears upon him and clothes himself in the righteousness of the Word. Only when he is clothed in the righteousness of the Word, he knows that the Word is put into use. Just like we use our clothes by being clothed in it. Whenever the enemy tries to deceive or fool us, we cannot fall for it, even though we live in this fallen world surrounded by the fallen angels of Lucifer, because we are clothed in the righteousness of the Word.

> *Well, no wonder! Even Satan can disguise himself to look like an angel of light! So it is no great thing if his servants disguise themselves to look like servants of righteousness. In the end they will get exactly what their actions deserve (2 Corinthians 11:14-15, GNT).*

Jesus lived our Father's name, Jehovah Tsidkenu, our Lord God, our Righteousness, in doing the right things the Father assigned Him to do. Even when the devil wanted to deceive Him, he couldn't get Him. Satan deceived Jesus with the scriptures for Jesus to prove His position as the Son of God, but Jesus lived the name of the Father by telling the devil the right things of what the scriptures say.

Every day, the enemy uses social media as his tool to twist people around by making them show others their images to prove who they are. We are to just live our Father's name, Jehovah Tsidkenu, in doing the right things of what our Father wants us to do.

June 12

~ Run the race of righteousness ~

And this word continues to work in you who believe (1 Thessalonians 2:13, NLT).

One winter's night, June 12, 2021, the television was on. I could hear the voices in the background, but wasn't paying attention. I know most people just put the television on and carry on doing whatever they want to do, like looking at their phone. It was almost 10 pm and my little family had all gone to bed. I was the one awake, chatting and messaging with a friend. I allowed the television to be on just to feel I had a companion present.

This is what the Holy Spirit taught me: Let the Word you contain within you always be your television and let it be on all the time, regardless of what you do and where you are. Let the right words of God inside of you flow out and fill the atmosphere outside of you so you will always be reminded to walk in the right path of God's way and will.

Just like someone who watches their favourite team on television and cheers, a good dad sits and always watches his loving Father's

Word and cheers on his household members to win in whatever battles life throws at them. Faith comes by hearing and hearing the Word of God. The heroes of faith always cheer other saints to run the race and complete it (see Hebrews 12).

> *If we say we live in God, we must live the way Jesus lived (1 John 2:6, ERV).*

Jesus the Word is the righteousness of God, and lived our Father's name, Jehovah Tsidkenu, our Lord God, our Righteousness. He has run the race of righteousness that the Father placed Him in so we can watch Him like a television and follow Him in every act of righteousness. He is now with the Father, not only cheering for us, but interceding for us as well. He has given us a rightful position with Him to rule and reign with Him as we live our Father's name, Jehovah Tsidkenu.

June 13

~ Connect your body to Christ as the head, and be dressed in the righteousness of God ~

> *They don't keep themselves under the control of the head. Christ is the head, and the whole body depends on him. Because of Christ all the parts of the body care for each other and help each other. So the body is made stronger and held together as God causes it to grow (Colossians 2:19, ERV).*

We have a beautiful massage chair that does everything from full body massage, spinal massage, relaxation massage, comfort massage, foot massage and even hot stone massage. On Christmas Eve of 2022, I was trying to start the massage chair, but it didn't work. I got off the chair and checked all the connections. One was not connecting, and that was where the problem lay. I put the connection back and the massage chair worked.

Hear what the Holy Spirit taught me: The massage chair was not broken, but the connection to make it work was not connected to where the power was coming from. When one part of our body is not connected well to make us become the complete body of Christ, we will not be moving, living and working as a body of Christ.

> *So stand strong with the belt of truth tied around your waist, and on your chest wear the protection of right living. On your feet wear the Good News of peace to help you stand strong. And also use the shield of faith with which you can stop all the burning arrows that come from the Evil One. Accept God's salvation as your helmet. And take the sword of the Spirit—that sword is the teaching of God. Pray in the Spirit at all times. Pray with all kinds of prayers, and ask for everything you need. To do this you must always be ready. Never give up. Always pray for all of God's people (Ephesians 6:14-18, ERV).*

Our heart is to be connected to the love of God, to love people with compassion, mercy and understanding them, that they are trapped and blind and do not know what they are doing. Our mind is to have the mind of Christ so we think heavenly things and pray without ceasing for all the body of Christ. This enables our body to connect well to Christ as the head. As a body of Christ, our hands have to find joy in everything it gives and our feet must fit in with peace so we can walk in peace. Ephesians 6 describes how a body of Christ is to be dressed in the righteousness of Christ, to stay connected to Christ as the head. When the enemy sees a body of Christ dressed in the armour of God that connects to the head of Christ he stays away. Enemies don't attack someone who is watchful and all dressed up for the battle.

Jesus came and lived our Father's name, Jehovah Tsidkenu our Lord God is our Righteousness. He lived in a body just like us and laid down His body just so He can reap from His body many bodies who will become the 'body of Christ'. He is the head, Himself, to which we, as His body, are connected.

Every new day we are to live our Father's name, Jehovah Tsidkenu and dress our body in the righteousness of God's Word to remain connected to Jesus Christ who is the head.

June 14

~ Always do the right thing all the time, even in an impossible situation ~

> *He that is unjust, let him be unjust still: and he which is filthy, let him be filthy still: and he that is righteous, let him be righteous still: and he that is holy, let him be holy still. And, behold, I come quickly; and my reward is with me, to give every man according as his work shall be (Revelation 22:11-12, KJV).*

I received a penalty fine from our local council for parking at the sign that says 'school bus zone'. Being a foreigner and not really used to the signs, I thought it was okay because I saw all the other cars parking there. My understanding was because I was doing a drop off and pick up, it should be okay. A month ago I received that penalty notice and today, June 16, 2021, I walked down to the gate to do pick up and realised that some cars had parked along the side where it said 'no stopping'.

This is what the Holy Spirit taught me by taking me back to the fine I received from parking at the 'bus zone' parking: Don't do it just because everyone is doing it. Always do the right thing, even if it means to go through some struggles, like difficulty in finding a spot to park. Your loving Father in heaven loves it when His children do the right things. To live in love is to live in righteousness. He is a righteous Father, Jehovah Tsidkenu. He is honoured when you behave and live in righteousness.

> *Jesus, our high priest, is able to understand our weaknesses. When Jesus lived on earth, he was tempted in every way. He was tempted in the same ways we are tempted, but he never sinned (Hebrews 4:15, ERV).*

Jesus lived the Father's name, Jehovah Tsidkenu, and always did the right thing with love, even if it meant standing alone. He stood alone to protect the woman caught in the adulterous act. At that moment, He was the only righteous man who had never sinned and had the right to throw the first stone on her. But instead, He forgave her and told her not to sin, but to live right.

Every day, be the one who stands out beautifully because you are a Tsidkenu. Put on the light of the Word that shows you are walking in the right path and live with love. To live and walk in love is to produce the fruit of righteousness of the Holy Spirit.

June 15

- Action the Word in the right way -

> *He shows how to distinguish right from wrong, how to find the right decision every time (Proverbs 2:9, TLB).*

A good dad is aware that when he has a dream, he is going to have distractions, but he won't allow them to direct his life. He sits in the direction of the light from the Father's Word to steer him in the right direction. People can be jealous of him and make him look bad, but as long as he has a good Father watching over him and his dreams, he is going to be that good father too. They can't keep him away from his dream, even if it is their dream to see downfall in his life.

Jesus lived the Father's dream and made His name to become alive. Not only was He the Word who has become flesh, but He lives our Father's name, Jehovah Tsidkenu, our Almighty Father is our Righteousness. It was the Father's dream to make us all become right again with Him, and Jesus accomplished it by becoming sin for us (see 2 Corinthians 5:21). He died and buried that sinful nature, then rose again with a new righteous life for us to live by faith. Faith comes by hearing and hearing the Word. The Word has become flesh, and so faith without action is dead. It is the Father's dream to make Jesus alive and live in us by making the Word become flesh. Therefore, we have to put into action the fruit of the Spirit. This is faith in action.

God made him who had no sin to be sin for us, so that in him we might become the righteousness of God (2 Corinthians 5:21, NIV).

Every new day comes with new opportunity to live our Father's name, Jehovah Tsidkenu. Our flesh must action the Word in doing the right things to reveal we are the Tsidkenu.

June 16

~ Invest and grow your trust in the righteousness of God ~

Those who trust in the Lord are steady as Mount Zion, unmoved by any circumstance (Psalm 125:1, TLB).

On the evening of June 16, 2022, as always, I tidied up some of the toys Blessed was playing with, some magnetic shapes he can build homes or anything his creative mind can take him to. I usually store them in a container box, but as I was putting them into the box, I realised it took me a little while to collect them from all over the place first, only for Blessed to come and empty the box out in a blink of a second. Normally, he just gets the container and pours it all out. This is what I heard the Holy Spirit say: You see, it's the same with trust. You can build up trust for someone, then one mistake from them and all the trust upon that person comes crashing down. Just like how it took you a while to put together Blessed's toys, what you build and put together for that person can come crashing down if they do something to ruin it.

This is why your loving Father in heaven doesn't want you to put trust in any of the things of this world or to build your treasures upon the things of this world. Your world will be crushed down because everything of this world is temporary and the force of evil works stronger in this world.

> *Some trust in chariots and some in horses, but we trust in the name of the Lord our God (Psalm 20:7, NIV).*

A good dad trusts completely in the Word of his loving Father in heaven, and never depends on what he thinks he understands of this world. The news of economic stress, pandemic crisis and inflation will never depress him because he knows His Father, and he completely trusts His Words. To walk in His righteousness is to walk in trusting Him. This is doing the right thing and living the Father's name, Jehovah Tsidkenu, our Lord God, our Righteousness.

Jesus is the righteousness of the Father and He lived among us in a physical nature to show us how to live with nothing, but to trust the Father, who is the source of life, to sustain your life. As long as we live right with the Father by putting first His kingdom and His righteousness, all the things we need will be given to us. All we have to do is just TRUST Him that He's got this.

Every day, we have to live our Father's name by seeking first His kingdom and His righteousness and completely trusting His Word that He will give to us everything we need. We need love, joy and peace, the fruit of righteousness, and this is what the world cannot give.

June 17

~ Live and seek first the kingdom of righteousness ~

> *Behold, I have engraved you on the palms of my hands; your walls are continually before me (Isaiah 49:16, ESV).*

One winter's morning, June 17, 2021, I was making fresh juice and thinking how it was a good thing I'd written down the recipe of that juice so I can always go back to my notes to refresh my memory and see how it is done, should I forget. The recipe was taken at a restaurant I ordered a juice from. This is what I heard the Holy Spirit say: You see, so it is with the Word of your Father. When your Father tells you something or make promises to you, He wants you to write it down.

> *The Lord gave me this answer: Write down clearly on tablets what I reveal to you, so that it can be read at a glance. Put it in writing, because it is not yet time for it to come true. But the time is coming quickly, and what I show you will come true. It may seem slow in coming, but wait for it; it will certainly take place, and it will not be delayed (Habakkuk 2:2-3, GNT).*

When you write it down, it is there to remind, refresh and renew your mind so you don't lose your hope and faith in the love and trust you have in the Word. Faith comes by hearing and hearing the Word, so the more you hear the Word of the Father, the more you will have great faith in Him that He will still do what He says He will do for you.

Your Father loves you so much, He has to engrave you right on His palms to show that His hands will always provide to you all the right things you need in your life. He is the Father of righteousness and wants you to seek first His kingdom of righteousness so all the things you wanted and have written down will be given to you (see Matthew 6:33). He has written you in His palms where He wants to use you as His hands to give.

Jehovah Tsidkenu, our Lord God, our Righteousness, has shown us His righteous hand by giving us His righteous, sinless Son to come and live in righteousness and die for our sin so we can be made right with the Father. Because of what He has done, we can also rule and reign with Him in the right hand of the Father—a place of righteousness.

Every day, take your place and position of righteousness in Christ where you can seek first the kingdom of God's righteousness and live the Father's name, Jehovah Tsidkenu. When you seek first the kingdom of God's righteousness, every right thing will be given to you.

June 18

~ Rise up every morning with righteousness in the joy and peace of the Holy Spirit ~

For the kingdom of God is not a matter of eating and drinking but of righteousness and peace and joy in the Holy Spirit (Romans 14:17, ESV).

Taken from my journal of 2019.

June 18, 2019, I woke up in the morning asking God what life is like in living the kingdom life and He mentioned Psalm 118:24 and Romans 14:17 to me.

> *This is the day that the Lord has made; let us rejoice and be glad in it (Psalm 118:24, NIV).*

What I am trying to say is that every answer to our life is written in God's Word. Of course, you can't find the answer to who that person you will marry is, but His Word is wisdom. When you read it, you will be filled with wisdom in making the right decisions, whether it's the right person to marry or not.

A good dad knows His Father in heaven is a good Father and He designs each day to overcome every evil around with the goodness of it. The flesh and blood that eat and drink are not his enemies. It is the principalities of darkness and their power which are the enemies, and they can be defeated by rising up with righteousness in the joy and peace of the Holy Spirit.

> *Christ is the power of God and the wisdom of God (1 Corinthians 1:24, NLT).*

Jesus was the righteousness of God and lived our Father's name, Jehovah Tsidkenu, our Lord God, our Righteousness. He is the kingdom of God, of righteousness of joy and peace in the Holy Spirit. He has now made us become the righteousness of the Father and the holiness of the Father in the Holy Spirit. Jesus is the wisdom and righteousness of our Father.

Our Father asks us to ask Him for wisdom so we can do the right thing in everything we do when we make decisions in our everyday life. Kingdom life is all about peace and joy in the Holy Spirit, which can silence the kingdom of darkness. As a Tsidkenu, this should be our way of living.

June 19

~ Live a story of love and passion in the righteousness of Christ ~

Therefore, if anyone is in Christ, he is a new creation. The old has passed away; behold, the new has come (1 Corinthians 5:17, ESV).

One cold winter's morning, June 19, 2021, I was looking at my devotional notes written in my notebook. Since I've been using it in 2012, the pages have rips and my handwriting has become worn out and faded. I thought, *now I need to re-write it in a new notebook.*

This is what I heard the Holy Spirit say: You see, it is the same with Jesus. He came on earth to live the name of the Father, to show His love. In the Old Testament days, they thought He was an angry Father who would just punish or put to death anyone who disobeyed Him. The laws He gave to Moses were to guide people to do the right things. Just like how you want to rewrite your old notes into a new notebook because it is all worn out and pages have been torn, Jesus came to rewrite our story from the old way of life which we were living under the laws. When the adulterous woman was caught and the crowd came with the law of Moses, which said to stone her to death, Jesus had to rewrite on the ground a new story of love for the adulterous woman—a story of compassion and love. Our Father is a loving Father and Jesus came to show that love and that there is no law under that love (see Galatians 5:22-23). What He has written is mysterious. All we know is it was love.

The Old Testament law of Moses on the stone tablet was to put her to death because she didn't do the right thing. Jesus, who is the righteousness of God, is the Living Stone, the Word of God who has become flesh. Jesus, the perfect, sinless righteous one who has never sinned, asked everyone, that whoever had not sinned should stone her first. Everyone left, leaving Jesus alone with her. He was sinless, the righteous one who was supposed to throw the first stone at her. Instead, He showed the love of the Father and forgave her sin and told her not to sin again. He bend down not to pick a stone to stone the adulterous woman to death, but to show that He is the Living Stone of the Father's love, to forgive and give life.

A good dad will always live His Father's name, Jehovah Tsidkenu, our Lord God, our Righteousness, in doing the right thing by taking responsibility for situations and not playing the blame game if something is not right in his household. Anything that is SIN is SIN and must be dealt accordingly with love, just like how Jesus dealt with love in the adulterous woman's case.

For all have sinned and fall short of the glory of God (Romans 3:23, ESV).

Every day comes with new favour from our Father to live the Father's name, Jehovah Tsidkenu, in producing the fruit of righteousness and not being judgemental, because we have all sinned and fall short of His glory.

June 20

~ Seek first the kingdom of God and His righteousness in all you do ~

In everything you do, put God first, and he will direct you and crown your efforts with success (Proverbs 3:6, TLB).

A good dad knows that to be successful he has to be success conscious in everything he does. Just as much as his loving Father wants him to be successful, he too wants to see his children be successful and to continue living the family's name in many generations to come by doing great things. He seeks the Father's kingdom of righteousness, so everything that is of success in nature, and great achievements, can come to him in the right way and in the right timing of the Father.

Our Father also wants us to live His name, and so He sent His Son, His righteousness in the right timing (see Galatians 4:4). We are the very chosen generation in this time to live our Father's name of righteousness, and so we have to seek His righteousness, who is Jesus.

> *Seek the kingdom of God above all else, and live righteously, and he will give you everything you need (Matthew 6:33, NLT).*

Jesus is the righteousness of God and lived our Father's name, Jehovah Tsidkenu, our Lord God, our Righteousness. He applied the fruit of the Spirit, which is the fruit of righteousness, into every situation He encountered. He was even kind to the authorities that crucified Him on the cross, even though He had the authority to have it the other way around. By seeking the Father's righteousness and living His name, Jesus was successful in what He came on earth to achieve. If He had never applied the fruit of righteousness, we would never enjoy the abundance of the LIFE IN THE SPIRIT.

Each day is a new day to live our Father's name, Jehovah Tsidkenu, and be that successful person. We are to apply and seek first the kingdom of God and His righteousness Who is Jesus, the wisdom of God.

June 21

~ *Plant righteousness wherever you go* ~

> *… and provide for those who grieve in Zion—to bestow on them a crown of beauty instead of ashes, the oil of joy instead of mourning, and a garment of praise instead of a spirit of despair. They will be called oaks of righteousness, a planting of the Lord for the display of his splendour (Isaiah 61:3, NIV).*

July 23, 2022, Angelilly and her three-year-old brother wanted to do something new, some kind of new play. They wanted their dad to be with them, so they asked him to stay with them in the room where they were going to play.

The Holy Spirit also reminded me that Jesus had to return back to the Father so He could come and stay with us. Wherever we are planted on earth is for us to grow and bloom in our Father's righteousness, like Angelilly and her brother wanting to do something new, and so they wanted their dad's presence. We too are in the presence of our Father, where our heart and spirit are new in the Holy Spirit, who is here to stay with us always.

A good dad understands that his loving Father in heaven has planted him right where he is, with what he has, to display the Father's character which is His name and Word. So he can be a good dad and live the Father's name to serve righteousness to all in his concern, care and connection in his life, he clothes himself in righteousness with garments of praise as he plants and sows the fruit of righteousness of the Holy Spirit. What he sows is what he reaps.

> *For the kingdom of God is not a matter of eating and drinking, but of righteousness, peace and joy in the Holy Spirit (Romans 14:17, NIV).*

Jesus lives the character of the Father by living His name, Jehovah Tsidkenu, our Lord God, our Righteousness. His flesh was the righteous Word of God woven from heaven to earth. He actions the right thoughts of God that are for our hope and future. The Father's tears were shown through the Son's compassion and pain he had for the lost, unrighteous soul that was separated from the righteousness of the Father. Jesus wore our sin so we could wear His righteousness by taking our sin upon Himself. We are now clothed in the righteousness of God in Christ in what He has done.

Every day, wear your crown of beauty, put on the oil of joy and dress in the garments of praise. The Holy Spirit lives in you and this is His lifestyle of living in righteousness.

June 22

~ Fix your brokenness in the righteousness of the Father ~

> *And behold, the curtain of the temple was torn in two, from top to bottom. And the earth shook, and the rocks were split (Matthew 27:51, ESV).*

June 22, 2021, I was playing with my second child, who turned a sweet two years and four months old. I gave Blessed a dolls' house that he wanted to play with. The house was torn in half, but could be put back together. There were also some cute flowers glued on it that he was trying to remove. I said, 'Don't remove anything, just fix the house and put it back together.'

This is what I heard the Holy Spirit say: You see, just like how you want Blessed to put back together that house which was torn in half, so are you. Jesus did not remove every good thing that your loving Father designed in you originally—He came to fix your brokenness. He died in His righteous blood to cleanse away your sin. His blood can remove it, but the sin and knowledge of evil nature is still within you. He only fixed it by giving you a new life to choose that life and live in it. You still have a choice to continue to clean your sin with His righteous blood or return back to your old sinful life. As long as you live in your flesh, you will have to make that choice every day. The Word has become flesh so our flesh can become Word by living and walking in it.

He said, 'I will break down this temple and rebuild it in three days.' The day He died, the curtains were torn in half. His death shows He came for that one purpose. He became sin for us and was torn apart like us. However, He is the righteous sacrifice from the Father for sin. His righteous blood was poured once to cleanse us so we can have access freely. The torn curtain shows there is an access now. He lived our Father's name Jehovah Tsidkenu, our Lord God, our Righteousness. He was the righteousness of the Father.

> *For I am sure that neither death nor life, nor angels nor rulers, nor things present nor things to come, nor powers, nor height nor depth, nor anything else in all creation, will be able to separate us from the love of God in Christ Jesus our Lord (Romans 8:38-39, ESV).*

A good dad will never tear apart his family. He can go broke and sacrifice himself just to see that his torn family is put together and bonded in love. He only sees what his loving Father in heaven does to His Son, Jesus, and follows that closely. When Jesus was in so much pain dying, the Father had to look away because He was broken too. The same brokenness the Son felt, the Father felt. The curtains were torn, but love was there to fix it. And nothing can separate us from the love of the Father. He sacrificed His one and only Son and went broken so we can be made right with Him. And this is what a good dad does, binding his torn family with love so they grow in the Father's love.

We have to live our Father's name of righteousness every day, and fix things where we can and bind things with our Father's love so our Father can get glory and praise in what we do. Get close to the broken people, just like your heavenly Father who is closer to the broken hearts.

June 23

~ Depend entirely in living in the righteousness of God ~

Wise men and women are always learning, always listening for fresh insights (Proverbs 18:15, The Mess).

On June 23, 2021, while tying my six-year-old's shoelace, I thought, *I will teach her to do it so she can know how to do it herself.* This is what the Holy Spirit taught me: Jesus poured out His righteous blood once and for all so we can use it to remain blameless. He is the righteousness of the Father who came on earth and lived His righteousness so we can learn from Him to live right with our Father.

Just like how I was trying to teach my child to learn how to be independent by depending on the knowledge I was going to teach her, Jesus came and lived as the greatest teacher to teach every child of God to be knowledgeable of the Father so we can be independent by depending on His knowledge in His Word, who is Jesus Himself.

To be a wise teacher to his household, a good dad depends daily on the teaching of his loving Father in His Word, so he can have a working knowledge of Him. His Father is always at work and he too must be at work upon His Word by walking in it.

> *All Scripture is breathed out by God and profitable for teaching, for reproof, for correction, and for training in righteousness, that the man of God may be complete, equipped for every good work (2 Timothy 3:16-17, ESV).*

Jesus has given us the Holy Spirit who is the spirit of knowledge (see Isaiah 11:2-3). He produces the fruit of righteousness within us, for us to live our Father's name, Jehovah Tsidkenu, our Lord God, our Righteousness. Being the Spirit of the Father, He knows everything about the Father and is our best teacher to help us live our Father's name.

Every day is just right for us to live our Father's name, Jehovah Tsidkenu, in Jesus name and overcome evil with goodness from the fruit of righteousness, and live right with everyone around us for the Father's glory.

June 24

~ Position yourself always in the righteousness of Christ ~

> *Stand your ground, putting on the belt of truth and the body armour of God's righteousness (Ephesians 6:14, NLT).*

I remember the morning of June 24, 2021. Blessed made a mess in his diaper and the smell of poo was there even after I cleaned him up. I removed the smell by spraying air freshener, which did great work by leaving its refreshing good smell over the bad smell. This is what the Holy Spirit taught me: The bad smell is there, but because you applied the freshener, its beautiful scent took over and drowned the smelly scent. This is also what happens when you apply goodness from the fruit of righteousness over the evilness around you, just like how the smell from Blessed's poo is there, but the power of the refreshing scent covers it. So it is with the righteousness from the blood of Jesus purchased for you, as it covers you from the evilness around you, even though evilness is still around.

Do not be overcome by evil, but overcome evil with good (Romans 12:21, ESV).

Jehovah Tsidkenu, our Lord God, our Righteousness, is our loving Father and wants us to be covered in the blood of Jesus and be clothed in His righteousness. Jesus came down and lived the name of the Father and gave Him all the glory due His name. He has now given the Holy Spirit to us with His fruit of righteousness to live the Father's name for His glory.

A good dad knows it is his birthright from being born again into His Father's kingdom to live in love and be fruitful in producing the fruit of righteousness from the Holy Spirit.

Be born again with the birth of every new day and seek first the kingdom of God and His righteousness and all that you seek and desire in all your days will be added to you.

June 25

~ Sow into something that is right for you to harvest the right things in your life ~

For God so loved the world that he gave his one and only Son, that whoever believes in him shall not perish but have eternal life (John 3:16, NIV).

February 26, 2021, I was trying to give something to someone and expected to see something come out of it; a seed I was to sow into them and wait to see the harvest of it.

This is what the Holy Spirit taught me: The kingdom of God is like this. God gave His only son because He expects something to come out of it. He wants to receive many sons.

A good dad sows into the life of someone he wants to become so he can be a great leader to lead his house. To be Christ-like, he has to sow into producing the fruit of the Spirit in his daily living. His personal time in Word and prayer nourishes and renews his mind to keep walking in the path of righteousness and produce the fruit of righteousness.

For the kingdom of God is not a matter of eating and drinking, but of righteousness, peace and joy in the Holy Spirit, because anyone who serves Christ in this way is pleasing to God and receives human approval (Romans 14:17-18, NIV).

Our loving Father in heaven desires for us to sow in producing the fruit of righteousness to live His name, Jehovah Tsidkenu, our Lord God, our Righteousness. Jesus lived our father's name.

He is the righteousness of God. We are now the righteousness of God in Christ for we house His Spirit. The Holy Spirit produces in us the fruit of righteousness for us to use and remain in the righteousness of Christ.

June 26

~ Serve the fruit of righteousness to everyone you come in touch with ~

And he said to them, 'Take care, and be on your guard against all covetousness, for one's life does not consist in the abundance of his possessions' (Luke 12:15, ESV).

February 3, 2021, someone bumped into my parked car. Thirty minutes before I discovered it, the Lord left in my heart the message of Job, about how the devil attacked especially his wealth and health. The message the Lord laid in me was actually about Job not going astray from the Lord because of the attack, as his life was not attached to the wealth he possessed.

When I saw the bump on my car I was at peace, because the Lord had already prepared me for that incident. I was not going to lose my moment of peace, joy and patience over a material possession. I also found out that the guy who bumped my car wrote an apology note and left it with his contact details, stating that he would fix everything. I sent him a text message and instead of being upset, I thanked him kindly for leaving his contact details so I could get in touch with him. He told me to go see the repairers and he would meet the cost of everything.

You see, when we walk in the righteousness of God, the right atmosphere of the presence of God is all around us. And so, everyone will do the right thing towards us and everything that is in our care and concern.

> *The Lord always does right and wants justice done. Everyone who does right will see his face*
> *(Psalm 11:7, CEV).*

A good dad walks in the righteousness of God in Christ. He abides in Christ by producing the fruit of righteousness of the Holy Spirit. As for him and his house, they will serve the Lord in serving the fruit of righteousness to everyone they come in touch with.

Our loving Father in heaven, Jehovah Tsidkenu, our Almighty Father is our Righteousness, loves us and teaches us what is right. If we have a learning heart we will see, hear and learn. Jesus lived our Father's name. He is the righteousness of God. We have inherited the name of our Father in Christ Jesus to live and carry the name of the Father from generation to generation.

June 27

~ *The Holy Spirit leads us on the path of righteousness* ~

> *For all who are led by the Spirit of God are sons of God*
> *(Romans 8:14, ESV).*

Our family took a week's holiday from January 25, 2021. While driving to visit a beautiful garden in Oberon, NSW, we had a white car in front of us. The car also wanted to go to the garden, because it turned into the sign that mentioned the way to the garden. We were right behind the car and every turn it made was towards the garden. This was what the Holy Spirit taught me: The kingdom of God is like this. You have to follow Jesus. He went to the Father and He sent forth the Holy Spirit as a helper to help you follow Jesus to the Father. The white car is leading the way to the same place you want to go. The Holy Spirit is also leading you to the same place where Jesus went. All you have to do is to live that kingdom life by being led by the Spirit. To be led by the Spirit, you have to be in the righteousness of Christ so you can be on the right path that leads to where Jesus is.

> *...to put off your old self, which belongs to your former manner of life and is corrupt through deceitful desires, and to be renewed in the spirit of your minds, and to put on the new self, created after the likeness of God in true righteousness and holiness (Ephesians 4:22-24, ESV).*

We have a loving Father who lives in heaven. His name is Jehovah Tsidkenu, our Lord God is our Righteousness. Jesus came on earth and lived our Father's name. He lived a life of righteousness, so we too can live our Father's name.

A good dad lives a righteous life by producing the fruit of righteousness in what he does in his household. His godly fatherly role is to lead his house in the right way to Christ, so he renews his mind and fixes it to set daily on what the Word of God teaches so he can have the mind of Christ (see 1 Corinthians 2:16).

Every new day is a new opportunity to live our Father's name, Jehovah Tsidkenu, and renew our mind in the righteousness of God so we can have the mind of Christ and be led by the Spirit.

June 28

*~ The Father made His righteous Word to become
flesh at the right time ~*

*Let your conversation be gracious as well as sensible,
for then you will have the right answer for everyone
(Colossians 4:6, TLB).*

On the evening of January 14, 2021, I was making spaghetti bolognese for dinner. Tom told me how nicely I prepare spaghetti bolognese and that he couldn't make it as good as I do. The specific flavours I use are what makes it good. This is what the Holy Spirit taught me: The kingdom of God is like this. To win people over, you have to season your words with grace according to the season of time they are passing through. It's the grace of God that saves them. You use the right specific flavours, and that is what makes the spaghetti bolognese tastier. So it is with wisdom. Wisdom is timely Word. When you speak wisdom to someone, you speak timely Word that is so gracious to them that they taste wisdom. They taste and see that the Lord is good (see Psalm 34:8).

A good dad remains in the righteousness of Christ and speaks only the right words at the right time. He doesn't talk too much unless he needs to. And when he does, he speaks the right timely word of wisdom that guides his household.

> *It is because of him that you are in Christ Jesus,
> who has become for us wisdom from God—that
> is, our righteousness, holiness and redemption
> (1 Corinthians 1:30, NIV).*

Our loving Father in heaven is the righteous holy one. Jehovah Tsidkenu is His name, the Lord God, our Righteousness. Jesus lived our Father's righteousness by making the righteous Word of the Father become flesh at the right time at all times.

Every new day is another right day to live our Father's righteous name in the name of Jesus and give Him glory in what we do.

June 29

~ *The sinless flesh has become Word to cloth our flesh with righteousness* ~

I put on righteousness, and it clothed me; my justice was like a robe and a turban (Job 29:14, ESV).

While waiting to pick up Angelilly from school one afternoon, I could see her among the other kids easily, simply because she is my child and I knew from how I dressed her to how she walks. This is also how our heavenly Father sees us among everyone. It is sin that hides us from Him. However, when we come to Jesus and receive Him, we are clothed in His righteousness. Our righteousness in Christ makes us become a son that He sees us. This is how we have favour around us. When our Father sees us, He see the righteousness of His dear Son in us.

It is because of your sins that he doesn't hear you. It is your sins that separate you from God when you try to worship him (Isaiah 59:2, GNT).

Jesus lived the Father's name, Jehovah Tsidkenu, our Almighty Father is our Righteousness. His sinless flesh has become Word for us to clothe our flesh in righteousness. The more we receive into us the Word, the more it does its work to keep us away from sin so we can walk in righteousness. Only God alone can clothe our nakedness with His righteousness. From the nakedness that the first man felt ashamed of, that he hid, the last man, Jesus Christ took that shame and offered Himself as the sacrifice to pay for that shame of sin.

Every day is another day to live our Father's name, Jehovah Tsidkenu, and continue to receive into us the Word of God so we can be clothed in righteousness and not sin against our Father in heaven.

June 30

~ Rest in the righteousness of Christ ~

But about that day or hour no one knows, not even the angels in heaven, nor the Son, but only the Father (Mark 13:32, NIV).

One winter's morning, June 30, 2021, I was waiting for a visitor to arrive. She was supposed to arrive between 10:30 and 11:00 am. After tidying the place and making it presentable, I made creamy chicken and corn soup for the cold day. I thought I'd just rest and wait for her, since everything was ready for our meeting and she was due to arrive any minute.

This is what I heard the Holy Spirit say: You see, the kingdom of God is like this. Jesus has done everything already for you, and so He said rest in me. All you have to do is make sure you are always clothed in righteousness and well-presented and ready for His coming, any hour of any day, as you rest in Him.

The Lord replied, 'My Presence will go with you, and I will give you rest.' (Exodus 33:14, NIV).

A good dad is always clothed in righteousness by producing the fruit of righteousness. Each day, when his loving Father in heaven presents to him a new day, he prepares himself to be well presented in the presence of the moment. He is always aware of the presence of his righteous Father who desires for him to rest in His righteousness. The peace and joy he gains in the Father's presence puts his soul, spirit and body to complete rest.

Jesus lived the Father's name, Jehovah Tsidkenu, our Lord God, our Righteousness, and lived a righteous life. He sowed righteousness on earth and has reaped righteousness in heaven by sitting and resting on the Father's right hand.

Let's make ourselves presentable for our new day, all the more by sowing righteousness while we are on earth. Every day, let's live our Father's name, Jehovah Tsidkenu, and action the fruit of righteousness of the Holy Spirit. The peace and joy from righteousness will dissolve all our worries as we find complete rest.

JULY

Jehovah El Shaddai! I AM Your abundance of supply, all sufficient.

Jehovah God-like Mind is a Good Father-like Character

OUR LORD GOD IS OUR ABUNDANCE.

~ The source of abundance now lives in us ~

Great is our Lord, and abundant in power; his understanding is beyond measure (Psalm 147:5, ESV).

I mentioned I was going to pay some bills that cost hundreds of dollars. Angelilly heard me and said, 'Mum, I can help you.' I said, 'Oh, really?' 'Yes—I have 10 cents,' she replied, then reached out to where she left her 10 cents and gave it to me. I gave her a heart-melting smile. It was all she had. It was small, but it was from a heart that wanted to help. I was reminded about the little boy with his small lunch that fed thousands of people. He was trying to help Jesus and brought his lunch to Jesus. He wasn't focusing on how big the number of people there to be fed was, but focused on giving his lunch to Jesus and who He was.

You see, Angelilly wasn't focused on the amount of the big bill, but on who her mother was and what she could do. She trusted me as her mother who has managed to give her what she wants. The little boy with the lunch was focused on who Jesus was and how great He is. Jehovah El Shaddai, our Almighty Father is our Abundance. This is His name and He is so big. We have to look at how big He is, and not how big our needs are.

A good dad knows how big His Father in heaven is, yet He can live in his little heart. There is no limit to His Word. The more a good dad sits in the abundance of His Word, the deeper and closer he moves into seeing how big His Father is.

Our Father in heaven came closer to us to show how big He is through Jesus. Jesus not only came closer to us, but paid a huge price so He can come into us so we can see and feel how big our Father is through the Holy Spirit we receive from Jesus. Jesus lived the Father's name, Jehovah El Shaddai, in showing how big the Father's love is that it can provide all that we need. The source of abundance is now living inside us.

> *This message is from the Lord. 'I am God, and I am always near. I am not far away. Someone might try to hide from me in some hiding place. But it is easy for me to see that person,' says the Lord, 'because I am everywhere in heaven and earth.' (Jeremiah 23:23-24, ERV).*

Each day of the month of July, and every day, live the Father's name, Jehovah El Shaddai. Don't look at how big your problems, struggles and tests are, but see how big and great your heavenly Father is, and who He has given as a helper to help you abundantly. The Holy Spirit is our helper to help us overflow in abundance in every area of life.

July 1

~ *The abundant life in Christ overflows when we sow more into the kingdom of God* ~

> *And Isaac sowed in that land and reaped in the same year a hundredfold. The Lord blessed him, and the man became rich, and gained more and more until he became very wealthy (Genesis 26:12-13, ESV).*

One morning, March 14, 2021, I was watching a documentary of the life of many Americans in suburbs where poverty and crime rates were high. This is what the Holy Spirit taught me: Many thoughts of evil and good will enter your mind because of the connections to the fruit of the knowledge of good and evil that gives you your nature. But it is now up to you to see that the fruit of good be served. There is another war also going on every day—the war of wealth and poverty caused by the spirit of greed. The spirit of greed is the bad spirit behind the rich getting rich and the poor getting poorer. The rich become greedy by trying to become even more rich by accumulating more wealth, and this makes a big gap between them and the poor.

The story is told of the rich man who wanted to follow Jesus, and Jesus asked him to give his riches to the poor so he could have treasure in heaven. The kingdom of God belongs to the poor, and when we give to the poor we are lending to the Lord because we are giving to the kingdom of God. The Lord Himself will reward us.

A good dad sows his wealth of funds upwards into the business of His Father in heaven, a place where the Word of the kingdom of God can reach out and connect with souls, a fertile soil where he can receive a hundredfold. Like Isaac, he plants and receives back a hundredfold. This is how he lives a blessed life of abundance. He knows and lives his loving Father's name, Jehovah El Shaddai, our Lord God of abundance.

> *Remember this: Whoever sows sparingly will also reap sparingly, and whoever sows generously will also reap generously. Each of you should give what you have decided in your heart to give, not reluctantly or under compulsion, for God loves a cheerful giver. And God is able to bless you abundantly, so that in all things at all times, having all that you need, you will abound in every good work (2 Corinthians 9:6-8, NIV).*

We must love to give freely with joy what enters our life, because we are grateful for the abundant life Jesus gave us freely. And so, we happily live our Father's name, Jehovah El Shaddai, in Jesus' name, and give where the Spirit leads.

July 2

~ After passing the test you reach a new, higher level of abundance ~

I came that they may have life and have it abundantly (John 10:10, ESV).

One winter's morning, July 2, 2021, I was thinking of defrosting the chicken for the family's dinner, and considering if I had time to leave it out to defrost by itself, or I'd need to put it in the microwave. To defrost in the microwave, heat has to be applied to give me what I want. This is what I heard the Holy Spirit say: The trials and tests you go through are applied to give what God wants to see in you. When you put the chicken in the microwave you do not know what is going on in there, but you know what time to set to give you the result you're after. So it is with your Father in heaven. He loves you so much that what He allows you to be put through is to bring the best that He designed you for. After you go through that test, and when it's time, you will come out with the best version of yourself. If you feel your heavenly Father is silent during a hard test you are sitting, remember there is always a silence in a test.

> *And I will put this third into the fire, and refine them as one refines silver, and test them as gold is tested. They will call upon my name, and I will answer them. I will say, 'They are my people,' and they will say, 'The Lord is my God.' (Zechariah 13:9, ESV).*

A good dad knows that as soon as he comes out of a test, the next one will be waiting for him. The higher the level he moves to, the harder the test will be. And so, he prepares himself daily in Word and prayer to go into the next test of life. He may fail the test given to him, but he knows his heavenly Father is love and His love never fails. This is what keeps him going. It's those tests in life that build him to receive the abundance of life.

Jesus lived our Father's name, Jehovah El Shaddai, our Lord God, our Abundance. He was the greatest teacher who taught the goodness of the Father and had to go through the challenging moments in life. And yet, He never failed the Father in any of those moments. He was flesh and could have walked away from death, but because He wanted to give us His life of abundance that the Father sent Him to give, He walked through and tasted that painful death.

Every new day comes with new challenges to build your faith. Walk in humbleness through those tests, knowing you're going to come out of the tests all built up to receive more abundance of life. If we are to share the glory of Jesus, we must look forward to sharing His suffering too. (See Romans 8:17).

July 3

~ Speak the life of the Word into your spiritual blessing of abundance and instruct it to be delivered to you ~

Blessed be the God and Father of our Lord Jesus Christ, who has blessed us in Christ with every spiritual blessing in the heavenly places (Ephesians 1:3, ESV).

On the evening of July 3, 2021, I was thinking of a friend who was supposed to send me some funds, but first she needed me to message and confirm how much she was to pay. This is what the Holy Spirit taught me: You see, she will never send the funds to you because she is waiting for you to give instructions of how much she should pay you. So it is with the spiritual blessings you have received in Christ. These blessings are in the spiritual realm and wait for you to give instruction in spirit and put life in them to be released into your life. Speak and instruct the Word. Jesus said, 'These words that I have spoken to you are not just words, they are spirit and life (See John 6:63). Renew your mind in the Word and pray in the Spirit to receive that abundance of spiritual blessings.'

A good dad allows the Holy Spirit to work through him by receiving into him the Word of His Father. He then renews his mind upon the Word. The Word is then opened and its light begins to show him the path to walk in victory to the path of receiving his spiritual blessing of abundance.

All the spiritual blessings of ours are in the Son whom the Father has given to us. Jesus came and lived the Father's name, Jehovah El Shaddai, our Lord God is our Abundance. He became poor for us so we can become rich (see 2 Corinthians 8:9). The kingdom of God belongs to the poor, and when we become like the poor and seek the righteousness of the kingdom of God to get a good life, all these things will be added to us to receive the riches of the kingdom of God who is Jesus, and all the treasure of God that is found in Him.

> *It is the Spirit who gives life; the flesh is no help at all.*
> *The words that I have spoken to you are spirit and life*
> *(John 6:63, ESV).*

Every day, get to live the Father's name, Jehovah El Shaddai, and live a life of abundance by seeking first the kingdom of the Father and His righteousness. Renew your mind and send forth the Word that is Spirit and life with instruction to bring to you your spiritual blessings.

July 4

~ *Connect to Jesus and remain connected with Him* ~

All things were made through him, and without him was not any thing made that was made (John 1:3, ESV).

The morning of December 7, 2022, I opened my laptop to work on the edited manuscript of this book and finalise it for the final stages of publication. It was trying to connect to the Wi-Fi and started showing on the screen as 'connecting'. I had to wait to use the Internet on the laptop until it said it was connected.

While I was looking on, this is what the Holy Spirit taught me: When we first receive Jesus into our hearts, we are now connecting to Him. We have to continue maintaining a relationship with Him in Word and prayer to remain connected with Him so we can be united with Him and have access into all our spiritual blessings in Him.

Hear this: Just like me trying to use the Internet and having to wait until my laptop is connected to the Wi-Fi, so it is with us. We have to keep connecting to Jesus in the Word until we are fully connected to His Spirit and our spirit becomes one with His Spirit. This is where we can easily hear the voice of the Holy Spirit through our spirit being.

But whoever is united with the Lord is one with him in spirit (1 Corinthians 6:17, NIV).

You see, once my laptop is fully connected to the Wi-Fi I can just download anything on the Internet. So it is with our life – once it's fully connected and become one with the Holy Spirit, we can easily hear His voice to lead and give us directions to walk in the path that leads to receiving all our spiritual blessings.

> *But just as he who called you is holy, so be holy in all you do; for it is written: "Be holy, because I am holy."*
> *(1 Peter 1: 15-16, NIV).*

Jesus came and lived our Father's name, Jehovah M'Kaddesh, our Lord God who Sanctifies. He set Himself apart to be holy while connecting Himself to the sinners because He wanted to connect them back to their original birthright that the enemy had stolen.

A good dad sanctifies himself to remain holy in this world where evil rises all the time. He remains in the righteousness of Christ and produces the fruit of the Holy Spirit to anyone who connects with him.

Every day, we are to live our Father's name, Jehovah M'Kaddesh, and set ourselves apart from not doing any sin. To do it victoriously, we have to connect to Jesus in His Word daily so we can remain connected with the Holy Spirit to produce His holy righteous fruit.

July 5

~ There is always an abundance of harvest when we sow in Jesus' name ~

> *The words I have spoken to you—they are full of the Spirit and life (John 6:63, NIV).*

One winter's night, July 5, 2021, I was looking at one of my dresses I had removed from the wardrobe when the Lord showed me a vision of a beautiful dress displayed on a mannequin. And this is what the Lord said: You see that dress on display—it is lifeless. But when a woman puts it on and moves in it, the dress becomes alive. When you put on the new life in Christ and move around in that life, the life of Jesus comes alive. The Holy Spirit put on the life of Jesus by resurrecting it and Jesus became alive, just like how a woman goes into a dress and makes the dress become alive in her. The Holy Spirit went into Jesus and resurrected Him. Jesus is now ALIVE forever.

The same Spirit that has resurrected Jesus now lives in us to make us alive in Jesus Christ. That dress will only fit well on someone who has the right height and weight for it. So it is with the life you have in Christ. He is the head and you, as His body, will fit completely into the head when you live in His righteousness. The kingdom of God is not about eating or drinking but of righteousness, peace and joy in the Holy Spirit.

> *For the kingdom of God is not a matter of eating and drinking, but of righteousness, peace and joy in the Holy Spirit (Romans 14:17, NIV).*

A good dad puts on the life of Jesus and moves and walks in His abundance of life. There is so much life in that LIFE that makes him look alive and glowing, as joy and peace flow like a river out from him. He will never be thirsty or hungry or need to seek after any desires of this world. He will seek first the kingdom of his loving Father and His righteousness that all things he needs in life will come running after him.

Jesus lived our Father's name, Jehovah El Shaddai, our Almighty Father is our Abundance. He had nothing in His possession but trusting the Father with the life He gave Him, and He used that life in an abundant way. He used the Word to declare abundance.

His Word was life. He spoke those Words into situations and abundance flowed out. The five fish and two loaves of bread were multiplied and overflowed by His Word when they entered His hands (see Matthew 14:13-21).

Every day is made by Jehovah El Shaddai, our Almighty Father of abundance. We are now to live our Father's name in Jesus' name to make abundance over nothing in our everyday living. Out of nothing our Father creates something. There is so much abundance of living our life in joy and peace because of the unconditional love of the Father poured into us through the Holy Spirit.

July 6

~ There is abundance in Jesus' name, live in it ~

You prepare a table before me in the presence of my enemies. You anoint my head with oil; my cup overflows. Surely your goodness and love will follow me all the days of my life, and I will dwell in the house of the Lord forever (Psalm 23:5-6, NIV).

Just like how any child believes in how big and great their father is, a good dad knows how big and great His Father in heaven is, Jehovah El Shaddai, all sufficient God, He is in abundance. He sees how His Father pours into his cup that overflows in abundance, and so he asks His Father to give him big and great dreams, to dream and lead him into.

Jesus overflowed the cup of the professional fisherman with fish with His Word. He is the Word of God who has become flesh. He showed the Father's love of how caring He is and lived His name, Jehovah El Shaddai, when He said the Word and the fisherman's fishing net almost broke with an abundance of fish.

When he had finished speaking, he said to Simon, 'Put out into deep water, and let down the nets for a catch.' Simon answered, 'Master, we've worked hard all night and haven't caught anything. But because you say so, I will let down the nets.' When they had done so, they caught such a large number of fish that their nets began to break (Luke 5:4-6, NIV).

There is abundance of overflowing blessings every day. We just have to live and remain in the name of Jesus, who lived the name of the Father, Jehovah El Shaddai, where the flowing of abundance flows through.

July 7

~ Abundance of life in God's instructions ~

Whoever heeds instruction is on the path to life, but he who rejects reproof leads others astray (Proverbs 10:17, ESV).

July 14, 2021, while doing home schooling with my then six-year-old, I told her she had to read instructions before she started doing the activities given, because she didn't pay attention to the instructions but went right away to do the exercises. This is what I heard the Holy Spirit say: You see, every new day, your loving Father in heaven gives special instruction and sets it out. Before you go into the day and do whatever activities for the day, you need to go into the Word of God, which is the instruction of life. Each day comes out with instructions from the Father for you to live your life.

A good dad sits in the Word to get instruction on how to carry his life through the day. Before he starts his day, he gets himself into the

Word so the Word can get into him to not only start his day well, but to end it well too.

The one whom each day was made for, and through Him everything was made, has come down Himself to live on earth. He was the very image of our Almighty Father of abundance, Jehovah El Shaddai.

> *Hear instruction and be wise, and do not neglect it (Proverbs 8:33, ESV).*

The very one who gives instruction to the new day to bring life to every living creature came down to show and give us access to live the abundance of life. He is the only way of the abundance of instructions, for us to remain in so we can go well through each day.

Every new day is instructed to give us the strength for the day. We have to live our Father's name of abundance, Jehovah El Shaddai, and remain in the abundance of the life of Jesus in the Holy Spirit.

July 8

~ God's abundance of life showing through His work of creation ~

> *My Father is always at his work to this very day, and I too am working (John 5:17, NIV).*

July 8, 2021, I woke up and looked out the window as dawn was breaking through. It's something I always do, first thing when I wake up. I look up to the clouds to see our Father at work. The clouds changing colours as the light of dawn comes through, the moving clouds. I look at it and smile, because that is how I see our Father's presence, who is at work.

I was thinking of how beautiful it was when the Holy Spirit spoke in my heart and said: You can see the light of a new day coming through the clouds. Your loving Father is at work, as always. He is putting on the light for a new day. You woke up because He put a new LIFE in you for this new day, just like how light was coming through this new day, remember that you live in a dark world. Your Father gave you life so you can put that light in you in this dark world of evil you are in, and others can see and know the Father of LOVE, Jesus of LIGHT and the Spirit of LIFE.

> *I am the light of the world. Whoever follows me will never walk in darkness, but will have the light of life (John 8:12, NIV).*

A good dad wakes up in the morning and is so grateful that he is alive, not because he can go and do what he can and live his day, but in knowing that he is alive to live in Jesus, in His flesh, and be doing what he has to do. He is drawn closer to his loving Father in receiving the light from the Word, Jesus, who has become flesh, so he can live the life of abundance in the Holy Spirit. Jehovah El Shaddai, our Almighty Father, is our Abundance.

Jesus came and gave us this abundance of love from the Father. He is the light that opened our eyes to see the amazing love from the Father that brings salvation and the gift of life from the Holy Spirit.

Every day, when you open the curtain of your eyes, see through the abundance of the Father's LOVE. Let the LIGHT of Jesus shine through your eyes so everyone can see the LIFE you carry in the Holy Spirit as you produce the fruit of the Spirit to meet all your needs.

July 9

~ Renew your mind in the abundance of the Word and contain it ~

Don't copy the behaviour and customs of this world, but let God transform you into a new person by changing the way you think. Then you will learn to know God's will for you, which is good and pleasing and perfect (Romans 12:2, NLT).

One cold winter's night, July 9, 2021, I made a hot vegetable soup. I took a bowl out from the cupboard, but because it was so cold, the bowl also was cold. After I poured the hot soup into the bowl, the bowl instantly became hot, as hot as the hot soup from the pot. This is what I heard the Holy Spirit say: You see, that bowl instantly changed and became what it contained. So it is with you—you become what you take into you and contain. What you take into you, you instantly become, just like the cold bowl that changed instantly after it contained the hot soup. This is why your loving Father wants you to constantly renew your mind in the Word and not to conform to the standards of this world. He is Jehovah El Shaddai, our Almighty Father is our Abundance. There is no limit to His Word. It is in abundance and is available all the time in its full goodness for us to renew ourselves in and contain it.

Whatever is inside of you is what will flow out from you and be poured upon, whoever you are in touch with. If you pour out that bowl of soup, out will flow the hot soup. If you renew your mind to remain in and contain the goodness of the abundance in God's Word, out will flow that goodness of God's Word.

A good man produces good deeds from a good heart. And an evil man produces evil deeds from his hidden wickedness. Whatever is in the heart overflows into speech (Luke 6:45, TLB).

A good dad focuses his mind to have the mind of Christ and renews his mind all the time in the Word. He renews his mind and settles it with peace from the Word whenever fears of the world target his way of living. The peace Jesus lived in the world is found in His Word and this is where a good dad fixes his mind on.

The flesh who has become Word is full of the abundance of love, light and life. He is now alive inside us in the Holy Spirit. We are to renew our mind to let His Word remain in us so we can contain Him and be filled of Him.

As each day renews into a new day, let your mind be also renewed into new thoughts from the Word that has no limit.

July 10

~ Overflow in abundance the compassion of our heavenly Father ~

He has blinded their eyes and hardened their hearts, lest they see with their eyes, and understand with their heart, and turn, and I would heal them (John 12:40, ESV).

One evening, July 10, 2021, I folded some clothes neatly, Blessed, my then two-year-old, came and messed them up. I looked at him and was about to raise my voice, when I saw him looking at me in a way that said there was nothing wrong in what he did. He didn't know what he was doing and had innocence all over his little face. Instead of raising my voice, I gave a laugh. I didn't know where it came from. The Holy Spirit spoke into my heart and said, 'That's joy you have expressed.'

And this is what the Holy Spirit taught me: When you are upset and about to throw it upon someone, just pause, look at them first with compassion, knowing that everyone is born into sin, evil being the nature, and what they do is a normal thing. The doer doesn't even know there is something wrong with what they are doing because they are blind. Just give out a laugh of joy and victory that you got this. Blessed didn't know he made a mess for you. There will always be someone who will try to mess you up without knowing what they are doing because they are blind to it.

A good dad knows he will still get angry over something he has no control over. This is where he applies PATIENCE and SELF-CONTROL to slow the movement of anger out from him. The anger will fade away when we slow it down. It's just like turning the volume of loud music down. The music is on, but its volume is down. Our anger also goes down instead of coming up and out from us, when we slow it down. Our loving Father is slow to anger and is full of compassion with kindness and goodness. It is his goal to become like the Father and be full of compassion.

> *The Lord then passed in front of him and called out, 'I, the Lord, am a God who is full of compassion and pity, who is not easily angered and who shows great love and faithfulness.' (Exodus 34:6, GNT).*

Jesus lived our Father's name, Jehovah El Shaddai, our Almighty Father is our Abundance. He was living a life overflowing with compassion where children were loved, strangers were loved and His enemies were loved and even forgiven by Him. Because Jesus now lives in us through the Holy Spirit, we too must live like Him by living our Father's name of abundance with compassion. We must be at peace and be patient with everyone around us, because they are blind and do not know what they are doing.

Each day, wake up and open your eyes to see, this is the day the Lord has made for you to rejoice and be glad with overflowing abundance of the Almighty Father's compassion. And so, you can have mercy to the blind people who bump into you and make life difficult for you.

July 11

~ *The love of the Father is so overflowing in abundance that there was never a time you were not loved* ~

I have loved you with an everlasting love; I have drawn you with unfailing kindness (Jeremiah 31:3, NIV).

July 11, 2021, I was thinking of a commitment I had, posting some things to a friend, and was trying to attend to it. This is what the Holy Spirit taught me: Your Father is also committed to loving you. God loves us so much and sent His only son into the world to save us. The love that loves us when we are in the world is for our FLESH. We receive His love and have the relationship with His Son in the Word (the Word who has become flesh) and He gives us His Holy Spirit. Our Father is still committed to loving us by pouring His love through the Holy Spirit (see Romans 5:5). This is a specific love for us believers who are committed to remain in the Word—the love for our SOUL, the eternal being, through the eternal Word of the Father. Then finally comes the LOVE that the Holy Spirit produces in us. This is the LOVE in our spirit being that our flesh has to action and produce, the love that shows our Father's love, that we receive Jesus and we have a relationship with the Father in His Word. This is the perfect love of the Father, where we live and walk, and can be able to love our enemies.

Our loving Father has a name, Jehovah El Shaddai, our Almighty Father is our Abundance is His name. His Love is in abundance and has filled the earth and heaven. There was never a time in all eternity when we weren't loved. We were loved before the foundation of the world (see Ephesians 1:3-6), we were loved when we were knitted together in our mother's womb (see Psalm 139:13), and we were loved on the day we were born (see Psalm 71:6). Nothing will ever separate us from God's love (see Romans 8:38-39). And we are loved at this very moment. God is LOVE. Every second of every minute of every hour we are loved because the Holy Spirit is producing His fruit of Love in us all the time.

July 12

~ Grow more to have Christ-like life by living in the abundance of His goodness ~

He is the radiance of the glory of God and the exact imprint of his nature, and he upholds the universe by the word of his power. After making purification for sins, he sat down at the right hand of the Majesty on high (Hebrews 1:3, ESV).

I remember the day, July 12, 2021, when I was managing some work with a friend assisting. I thought how it was only the both of us, but work was being done every day and flowing well. As I pondered that thought, I heard the Holy Spirit say: Your Father, too, is interested to see the image of His Son, even if it is only one soul who has the image of Christ. He is glorified when He sees the image of Jesus in whatever one does. Therefore, whenever you do something, remind yourself how and what would Jesus do if He was doing it.

Jesus came and lived our heavenly Father's name on earth, Jehovah El Shaddai, our Almighty is our Abundance. He was overcoming evilness with the abundance of the Father's goodness. He was interested in only one sheep, and had to leave alongside the ninety-nine to find that one lost one. Just one sheep who would become like Him is who Jesus is looking for.

> ...how God anointed Jesus of Nazareth with the Holy Spirit and with power. He went about doing good and healing all who were oppressed by the devil, for God was with him (Acts 10:38, ESV).

Even though Jesus was the only Son, He was the very image of the Father, the Word who became flesh. The Father saw all of Himself in there and was glorified through every work He was doing. For the Father to reap many sons, He sowed His one and only Son into the world.

Every child has only one dad on earth, chosen by our heavenly Father. A good dad knows he is chosen to become more like Christ and give our heavenly Father glory in whatever work he does to provide for his household. Everything he does is for the Father and not men.

Every day is another day to go out and work in living our Father's name in whatever we do. We are to become more in the image of Christ by living in the abundance of His goodness and overcoming all kinds of evil.

July 13

~ Sharpen yourself in the Word every day ~

> *For the word of God is alive and active. Sharper than any double-edged sword, it penetrates even to dividing soul and spirit, joints and marrow; it judges the thoughts and attitudes of the heart (Hebrews 4:12, NIV).*

July 13, 2021, another day of home schooling my six-year-old. While sharpening her colour pencil, I told her, 'I will sharpen all these colour pencils and have them ready for you to just use.' This is what I heard the Holy Spirit say: You see, so it is with you. When you sharpen yourself in the Word, you are preparing yourself to be used by your Father. The Word is sharper than any double-edged sword, to sharpen you up and get you ready for the good work in Jesus Christ.

To be like his good, loving Father in heaven, a good dad sharpens himself in His Father's Word. He lets the light of the Word penetrate through every darkness to do its work of sharpening. Jehovah El Shaddai, our Almighty Father is our Abundance. He has in abundance good thoughts and plans to give us hope and a future to be successful in our journey we call life.

Jesus lived our Father's name, Jehovah El Shaddai, by creating an abundance of goodness in the work of His ministry for us to carry it further. He has given us the Holy Spirit to sharpen us in the Word to be ready all the time to be used in the goodness and mercy of the Father to the ungodly people.

> *All Scripture is God-breathed and is useful for teaching, rebuking, correcting and training in righteousness, so that the servant of God may be thoroughly equipped for every good work (2 Timothy 3:16-17, NIV).*

Each day is another opportunity to sharpen up in the abundance of the Word of the Father. You are a threat to the kingdom of darkness when you get sharpened up and ready to be used. What the enemy sees is you are ready to attack any of his work he plans to carry out.

July 14

~ Shine the light of the Word in abundance ~

Your words are a flashlight to light the path ahead of me and keep me from stumbling (Psalm 119:105, TLB).

July 14, 2021, while in lockdown due to the COVID-19 pandemic, I was doing home schooling with my then six-year-old. My two-year-old was there too, and I gave him a picture book to keep him part of our learning. I showed him what was in the book, then got a real mushroom, carrot, tomato and onion to go with the pictures he saw in the book. As we were going through it, the Holy Spirit taught me this: You are the image of what the Word says of you. You have to actually be alive in the Word and show the real you, just like how you are showing your two-year-old the actual vegetables that are in the book. You have to make the Word become alive and bring into action everything that the Word has written of you.

I then remembered a movie I watched, called, *Baby's Day Out*, where a little baby of about eight months old was kidnapped. He had a little book that the nanny used to read to him every day, so the little baby knew every picture and every place in that book. After he got kidnapped, he escaped from his kidnappers and decided to go to all the places in his picture book by crawling to them. He was following the book. You see, he made his picture book come alive. We all have a story that God has written down in His Word for us to read every day and live that story, just like the little baby who was living the story of his book.

A good dad sits daily in the Word of his loving Father in heaven so he can know his story and live in it by rewriting it on the pages of each day. The Word is the light to brighten up each story of our life. Our good Father's name is Jehovah El Shaddai, our Almighty Father is our Abundance. He is the Father of light. There is abundance of light in His presence. We only contain the level of light according to how much we spend time in His Word and know Him.

> *For you have a new life. It was not passed on to you from your parents, for the life they gave you will fade away. This new one will last forever, for it comes from Christ, God's ever-living Message to men (1 Peter 1:23, TLB).*

Jesus came and lived on earth our Father in heaven's name, Jehovah El Shaddai. He was the light of the world. He came and showed us the way, the truth and life with the light from the Father so we too can live our story and make the Word become our flesh by living our story written on it.

Every day, let's rise up and live our Father's name, Jehovah El Shaddai, and shine in abundance the light from the Word and live our story that was written.

July 15

~ Live an abundant life of patience and faithfulness in living the Father's name ~

> *Fear of the Lord leads to life, bringing security and protection from harm (Proverbs 19:23, NLT).*

I always share with any Christian parents who are believers and have lost their child to the world that their children may go out in the world, but the fear of the Lord installed in them will bring them back to the right path. They will taste and see how the world is and realise the presence of the Lord is the best, and will begin to appreciate more the goodness of the Lord.

One evening, July 15, 2021, the Lord opened my eyes to make me understand this more. I was in the kitchen, which was filled with the smell of the delicious food I had cooked. Since I was in the kitchen the smell was part of me, so I didn't pay attention or take notice of how delicious the food smelt. When I walked out of the kitchen, I was no longer with the food and its smell. However, when I returned to the kitchen, the nice smell started filling me. This is what the Holy Spirit taught me: We may leave the presence of the Father, depart from it and have nothing to do with it and start living a separate life. But the day we come back into His presence we will have a meltdown in Him, knowing how good, patient and faithful He is. He patiently and faithfully waits for us, just like how I walked back into the kitchen and its good, delicious smell filled me up again.

Any dad can get distracted and move away from the presence of the Father, but a good dad will return because he has tasted and seen the goodness of the Father. In the Father's presence there is always joy. It's the fear of the Lord that was installed in him which goes off like a warning alarm to bring him back into the Father's presence.

Jesus lived an abundant life of patience and faithfulness in living our Father's name, Jehovah El Shaddai, our Almighty Father is our Abundance. He was patient in living on earth which was so full of evil, though He knew what heaven was like and would like to be back in heaven. He remained faithful until He finished the work the Father had given Him to do.

Every day, let's live in abundance with the patience and faithfulness of the Father in living His name, Jehovah EL Shaddai, and giving glory back to Him.

July 16

~ Allow the abundance of wisdom from God to leak out from you every day ~

Be kind and compassionate to one another, forgiving each other, just as in Christ God forgave you (Ephesians 4:32, NIV).

One morning, July 16, 2021, I saw that the bathroom tap was leaking water. I put a bucket under the tap so the leaking drop of water was not wasted. Suddenly, the Holy Spirit started teaching me: You see, every day the love of God flows out from His Word from you. You must not waste it. Just like the water leaking out in drips and you don't want it to be wasted, so is the word, coming out from you through the air you are living, which is the breath of God. Let it not go to waste—speak a word or an act of kindness to people around you. Let everything that has breath praise the Lord.

You may think it's little, but that little kindness goes a long way in helping someone to take them through. For the person receiving, the words of kindness keep the mind glowing with new life. The act of kindness tells them we have a loving Father who cares.

A good dad is a mouthpiece of His Father in heaven. He connects to the mouth of His Father in His Word so something good can come out from him all the time. A timely word is wisdom and he makes sure wisdom leaks out in kindness to everyone around him who drinks in this fountain of life that he provides.

Everyone enjoys giving good advice, and how wonderful it is to be able to say the right thing at the right time! (Proverbs 15:23, TLB).

Jesus lived the name of our Father in heaven on earth, in abundance. He became poor so we can be rich. He became sin so we can become righteous. Jehovah El Shaddai, our Almighty Father is our Abundance and self-sufficient is His name, and Jesus lived it. He was the Word who became flesh. His words were always full of kindness and His flesh always acted in kindness in every possible way. With man it is impossible, but with God it is possible. When we connect to the possible God, nothing becomes impossible to do.

Each day, live the Father's name, Jehovah El Shaddai, and connect to the living water and let it leak out from inside of you, the abundance of living water who is Jesus.

July 17

~ Faith of a fish is about abundance ~

They caught so many fish that they could not pull the net back into the boat (John 21:6, ERV).

Living the faith lifestyle of a fish is a life of multiplication and abundance. Whenever fish are mentioned in scriptures they demonstrate abundance. A good dad lives that faith of a fish lifestyle. There will always be abundance where he lives. Like a fish that will only survive in its home of the vast ocean, he can only survive and live in the vast ocean of his heavenly Father's Word—the Word that has no end. Our Father has a name and His name is Jehovah El Shaddai, our Almighty Father is our Abundance. He lives the name of the Father and His Word, because the Father has placed above everything His name and His Word. Whatever daily business of his life on earth, a good dad uses it as his fishing boat. And like Peter, who invited Jesus into his boat and caught an abundance of fish, he lets Jesus also into his boat so there will always be an abundance.

*I bow down toward your holy temple and give thanks to
your name for your steadfast love and your faithfulness,
for you have exalted above all things your name and your word
(Psalm 138:2, ESV).*

Jesus lived our heavenly Father's name on earth, Jehovah El Shaddai, our Almighty Father is our Abundance. He created an abundance out of nothing wherever He was. Every miracle He performed was with a purpose. He made known the purpose of His life on earth with each miracle performed. When He spoke the Word and Peter caught an abundance of fish, the purpose was for Peter to catch an abundance of souls in his career. When Jesus multiplied the two fish into an abundance with leftovers, the purpose was for us to know He will always multiply what we have in our hand, when we place it into His hands.

Every day is a new day given to you for your hands to work. Give your day into the hands of your Father to give in abundance what your hands find to do.

July 18

~ An abundance of patience can be built from waiting ~

*I wait for the Lord, my soul waits, and in his word
I hope (Psalm 130:5, ESV).*

It was July 8, 2021, and because I was expecting a parcel during the week I was constantly checking the letter box. I live along a main road and wanted to make sure my parcel wasn't snatched by someone walking along the pathway. While I was constantly checking, the Holy Spirit taught me this: If you also ask the

Father for something you really want, you have to check on Him constantly to see if what you are expecting from Him comes to pass. Remind yourself what He promises in His Word, and use it as a declaration by declaring it in prayer.

A good dad patiently waits on his heavenly Father in all that he requests from Him. He declares with delight in his heart the promises of the Father. The more he waits on the Father, the more he develops an abundance of patience that cannot run out.

Jesus showed us how to live a life of abundance in patience. He lived the Father's name, Jehovah El Shaddai, our Almighty Father is our Abundance. An abundance of patience overflowed from Him as He went through each day, never running out of patience with everyone wanting to see Him—and all at the same time. Jesus also endured the pain with patience to give us eternal life.

He understands we will all need Him now, and so He made available the eternal life by giving us the Holy Spirit, who can personally live inside of us and attend to us all at the same time in different places. Not only can He attend to us personally anytime and anywhere, but He produces an abundance of eternal patience that will never run out. Patience is a fruit of the Holy Spirit and we need His help to help us constantly to produce it.

> *You also, be patient. Establish your hearts, for the coming of the Lord is at hand (James 5:8, ESV).*

Every day is all about waiting for Jesus to return or for something good to happen in our life, and it's a great opportunity to live our Father's name, Jehovah El Shaddai, and build an abundance of patience in that wait.

July 19

~ God has an abundance of gifts in store for us ~

For the wages of sin is death, but the free gift of God is eternal life through Jesus Christ our Lord (Romans 6:23, TLB).

Many times, I get frustrated because I think I deserve what I'm asking God to give me and I don't understand why He isn't granting it to me or answering my prayers as soon as possible. We are all emotional beings, so this happens when we get so focused on what we want and don't control our emotions.

July 14, 2021, was one of the days I was practising the fruit of 'patience' and how to master it. Someone was trying to give me a gift in the form of cash. I thought *it's a gift they said they'd give me, so I am going to patiently wait, and while waiting I have to be grateful and thankful to the Lord that I would be receiving the gift.* Also, it's not a kind thing to go and hurry the person giving the gift. I had received it already by WORD, and just had to wait for them to take action.

While waiting to receive that gift, I was being grateful, knowing that I didn't work hard to receive it. The Holy Spirit spoke into my heart and said: Someone promises to give you a gift and you wait patiently with a grateful heart. The same about your Father in heaven. What He promises to give is all in the gift of Jesus, the WORD who has become flesh. What you want is in Jesus' name, in His flesh, and if you abide in Him you will receive it. So with a heart of gratitude, wait patiently that all the promises of God are yes and amen in Jesus (see 2 Corinthians 1:20).

You see, the word was given to me by my friend that I was to receive the gift of cash. For me to receive that gift, I had to stay connected to her so she could contact me to tell me she had sent my gift of cash into my bank account. So it is with Jesus. He is the Word. We have to abide in Him and connect with Him to receive whatever we ask.

Our loving Father is of abundance. His name is Jehovah El Shaddai, our Almighty Father is our Abundance. He provides to us what we need for the moment, while we wait patiently with a grateful heart to receive all His promises concerning us. He is a NOW Father. "I AM Jehovah El Shaddai" is His name.

Jesus lived our Father's name, Jehovah El Shaddai, the very gift of God, His WORD. There is no limit to the Word. It is overflowing and of abundance.

> *Everything has its limits, except your commands (Psalm 119:96, ERV).*

Each day, we must wake up knowing we have a purpose to live the gift of the Father in abundance and action it. This is the gift and life of Jesus.

July 20

~ Renew your mind in the abundance of God's good thoughts ~

And now, dear brothers and sisters, one final thing. Fix your thoughts on what is true, and honourable, and right, and pure, and lovely, and admirable. Think about things that are excellent and worthy of praise (Philippians 4:8, NLT).

It was a cold Friday morning, July 9, 2021, a school holiday winter's morning. I put on 'Caillou', one of my kids' favourite cartoons, to watch on YouTube on my laptop. As usual, while we were trying to watch, the ads came on, something we normally get all the time. My six-year-old was trying to press the arrow key to skip the ad so we could go straight into watching the program we were focusing on. While she did that, this is what I heard the Holy Spirit say: You see, the 'ad' automatically appears on the screen, which you have no control over. But you do have control over whether to continue watching that ad or skip it. So it is with your thoughts. You have no control over the thoughts that get into your head from what you hear or see, but you do have control whether to let it remain or let it out. Whatever that is godly, let it remain. Whatever is ungodly, let it out.

A good dad focuses on the godly nature of our loving Father to guide his thinking (see Philippines 4:8). He lives an abundant life upon the beautiful thoughts that he allows to remain in his life. As a man thinketh, so is he (see Proverbs 23:7).

Above all else, guard your affections. For they influence everything else in your life (Proverbs 4:23, TLB).

Our loving Father has a name. He is Jehovah El Shaddai, our Almighty Father, is our abundance. He is a good Father and He has beautiful, wonderful, good thoughts towards us that are like the sands on the shore. All His good thoughts towards us bring goodness out of anything bad we may go through.

Jesus lived our Father's name, Jehovah El Shaddai, with an abundance of goodness flowing out from Him to all He came in contact with. The very own image of the Father's love in the flesh form has now come back to live in us through the Holy Spirit, for us to continue living an abundant life of goodness by producing the fruit of 'goodness in us'.

Each new day is filled with an abundance of goodness from our loving Father, for us to use to overcome evil. We just have to think only godly thoughts and let it remain in us to overcome the evilness around us.

July 21

~ There is an abundance of goodness within you to use to conquer the evil of the day ~

You can identify them by their fruit, that is, by the way they act (Matthew 7:16, NLT).

On a cold winter's day, July 8, 2021, I was walking with the kids when I noticed a similar car to their grandmother's. I looked instantly at the plate number of the car because I know it by heart. When you always see someone, you get to know them so well that you even know the kind of car they drive. As I was looking at the plate number to confirm if it was hers, I heard the Holy Spirit say: All of the ministry that preach the gospel of Jesus Christ can look the same. Everyone is doing it for Jesus, and like you, looking at the plate number to see if it is your mother in-law. All the creation of God is awaiting the sons of God to be revealed. You are known as a son, a very image of Christ by the fruit of the Spirit you produce, not your gifts. It's your characters that determine whether you are Christ-like in your actions.

When God gives you a gift He doesn't take it back (see Romans 11:29). You can receive the gift of moving mountains with your faith or prophecy, but if your character is not of love, which is the fruit of the Spirit, then you don't carry the image of Christ. Jesus Christ is love (see 1 Corinthians 13).

> *For the earnest expectation of the creation eagerly waits for the revealing of the sons of God (Romans 8:19, NKJV).*

Any dad can make a father figure at home, but to be a good father like His Father in heaven, he has to be good in overcoming evil around him. A good dad sits in the Word and prays to be led in the abundance of goodness in the Word. He refills himself all the more and actions the fruit of the Holy Spirit, goodness. To show the goodness of the Father, He is merciful all the time in how he treats his families and servants.

Jesus lived our Father's name, Jehovah El Shaddai, our Almighty Father is our Abundance. He is the very image of our good Father. There was never a day that He saw as a bad day, because every day He found something good to do. Every day, Jesus performed the abundance of goodness to everyone that needed it.

> *True, God made everything beautiful in itself and in its time (Ecclesiastes 3:11, MSG).*

We have inherited all the good things in the Father's name that Jesus lives. In Jesus' name we can now perform goodness to our everyday living. There is an abundance of goodness in our every day to overcome the evil of the day. This is the day that the Lord has made, and everything God made is beautiful in its time.

July 22

~ Remain in the abundance of God's promises ~

> *Great is our Lord, and abundant in power; his understanding is beyond measure (Psalm 147:5, ESV).*

July 22, 2021, I was sitting down and having a great time just watching my kids playing with the sand on the beach. It was low tide with the water going back. The Holy Spirit started showing me how some things are not for you to go and do. Showing me the ocean, the Lord started saying to me that a person who cannot swim will not go into the ocean where it is too deep for them. In everything, you are limited according to your ability. The ocean too has its limit. It cannot cross its boundaries where it is marked to stay, because if it does there will be disasters.

> ... when he gave the sea its boundary so the waters would not overstep his command, and when he marked out the foundations of the earth (Proverbs 8:29, NIV).

The Holy Spirit began to open the heart of my eyes to see that we cannot cross over to someone's path and see how they live, or want to live the way they live. Everyone has their own calling to walk their own path in this journey we call life. When we start crossing over to someone else's path and get in their way, we only stop our progress and development.

To live as a good father to his household, a good dad only looks up to our loving Father in heaven. God's Word has no limit. This is where a good dad stands firm and anchors himself, allowing the will of the Word to take him on the path of what he is called to do. He lives in the abundance of the Word of the Father.

> *Everything has its limits, except your commands (Psalm 119:96, ERV).*

Jesus lived our Father's name of abundance, Jehovah El Shaddai. He was the very Word that has no limit. He chose and calls each of us to live the life He has laid down for us. We just have to find rest in the promises of the Father and remain in Christ, because apart from Him, we can do nothing.

Every day is another new day to live our Father's name, Jehovah El Shaddai, and remain in the abundance of His promises. What He said, He will do. Our Father doesn't lie.

July 23

~ Add on the abundance of life within you to live ~

Because you have these blessings, do all you can to add to your life these things: to your faith add goodness; to your goodness add knowledge; to your knowledge add self-control; to your self-control add patience; to your patience add devotion to God; to your devotion add kindness toward your brothers and sisters in Christ, and to this kindness add love (2 Peter 1:5-7, ERV).

Another winter's day, July 23, 2021, as I was trying to change into some fresh clothes, the Holy Spirit taught me this: When you change into new fresh clothes, you wear inside clothes, and outside ones which can be seen. The kingdom of God is like this. When you are born again, you are focusing on changing from inside to outside. You want to put on clothes that fit you and make you feel and look your best inside, and wear outside clothes that are of good quality and don't tear off easily. You also must clothe yourself with the armour of God in your outer being so you don't stumble easily when arrows of evil come your way. Your outer flesh must be clothed in a way that it doesn't respond in defeat to the attacks of the dark forces, but maintains calmness and peace. The dark forces come with a strong unseen force and you often don't see where its form of evil is coming from. The Almighty Father of Abundance is His name, Jehovah El Shaddai, and He has designed your inner being with an abundance of overflowing goodness to reach within and conquer evil.

A good dad wakes up each day and clothes himself with faith on his inner being (see 2 Peter 1:5-7).

On his clothing of FAITH he adds GOODNESS, then KNOWLEDGE. He then adds SELF-CONTROL, and adds PATIENCE on self-control. This is so he disciplines himself to endure the KNOWLEDGE of the fruit of GOODNESS and overcomes evilness. Add DEVOTION TO GOD, by devoting and committing himself to God, add KINDNESS and add LOVE.

KINDNESS ADDS LOVE on. The appearance of LOVE is where KINDNESS is. This is how he creates his new inner self in the image of Christ.

His mind is in a renewing process to always remind him of what he is wearing, while his mouth is breathing out praises to his loving Father in heaven. For his outer wear, he is clothed with Ephesians 6:10-18 so he doesn't stumble or fall at the arrows of the wicked attacking him.

Jesus was the life of abundance and had life in abundance. He lived our Father's name, Jehovah El Shaddai, our Almighty Father is our Abundance. He gave us this life in abundance within us through the Holy Spirit, who produces the nine fruit of righteousness. We are to be clothed with righteousness, from inside to outside by serving it to all we come into contact with, who are in need of it.

Every day is a new day to create that new you in living our Father's name of abundance, in the name of Jesus, to the Father's glory.

July 24

~ *Faith of an ant! Abundance* ~

Take a lesson from the ants, you lazybones. Learn from their ways and become wise! (Proverbs 6:6, NLT).

A good dad has the faith of an ant. He learns his life from the way ants live and work. He works and lives the name of His Father. Our heavenly Father is always at work. With his faith of an ant, he too must be at work without being told to. He imitates the way Jesus came and lived the Father's name, Jehovah El Shaddai, our Lord God is our Abundance. Our Father in heaven supplies and meets our every need when we are working and glorifying Him in whatever work we do.

The faith of an ant is all about making sure whatever food they find and collect must be carried to their destiny and stored. They make every effort to make sure the food reaches its destiny. Our loving Father in heaven is working to see that His Word accomplishes its purposes it is designed for. The Word is full of the abundance of life to give us life that is alive forever. Jesus is the Word who has become flesh to give us this abundance of life. Our Father is watching to see that His Word reaches its purpose it is designed for.

The Lord said to me, 'You have seen correctly, for I am watching to see that my word is fulfilled.' (Jeremiah 1:12, NIV).

Every day, live the Father's name, Jehovah El Shaddai, our Lord God is our Abundance, and keep collecting and collecting the Word of God and store it within your heart so you won't sin in this sinful world.

July 25

~ Let the abundant life of light shine out from you and light up someone's life ~

Satan, who is the god of this world, has blinded the minds of those who don't believe. They are unable to see the glorious light of the Good News. They don't understand this message about the glory of Christ, who is the exact likeness of God (2 Corinthians 4:4, NLT).

One sunny morning, July 25, 2021, I was near the bathroom window when the morning light was shooting through. With my eyes closed, I could still see the presence of light. But when I drew away from the window where there was no light, with my eyes closed I could only see darkness. This is what I heard the Holy Spirit say: Every one of us has been born into this world of darkness. When we were born and started growing up, the devil tried to blind us to this dark world so we would remain in the darkness. Our enemies are the principalities of these dark forces. Jesus even told the Pharisees that you can see, but you are blind. Jesus was the very light from the Father, yet they could not see the truth. The light was there shining, but because they were in the dark and their eyes were closed they couldn't see Jesus, the light of the world. It was like how the light was shooting in through the bathroom, but because I was in the dark part of the room with my eyes closed, I couldn't see the light.

Jesus lived an abundant life of power. He was the power of light, life and love in abundance and overflowing. He lived our Father's name, Jehovah El Shaddai, our Almighty Father is our Abundance with overflowing of good light to give sight to the blind and show us the way to the Father.

A good dad stays connected to the Word of his good Father in heaven to receive the power of light, life and love so he can see well the path of life he is walking through. He doesn't allow the things of the world to blind him, rather, he binds the things of the world that try to lure him away from the presence of light.

Light, life and love from our loving Father in heaven enters another day and brings light and life to us. This is the day the Lord has made. Every day, we are to live our Father's name, Jehovah El Shaddai, and live that abundant life by allowing the power of light which is the Holy Spirit who lives in us to shine out from us and light up someone's world.

July 26

~ Produce a fruitful abundance of life by abiding your flesh in the Word who has become flesh ~

Abide in Me, and I in you (John 15:4, ESV).

Like a tea bag in hot water abides until the water takes the flavour of the tea bag, so it is with a good dad. He abides in the living water who is Jesus, until he takes the taste and flavour of the living water into him. For him to bear fruit of the abundance of life and make his life alive and living, he remains in the living water.

It is not the branch that produces the fruit, but the vine. As long as the branch remains in the vine it will produce the fruit. Jesus is the vine who produces the fruit. As the branch, we are to bear the fruit that is produced. For us to be able to bear the fruit in all seasons, we have to go through pruning and be moulded in the design purposed by the Father. The branch doesn't produce the fruit; it bears the fruit. It's the vine that produces the fruit. And Jesus said,

'I am the vine, you are the branches. He who abides in Me, and I in him, bears much fruit; for without Me you can do nothing.' (John 15:5 NKJV).

Jesus lived our Father's name, Jehovah El Shaddai, our Lord God is our Abundance. He gave His flesh to us for us to abide in His flesh so we can produce a life of abundance. We are to live our Father's name, Jehovah El Shaddai, by letting our flesh abide in the flesh of Jesus, who is the Word, so we can produce a fruitful life of abundance.

Every day is another opportunity for us to abide more in Jesus, who is the vine, and go deeper in Him so the Word can permeate into us.

July 27

~ Live a life of multiplication and addition from a place of blessings ~

Then God blessed them and said, 'Be fruitful and multiply. Fill the earth and govern it. Reign over the fish in the sea, the birds in the sky, and all the animals that scurry along the ground.' (Genesis 1:28, NLT).

A good dad is good at making multiplication and addition to his resources because he knows his Father in heaven and that His name is Jehovah El Shaddai, our Almighty Father is our Abundance. He has given him access to abundance through the life of Jesus. The foot of the cross is where this life begins. The cross indicates to him the sign of multiplication and addition to view life in all directions.

Whatever little he has is multiplied, and more added, and flows back to him in abundance when it is put into the Father's hands for

His blessing. There is blessing in his hands on everything he touches because he trusts the hands of the source from where his blessings flow, and the blessings do overflow.

The life Jesus laid down at the cross is a life of abundance. He lived our heavenly Father's name, Jehovah El Shaddai, our Almighty Father is our Abundance, and in Jesus' name we too can live our Father's name of abundance.

The Holy Spirit of God is the source of blessing that forever flows from the new life of Jesus, from whom comes the abundance of life. He is the same Spirit that raises up this abundant life and He now lives inside our lives.

> *The thief comes only to steal and kill and destroy.*
> *I came that they may have life and have it abundantly*
> *(John 10:10, ESV).*

The enemy cannot destroy the new life of abundance Jesus gave us. We are now to use that life to defeat the enemy every time he lies to us. This is the life of truth and will set us free from the lies of the devil. The Spirit of truth lives in us.

July 28

~ There is abundance of life in the Word which is life ~

> *I came that they may have life and have it abundantly*
> *(John 10:10, ESV).*

July 23, 2022, I was going to go into the kitchen to make fried rice, but since Tom was already there I asked him to cook the rice, saying I would do the rest. This is what I heard the Holy Spirit say:

Wherever I am, I have to do what needs to be done with what is in my hand. God will do the rest.

You see, it doesn't matter where we are, whatever we desire to have in abundance is what we have to sow to reap its kind. As long as we seek first the kingdom of God and His righteousness, all these things will be added to us to sow more and reap in abundance.

A good dad is so hungry for righteousness that he seeks the Word of God more so the Holy Spirit can fill him with abundance of life from the Word (see John 6:63).

To make money, you need more money to invest into making it. To make life in you, you need more life to invest into making it. And so a good dad invests more of his life into the Word, which is LIFE.

> *Blessed are those who hunger and thirst for righteousness,*
> *for they will be filled (Matthew 5:6, NIV).*

Jesus came and lived our Father's name, Jehovah El Shaddai, our Lord God of Abundance. He gave us His life in abundance of righteousness. The same Spirit who resurrected His life is given to us with His fruit of righteousness in abundance that we will never run out of, and it's the nine fruit of the Spirit, which is of righteousness, that gives life to the giver as well as the receiver.

When you feel like you are running out of the fruit of the Spirit, especially patience, run into the Holy Spirit and ask Him to help you produce His fruit.

Every day is a new day with an abundance of life as a gift from the Father for us to have enough strength and joy to see us through.

We have to live the Father's name, Jehovah El Shaddai, knowing that there is so much life, love and light to live for the day.

July 29

~ Springs of living waters flow within us to grow us in the characters of Christ ~

Therefore, if anyone is in Christ, he is a new creation. The old has passed away; behold, the new has come (2 Corinthians 5:17, ESV).

Early one morning, April 14, 2021, while praying in the kitchen, the Holy Spirit spoke through me of a particular plant I have in the kitchen, a small living plant, just above the tap. It had grown new shoots of leaves while the old leaves got a little dry and fell off. The new leaves kept growing, higher and higher. This is what the Holy Spirit taught me: Once you are new in Christ, your life starts to grow its new Christ-like character and the 'old you' starts leaving you. Like how you take care of that plant and give water and sustain it, the more you drink the living water from Jesus, your life is sustained and you grow in your new Christ-like character. Your old character starts leaving you like how the old leaves of the plant fall off, and the new character of Christ starts growing in you like those new shoots from the plant.

A good dad plants himself in the teaching of His Father in heaven to be like Him. To have an abundance of life and enjoy his fatherly role, he remains connected to the Father and obeys His teachings. His Father has a name, Jehovah El Shaddai, our Lord God, is our Abundance. He praises and gives glory to the name of the Father in Jesus' name.

Whoever believes in me, as Scripture has said, rivers of living water will flow from within them. By this he meant the Spirit, whom those who believed in him were later to receive. Up to that time the Spirit had not been given, since Jesus had not yet been glorified (John 7:38-39, NIV).

Jesus lived our Father's name, Jehovah El Shaddai, in giving us a life of abundance. He is the living water who gave His life so the spring of living water can flow in abundance from within us. The gift of the Holy Spirit from Jesus is inside us as the living water to sustain, and to grow us more to be like Christ.

Every day, sustain yourself in the living water to stay fresh and to refresh others who are thirsty.

July 30

~ Live in the abundance plan of God and achieve little goals that lead to big dreams ~

He must become greater; I must become less (John 3:30, NIV).

One night, April 4, 2021, I was sorting out my kids' clothes and I thought I'd give away the clothes that were small on them, and keep the ones that fit them or were bigger for them to grow into.

This is what the Holy Spirit taught me: The kingdom of God is like this. Be Joseph the dreamer and dream big goals to achieve. Write down your dreams and what goals you need to action to achieve them. Like you remove your kids' clothes that are small, remove also any smaller dreams and small-minded people in your circle that will belittle you. You have a bigger and great God working His power within you to do big things. Dream big and write down big goals to achieve them. Grow into it to be in it, just like how your kids will grow into those big clothes and fit into them.

Every child sees their dad as big and great, able to do anything for them. A good dad looks up only to His Father in heaven. The more he spends time in His Word, the more he grows closer to Him. The closer he is to His Father, the more he sees Him as so big. He is all sufficient and abundance. Jehovah El Shaddai is His name, our Lord God of Abundance. He can supply to him anything of which he dreams.

Jesus lived our Father's name. He came that we may have life in abundance. The enemy comes to steal, kill and destroy that life, and our dreams when we are not fully living our life in abundance and making the most of it.

Look for any opportunity every day and make the most of it. Live in abundance your new life in Christ by achieving little steps, little goals towards that big dream.

July 31

~ Love from the abundant love of our Father in heaven ~

Dear friends, since God so loved us, we also ought to love one another (1 John 4:11, NIV).

One winter's morning, July 31, 2021, I was doing home schooling with Angelilly. After she wrote her answers, she tried her best to do perfectly what I instructed her to do. I could still see the little mistakes she did in her work. But then I thought *it's okay, because it shows that it's her work, her own handwriting and the level she is at.*

This is what I heard the Holy Spirit say: This is also how the Father sees us every time we don't love someone perfectly like He does. He is not upset. He looks at us and sees how we are trying our best to love like Him. We are trying to be like Him, but we are still making some mistakes in our trying to be like Him. We are a work in progress. The Love of our Father has no ending. It's an ongoing thing that must continue in our life.

Every dad will show their love in their actions, even if they don't tell their children. A good dad loves with understanding. He will continue to love his family regardless of how unappreciative they are towards him in what he provides. He loves from the Love of his heavenly Father who is committed to him. As long as he is committed in Word and prayer he is able to love in abundance, because the Word of God is in abundance and has no ending.

> *The faithful love of the Lord never ends! His mercies never cease (Lamentations 3:22, NLT).*

Jesus is the abundant Word of the Father who came and lived the name of our Father in heaven. The Word who has become flesh. His flesh was committed in performing and producing the fruit of the Spirit which is love. He is now knocking on our hearts to come in and live in us so we can love in abundance.

Each new day is another day to live our Father's name, Jehovah El Shaddai, and practice the new commandment of our Father, and that is to love with His love of abundance.

AUGUST

Jehovah M'Kaddesh! I AM your Sanctifier.

Jehovah God-like Mind is a Good Father-like Character

OUR LORD GOD WHO SANCTIFIES.

~ The pain gives you strength to birth new beginnings you carry within you ~

> *What we do see is Jesus, who for a little while was given a position 'a little lower than the angels'; and because he suffered death for us, he is now 'crowned with glory and honour'. Yes, by God's grace, Jesus tasted death for everyone (Hebrews 2:9, NLT).*

April 26, 2022, I was thinking of how I was going to go through the pain of birthing the life I carried inside of me. After the birthing of Christos, my third born child to be, I knew what joy that would bring. This is what I heard the Holy Spirit say: The kingdom of God is like this. God will conceive a seed of the desires of your heart, a dream or vision for you. But for you to give birth to that dream, you have to go through some pain and discomfort.

Carrying the life inside of me I had to go through many uncomfortable moments. The pains started coming in when the baby started growing bigger and the discomfort increased. When your dream is about to become reality, as it comes closer to you, this is where you get much adversity, criticism and perhaps some knockdowns. Don't allow that to kill your dream. Keep on persevering with it. You are going through the pain of giving birth to it.

> *Dear brothers and sisters, when troubles of any kind come your way, consider it an opportunity for great joy. For you know that when your faith is tested, your endurance has a chance to grow. So let it grow, for when your endurance is fully developed, you will be perfect and complete, needing nothing (James 1:2-4, NLT).*

Jesus lived our Father's name, Jehovah M'Kaddesh, our Almighty Father who Sanctifies. He carried in Him the eternal life that He was going to give us once and for all. When the time came for Him to lay down His life, He went through the uncomfortableness, and finally the pain and suffering, so He could lay down His holy life to give us one. We have been sanctified through His holy life.

Every day, and each day of the month of August, live the Father's name, Jehovah M'Kaddesh, in Jesus' name and set yourself aside to do the will of the Father in whatever work you do. Work towards your dream and face the uncomfortableness. When you are about to give birth, embrace the pain. It only makes you stronger to give birth to your dream.

August 1

~ Clean yourself and be ready to be used by the Father ~

> *He saved us and called us to be his own people, not because of what we have done, but because of his own purpose and grace. He gave us this grace by means of Christ Jesus before the beginning of time (2 Timothy 1:9, GNT).*

One morning, August the first, 2021, I was thinking of how I was cleaning up the dishes so I could have them ready to be used again. This is what I heard the Holy Spirit say: You see, your loving Father in heaven's name is Jehovah M'Kaddesh, the Lord God who Sanctifies. He is always making you clean so He can set you apart for His special use. No one would want to eat food from a place that is dirty, and so when He wants to send forth His Word to you to feed someone who is losing hope, He makes sure you are clean and set apart and be ready to be used.

A good dad always cleans himself in the Word of his loving Father by renewing his mind in the Word so he has the mind of Christ and is ready to be used by our Father in heaven.

Jesus lived our Father in heaven's name on earth by coming down and making us clean. Jehovah M'Kaddesh, our Almighty Father who Sanctifies, said His Word to us already and made us clean. He is the Word and He said we are clean.

> *You are already clean because of the word I have spoken to you (John 15:3, NIV).*

Every day, we have to live the name of our Father in Jesus' name and clean someone so they can also become of good use. We are sanctified by our Father in heaven through the work of Jesus on the cross.

August 2

~ *Sanctify yourself as a Jasper, the Holy City of God to dwell* ~

> *The wall was made of jasper, and the city of pure gold, as pure as glass. The foundations of the city walls were decorated with every kind of precious stone. The first foundation was jasper, the second sapphire, the third agate, the fourth emerald, the fifth onyx, the sixth ruby, the seventh chrysolite, the eighth beryl, the ninth topaz, the tenth turquoise, the eleventh jacinth, and the twelfth amethyst (Revelation 21:18-20, NIV).*

We are the holy city of God which His Holy Spirit is to live in. Every day, we have to live our Father's name, Jehovah M'Kaddesh, our Almighty Father who Sanctifies. Being the Holy City we are made of Jasper, one of the precious stones, and Jesus is the living stone who lives our Father's name so we can live our Father's name in Jesus' name and be set apart like the precious stone Jasper.

And the one who sat there had the appearance of jasper and ruby. A rainbow that shone like an emerald encircled the throne (Revelation 4:3, NIV).

Jasper symbolises the glory of God: His splendour, brightness, magnificence and beauty. Jasper symbolises the blood atonement we have through the sacrifice of Jesus Christ and the passing over of God's judgement. It also represents royalty, prosperity, prestige and valiance.

The wall was made of jasper, and the city of pure gold, as pure as glass (Revelation 21:18, NIV).

Our wall of Jasper is the blood of Jesus that silences all the negative energy and protects us from it.

See, I have engraved you on the palms of my hands; your walls are ever before me (Isaiah 49:16, NIV).

Every day, we are to live our Father's name, Jehovah M'Kaddesh, and set our life apart as a Jasper, to which the Holy City of God was founded.

August 3

~ We are the chosen ones to be set apart as God's holy people ~

Therefore, if anyone cleanses himself from what is dishonourable, he will be a vessel for honourable use, set apart as holy, useful to the master of the house, ready for every good work (2 Timothy 2:21, ESV).

August 3, 2021, while doing home schooling, the Holy Spirit pointed out to me how Angelilly's school work was set aside for her under her school account name which belongs to her.

Our Father is Jehovah M'Kaddesh, our Almighty Father who Sanctifies. He is Holy and wants to set us aside, and so He chose us to be His holy people. This is why we are born in this time, where the Holy Spirit is being sent down to us to live in us. Because our loving Father is Holy, so is His Spirit who is the Holy Spirit, the Spirit of truth. You see, just like Angelilly having an account set aside for her to access and do her school work, so it is with us. We are chosen by our Father to be born at this time and are set aside to access the Holy Spirit within us to do good work.

A good dad sets his life aside to remain in the holy Word of His Father in heaven. His life remains in Christ so he can easily connect to the Holy Spirit and be holy like Jehovah our Father.

Jesus was a good man, showing us the loving goodness of the Father. He gave us the Holy Spirit to live in us so we can produce the fruit goodness. But Jesus never wasted His time proving to anyone that He was good. He made us holy by coming into our life through the Holy Spirit. Every day, the Holy Spirit is willing to make us holy like our loving Father if we ask Him to and set ourselves wholly for His use. Our spirit is willing but the flesh is weak (see Matthew 26:41).

> *But now he has made you his friends again. He did this by the death Christ suffered while he was in his body. He did it so that he could present you to himself as people who are holy, blameless, and without anything that would make you guilty before him (Colossians 1:22 ERV).*

Every day, live the Father's name, Jehovah M'Kaddesh, in Jesus' name. Set your spirit, which is willing, into the will of the Holy Spirit, which is to be holy like the Father.

August 4

~ Renew your mind in the Word and focus on being holy ~

...for it is written, 'Be holy, because I am holy.'
(1 Peter 1:16, NIV).

August 4, 2021, I was doing home schooling with Angelilly and we were to read some passages, then answer questions relating to them. I was trying to make her focus her mind on what the passage was trying to explain. The reading passage was about the white sharks, considered the aggressive shark of the ocean. This is what the Holy Spirit taught me: You see, you are trying to make your child focus her mind on the passage so she can understand what it is. So are you. You have to renew your mind on what the Word of God says of you so you will have the understanding to live your life. The Word is the manual guide of the new eternal life you are born again of.

> *Fix these words of mine in your hearts and minds; tie them as symbols on your hands and bind them on your foreheads (Deuteronomy 11:18, NIV).*

A good dad is always conscious of the Word of God. He is committed to it every day and reflects himself in the Word so he can have the mind of Christ. He sets his mind upon it as he goes forth through the day. He knows His Father's name is Jehovah M'Kaddesh, our Lord God who Sanctifies. He sets, focuses and fixes his mind for His Father to make it holy so he can think holy and live a holy life like Him.

Jesus came and lived our Father's name, Jehovah M'Kaddesh, our Almighty Father who Sanctifies. He was holy, yet walked and lived among us, the sinners, so He can take us out of this world and set us apart, away from the kingdom of darkness and into the kingdom of light, to work in us and make us holy like Him. If He could be holy while on earth, we can also be holy like Him.

Every day is made by our Holy Father to live His name, Jehovah M'Kaddesh, and remain in His Holy Spirit and be holy.

August 5

~ Be still and set yourself apart to be used by the Father's holy purposes ~

The steadfast love of the Lord never ceases; his mercies never come to an end; they are new every morning; great is your faithfulness (Lamentation 3:22-23, ESV).

August 5, 2021, the Lord was showing me images of photos I'd taken, and that how I look in the moment captured of each photo will never change. This is what the Holy Spirit taught me: This is how the image of Christ is. He never changes. The moment we create our image to be like Him, we remain the same, just like the photos captured, except that we become new all the time. And this is why, many times, you will see a man of God look like they have hardly aged, they only look fresher in their appearance. The Word of God is new all the time to be timely, and when we take in the Word, it rebirths us and makes us newborn in the Word. This is why we have to crave God's word like a newborn baby, so we remain new and the same in the Word.

A good dad creates his new image in the image of his loving Father every day in His Word. He knows His Father is the same yesterday, today and forever. He is Love, and His love is rich in mercy, which is new every day. To make a good image, one has to be still, and so in the midst of fear and chaos we have to remain still and know that our Father is Jehovah M'Kaddesh, our Lord God who Sanctifies.

Jesus, the visible image of God, lived our Father's name, Jehovah M'Kaddesh. He is the very image of our loving Father who came down and took away our sin, and set us apart to continue to work in creating us to be holy like our Father. He gave us the Holy Spirit to remain in us so we can live in the holiness of the Holy Spirit and be readily available all the time to be used by our Father.

> *A new commandment I give to you, that you love one another: just as I have loved you, you also are to love one another. By this all people will know that you are my disciples, if you have love for one another (John 13:34-35, ESV).*

Every day is another new day for us to love more with our Father's mercy which is new. We are being set apart to live our Father's name, Jehovah M'Kaddesh, and be sanctified to become more and more in the image of Christ.

August 6

~ Commit your life to stay away from sin ~

> *Jesus gave them this answer: 'Very truly I tell you, the Son can do nothing by himself; he can do only what he sees his Father doing, because whatever the Father does the Son also does (John 5:19, NIV).*

January 30, 2022, while having breakfast, Blessed, my almost three-year-old, started copying everything his seven-year-old sister was doing. He ripped off the skin of the sausage and followed the way his sister was eating. Angelilly complained to me that Blessed likes to copy everything she does. I told her, 'This is why I keep telling you to do the right things only, so Blessed too will do the right things.' As soon as I spoke I heard the Holy Spirit say: Jesus came and did only good and the right things so we too can also do that. Jesus told us He is doing only what He sees from what our Father is doing.

Jesus lived our Father's name, Jehovah M'Kaddesh, our Almighty Father who Sanctifies. He was sinless and lived among the sinners, and yet He had never sinned. As the righteous one from God, He set Himself apart and did not commit any sin. Jesus said we can do what He did, and even greater things than He did (see John 14:12). We too can live our Father's name, Jehovah M'Kaddesh, and set our lives apart from committing to doing any evil that is around us. Just like how we do not want ourselves or our loved ones to come in contact with someone wicked and evil who will harm us, let us also abstain from coming in contact with or doing anything that is ungodly and unholy.

> *This day is holy to our Lord. Do not grieve, for the joy of the Lord is your strength (Nehemiah 8:10, NIV).*

Every day is holy because a holy God has made it, but as soon as it is received by us in the evil world it starts to become ruined. We have to protect our every day given to us and keep it holy and set it apart from any evilness.

August 7

~ Remove away the old life of nature so you can move forward in the new life ~

> *Therefore, if anyone is in Christ, the new creation has come: The old has gone, the new is here! (2 Corinthians 5:17, NIV).*

One morning, August 7, 2021, I was trying to send a text message. I opened my messages and realised there was another message waiting for me to send first. I thought *I have to attend to that message and send it off before I do a new one.* This is when the Holy Spirit pointed out to me that before you move on to something new, you have to sort out any old issues not yet sorted. If you bring your gifts to the altar and realise you have not forgiven a brother, leave your gifts and go back to the brother and ask for forgiveness. You see, I couldn't send a new text message because an old one I typed was in the way. I had to send it or delete it to have access to type my new message. We too cannot move forward into our new life in Christ if something in our old life is in the way and needs attending to first.

We have a loving Father who loves us and forgave us for all our sin. He chose us before the creation of the world for Himself. He is Jehovah M'Kaddesh, our Almighty Father who Sanctifies. He took us apart from ungodliness around us, and works on us to make us holy like Him because He wants us to be just like Him.

Jesus lived our Father's name. He set Himself apart from the world. Divine virgin birth into a sinful world, He was sinless and remained sinless until His death and resurrection so we can remain in this new life He gave us. This new life is now made accessible to us to be set apart to action the holy fruit of the Holy Spirit. For us to move forward in our new life in Christ, Jesus had to do away with our old life that is going to be in the way. It is just like how I had to deal with the old text message in the way before I moved on in the new text message.

I press on toward the goal for the prize of the upward call of God in Christ Jesus (Philippians 3:14, NASB).

Every day, time is moving and not waiting. Let's live our Father's name, Jehovah M'Kaddesh, in Jesus' name, and move out what is not meant to be in our life so our lives can be set apart to be holy and live the new life in Christ.

August 8

~ Set yourselves apart for the Holy Spirit to do His Holy work in you ~

For he has rescued us out of the darkness and gloom of Satan's kingdom and brought us into the Kingdom of his dear Son (Colossians 1:13, TLB).

One cloudy, dull day, August 8, 2021, we drove by one of our beautiful beaches, and I thought *it's not a good time for me to go out and get a good photo.* The capture of the image wouldn't be good, but I had the lighting feature in the phone's camera to make the image brighter and still show its beauty.

This is what I heard the Holy Spirit say: You see, in your dull days and storms, the light from the Word you receive into you keeps you lit up and beautiful in the image of Christ you are becoming. Just like your phone camera that has different lighting features for you to choose, so it is with God's Word. The Word of God is the light and has many different promises to add light to your dull life during the storms (see Psalm 119:105).

Jesus is the light of the world from the Word of our loving Father. He came and lived our Father's name, Jehovah M'Kaddesh, our Almighty Father who Sanctifies. He is the light that took us away from the kingdom of darkness into the light of the kingdom of the

Father to make us holy. The holy kingdom of the Father, who is the Holy Spirit, is now in us through what Jesus has done for us.

> *I have come into the world as light, so that whoever believes in me may not remain in darkness (John 12:46, ESV).*

Each day is another day to live our Father's name, Jehovah M'Kaddesh, and set ourselves apart for the Holy Spirit to begin His holy work in us.

August 9

~ *Set your old rebellious life away from your new resurrected life* ~

> *Seek his will in all you do, and he will show you which path to take (Proverbs 3:6, NLT).*

I remember a winter's night, August 9, 2021. Everyone was asleep and I was trying to go to sleep. Tom had cooked, but didn't turn the stove off after cooking and it was already two or three hours later. I was going to go off to sleep when I went to get something in the living room. I walked past the kitchen and felt a strong urge to look to the stove where the lights go on to indicate that the stove is on. I couldn't see whether the pot was burning or not, but I could see the red light on from where I was. I rushed over to have a look, only to see a burning frying pan and its lid. I quickly turned the stove off.

The old me could be so upset, raising my voice to Tom and telling him how careless he was—words to put him down that could blame and shame him. Instead, I only made mention to him how he'd left the stove on without knowing. I heard the Holy Spirit talking gently to me: When we set our SELF away from our old rebellious life and focus on being in the presence of Jehovah, our life can never go wrong. Nothing goes bad in the goodness found in the presence of Jehovah. The Holy Spirit is there to always warn us of dangers, not only in our spiritual concerns, but also in our physical concerns. So always make the Word become your flesh.

We are to live our Father's name, Jehovah M'Kaddesh, our Almighty Father who Sanctifies. When we set ourselves for Him to work on, no harm or trouble of any kind will come to us because nothing must destroy the work He is doing in our life.

> *Your ears will hear a word behind you, saying, 'This is the way, walk in it,' whenever you turn to the right or to the left (Isaiah 30:21, NASB).*

Jesus lived our Father's name, Jehovah M'Kaddesh, our Almighty Father who Sanctifies. He laid down His life for us so we can also lay down our old life and receive His new life. We can now set our new life in Him apart for our Father to work on it and keep it holy. The Holy Spirit we receive set us apart to be kept in the holiness of the Father.

Every new day is a new opportunity to live our Father's name, Jehovah M'Kaddesh, and be set apart for the Holy Spirit to work in us and keep us holy like our Father.

August 10

~ Make the new image of Christ in you to be holy in the Holy Spirit ~

> *Create in me a pure heart, O God, and renew a steadfast spirit within me (Psalm 51:10, NIV).*

On August 10, 2017, while I was at the twelve items or less checkout, I realised the lady in front of me had more than twelve items—she had a trolley full of groceries! I thought to myself *some people can't just do the right thing*. I started feeling irritated and impatient. This is what I heard the Holy Spirit say: Now you know exactly how God feels towards everyone not doing the right thing, but yet He is patient with them, because He is love. And love is patience.

I had to renew my mind and wait patiently to be served. If we fail along the way, we have another opportunity to try better to produce the fruit of love. God's love will never fail us. It is full of kindness and goodness to be patient with us. When we give someone patience we give the goodness and kindness in us as well. A good dad knows that the moment he allows Jesus into His heart he has set himself away from the old way of living, and so he renews his mind to keep it blameless and holy. He thinks thoughts of a holy nature so his heart can be filled with things of the Holy Spirit who resides in him. Therefore, he focuses on producing the fruit of the Holy Spirit wherever his steps lead him to.

Jesus lived our Father's name, Jehovah M'Kaddesh, our Almighty Father who Sanctifies. He came down to sanctify us and make us become a pure bride for Himself. His best man, the Holy Spirit, is holy and He lives in us. The Spirit and the bride say come, Lord Jesus (see Revelation 22:17). He is the Spirit of our Father who knows when our Master will come for us. He lives in us to make us holy from the inside out so we can be spotless and blameless for our Master.

> *… to make her holy and clean, washed by baptism and God's Word; so that he could give her to himself as a glorious Church without a single spot or wrinkle or any other blemish, being holy and without a single fault (Ephesians 5:26-27, TLB).*

Every day is a new day to set ourselves apart for the Holy Spirit to keep us in His ways. We are here to live our Father's name, Jehovah M'Kaddesh, and make the new image of Christ in us to be holy in the Holy Spirit.

August 11

~ Set your life aside to keep it holy for God's purposes ~

> *For it is written: Be holy, because I am holy*
> *(1 Peter 1:16, NIV).*

God's will for us now is that our lives should indeed become holy, just as God is holy. This is the specific usage of the name Jehovah M'Kaddesh—to indicate that God is the Lord who sanctifies us. When something is set apart, it is for that thing to be put aside from the rest because a work is going to be carried out on it. I had decided to pack aside some clothes because I had some work to do on them. I told Tom and the kids to leave them alone and not to touch it. Or sometimes I buy specific foods for a certain recipe and put them in the fridge, telling my household members not to touch them as I have work to do with them.

> *God the Father knew you and chose you long ago, and his*
> *Spirit has made you holy. As a result, you have obeyed him*
> *and have been cleansed by the blood of Jesus Christ. May*
> *God give you more grace and peace (1 Peter 1:2, NLT).*

You see, our Father bought us with the holy blood of Jesus and choose us and set us apart so He can work on us. He is always at work and He is Jehovah M'Kaddesh, our Almighty Father who Sanctifies. He is working on us to make us holy with His perfect love in the Holy Spirit so we can become holy like Him.

A good dad is not perfect. He needs the perfect love from his loving Father from above to work in driving out fears of his imperfection. He spends his daily time in the Word and loves living a life of producing the fruit of the Spirit. He sets his eyes apart to see and look with compassion, not judgement.

The perfect love of the Father, Jesus, lived our Father's name and brought glory to His name to show us how to do the same. Every day, spend time in the Word and set the Word to do its purpose in that area of your life that needs work to be done.

August 12

~ Hide your flesh in the Word who has become flesh ~

> *Those who live in the shelter of the Most High will find rest in the shadow of the Almighty (Psalm 91:1, NLT).*

April 12, 2022, one beautiful autumn night, I walked out to the porch of the house. As I looked into the backyard, the shadow of my appearance became so big. This happened because of the reflection of the porch light I was standing under. My shadow was so big it covered the whole yard. This is what I heard the Holy Spirit say: God is so big and great that we are hidden in Him. He appeared in the flesh by Word becoming flesh, Jesus Christ. Our whole being can now be hidden in the flesh of Christ. Jesus lived our Father's name, Jehovah M'Kaddesh, our Almighty God who sanctifies. He is the light of the world who came to set us apart in Him. Just like the light of the porch made a big shadow of me and everything was in my shadow, the light of Jesus in this dark world also sets us apart in Him, to remain in Him and be prepared to be used for the Father's glory. We are hidden in the shadow of His wings.

This is the prayer of a good dad:

> *Guard me as you would guard your own eyes. Hide me in the shadow of your wings (Psalm 17:8, NLT).*

Every day is another day that falls into this dark, fallen world for us to live. Live daily the Father's name, Jehovah M'Kaddesh, by setting yourself apart from this dark world and be in the light of the Word.

August 13

~ In the heat of the moment, set yourself apart to maintain holiness ~

> *A wise man controls his temper. He knows that anger causes mistakes (Proverbs 14:29, TLB).*

August 13, 2021, I felt so bad. While home schooling, I lost my patience with my six-year-old over something I should not have. She asked me to do something for her on the laptop, and after rushing through to set her up she changed her mind. I raised my voice because after she asked me to use the laptop and I had it set up for her, she wanted something else again. I felt like I had no time to do this and that, and she had to make up her mind once and for all.

I become conscious right away for doing it and repented. I asked the Holy Spirit to help me more and asked how I could improve. What the Holy Spirit revealed and opened my eyes to see left me in awe: The accuser, Satan devil, roams around with a strong force of anger and impatience because his time is running out. The force of his dark energy is around us, everywhere. When you are running out of time to do something, you will lose patience, anger will creep in and you will start getting frustrated.

This is the moment to live our Father's name, Jehovah M'Kaddesh, our Almighty Father who Sanctifies. When our anger tries to rise, let it rise up in holiness. Every area of our life has to be set aside for holiness. Even our anger is to be holy anger, where we pause and stop the flow of anger. When we stop and pause we are controlling anger, stopping it from travelling to the wrong path which can cause damage to both parties, like how two cars moving with force collide into each other.

Losing your temper causes a lot of trouble, but staying calm settles arguments (Proverbs 15:18, CEV).

Jesus lived our Father's name, Jehovah M'Kaddesh, our Almighty Father who Sanctifies. He set His whole sinless life apart into a new life for us in the Holy Spirit. We are now to set our life apart in NINE ways in producing the nine righteous fruit of the Spirit by living our Father's name.

Every new day, set it apart as holy to live the Father's name, Jehovah M'Kaddesh. Make everything concerning your life holy, even your anger and impatience. There will be wisdom and understanding in how to approach life in the heat of the moment.

August 14

~ Set your mind apart to purify words or images to be godly and holy ~

The Son is the radiance of God's glory and the exact representation of his being, sustaining all things by his powerful word. After he had provided purification for sins, he sat down at the right hand of the Majesty in heaven (Hebrews 1:3, NIV)

August 14, 2021, I was looking at the tap in the shower that morning, and after a while some bad images ran through my mind about it. This is what I heard the Holy Spirit say: Whatever is in your heart flows out when you see something. Fill your mind with good things. It took me a while for some bad thoughts to create an image. Our eyes see an image and create something out of it instantly. Our ears hear something and words flow out of us right away. What we contain within us flows out from us when we take into us words and images. You see, because we are in the old self nature of evil, it is that nature that rushes out quickly from us.

Our Father in heaven loves us so much and wants us to be restored to our original image which He made us to be like Him. He sent His Word, His Image to become flesh, so our eyes can see the image of Jesus and have an insight of the Father's love. And when our ears hear something, His Word will flow out from us because it is what we contain within us.

Jesus lived our Father's name, Jehovah M'Kaddesh, our Almighty Father who Sanctifies. He is the Word, the visible image of the Father who became flesh. Jesus was in the Father and set Himself apart because He is the very image of the invisible Father. He has chosen us in His Word who becomes flesh so we, flesh, can be in Him in the Holy Spirit to be the image of the Holy Spirit and be holy.

> *Instead, let the Spirit renew your thoughts and attitudes. Put on your new nature, created to be like God—truly righteous and holy (Ephesians 4:23-24, NLT).*

Every day our mind processes words through our hearing and images through our sight. We are to live our Father's name, Jehovah M'Kaddesh, and set our mind apart to purify words or images to be godly and holy.

August 15

~ Set yourselves apart to be filled from the Father's cup of love so you can be able to give out love ~

You prepare a table before me in the presence of my enemies. You anoint my head with oil; my cup overflows. Surely your goodness and love will follow me all the days of my life and I will dwell in the house of the Lord forever (Psalm 23:5-6, NIV).

August 15, 2021, I was sorting out a tea cup set. It had three pieces, with a little plate and saucer and the tea cup. The plate was a little bit bigger than the saucer, and the cup was sitting nicely on the saucer which was on the plate. This is what the Holy Spirit taught me: The little plate is like our Father in heaven, which Jesus is in, and the cup is the Holy Spirit which was given to us through Jesus. The Holy Spirit receives from Jesus and pours into us what He receives from Him. He is of abundance, and when He pours into us, our cup overflows. It is impossible to pour out from an empty cup. This is why we must always remain connected to the Holy Spirit and receive into us the Word of God.

A good dad desires to be like His Father in heaven that he sets himself apart to be committed to receiving the love of the Father, by committing to His Word. He is thirsty for the Word to fill his cup so he can pour out to his household.

Jesus came and lived our Father's name, Jehovah M'Kaddesh, our Almighty Father who Sanctifies. In a home there are special utensils that are kept apart to be used on special occasions. He has come to set us apart to be that special cup to be used for His special purpose.

He made us clean and purified us in His blood for us to remain clean in Him. He gave us the Holy Spirit so He can reside in us to keep us holy, and be away from the unholiness of this world.

> *In a wealthy home some utensils are made of gold and silver, and some are made of wood and clay. The expensive utensils are used for special occasions, and the cheap ones are for everyday use. If you keep yourself pure, you will be a special utensil for honourable use. Your life will be clean, and you will be ready for the Master to use you for every good work (2 Timothy 2:20-21, NLT).*

Every day is the day our Father has made for us to live His name, Jehovah M'Kaddesh, and set ourselves apart to be filled from His cup of love so we can give out love in the form of the fruit of righteousness.

August 16

~ Set yourself apart from the mess of this world ~

> *For I was born a sinner—yes, from the moment my mother conceived me (Psalm 51:5, NLT).*

April 15, 2022, the Lord showed me how every one of us born into this world falls into a fallen world of sickness and disease. A few days ago, back in my country of Papua New Guinea, there was news showing people diving into a sewerage waste swamp looking for money, as it had been said that money had been washed into that swamp. The people who dived in had waste and whatever filled the swamp stuck on their bodies.

This is what the Holy Spirit pointed out: Every one of us born into this world is born into a fallen, cursed world that is full of sickness, disease, pain, sorrow and heartache. All this gets stuck on us and makes us sick or in pain. Jesus came so we can be born again into our loving Father's kingdom. Born out of poverty, sickness and pain that the world is full of, He bought us with His precious holy blood that is sinless.

> *Yet it was our weaknesses he carried; it was our sorrows that weighed him down. And we thought his troubles were a punishment from God, a punishment for his own sins! But he was pierced for our rebellion, crushed for our sins. He was beaten so we could be whole. He was whipped so we could be healed (Isaiah 53:4-5, NLT).*

Just like the people who dived into the sewerage swamp and got mess all over their bodies, so are we. We too were born into this world full of wicked and evilness that is messing up our lives. Jesus lived our Father's name, Jehovah M'Kaddesh, our Almighty Father who Sanctifies. He bought us out from this mess with His sinless holy blood. His body went through pain and suffering to bring healing to our bodies.

Be born again with the birth of every new day so your day is not messed up by how the world runs its course. Fill out your days with the holiness of the Father, and give no space to the unholiness of this sick world.

August 17

~ Set your life apart and make it holy to serve our Holy Father ~

Before they call I will answer; while they are still speaking I will hear (Isaiah 65:24, NIV).

August 17, 2021, I was doing home schooling with Angelilly. We were reading a story about the gingerbread man, which she had to write a story about. After we read the story, we decided to answer the questions. Before I could read the questions to her, she gave me her answer to them. I said, 'Well done, you gave me the answer before I even asked you the question.'

This is what I heard the Holy Spirit say: Your Father in heaven already gave you answers to what you are praying and asking for. Even before you call, He will answer (see Isaiah 65:24). He knows you and knows everything about what you will need. He is Jehovah M'Kaddesh, our Almighty Father who Sanctifies. He set you apart and is working on you and knows exactly what you will need. But because He is the one working on you, He knows what you need, not what you want.

A good dad knows all the answers to his questions have been answered by His loving Father before he even knows those questions himself, just like how His Father knew him before he was formed in his mother's womb. He knows his needs before he even asks. The more he formed himself to be in the image of his good Father to be a good dad, the more he is at peace in all his requests in prayer that he has asked the Father.

> *But God demonstrates his own love for us in this: While we were still sinners, Christ died for us (Romans 5:8, NIV).*

Jesus lived our Father's name, Jehovah M'Kaddesh, our Almighty Father who Sanctifies. He made known to us our Father's pure, perfect love that can purify us and perfect our imperfect love towards others. We can only know our Father by living and walking in the way Jesus showed us. The love of our Father knows and accepts us in our rebellious, sinful nature so it can purify us. We are a work in progress to be holy, because the one who is working in us is holy.

Every new day is holy because a holy, awesome God made it. In every day of your life, live the Father's name by setting your life apart and make it holy to serve our holy Father.

August 18

~ Our life has been set apart and predestined for greatness ~

Blessed are those who keep his statutes and seek him with all their heart—they do no wrong but follow his ways (Psalm 119:2-3, NIV).

One beautiful morning, August 18, 2021, while doing home schooling with Angelilly, I told her to let me know before she wrote her answer, just so I could confirm whether it was right or not. God also wants us to seek Him before we make any decisions. I knew what the questions were on my child's question paper, and I knew the answers, but I wanted her to let me know what she was going to do before she did it, because I didn't want her to do the wrong thing. This is how our loving Father's love is towards us. He knows everything about what is ahead of us, and what we plan to do, but before we go ahead and do it. He wants us to commit our plans to Him and seek His counsel first. This is so He will lead us into doing the right thing so we can be successful in carrying it out.

Trust in the Lord with all your heart; do not depend on your own understanding. Seek his will in all you do, and he will show you which path to take (Proverbs 3:5-6, NLT).

Our life has been set apart and predestined for greatness. For that to come to pass, we have to seek the Lord's counsel every day. Jesus came and lived our Father's name, Jehovah M'Kaddesh, our

Almighty Father who Sanctifies. He laid down His life only to get it back and give it to us, for us to set it apart for the holy purpose of our loving Father in heaven. The abundant life of Jesus in us is for us to sanctify it more in the Word and seek our Father to lead us in the path of righteousness and holiness.

Set each day apart to live the Father's name, Jehovah M'Kaddesh, and sanctify your day in the holy beauty of the Father.

August 19

~ Renew your mind and set it apart to be holy ~

> *But we have the mind of Christ*
> *(1 Corinthians 2:16, NIV).*

One afternoon, August 12, 2021, I swept away some crumbs from the kitchen. Then I took out the bread toaster to toast some bread, only to have more crumbs came out of the toaster. This is what I heard the Holy Spirit say: You can renew your mind, but as long as your mind is thinking, it is at work and will still receive crumbs from anything. You must continue to empty those crumbs of thoughts that can ruin you. If you do not empty it, those crumbs can find a home in your heart to settle permanently. And this is why your heart can be deceitful above anything. Therefore, you need to renew your mind to have a new heart constantly. Just like how I just cleaned out the crumbs and there were new ones again, you can renew your mind, but there will be new thoughts again. Set and fix your mind to be devoted to God and be renewed constantly.

> *The heart is the most deceitful thing there is and*
> *desperately wicked. No one can really know how bad it is!*
> *(Jeremiah 17:9, TLB).*

Jesus lived our Father's name, Jehovah M'Kaddesh, our Almighty Father who Sanctifies. He, who is sinless, became sin for us and gave us a new beginning so we can have his mind—the mind of Christ. Our mind is to be set apart for our Father who is holy to make it holy. We house the Holy Spirit in our heart, so we must make sure we have the mind of Christ, where holy thoughts only can enter our heart.

Each day is another new day to keep having the mind of Christ with something new from the Word. We are to live our Father's name, Jehovah M'Kaddesh, and allow the holy Word of our Father to renew our mind and make it holy.

August 20

~ Focus your life to carry the life of Christ ~

Therefore do not worry about tomorrow, for tomorrow will worry about itself. Each day has enough trouble of its own (Matthew 6:34, NIV).

January 24, 2022, I was into my fourth month of pregnancy with baby number three and carrying heavy stuff. I realised the heavy stuff could destroy the fragile life I carried within me, so I stopped right away. This is what the Holy Spirit taught me: The kingdom of God is like this. When you carry the new life of Christ in you, do not carry any heavy burdens of the world, especially the concerns of life that will cause you to worry and pull you down, for it can kill the new life Christ has in you. The enemy comes to steal, kill and destroy. He knows he has completely destroyed you when he kills the new life in you.

Jesus spoke about this in the parable of the sower in Mark 4:

> *Still others, like seed sown among thorns, hear the word; but the worries of this life, the deceitfulness of wealth and the desires for other things come in and choke the word, making it unfruitful (Mark 4:18-19, NIV).*

We have to crave God's spiritual milk, His Word, like a newborn baby who needs to grow. It doesn't matter how long we have been in a relationship with Christ. Hearing and seeing God five years ago doesn't matter—it's hearing and seeing God in His Word five minutes ago.

Jesus lived our Father's name, Jehovah M'Kaddesh, our Almighty Father who Sanctifies. He set His holy life apart and laid it down for us so we can be knowledgeable of who our Father is. We have a loving Father who is rich in mercy and love. With lack of knowledge a person perishes (see Hosea 4:6).

Every new day, become like a newborn baby again so you can crave God's spiritual milk, His Word, so you can grow and be strong to carry anything the world throws in your way.

August 21

~ Set yourself apart to grow bigger and better in the Word of God ~

He must become greater; I must become less (John 3:30, NIV).

January 27, 2022, a beautiful morning, I was making breakfast for the kids. I made a big portion for my seven-year-old and a small portion for my almost three-year-old. As a mother, I knew who was going to eat a lot and who was going to eat just a little. Also, I knew the bigger child would eat more than the smaller one.

This is what the Holy Spirit taught me: The kingdom of God is like this. The more you grow bigger in the Word, the more God feeds you by giving you deeper insights into His Word, and this is where you face more battles and challenges in life too. God fights for you because you have become less and He has become great.

> *The Lord will fight for you; you need only to be still (Exodus 14:14, NIV).*

Our loving Father's name is Jehovah M'Kaddesh, our Lord God who Sanctifies. Jesus lived His name to show us the way to also live our Father's name in His name. He is the living bread of life that we are to feed our flesh upon more. The Word has become flesh, and the more we feed on the Word, the more He becomes great and we become less in our fleshly desires. The Father has given authority and power to the name of Jesus because Jesus has lived the Father's name and brought glory to Him.

Every day is another new day to set ourselves apart to feed on the living bread so Christ can grow greater and we become less. We are clean because of the Word Jesus has already spoken to us (see John 15:3).

August 22

~ *Put on the armour of God to fight the good fight of faith* ~

> *Put on the full armour of God, so that you can take your stand against the devil's schemes (Ephesians 6:11, NIV).*

One Saturday morning, January 29, 2022, as we took Angelilly to her swimming class we stopped right in front of the building. Tom didn't put the brakes on, so I said, 'You put on the brakes.' As soon as I said that, I heard the Holy Spirit say: When you put 'on something' you apply a force to it. So it is, when you put 'on' the amour of God, as mentioned in Ephesians 6: 10-18, you apply the force in the truth of God's Word upon your life. The car came to a stop when the brake was put on. The devil also comes to a stop in attempts to attack you when you put on the armour of God in your temptations. He sees you in the armour of God and stops getting in your way. You are armed with the sword of the Spirit, the Word of God. The Word of God is the double-edged sword that cuts through.

You see, when we are driving on the road we put on the brakes because we don't want to cause any accidents. If we don't put on the brakes we will get into an accident that will affect both parties involved. When we also do not put on the armour of God, we will most likely cause accidents to ourselves and whosoever flesh and blood the devil has used to attack us, but when we put on the armour of God we will defeat them. No one in their right mind will attack someone who is fully armed. Put on the armour of God.

> *The weapons we fight with are not the weapons of the world. On the contrary, they have divine power to demolish strongholds (2 Corinthians 10:4, NIV).*

Jesus lived our Father's name, Jehovah M'Kaddesh, our Almighty Father who Sanctifies. He is the Word, the Sword of the Spirit who has become flesh. His righteous blood that came out of His flesh has sanctified and purified us to be holy, to be set apart and always armed with the armour of God, ready to fight the good fight of faith which we have already won in Christ.

Every day, remind yourself that you have already won every battle through the finished work of Christ. All you have to do is put on the full armour of God and make sounds of joy and celebration in praising the Father.

August 23

~ Make space to build yourself in Christ by removing anything that is not of Christ's nature ~

And it will be said: 'Build up, build up, prepare the road! Remove the obstacles out of the way of my people.' (Isaiah 57:14, NIV).

On the morning of January 30, 2022, I removed something from the kitchen because it had no use and was just occupying space. This is the what the Holy Spirit taught me: The kingdom of God is like this. You have to get rid of things that are of no use to your life and take up space. When the rich young man wanted to follow Jesus, He told him to go give his riches to the poor and follow Him. His riches would be put to use and given to the poor, as he followed Jesus and Jesus wanted him to remove from him anything that would draw him away from Him.

There are many things in our life that we have but are not using for the kingdom of God. It's not always money. How we use our time and live by our character is also very important—Jesus wants us to use it as we follow Him. The reward we will get from laying down the riches of this world and following Jesus is priceless. No eyes have seen, no ears have heard and no mind has perceived what God has prepared for those who love Him (see 1 Corinthians 2:9).

Jesus came and lived our Father's name, Jehovah M'Kaddesh, our Almighty Father who Sanctifies. Just like how I got rid of things taking up space and of no use to me, Jesus got rid of laws that had put man into slavery to sin and gave us His Spirit to live in us and be free. There is no more law to make us earn righteousness. Jesus has paid the price, and we no longer live but Christ lives in us. We are the righteousness of God in Christ and the holiness of God in the Holy Spirit. Jesus has sanctified us and set us free. There is no law in the fruit of the Holy Spirit.

> *But the fruit of the Spirit is love, joy, peace, forbearance, kindness, goodness, faithfulness, gentleness and self-control. Against such things there is no law (Galatians 5:22-23, NIV).*

Every day is another new day to showcase our exciting new life, knowing that Christ is alive and living in us by producing the fruit of the Spirit for our contacts who need it. We have to remove whatever is not of Christ which is taking up space in us.

August 24

~ Be prepared by keeping yourself holy for the King's return ~

> *Therefore keep watch, because you do not know on what day your Lord will come. But understand this: If the owner of the house had known at what time of night the thief was coming, he would have kept watch and would not have let his house be broken into (Matthew 24:42-43, NIV).*

One beautiful morning, January 31, 2022, I was thinking of how I didn't need to rush around for school stuff for my seven-year-old who was starting year two the next day. I had already prepared myself during the holidays to make sure she had everything needed. This is what the Holy Spirit taught me: The kingdom of God is like this.

Always be prepared, every day, for the day Christ will return and take you in His flesh to reign in His glory. Every moment of being alive is a new blessing to remind us to keep ourselves apart from ungodly things and be holy like our Father in heaven who is holy.

Jesus came and lived our Father's name, Jehovah M'Kaddesh, our Almighty Father who Sanctifies. He prepared His flesh and set it apart to live the Father's name and bring Glory to His name. His resurrecting flesh can now give life and resurrect our life in our flesh to be like Himself. He showed it through the sacrifice of His flesh.

> *Do not be afraid of those who kill the body but cannot kill the soul. Rather, be afraid of the One who can destroy both soul and body in hell (Matthew 10:28, NIV).*

Every new day we are to prepare ourselves to live a godly and holy life with the help of the Holy Spirit. This is so we are not afraid of death or the pains, suffering and increase of evil caused by man, which are the signs of the return of our King. We are well prepared to meet our coming King.

August 25

~ Your mustard seed of faith makes you great in doing big things ~

> *In addition to all this, take up the shield of faith, with which you can extinguish all the flaming arrows of the evil one (Ephesians 6:16, NIV).*

In the early hours of April 4, 2022, I was in my last trimester of pregnancy, so my body was getting bigger and bigger, preparing for the arrival of the newborn baby. This is what I heard the Holy Spirit say: You have a tiny little unborn baby within you, but you are growing so big because the time for you to give birth to a new life is coming soon. This is how the enemy sees you: Even with your small mustard seed of faith, you may think you are small, but the enemy sees you so big and about to give birth to a new life and beginnings. And this is why he attacks you from all directions.

You see, the enemy can see how big we are in Christ with our mustard seed of faith and he will come for us from all directions. As long as we set ourselves aside and renew our mind in the mind of Christ, we will never fall for the arrows of attack from the enemy. We shall mount up like eagles, taking our shield of faith and extinguish all the flaming arrows of the evil one. We will be silencing the devil with the blood of the Lamb—the blood that has sanctified and purified us.

Our people defeated Satan because of the blood of the Lamb and the message of God. They were willing to give up their lives (Revelation 12:11, CEV).

Jesus came and lived our Father's name, Jehovah M'Kaddesh, our Almighty Father who Sanctifies. He cleansed and purified us to set us apart to be holy for His holy purpose, to which we are able to give birth to great beginnings.

August 26

~ Words have power—use it wisely ~

How can a young man keep his way pure? By guarding it according to your word (Psalm 119:9, ESV).

Not only a good dad, but a wise one, said this:

'To think that as a parent, I can choke my child with the words I use on them, is unbearable. And yet, we are the nicest people at work, in public or in church. Upon reflecting on ourselves, I hope that Elizabeth and I have been good, loving and nurturing parents, instructing all our children in the ways of the Lord with love and care. We know these young ones face challenges that we did not experience in our time. Nevertheless, we have put our trust in the one thing that has stood the test of time —the Word of God. The Word has been consistent and sufficient for all times and the fundamental principles laid down by the Creator have not changed, and will not change. They are eternal, they exist independent of time, beyond any culture and certainly beyond any human society. To all you young people—do not depart from the truth of the Word (Bible); it's the only thing that is true.'

Dean Kuri, father of three children and grandfather to three children.
CEO Papua New Guinea Airlines, Accident Investigation Commission.

God's laws are perfect. They protect us, make us wise, and give us joy and light. God's laws are pure, eternal, just (Psalm 19:7-9, TLB).

Jesus came down and lived our loving Father's name, Jehovah M'Kaddesh, our Almighty Father who Sanctifies. He sanctifies and purifies us in His Word. His Word is pure. When we get into the Word, the Word gets into us and starts its work of purification. For the Word to be made pure, it is up to us to renew our mind in the Word. The more we take in the Word, the more it makes us become conscious to remain pure, because the Word of God is alive and active.

Every day, let's live our Father's name and set ourselves apart and away from the lust of the world. It's a new day for us to let the purification of the Word be taken into us and purify us for the day. We must always renew our mind to use the Word of God to build others up.

August 27

~ Set yourself apart for wisdom and truth ~

> *… and they saw the God of Israel. There was under his feet as it were a pavement of sapphire stone, like the very heaven for clearness (Exodus 24:10, ESV).*

The twelve precious stones that the holy city of God was built from are the stones that God would appear on when delivering His messages. Sapphire was the second stone in the foundation of the Holy City (see Revelation 21), and Sapphire represents wisdom.

Sapphire is said to stimulate communication, insight, intuition, divination, inspiration and stillness. A stone of wisdom and truth, it clears away distortions and brings forth spiritual knowledge. This could be one of the reasons why God makes His appearance in the beauty of the precious sapphire stone.

> *And above the expanse over their heads there was the likeness of a throne, in appearance like sapphire; and seated above the likeness of a throne was a likeness with a human appearance (Ezekiel 1:26, ESV).*

We are the holy city of God and are to live our Father's name, Jehovah M'Kaddesh, our Almighty Father who Sanctifies. We are to be made holy like the precious stone sapphire in the holy city of God, and build ourselves up as that Holy City for the Holy Spirit to dwell. Therefore, we need to run after and seek wisdom and set ourselves apart in the truth of wisdom, which is Jesus Christ.

August 28

~ Set your body apart as a living sacrifice to be holy for the Holy Spirit to dwell ~

Since we have these promises, beloved, let us cleanse ourselves from every defilement of body and spirit, bringing holiness to completion in the fear of God (2 Corinthians 7:1, ESV).

A beautiful morning, September 2, 2021, I was lying face-up on the rug and noticed the red hanging decor of shells on the ceiling was catching dust and needed a clean. While I was thinking of how I would need to wash the shells individually, I heard the Holy Spirit say: You see, Jesus too had to wash the feet of His disciples individually. He chose them, then set them apart individually and washed them. Even to the point where He was going to be betrayed and death was approaching, He was there for His chosen ones. In Jesus' name we are to live the Father's name, Jehovah M'Kaddesh, our Almighty Father who Sanctifies. We are to set our self apart and remain clean in the Word of Jesus every day. Jesus did it once and for all for us to do it every day, because every day is a new day to continue remaining new and clean in Jesus.

My prayer is not that you take them out of the world but that you protect them from the evil one. They are not of the world, even as I am not of it. Sanctify them by the truth; your word is truth. As you sent me into the world, I have sent them into the world. For them I sanctify myself, that they too may be truly sanctified (John 17:15-19, NIV).

Just like how I was thinking of washing those hanging shells individually, every individual part of our body has a role in the body of Christ and must be set apart for its holy purpose. Our body is the temple of the Holy Spirit and has to be kept holy.

Our Father is Holy and we are called to live His name, Jehovah M'Kaddesh, and so everything we do for Him has to be holy to bring glory to His name.

August 29

~ Every day is a holy day to remain in the righteousness of Christ and the Holiness of the Father in the Holy Spirit ~

God made him who had no sin to be sin for us, so that in him we might become the righteousness of God (2 Corinthians 5:21, NIV).

I have some cleaning cloths that I keep for cleaning around the house. When I want to clean dirty spots I normally use those cloths, so they are worn out and old. April 3, 2021 was a beautiful Saturday morning, Easter Saturday. I was trying to clean up a dirty spot in the kitchen and decided to use a dirty cloth instead of the new clean ones I had, because eventually it would be dirty anyway. This is what the Holy Spirit taught me with an Easter message: You see, God had to make Jesus also a sinner and die to clean you from sin and death. He became a sinner for you. Just like how you are trying to use a cloth which has already been used for cleaning dirt, our Loving Father had to make His sinless Son become sin just so we could be made right.

A good dad knows how dirty and sinful he is, but because of the loving Father who wants to give him hope and future, a way was made for him. Jesus Christ the Holy One came into the world and became a sinner and did away with sin. Even though He was tempted, He never sinned, but set Himself apart from sin and lived a life of holiness.

> *And such were some of you. But you were washed, you were sanctified, you were justified in the name of the Lord Jesus Christ and by the Spirit of our God (1 Corinthians 6:11, ESV).*

Jehovah M'Kaddesh, our Lord God, our Sanctifier is our Father's name, and Jesus lived that name by keeping and setting Himself apart to remain holy and do His Father's will. Jesus has now given us the Holy Spirit through His resurrection after death to sanctify us to remain in His holiness.

Every day, see it as a holy day for the Lord and walk in the holiness of the Holy Spirit. Set yourself aside to be in the righteousness of Christ in the Holy Spirit so you can be the holiness of God in Christ.

August 30

~ Set yourself aside to remain and be maintained in the Word ~

Never give up praying. And when you pray, keep alert and be thankful (Colossians 4:2, CEV).

January 10, 2021, a friend of mine bought a beautiful sea-view home. She invited me over to her house and showed me around. I was there to share her moment of happiness. The garden, everything, was well maintained and beautiful. She showed me around and said everything was already fixed and done. So I said, 'Oh, you don't really need to do anything. You just have to maintain what you bought.' This is what I heard the Holy Spirit say: Jesus bought you with His blood for you to house His Spirit. You also don't need to do anything. You just have to maintain it by having a solid daily relationship with Him and nurture your life with Word and prayer. When we nurture our life in Word and prayer we are setting ourselves aside to be in the will of God and accomplish the purpose we were designed for.

> *Jesus said to the people who believed in him, 'You are truly my disciples if you remain faithful to my teachings.' (John 8:31, NLT).*

Jesus lived our Father's name, Jehovah M'Kaddesh, our Almighty Father who Sanctifies. Even though He was the Word Himself, God in the form of flesh, He maintained His God-like character and connection to our Father in heaven while living on Earth. If God in Word and flesh who walked on earth can remain in prayer, how much more do we need to spend time in our prayer life to connect to our Father in heaven?

Every day is another day of opportunity to live our Father's name, Jehovah M'Kaddesh, and set ourselves aside to remain and be maintained in Word and prayer so we can connect to our Father in heaven to be used for His glory. Just like how we set the time to wake us up on time, we also need to set our lives apart from the lifestyle of the world when we wake up every morning.

August 31

~ Set yourself aside from any evil that is around ~

> *Do not be misled: Bad company corrupts good character (1 Corinthians 15:33, NIV).*

One winter's night, August 31, 2021, I wanted to use some beans I had in the fridge before they went completely off. There were already some which have gone off, so I started choosing the good ones and separating them from the rotten and bad ones. This is what I heard the Holy Spirit say: You see, this is what happens when bad company corrupts good habits. The good habits you have can become rotten and bad when you hang out with toxic people. In this world, where you are surrounded by evil, you have to set your life apart from that and away from the evil that causes worries, fears or guilt.

Just like how I was choosing only the good beans, our good loving Father also chose and separated us for His own good work He planned, even before we were born, as God knew we were going to be born and He has great plans for us to be change makers.

> *For God saved us and called us to live a holy life. He did this, not because we deserved it, but because that was his plan from before the beginning of time—to show us his grace through Christ Jesus (2 Timothy 1:9, NLT).*

Jesus lived our Father's name, Jehovah M'Kaddesh, our Almighty Father who Sanctifies. In Him we are set apart and chosen to do the good work in Him that He did while He was here on earth. Every day is created by our holy Father and is holy for us to set it apart and live a holy life in the Holy Spirit by producing His fruit of love.

SEPTEMBER

**Jehovah Shammah! I AM There for you!
Your ever-present help!**

OUR LORD GOD WHO IS THERE!

~ Point out Jesus to someone who couldn't see Him there ~

And even if our gospel is veiled, it is veiled only to those who are perishing. In their case, the god of this world has blinded the minds of the unbelievers to keep them from seeing the light of the gospel of the glory of Christ, who is the image of God (2 Corinthians 4:3-4, ESV).

December 8, 2021, I was trying to show Blessed where his dad was and was pointing it out for him. The Holy Spirit taught me this: Jesus came down on earth to open our eyes to see who the Father is through Him. No one has ever seen the Father, except the Son. You see, Blessed's dad was there, but he couldn't see him until I showed him. Our heavenly Father is Jehovah Shammah, 'the Lord is there'. Jesus came to open our eyes to show us that our Father is there and will always be there for us. And because He lived the Father's name, He is the only way to the Father.

A good dad is a good role model to his children. He will always be there to show them his goodness of being that loving dad. For him to do it right, he absorbs the good news of his heavenly Father's Word and actions it, because children see and follow examples.

For God, who said, 'Let light shine out of darkness,' has shone in our hearts to give the light of the knowledge of the glory of God in the face of Jesus Christ (2 Corinthians 4:6, ESV).

Our heavenly Father is there for us through Jesus Christ. Jesus came and lived the name Jehovah Shammah, our Lord God is there.

Every day, and each day of the month of September, live the Father's name, Jehovah Shammah, our Almighty Father who is there, and be there for someone you know who is in need. Reach out in prayer or encourage them in the Word of God. Your time in doing that will be measured back to you in one hundredfold and you will live to a good old age.

September 1

~ The peace of God is there for us through the Holy Spirit within us ~

When you pass through the waters, I will be with you; and when you pass through the rivers, they will not sweep over you. When you walk through the fire, you will not be burned; the flames will not set you ablaze (Isaiah 43:2, NIV).

March 23, 2021, I was looking into the bathroom mirror. The Holy Spirit reminded me of a hotel I stayed at during my visit to London in 2019. A hotel in the city, their mirror was designed in a way that you could have a really hot shower and get the whole place clouded with hot air, but it didn't affect the clear view of the mirror. It was designed in a way that the heat from the light was directed to it so when you came out of a hot shower you could still see yourself clearly in the mirror.

This is what I heard the Holy Spirit say: You see, after you go through the heating process, you will step out clean and clear so you can see the original image and design of who you really are. It is in the heating moments of your life that you find Christ in there. Jesus Christ is the light of the heat for you so you can see yourself becoming like Him in the fire, just like how the heat of that light in the bathroom caused the mirror to still give you a clear view of yourself. When Daniel and his friends were in the fire, Jesus was there with them.

> *'Look!' he answered, 'I see four men loose, walking in the midst of the fire; and they are not hurt, and the form of the fourth is like the Son of God.' (Daniel 3:25 NKJV).*

All the time Jesus is with you there, but because you are having a good time you do not see a clear picture of Him. Only when you walk through fire and start to think you will burn, then you will truly see Him.

A good dad will always be there for his household when they go through the burns. He will not abandon them and vacate. He will stay with his family and see that no one is hurt. In order for him to be the greater fighter in the fire, he fights the good fight of faith by staying connected to the Word of God. He knows his loving Father is Jehovah Shammah, our Lord God who is there.

Jesus lived that name and was here for us on earth. He left peace to be with us before He went back to the Father. Jesus is right there for us anytime, everywhere and all the time through the Holy Spirit inside of us. The peace of God from Christ is there for us in the Spirit of God. He is Jehovah Shammah. Let the peace of Christ reign in our every new day that we step into.

September 2

> *~ God's presence is there for us every day to enjoy the joy and peace of the moment ~*

> *The thief comes only to steal and kill and destroy. I came that they may have life and have it abundantly (John 10:10, ESV).*

March 25, 2021, I remember receiving advertising messages from my phone, especially from travel sales agents wanting to sell their products so they could have money in the PRESENT, but the deal was for you to book and travel sometime in the FUTURE. Sometimes, I think *am I going to trust that travel agent to risk my money into booking those holiday deals?* And so I try to look to the PAST records of the pros and cons by reading other people's reviews. This is what the Holy Spirit taught me: The enemy is interested in robbing you of your PRESENT joy and peace, like the travel agent who wants your money now for their financial growth.

Neither the travel agent nor I know what the future holds because of the way the world is heading, with borders opening and closing due to the COVID-19 pandemic. The enemy knows that when he robs your present joy and peace you have no hope and future. He wants to destroy God's plan of giving you that hope and future, which he normally does by reminding you of all the negativity of your past, so you will accept his offer of what he will do for you in your present life. And that is to rob your moment of peace.

A good dad is present every day in the presence of his loving Father in heaven, so the enemy can't even steal his present joy and peace. Every day he rises and declares, 'This is the day the Lord has made. I will rejoice and be glad in it.' He knows His Father's name, Jehovah Shammah, our Lord God who is there. He is ever-present all the time with him.

Because our Father loves us so much, He made a way for Jesus to come live His name on earth. The Father was there for us through Jesus. Jesus lived the Father's name, Jehovah Shammah, and made a way that the Father can come and live with us through what Jesus has done. Jesus died and gave up His Spirit to the Father. The Father rose Jesus up by the power of the Holy Spirit. Jesus had to go back to the Father so the Father's Spirit could come and live in us.

Before Jesus returned to the Father, He said, 'I will be with you to the end. He is now ever-present with us through the Holy Spirit.'

> *You will show me the way of life, granting me the joy of your presence and the pleasures of living with you forever (Psalm 16:11, NLT).*

Our Father in heaven creates each new day. His presence and life is there in that day for us to rejoice and be glad in it. He is Jehovah Shammah.

September 3

~ The beauty of life is always there for us to enjoy in the Holy Spirit ~

> *There is a time for everything. God made every thing beautiful in its time (Ecclesiastes 3;1, 11).*

This is the prayer of a good dad:

> *Everything you do is beautiful, flowing from your goodness; teach me the power of your wonderful words! (Psalm 119: 68 TPT).*

On the morning of September 23, 2021, Angelilly asked me for some good flowers we had for home decoration in the house. She wanted to use them to do some craft work. I told her she could instead go out of the house and collect some of the nice fresh flowers that had just fallen. Their beauty was still there because they had just fallen. This is what the Holy Spirit taught me: So is your life. Life is beautiful. Whether it's broken and fallen like the flower, the beauty of life is still there.

> *The one who does what is sinful is of the devil, because the devil has been sinning from the beginning. The reason the Son of God appeared was to destroy the devil's work (1 John 3:8, NIV).*

Your loving Father in heaven has wonderfully and fearfully created you. He has made everything in its time. There is a time for everything under the sun: A time to be broken and fallen and a time to mend and rise up. His name is Jehovah Shammah, our Almighty Father who is there. When we are broken and fallen and feel abandoned, He is there, through the Holy Spirit within us. Like that flower fallen off yet still beautiful, so is our life. Though we have been broken or fallen away from the presence of God, we are still beautiful and of great value in our Father's house.

This is why the enemy wants to steal us by making us fall away from our Father. Then he will want to kill us, because he knows once he kills us he has destroyed us (see John 10:10). Our Almighty Father, Jehovah Shammah, is there and will always be there for us, and that is His name. He is there with us forever because Jesus has lived His name. Jesus was here on earth for us and destroyed the work of the devil, which is death.

He has given us the eternal life of the Holy Spirit, who is now in us all the time. When we feel like we have fallen away from the path of righteousness, we can always get back onto the right path and walk in the fruit of righteousness.

Every day, whatever we do, we have to thank our Almighty Father, Jehovah Shammah, and live His name to be there and connected to the Holy Spirit who is there for us. We have to thank Jesus for what He has done so we can enjoy the eternal life in the Holy Spirit who lives in us.

September 4

~ Be there to live your purposes each day ~

Before I formed you in the womb I knew you, and before you were born I consecrated you; I appointed you a prophet to the nations (Jeremiah 1:5, ESV).

September 4, 2021, I was using one of the soaps that was given to me. I don't really like that soap because it has no sweet scent, however, I thought *I am not going to just leave it there, I still have to make use of it.* In that way, I felt better after using the soap, knowing it had served its purpose well.

This is what the Holy Spirit taught me: Many of us have a purpose to be used by God, but we just don't allow God to use us. We think that we don't have gifts, talents or money, so what good use are we going to be? These thoughts are lies from the devil to keep us where we are and not living our purpose in life. If you think you will serve God and help people when you have lots of money, and right now you can't do anything but wait and pray for God to give you some money first—then what you hear in your thoughts are the devil's lies.

You see, you have to do something while waiting to show that you are able to be faithful to little things, because when you are faithful to the little you have, God will bless you with bigger things to manage.

Jehovah Shammah is His name, our Almighty Father who is there. He is always there for us and always has been, even before we were born. He has a purpose and a future for us for His good works.

> *... great are your purposes and mighty are your deeds. Your eyes are open to the ways of all mankind; you reward each*

person according to their conduct and as their deeds deserve
(Jeremiah 32:19, NIV).

Every day, our Father is there for us to live His name, Jehovah Shammah, for that day. We have to wake up, dress up and live our Father's name, and be there for whatever purposes we are designed and created for.

September 5

~ God is right there in meeting our needs when we pray ~

Then he returned to his disciples and found them sleeping. 'Couldn't you men keep watch with me for one hour?' he asked Peter. 'Watch and pray so that you will not fall into temptation. The spirit is willing, but the flesh is weak.'
(Matthew 26:40-41, NIV).

In October 2015, I remember travelling on the freeway at a speed of 110km/h. As usual, the big trucks were on the left. As we were driving, the Holy Spirit prompted me to pray, to just pray for our travelling protection. This is something I would normally do already, however, at that very hour the Lord wanted me to pray. So I prayed. As soon as I said amen, a few minutes later, Tom took the inside lane—and a huge 20-foot container truck, which was on the left outside lane, came into the inside lane at the same time! We were right into its back, but tell you what—that prayer the Holy Spirit prompted me to pray in that hour saved us. I could literally *see* we had been held a little bit back, with smoke coming from the tyres.

A good dad watches over his loved ones every day in his household and makes sure everyone's wellbeing is taken care of. He uses preventive measures in his house to prevent them from getting into trouble. He stays connected to the Holy Spirit in God's Word, and he can sense in his spirit if trouble will occur. He is always there for his house in prayers. God doesn't slumber; He watches over our life. A good dad knows his loving Father, Jehovah Shammah, our Lord God, is there. Every time we pray, our Father is there to destroy anything the enemy can use as an opportunity to destroy us.

> *He will not let your foot slip—he who watches over you will not slumber (Psalm 121:3, NIV).*

Jesus has lived our Father's name, Jehovah Shammah. He is now always there for us, through the Holy Spirit inside of us. He knows our every move and will warn us should we face any troubles coming up in the next hour. He will warn you to quickly pray to destroy the work of the dark forces.

This is what Jesus was doing in the garden of Gethsemane. In the coming hour of His death, He was praying and not sleeping, He even told His disciples who were with Him to pray as well. It was His prayer that gave Him the strength to endure the walk to the cross (see Matthew 26:42-46).

> *The reason the Son of God appeared was to destroy the devil's work (1 John 3:8. NIV).*

Every day, pray and pray to keep God working in you. God will work in you when you pray.

September 6

~ Be there for Jesus to win souls ~

> *I tell you that in the same way there will be more rejoicing in heaven over one sinner who repents than*

> *over ninety-nine righteous persons who do not need*
> *to repent (Luke 15:7, NIV).*

September 6, 2021, I was watching on television news how a family celebrated in victory after finding their three-year-old boy who'd been lost. They were overjoyed because they'd found him alive after four days. The celebration and dancing I saw was overflowing. This is what the Holy Spirit taught me: This is what happens in heaven when one soul is found alive for Jesus to save. And it also explains why there is sorrow when one soul dies without receiving Jesus. That soul is lost for eternity.

Our loving Father's name is Jehovah Shammah, our Almighty Father who is there. Any dad can be around for their children, but a good dad is always faithful and makes sacrifices to be there for his children. Jehovah Shammah is our Almighty Father's name and He sacrificed His Son by being there for us in the flesh of His Son. Because He is the Word, He made the Word become flesh. The sacrifice Jesus made was to be there for us all the time, everywhere, anywhere, by giving up His life for us so we can have the Holy Spirit, who will always be there for us. He lives in us and He produces the fruit of faithfulness to remain faithful by being there for us all the time. Even death will not separate us from His Love, and we cannot even be separated from the Holy Spirit who is LOVE (see Romans 8:38-39).

> *Who, though he was in the form of God, did not count equality with God a thing to be grasped, but emptied himself, by, taking the form of a servant, being born in the likeness of men. And being found in human form, he humbled himself by becoming obedient to the point of death, even death on a cross (Philippians 2:6-8, ESV).*

Every day is another day of great opportunity to live our Father's name, Jehovah Shammah, and be there for lost souls to bring them to heaven so there can be celebration.

September 7

~ Connect with God every day by being always there in Word and in prayer ~

The Lord God is my strength; he will give me the speed of a deer and bring me safely over the mountains (Habakkuk 3:19, TLB).

The Lord wants to remind you that it is in your battles and storms that He wants to build His new strength within you. So if your health is failing, you come out in your strength that will make your flesh stronger and youthful. Continue practising patience, kindness and goodness in your battlefields.

When you buy a product from a manufacturer, under the warranty you have the right to take it back to them to have it fixed if it is not working in the way it was designed for its purpose. So it is with us. We are designed by our Creator to carry out His purpose He has for us. The battles and storms are part of our life so we can go back to Him to work on us, putting in new strength so we can continue to live and reach new levels in our lives. Appreciate and be grateful for storms, because they come to bring you to a new level of your potential. You are growing from glory to glory for the Father's glory, and from strength to strength from His strength.

A good dad knows His Father in heaven is always there for Him. He is Jehovah Shammah, our Almighty Father who is there. Before he goes into his storms, His Father is there. All he does is remain in Word and prayer so he can rest in peace as he travels through his storms.

> *Now may the Lord of peace himself give you peace*
> *at all times in every way. The Lord be with you all*
> *(2 Thessalonians 3:16, ESV).*

Jesus lived our Father's name. He was always there for everyone who needed him, even when He was interrupted. He is now forever with us through the Holy Spirit who lives in us. Our Father in heaven, Jehovah Shammah, is there for us in flesh through Jesus and is there for us in Spirit through the Holy Spirit.

Whenever you go through the storms, let your flesh remain in the Word who has become flesh and pray in your spirit in the Holy Spirit at all times.

September 8

~ We carry the light of the Father to be there,
where darkness is ~

> *The light shines in the darkness, and the darkness has not*
> *overcome it (John 1:5, ESV).*

September 8, 2021, I was with Blessed, watching the pelicans at the park. One of the pelicans flew right up and went to the light post and sat there. I was explaining to Blessed that it was a light post and the light comes on in the night, when it is dark.

While I was teaching Blessed, this is what the Holy Spirit taught me: We are also the power post light of Jesus and our light is meant to shine in the dark. The dark moments of our life that we go through are for us to put that light on. We serve a purpose, and our purpose is to do that, this is why we face many dark days in our life. As soon as one dark moment ends another comes around. That is perfectly fine and normal, because we need to continue to keep the light of Jesus from His Word shining out for others to see. To overcome the dark moments of our life, we have to put the light of the Word into that situation, because darkness cannot overcome the power of light.

In the same way, let your light shine before others, so that they may see your good works and give glory to your Father who is in heaven (Matthew 5:16, ESV).

Our loving Father's name is Jehovah Shammah, our Almighty Father who is there. He is there in our darkest moments, but because we are absorbed in our darkest hour, we cannot see Him well, so we think we are lost and drowning with more troubles and problems. He is ever-present when we put on the light from the Word who is Jesus. We see the grace, love, strength and compassion of the Father with us in the dark moments. And because the light is on, others will also see the light and give glory to our Father in heaven.

Jesus lived our Father's name, Jehovah Shammah, and is always there, ever-present in our flesh through the Holy Spirit who lives within us. We are also to live our Father's name, Jehovah Shammah, and be always there to put on the light of Jesus everywhere. But most of all, it is in our dark hours that we must shine out that light, because not only our light shines brighter and very well to see, but where the light is, darkness cannot exist.

September 9

~ Produce the fruit of love right away and do not delay ~

Above all, love each other deeply, because love covers over a multitude of sins (1 Peter 4:8, NIV).

On the night of September 9, 2021, I was trying to make fresh fruit. I prepared and cut the fruits, but after doing other things around the house I felt so tired that I went off to sleep. The next morning, I woke up to find the prepared fruits from the previous night were not looking fresh. I thought, *I have to start right away and make the fresh juice, because the more it stays out like this, the more it will dry up.*

This is when the Holy Spirit started teaching and pointing out to me things of the kingdom of God: Our life is like this when we don't remain in the Holy Spirit who produces the fruit of love. When we remain in Jesus, we remain in the Holy Spirit and He produces His fruit which is new and fresh. When someone hurts us, or causes evil to us, let's give them the fresh love of God that the Holy Spirit produces within us right away, without delay. We must think about forgiving them and pray right away for the Holy Spirit to help us in producing the love towards them. I didn't attend to my fruit right away and it was not fresh, and so it is with us. When we don't forgive right away, resentment can build up in our life and make our life wither away.

Jesus lived our Father's name, Jehovah Shammah, our Almighty Father who is there. He showed us how to produce the fruit of love right away when He was in pain and dying on the cross. He looked with compassion to the world that crucified Him, and before He died, with His last breath He blessed the world with forgiveness. Jesus wasn't thinking about whether to forgive the world for crucifying Him, rather He prayed right away and forgave them. The Holy Spirit is there for us all the time for us to produce His fruit of love right away and not to procrastinate.

We love because he first loved us (1 John 4:19, ESV).

You see, just like how I cut the fresh fruit and never used it, and it was starting to wear out, we too must always use the fruit of the Spirit right there where it is needed and not put it aside to do it later. When persecution and tribulations come upon us we have to live our Father's name, Jehovah Shammah, and be there to approach it with love. Love conquers everything.

September 10

~ The love of the Father is there to help us all the time through His Spirit who is our helper ~

Therefore, as God's chosen people, holy and dearly loved, clothe yourselves with compassion, kindness, humility, gentleness and patience (Colossians 3:12, NIV).

One beautiful evening, September 9, 2021, Tom was getting our two-year-old into his car seat. Like every toddler, he took so long to go into his seat. He was busy trying to get whatever was around him. I was seated in the front of the car and heard his dad speaking so gently to him to put him into his seat. I thought to myself, *you can't move a toddler that quickly if you are so patient and talking so gently to him. Just carry him and put him in his seat, or talk to him in a way that he will do it quickly.*

As I prepared to tell Tom to just tell him to get into his car seat, and be quick, the Holy Spirit opened my eyes to see things differently. He spoke into my heart: The dad being gentle to him is not about your toddler, it's about himself. He has to be gentle with things. He doesn't want to stress over little things like this. How you react to a situation is not about that situation, but who you are. You can be so rebellious, but God's love is still waiting to receive you and forgive you. It's not about you but about God, and He is love and He is committed to loving you. The way you do things will never change the way God is with Himself.

> *... if we are faithless, he remains faithful, for he cannot disown himself (2 Timothy 2:13, NIV).*

Jehovah Shammah, our Almighty Father who is there, is the same yesterday, today and forever. He is always there for us. No situations or circumstances in our life will stop Him being there for us when we need His help. It is only our sin that keeps Him away from us (see Isaiah 59:1-2). This is why Jesus had to come and take away sin from us so our Father will always be there for us.

Jesus lived our Father's name, Jehovah Shammah. He was there for us to pay the price of our punishment so we could be set free. He gave us the Helper, Holy Spirit, to be there and help us always.

September 11

~ Always be there for someone by giving life to them ~

If you remain in me and my words remain in you, ask whatever you wish, and it will be done for you (John 15:7, NIV).

One evening, September 11, 2021, I was trying to make noodle soup for my kids, and was trying to put the noodles and spring onions into the pot. I grow fresh spring onions from my little garden, but decided to use the ones a friend had given me a day earlier. They were not as fresh as from the garden, where I was going to dig them out of the soil. This is what the Holy Spirit taught me: When we abide in the Word, we also produce the fresh fruit of the Spirit. When someone is wearing out our patience, we have to reach within and produce that fresh patience. When someone is unkind to us, we have to reach within to produce that fresh kindness. It's the freshness and newness in something that makes the receiver feel so renewed.

Jesus lived our Father's name, Jehovah Shammah, our Almighty Father who is there, and became the Word who has become flesh (see John 1:14). He now asks us to abide in Him, in His Word, so we can be right where He is. He is at the right-hand side of the Father at this very moment. He has given us the Holy Spirit who brings LIFE and makes the Word, who is Jesus alive in us. The Holy Spirit will never leave nor forsake us. He is right there in us and will always be there for us. He is our helper, teacher, comforter, sustainer, healer and everything the Father is, because He is the Spirit of the Father.

Just like how the spring onion remains fresh in the soil it is planted in, we too remain fresh when we abide in Jesus because our Father is the gardener and He will make us flourish with care and love.

But new wine must be put into fresh wineskins
(Luke 5:38, ESV).

Every day is another day to be always there for someone and live our Father's name, Jehovah Shammah. Just being there for them and talking with them brings life into their lives.

September 12

~ Our Father is there to meet our little needs for the moment ~

My God will use his glorious riches to give you everything you need. He will do this through Christ Jesus (Philippians 4:19, ERV).

Earlier on during the week of January 18, 2021, God was speaking to me about not worrying about anything as He will always be there for me with what I need in my time of need. I was thinking about what to take for the morning tea I was rushing to. I checked the fridge and grabbed the rock melon fruit (it was the only fruit available). This is what the Holy Spirit reminded me: You see, that is why God says not to worry about anything, as there will always be something in that time of your need. Fast forward some hours of hearing this from the Lord: I took scissors into the car to use, but didn't need to use it. It was then that the kids needed the scissors to cut something, and I realised that we needed the scissors.

I want to remind us again that whatever we need will always be there when we connect to our Father in heaven. His name is Jehovah Shammah, and He will always be there for our need, even before that needs arises. You see, the scissors were already there, before the need of them arose, and that is what our Father does. These may be small things I have encountered, but they were teaching me a lesson of how God is there in meeting our needs. The ants are the smallest animal, but God asks us to learn a lesson from them. He knows what we will need and He is already there meeting it, we just have to step into it.

> *So don't be anxious about tomorrow. God will take care of your tomorrow too. Live one day at a time (Matthew 6:34, TLB).*

A good dad is always there meeting his children's needs. He takes responsibility as a father. To make sure that his responsibility is reliable to his children, his relationship with His Father in heaven is well established through his time in Word and prayer.

Every day when we wake up, remember that if our Father wants us to see this day, He will always be there to see that our needs for the day are met. He is Jehovah Shammah. It may be the little things He meets, but it is what we need for the moment.

September 13

~ Your Father is there for you, to provide and heal you in every way ~

It is the Lord who goes before you. He will be with you; he will not leave you or forsake you. Do not fear or be dismayed (Deuteronomy 31:8, ESV).

Jehovah Shammah, our Lord God who is there. He is already there to save, rescue and protect us, even before we are there. He is there because we live, move and have our being in Him, and He knows even before we do what will be in that place, at that particular time.

Hear this godly mumma share on how our loving Father in heaven approached her with His name, Jehovah Shammah, our Almighty Father who is there.

****

I have three daughters and two sons. We were attending the wedding of one of my beautiful daughter's in Brisbane, Australia. It's truly amazing how God helps us when we are in desperate need.

One of my sons, Junior Willie, is allergic to prawns. We were all eating prawns around the table that day. Fifteen minutes after eating the prawns, we all decided to go for shopping at Westfield Shopping Center. Instead of going there, we mistakenly went to another smaller shopping center. As soon as we entered, Junior began having an allergic reaction to the prawn he ate, with shortness of breath, and itchiness in his throat and neck. He was swelling and was about to stop breathing. Great panic gripped us all as we didn't know what to do. Then we realised there was a medical clinic right in front of us. We raced Junior into the medical clinic and he was quickly rushed upstairs, as any moment he could stop breathing from the condition he was in.

You see, Jehovah Shammah, our Lord God who is there is His name, was already there for us, even before we walked through that storm on that day. We arrived at a shopping center we hadn't planned to go to, but it was all the Lord's doing as He knew ahead what was to come, and He was there already for us.

> *We can make our plans, but the Lord determines our steps (Proverbs 16:9, NLT).*

Our Father was not only there for us, but He also provided for us. When God shows up as Jehovah Shammah, He also shows us, He is Jehovah Jireh. He will always provide whenever He is there for us. Not only was Junior well and fine, our Father, Jehovah Rophe, our Almighty Father who is our Healer, healed him, and the spirit of death left instantly, but we were never charged with any ambulance fee or hospital bills because our Father is Jehovah Jireh, our Almighty Father who provides. He was there for us (Jehovah Shammah) and He healed Junior instantly (Jehovah Rophe). We are grateful for the medical staff involved also, because in everything we saw the mighty invisible hand of the Father working through them to bring healing, delivery and restoration.

~ Elizabeth Edo ~

****

Jesus lived our Father's name, Jehovah Shammah, our Almighty Father who is there. He was there for the woman at the well before she arrived there (see John 4 for full story). Jesus delivered and set her free from the unsatisfying lifestyle she was living. She was so thirsty for a faithful, loving relationship that she went from relationship to relationship with five different men. Jesus provided her the living water and healed her of her thirst for a relationship.

> *Jesus answered, "Everyone who drinks this water will be thirsty again, but whoever drinks the water I give them will never thirst. Indeed, the water I give them will become in them a spring of water welling up to eternal life."*
> *(John 4:13-14, NIV).*

Every day, our Father's love is there for us to provide and heal us in every area of our life. When God shows up as Jehovah Shammah, He also provides what we need right where He is there for us. He is there with all our providence to heal, restore, save and deliver us from any situations.

September 14

~ A child will always believe the words of his father to him ~

> *Don't be afraid, for I am with you. Don't be discouraged, for I am your God. I will strengthen you and help you. I will hold you up with my victorious right hand*
> *(Isaiah 41:10, NLT).*

In the country of Armenia, in 1988, Samuel and Danielle sent their young son, Armand, off to school. Samuel squatted before his son and looked him in the eye. 'Have a good day at school, and remember, no matter what, I'll always be there for you.' They hugged and the boy ran off to school.

Hours later, a powerful earthquake rocked the area. In the midst of the pandemonium, Samuel and Danielle tried to discover what happened to their son but couldn't get any information. The radio announced that there were thousands of casualties. Samuel then grabbed his coat and headed for the schoolyard. When he reached the area, what he saw brought tears to his eyes. Armand's school was a pile of debris. Other parents were standing around crying.

Samuel found the place where Armand's classroom used to be and began pulling a broken beam off the pile of rubble. He then grabbed a rock and put it to the side, and then grabbed another one.

One of the parents looking on asked, 'What are you doing?'

'Digging for my son,' Samuel answered.

The man then said, 'You're just going to make things worse! The building is unstable,' and tried to pull Samuel away from his work.

Samuel just kept working. As time wore on, one by one, the other parents left. Then a worker tried to pull Samuel away from the rubble. Samuel looked at him and said, 'Won't you help me?' The worker left and Samuel kept digging.

All through the night and into the next day, Samuel continued digging. He dug for thirty-six hours. Parents placed flowers and pictures of their children on the ruins. But, Samuel just kept working. He picked up a beam and pushed it out of the way, when he heard a faint cry.

'Help! Help!' Samuel listened, but didn't hear anything again. Then he heard a muffled voice, 'Papa?'

Samuel began to dig furiously. Finally he could see his son.

'Come on out, son!' he said with relief.

'No,' Armand said. 'Let the other kids come out first because I know you'll get me.'

Child after child emerged, until finally, little Armand appeared. Samuel took him in his arms and Armand said, 'I told the other kids not to worry because you told me that you'd always be there for me!'

Fourteen children were saved that day because one father was there for his child.

Author Unknown

This is a good father who was there for his child. A man of faith who was faithful and patient, his good character was shown through his child who let other kids out first. This child put the interest of others over his own.

Jehovah Shammah, our Almighty Father who is there, is the name of our heavenly Father. Jesus lived our Father's name, Jehovah Shammah. He promised that He will never leave us nor forsake us, and He will always be there for us. He came to us in the Word who has become flesh and is always there for us in the Word who is Spirit and life through the Holy Spirit (see John 6:63).

Every new day, our Father shows us that He is there for us by calling us to wake up. Wake up each day and know that Jehovah Shammah, our loving Father, is there for us in that new day to give Him glory.

September 15

~ Our heavenly Father is always there to strengthen us in the Holy Spirit ~

No temptation has overtaken you except what is common to mankind. And God is faithful, he will not let you be tempted beyond what you can bear. But when you are tempted, he will also provide a way out so that you can endure it (1 Corinthians 10:13, NIV).

February 28, 2022, I was doing the dishes. It is in the kitchen mostly where I hear the Holy Spirit, teaching me in my everyday chores. I was washing the lid of a pot. Stained with a bit of grease, I scrubbed it, but it didn't come out completely clean. But when I applied pressure on it and scrubbed, it came out easily, leaving the lid of the pot sparkling clean. This is what the Holy Spirit taught me: The kingdom of God is like this. God will allow and put some sort of pressure upon you as you go through the test of your faith. This is so you can put away all the filth of your old life and come out clean. With the pressure you are put through, you are also provided with the strength to be capable of making it through. Just like how I applied pressure and strength to get the lid of the pot to a clean state, so it is with us. When you go through the pressure of life, God will provide you the strength to make it through and He will also allow only what you are capable of handling.

So do not fear, for I am with you; do not be dismayed, for I am your God. I will strengthen you and help you; I will uphold you with my righteous right hand (Isaiah 41:10, NIV).

Our Father's name is Jehovah Shammah, our Almighty Father who is there. Jesus came and lived His name and promises us that He will never leave us nor forsake us. For Jesus to never leave us, He has to go back to the Father so they can send forth the Holy Spirit who has the power to live within us, in everyone, everywhere, all the time and at the same time. Whenever the pressure of life's concerns challenge us, we must always bring all our concerns to Jesus and rest in the Holy Spirit who is always there within us.

Every day, our loving Father in heaven gives us a new life to remind us that He is there for us. He is Jehovah Shammah.

September 16

~ We have a reason to celebrate the joy of freedom in Christ every day ~

So Christ has made us free. Now make sure that you stay free, and don't get all tied up again in the chains of slavery to Jewish laws and ceremonies (Galatians 5:1, TLB).

September 16, 2021, as I was celebrating the 46th anniversary of independence of my country, Papua New Guinea, I asked the Lord to lay a message in my heart. This is what the Holy Spirit laid in my heart: You are celebrating the date of the day your country became independent and was set free from the rule of another country. Jesus also came down to set you free from the rebellious life that has control over you. He gave you freedom to be set free from being the slave of sin by giving His life of righteousness. This explained how our old life has laws that govern us to make us righteous or some rituals to go through to cleanse our sin. But Jesus has set us free, once and for all, and cleansed us from all unrighteousness. We just have to receive this by faith and live in His righteousness. We have the free will to choose goodness to conquer evil around us, or do nothing and let evil continue around us.

This Word from Romans 7:15-25 (CEV) explains everything the way we are:

> *In fact, I don't understand why I act the way I do. I don't do what I know is right. I do the things I hate. Although I don't do what I know is right, I agree that the Law is good. So I am not the one doing these evil things. The sin that lives in me is what does them. I know that my selfish desires won't let me do anything that is good. Even when I want to do right, I cannot. Instead of doing what I know is right, I do wrong. And so, if I don't do what I know is right, I am no longer the one doing these evil things. The sin that lives in me is what does them.*
>
> *The Law has shown me that something in me keeps me from doing what I know is right. With my whole heart I agree with the Law of God. But in every part of me I discover something fighting against my mind, and it makes me a prisoner of sin that controls everything I do. What a miserable person I am. Who will rescue me from this body that is doomed to die? Thank God! Jesus Christ will rescue me. So with my mind I serve the Law of God, although my selfish desires make me serve the law of sin.*

The sin living in me will always want to do what it wants to do. And if I do it, then the Law is at work. Jesus came and lived our Father's name, Jehovah Shammah, our Loving Father who is there. Jesus is there for us right now in the Holy Spirit who lives in us, and every day we have a reason to celebrate this life of being set free from living in sin and from evil which is there. Countries who have control over another set up laws for that country to follow.

Our old life has laws that were governing us on what to do, to do this and that, but with the new life there is no law in the fruit of righteousness in the Holy Spirit (see Galatians 5:22-23).

We are free to choose and practice the fruit of the Spirit. That is what love is. Our loving Father, Jehovah Shammah, our Almighty Father is there with His love, and nothing can separate us from His love (see Romans 8:38-39).

Every day is a new day to celebrate the freedom of living in the new life of Christ, knowing that our Father, Jehovah Shammah, is there for us.

September 17

~ God's invisible power is there for us to do mighty powerful work ~

Now to the King eternal, immortal, invisible, to God who alone is wise, be honour and glory forever and ever. Amen (1 Timothy 1:17, NKJV).

One night, February 24, 2022, I was watching bedtime stories on YouTube with my two children. I normally watch the English fairy tales with them before they go to sleep. This story was about an 'invisible man', a clever college student who graduated in science and went on to do experiments and made himself invisible. He started using his invisible power to rob banks and get what he wanted. Nothing was impossible for this invisible man. He appeared one time to an old school friend in his invisible nature. His confused friend asked him why he would do something like this? He said, 'because an invisible man is the most powerful man.'

This is what the Holy Spirit taught me about His power and His invisible nature within us: This invisible man in our bedtime story has no flesh, he is just air, but puts his invisible form in some clothes. You can see an invisible figure of a man in the shape of the clothes he wears. The Holy Spirit within us is more powerful and needs our flesh to use His power through us. He needed a flesh form. Jesus had to become the flesh to provide that flesh to us so the Holy Spirit can dwell in that flesh. Unlike the invisible man in the story who was using his power for evil, the Holy Spirit produces the fruit, 'goodness', and He wants to use His power of goodness through us so we can overcome evil around us.

Jesus lived our Father's name, Jehovah Shammah, our Lord God who is there. His flesh is given to us so the Holy Spirit can live in us. It was the power of the Holy Spirit who resurrected the flesh of Jesus. That same power is within us to rise us up to do goodness to all evil around. The invisible power of the Holy Spirit can be with us all at the same time, anywhere, and connect us to be in alignment with our Father's move for each season. Jehovah Shammah, our Almighty Father is there all the time in a powerful way.

> *...even the Spirit of truth, whom the world cannot receive, because it neither sees him nor knows him. You know him, for he dwells with you and will be in you (John 14:17, ESV).*

Every new day comes with new opportunities to walk on the path of God's Word, which is always there for us. Our loving Father in heaven is always there for us in His invisible, powerful Spirit through Jesus Christ, the Word who became flesh.

September 18

~ Our Father is there with a great plan for us ~

This plan of mine is not what you would work out, neither are my thoughts the same as yours! For just as the heavens are higher than the earth, so are my ways higher than yours, and my thoughts than yours (Isaiah 55:8-9, TLB).

December 29, 2020, I was driving to go pick up Angelilly's birthday cake as she was going to turn six the next day. I was thinking about how someone disconnected herself from me because I wasn't doing what she wanted. She wanted me to do certain things in the way she wanted. But it was not what I wanted because I was not at peace to do it. While I was pondering on it, I heard the Holy Spirit say: You see, many people disconnect with God because they want things to be done their way, according to their will. If you ask God for something, He wants it His way, and as a loving Father who adores His children, He only wants to give us the best future He planned for us. But because He had to work on our characters, we do not want it His way but our way, and so we disconnect ourselves from Him.

He is Jehovah Shammah, our Lord God who is there, an ever-present Father who is there for us by giving us every day so we can connect back to Him and get back to where He wants us to be. It doesn't matter how messed up we are, when we connect to Him and ask for His will to be done, He will take us from where we are and start something great in our life.

This is the confidence we have in approaching God: that if we ask anything according to his will, he hears us. And if we know that he hears us—whatever we ask—we know that we have what we asked of him (1 John 5:14-15, NIV).

A good father doesn't go by his own will. He sits in the Word of God to direct his will into His Father in heaven's will. And when He prays for his house, his prayers are answered because it is the will of the Father.

September 19

~ *Dealing with your burdens right away* ~

But if we confess our sins to him, he is faithful and just to forgive us our sins and to cleanse us from all wickedness (1 John 1:9, NLT).

There are certain delicate dresses I have that I don't usually put in the washing machine, but hand wash instead. September 19, 2021, after hand washing these dresses, I hung them on the clothes line while thinking if I'd just washed them right away after I wore each of those dresses, it would not be a burden to wash everything that had piled up. This is what I heard the Holy Spirit say about the many burdens of life that we try to carry all at once: Whenever an issue or burden arises, deal with it right away, don't put it aside and carry on in life as if everything is alright. If today you see you are not clothed right in patience with someone, ask for forgiveness and work on improving yourself to do it better. If you are unkind to your kids or spouse and react in anger, apologise, say sorry right away and realise your mistake.

You see, if I had just dealt right away with washing my delicate dresses rather than piling them up, I would never go through the extreme burden of hand washing them all. So it is with our dirty actions towards others—if we just deal right away, ask for forgiveness and try to do the right things, we are not only freeing ourselves from carrying the guilt of burdens, but we also build a good relationship with our loved ones.

God is our refuge and strength, an ever-present help in trouble (Psalm 46:1, NIV).

Jesus came and lived our Father's name, Jehovah Shammah, our Almighty Father who is there. He is ever-present with us through the Holy Spirit, who is our helper to help us do the right things right away. Let's deal with it without delay whenever we do something which is a burden to carry.

Every day is another opportunity to live our Father's name, Jehovah Shammah, our Almighty Father who is there. In Jesus' name, we are going to take responsibility for our actions by being there and solving issues with the love of the Father. When our Father was in the garden to deal with the first sin, the man blamed God for the woman He gave him, because she was the one who made him do it. The woman then blamed the serpent. The love of the Father came to us in flesh form and carried the blame, shame, guilt and punishment to the cross and hanged it there, then went to the grave and buried it with death.

September 20

~ You sow your time by being there for someone who is in need ~

God is a safe place to hide, ready to help when we need him. We stand fearless at the cliff-edge of doom, courageous in sea storm and earthquake (Psalm 46:1-2, MSG).

First day of winter, June 1, 2021, I was going to do something when I realised Blessed's fingernail needed trimming. I dropped everything I was doing and attended to it. This is what I heard the Holy Spirit say: You see, the kingdom of God is like this. God will come quickly to you and attend to you when you have need of His complete attention. If you are about to get into an accident He will always be there, He is ever-present. So take that leap of faith and jump off your cliff. Yes, jump into that thing you have always wanted to do to get what you desire. This is walking by faith and receiving by faith, like Peter, who walked on the waters like Jesus by faith. The moment he lost focus on faith who is Jesus, he sank into the water. Faith comes by hearing and hearing the Word, and Jesus is the Word who has become flesh. Faith without action is dead. Your flesh must action the Word for your faith to be alive in you.

For we walk by faith, not by sight (2 Corinthians 5:7, ESV).

A good dad walks by faith, not by sight. He uses what He sights to walk more miles by faith. Faith comes by hearing and hearing the Word. He stays connected to His Father in heaven in hearing the Word and walking in obedience to the Word. To walk by faith is to walk by the Word. He may not see it, but his focus is on Jesus and he will not lose sight of Him.

Each day, we have to live our Father's name like Jesus, Jehovah Shammah, our Lord God who is there, by being there for anyone we know who needs help. Let's be kind, as that is what our Father is rich in, and that is what we should be rich in too.

September 21

~ *Our loving Father is there to catch us when we fall* ~

He cuts off every branch in me that bears no fruit, while every branch that does bear fruit he prunes so that it will be even more fruitful (John 15:2, NIV).

One beautiful morning, September 21, 2021, I saw two of my succulent flower pots were growing so fresh, green and big. The only problem was they were growing downwards, not up. I thought to hold them upwards and put something to make them stand upright, but they broke in my hand when I took them to stand them up. I was so sad for the fresh, nice-looking succulents to break away.

This is what the Holy Spirit taught me: The plant will grow better again as it still has its roots abiding in the soil. The same with your life, and how your heavenly Father in heaven prunes you. You'll notice how well you are blooming and growing in life, then all of a sudden things get cut off from your life. This is a fallen world, and as you grow up in your faith, things in your life will also start to fall down. For your Father to keep you going up only, He will remove all things falling down and not bearing fruit in your life. God puts law upon all His creation. The law of gravity states that anything that goes up will fall down. This is a fallen world and everything will still fall and fail us, but as long as we remain in the Word we are rooted and will grow new roots and strength to move upward.

> *Dear friends, you already know about this. So be careful. Don't let these evil people lead you away by the wrong they do. Be careful that you do not fall from your strong faith. But grow in the grace and knowledge of our Lord and Saviour Jesus Christ. Glory be to him, now and forever! Amen (2 Peter 3:17-18, ERV).*

Jesus lived our Father's name, Jehovah Shammah, our Almighty Father who is there. He came into this fallen world and was there in every path we travelled. He went through everything we are facing today. He is there now in the Holy Spirit in us and knows and sees our falls every day. But as long as He is there, He is our ever-present help to hold us up and prune us to grow stronger and better.

Every day, stay rooted in the Word, and when you feel like falling, fall more into the promises of the Father and know He is Jehovah Shammah, He is there in the Word that you abide in and will make His Word become flesh on your flesh.

September 22

~ We are to be born again to be there in the Father's kingdom to receive our spiritual blessings ~

There is a right time for everything (Ecclesiastes 3:1, TLB).

September 22, 2021, I put aside a nice new dress to gift to a friend on her birthday. I wanted to see that friend today and thought I would give her gift on her birthday, which was a month away. This is what I heard the Holy Spirit say: All your spiritual blessings in the gift of life are there. In that right time, when you are mature enough to receive it, then you shall get it. I was trying to give to that friend the dress on her birthday when she'd turn a year older, and here the Lord is also saying that on that day when you get older and mature, you will receive your inheritance.

Our loving Father is Jehovah Shammah, our Almighty Father who is there. There is a time for everything, as He has appointed. We are to only grow our character to be Christ-like and be matured to receive it. You see, that time we are matured to receive our gift is the day we are born again into it and we will receive it as our birthright. That day is our birthday in the spiritual realm as we receive the spiritual blessings of gifts. We have to enter the kingdom of God to receive what is in our Father's kingdom. When we are born again, we will see it.

As for me, I wanted to give that gift on my friend's birthday as she turned a year older. Our Father also has our spiritual gift of blessings to give us on that day we are born again and become matured to be able to use it.

> *But when the right time came, the time God decided on, he sent his Son, born of a woman, born as a Jew, to buy freedom for us who were slaves to the law so that he could adopt us as his very own sons. And because we are his sons, God has sent the Spirit of his Son into our hearts, so now we can rightly speak of God as our dear Father. Now we are no longer slaves but God's own sons. And since we are his sons, everything he has belongs to us, for that is the way God planned (Galatians 4:4-7, TLB).*

Jesus lived our Father's name, Jehovah Shammah, our Almighty Father who is there. He is the very treasure where the spiritual blessings of the Father are. He walked and lived in love, giving the spiritual blessings. He is there now in us through the Holy Spirit. We only are to be born again into being matured to receive those spiritual blessings of gifts.

September 23

~ *Don't stretch out your stress. Our loving Father is always there to provide for us* ~

> *Have I not commanded you? Be strong and courageous. Do not be frightened, and do not be dismayed, for the Lord your God is with you wherever you go (Joshua 1:9, ESV).*

This is the prayer of a good dad to all in his care and concern:

> *For this reason, since the day we heard about you, we have not stopped praying for you. We continually ask God to fill*

> *you with the knowledge of his will through all the wisdom and understanding that the Spirit gives, so that you may live a life worthy of the Lord and please him in every way: bearing fruit in every good work, growing in the knowledge of God (Colossians 1:9-10, NIV).*

On the morning of September 23, 2021, I was looking at a video of a new recipe on how to make broccoli become delicious for my kids to eat. If I practised the recipe, I'd have to go through and experience how it is made with my hands. Amazingly, this is what the Holy Spirit taught me: You see, so it is with the new life you have in Christ. A new life to learn in the Holy Spirit is just like a new recipe you are about to learn—every day there is something for you to learn, but you have to go through and experience what the new Christ-like life is yourself. This is where you have to practice the characters of Christ in your new life in the situations you approach. You have the fruit of the Holy Spirit, self-control, to help you control what you can control, and you have also the fruit of peace to help you walk out in peace on any matters you cannot control.

Jesus came and lived the name of our Father in heaven, Jehovah Shammah, our Almighty Father who is there. The life He lived and laid down for us is there through the nine fruit of the Holy Spirit. This is the life we have to live. Every day, we are to learn how to use the fruit of the Holy Spirit in those situations so we can grow our characters. It's a learning process. We may fail, but God's love will never fail us. It is always there for us to walk and live in it towards eternity.

Each day is another day to live the Father's name, Jehovah Shammah, in the name of Jesus. Our Father is there already in what we are about to go through. We just have to walk through it and practice the fruit of love in there.

September 24

~ The voice of the Father is speaking all the time through His Spirit ~

Only be strong and very courageous, being careful to do according to all the law that Moses my servant commanded you. Do not turn from it to the right hand or to the left, that you may have good success wherever you go. This Book of the Law shall not depart from your mouth, but you shall meditate on it day and night, so that you may be careful to do according to all that is written in it. For then you will make your way prosperous, and then you will have good success. Have I not commanded you? Be strong and courageous. Do not be frightened, and do not be dismayed, for the Lord your God is with you wherever you go (Joshua 1:7-9, ESV).

While doing a road trip on March 6, 2021, I was driving in a new place that I don't know. I asked Tom to give me the direction to our destiny. This is what the Holy Spirit taught me: You see, you don't know the place and the surroundings, but you just have to go through it and get the direction from the voice of Tom. You are the one who will make the move and follow the voice until you arrive at your destiny. So it is with your life in living in the kingdom of God. It's a new place where you need to follow the voice of the Holy Spirit to move to your destiny God designed for you. You will always reach your destiny when you live in the kingdom of God, in God's righteousness. The way to your destiny that God purposed for you is through the kingdom of God, and so you have to be born again to enter the kingdom of God.

A good dad understands that he moves and has his being in his loving Father. His Word is Him and so he pays more attention to

His Father in heaven's voice through His Spirit. The more he spends time in His Word and in prayer, he develops the confidence and courage to move in the direction of the Voice of the Word. It's not just a Word, it is the Word of His Father, and it is life and spirit. He knows he has to take the first step of faith in whatever he is unsure of, because the Word contained within him will always be there for him to give him life, light and lead him on the right path to his destiny of success.

> *For in him we live and move and have our being (Acts 17:28, NIV).*

Jehovah Shammah, our Lord God who is there. Jesus will always be there for us. He is the Word who has become flesh. He Said, 'I will be with you until the end of times,' (see Matthew 28:20). Our Father was there for Him and was with Him while Jesus was living in this world. In the name of Jesus, to the glory of our Father's name, Jehovah Shammah, with whom Jesus is now seated on the right-hand side, He is ever-present with us forever through the Holy Spirit who lives inside of us.

Every new day given was made in the presence of the Father, Son and Holy Spirit and is a present and gift to confirm His promise that He is always there for us in that day.

September 25

~ The blood of Jesus is always there to cleanse us from all unrighteousness ~

> *But if we confess our sins to him, he is faithful and just to forgive us our sins and to cleanse us from all wickedness (1 John 1:9, NLT).*

This is the prayer of a good dad:

> *But as for me, I will be on the watch for the Lord; I will wait for the God of my salvation. My God will hear me. Do not rejoice over me, enemy of mine. Though I fall, I will rise; Though I live in darkness, the Lord is a light for me. I will endure the rage of the Lord because I have sinned against Him, until He pleads my case and executes justice for me. He will bring me out to the light, and I will look at His righteousness (Micah 7:7-9, NASB).*

I left some scraps of food on a plate which I didn't clean up at night. I woke up to it in the morning of September 25, 2021, when I saw ants gathering around and feasting on it. I was the one who left the scraps and didn't clean them up, and this gave access to the ants. This is what the Holy Spirit taught me: When you also don't confess and clean out any bad habits you have in your life, the enemy can access it and have its way into and around your life.

Every time the Holy Spirit convinces you that something isn't right, and that you've walked away from the path of righteousness, get back on the track. Don't get stuck in your traps of evil desires. So often, we unconsciously do some of the bad habits because it is so natural to do. Jesus lived our loving Father's name, Jehovah Shammah, our Almighty Father who is there. Jesus is there with the love of the Father to forgive us, the love that He has paid us with His pure, sinless blood. We just have to confess our sin and mistakes right away and be clean and have a mind of clear consciousness. You see, if I had cleaned up the scraps of food, the ants would never have been there. If we confess our sins instantly, the blood of Jesus is there all the time to clean us right away. When cleaning by the blood of Jesus is going on in your life, the enemy will not have access into your life. Like how a public toilet can be closed when cleaning is going on, our life too will be closed to shut out any disturbance from this fallen world.

Each and every day, live for Jesus' name, who lives the name of the Father, Jehovah Shammah, through the Holy Spirit. The Holy Spirit, our Helper, is always there to help us immediately, to encourage us to confess any unrighteous acts so we can remain clean in the fruit of righteousness produced by Him.

September 26

~ The Word of God is new and there for us all the time in our challenges ~

The steadfast love of the Lord never ceases; his mercies never come to an end; they are new every morning; great is your faithfulness (Lamentations 3:22-23, ESV).

March 22, 2021, I was doing a reading book with Angelilly, during one of our home schooling days. The book was called *Chug the Tractor*, about an old tractor who couldn't do farm work, especially going up the hill. The farmer brought in a new tractor and got rid of the old one by taking it to the park for the children to play with. In the story, the old tractor said to himself, 'I am old and the farmer and no one wants me anymore.'

But when the farmer left him at the park, all the children shouted delightfully and said, 'Come on, let's check out the new tractor,' and ran to it happily. Then the old tractor smiled to himself and said, 'Even though I am old, the children are enjoying me.' This is what the Holy Spirit taught me: The Word of God is ancient, but it is new all the time for us to enjoy. That old tractor thought it was old, but it became new in a new situation and was enjoyed. The same old Word of God is new to every new situation and challenges in our lives. The Word of God will always be there. Jehovah Shammah, our Lord God who is there. This is our Father's name and it is of His character to be there for us.

> *... and have put on the new self, which is being renewed in knowledge in the image of its Creator (Colossians 3:10, NIV).*

A good dad renews himself in the Word of His Father in heaven all the time. He knows His Father is always there for him, even before he calls out to Him. Many times, he thinks he is all worn out and can no longer do it, but with the ever-present renewed Word of the loving Father in heaven, it renews him with new strength to do everything in Christ.

Jesus lived our Father's name. He is always here and will be there for us in meeting all our needs through the Holy Spirit inside of us. This is why He said, 'I must go to the Father so the Holy Spirit can come to us.'

September 27

~ Store the Word to attract the Holy Spirit to it ~

> *God is our refuge and strength, an ever-present help in trouble (Psalm 46:1, NIV).*

One winter's night, July 3, 2021, I was trying to write down ways in which the Holy Spirit helps us in praying. One of the ways is He puts the Word in our mouth to pray. Whatever is within our heart flows out of our mouth. The more we have the Word of God in our heart, the easier it will be for the Holy Spirit to bring the Word into our mouth to use in our time of need. The Word is light unto our path and it keeps us and all our loved ones in safety. This is what the Holy Spirit pointed out to me: On the day before, at around 1pm, I remember all of a sudden, the Holy Spirit put in my spirit to pray over a friend, so I did. An hour later, she messaged to tell me she missed being hit by a big truck. Prayers get God to work right away. At that hour, the word the Holy Spirit put into me to pray over her began the work of rescuing her. In my spiritual eyes, I can see that the moment I started praying, God sent for the angel to rescue her.

A good dad stores the Word of His Father in his heart so he may not sin against Him, and this word can protect and keep him camouflaged in His Father's presence, where he will be safe. Our Father loves us so much He is everywhere at the same time for all of us. The more we abide in Jesus in His Word, the more we connect to Him and He is present everywhere.

Jesus came and lived our Father's name, Jehovah Shammah, our Lord God who is there. Our Father is always there for us to protect, shelter and feed us. Jesus was always there for anyone and everyone who needed Him. He healed, fed and restored everyone. He was even there for the little children and protected them. He showed the Father's love for being always there for His children. He was even there for us at the grave to conquer it, so we will not be afraid of death anymore. He gave us the greatest gift, who is the Holy Spirit, so we can connect and rule and reign with Him in heaven through the Holy Spirit in us.

Every day, we must live our Father's name, Jehovah Shammah, our Almighty Father who is there, by being there in Word and prayer for everyone we are connected with.

September 28

~ Trusting God that He is always there for us ~

But blessed are those who trust in the Lord and have made the Lord their hope and confidence. They are like trees planted along a riverbank, with roots that reach deep into the water. Such trees are not bothered by the heat or worried by long months of drought. Their leaves stay green, and they never stop producing fruit (Jeremiah 17:7-8, NLT).

February 6, 2020, after dropping off Angelilly (my five-year-old then) at school I thought, *okay, I just don't need to worry about her until school ends.* This is what I heard the Holy Spirit say: When you also lay down your life down and live the life of Christ, you don't need to worry about anything until the world ends. And because Jesus lived the Father's name, Jehovah Shammah, our Almighty Father who is there, He promised us that He will always be there for us until the end of times.

A good father brings and offers to His Father in heaven all the days of his household, and he doesn't worry about what the future holds for them, because he trusts the hands that are holding his future. When the hour of his need arrives, his Father will be there to meet it. He knows His Father is Jehovah Shammah, the Lord God who is there. Because of what Jesus has done, our Loving Father in heaven can meet all our needs in Christ Jesus who is His glorious riches when the need arises.

Do not be anxious about anything, but in every situation, by prayer and petition, with thanksgiving, present your requests to God. And the peace of God, which transcends all understanding, will guard your hearts and your minds in Christ Jesus (Philippians 4:6-7, NIV).

The more you spend time with your Father in heaven in His Word and in prayer, the more you will see Him at work for you everywhere. He is Jehovah Shammah. He will always be there for you when your moment of need arises.

September 29

~ God was there in your past mistakes and will always be there to help you ~

Consider it pure joy, my brothers and sisters, whenever you face trials of many kinds, because you know that the testing of your faith produces perseverance. Let perseverance finish its work so that you may be mature and complete, not lacking anything (James 1:2-4, NIV).

A good dad knows that even when he comes out from yesterday's trial, today might bring him another trial and he is heading towards the next one tomorrow. This is what his new life in Christ is all about. He must go through all this so his better version of a good dad that His Father in heaven designed him to be will come forth. The love of God and the peace of the moment from Jesus, with the Joy from the Holy Spirit, is the same yesterday, today and forever. A good dad considers all his trials as joy and is at peace, because it is building his character to be Christ-like. He knows he has a loving Father in heaven who is there for him and will never leave nor forsake him.

The Lord himself goes before you and will be with you; he will never leave you nor forsake you. Do not be afraid; do not be discouraged (Deuteronomy 31:8, NIV).

Jehovah Shammah is His name, our Lord God who is there, and He is our loving Father in heaven. Jesus lived our Father's name.

He said, 'I will be with you until the end of times.' Jesus is always with us in all our trials. And Jesus Christ is the same yesterday, today and forever.

Every new day is another opportunity to learn from our mistakes, trials, tests and temptations of the past to make good decisions in becoming a better version of who we are in Christ.

September 30

~ God is right there where we are, we just have to connect to Him ~

He told them, 'The secret of the kingdom of God has been given to you. But to those on the outside everything is said in parables so that they may be ever seeing but never perceiving, and ever hearing but never understanding; otherwise they might turn and be forgiven!' (Mark 4:11-12, NIV).

Tom and I have this particular friend who stopped communicating with us. One time Tom met her and started getting into a deep conversation, telling her all about us. I was there, and I warned him not to talk too much as she was no longer part of our life, of where we are.

This is what I heard the Holy Spirit say: The kingdom of God is like this. The things of the kingdom will only be revealed to you in the moment when you are connected and communicate with God every day. If you lose connection and stop communicating with God, you will no longer receive deep insights of the secrets of the kingdom of God. When God sees that you have become one of them, that is, when you take the nature of Christ, secrets things from the throne of God will be revealed as you are one of them now.

God is our loving, kind Father in heaven. He is there for us because He is Jehovah Shammah, our Lord God who is there. Wherever we are or are heading towards, He is there. All He wants is for us to reconnect to Him so we can see Him. Jesus lived our Father's name. The disciples didn't connect to Him in the boat during the storm, even though He was there. After they connected and communicated with Him, He was right there in the storm, calming the storm.

A good dad will always stay connected and communicate with His Father in heaven to be strengthened in His Word so he can see His glory from glory to glory. Like Moses, he leads his house through the journey of God's promises, and so he meets His Father every day in Word and prayer to be strengthened.

God's glory goes from glory to glory and strength to strength. What He showed you five years ago to strengthen you can be a new joy again if He reveals it to you now, or five minutes ago. You need new, fresh revelation, and to receive that you need to stay connected to God every day so you can see the glory of the day.

OCTOBER

Jehovah Rophe! I AM Your Healer!

OUR LORD GOD IS OUR HEALER.

~ Take care of the life you carry in you ~

This happened so that what was spoken through Isaiah the prophet would be fulfilled: He Himself took our illnesses and carried away our diseases (Matthew 8:17, NASB).

January 24, 2022, I was into my fourth month of pregnancy and carried some heavy stuff that I shouldn't have. I didn't want to face any problems, as I was carrying a life in me which was at a vulnerable stage, and if I was not careful with myself I could harm that life. This is what I heard the Holy Spirit say: When we carry the new life of Christ, we are never to carry any heaviness of this world, especially the concerns of life that will worry and pull us down, because it can kill the new life we have in us. We have to focus on growing the life of Christ within us to maturity state. It's a newborn state and needs milk, which is the Word of God.

You see, my body and flesh carried the new life in me that I couldn't see, but I knew a likeness of me was about to be born, and that gave me the hope and joy of waiting for that day to come. Therefore, I had to be careful and not carry any heavy things, because I could terminate or cause a miscarriage. So it is with us. When we carry the problems, concerns and worries of the world in our life, we carry the burden and heaviness of the world. This not only puts burdens on our body and has us feel aches and pains, or even sick, but we also do not grow and mature in our new life in Christ. Jesus keeps telling us not to worry. When we continue to worry, it can build up illness and sickness, causing us not to live and see long days of life.

You cannot add any time to your life by worrying about it (Matthew 6:27, ERV).

Jesus came and lived our Father's name, Jehovah Rophe, our Almighty Father is our Healer. He has healed us already by carrying our sin in His body, and every curse-related issue that connects to sin such as illness, sickness and disease. We are never to carry any worries or burdens upon us, because Jesus carried it on His flesh and nailed it to the cross. The pouring of His sinless blood is the witness and speaks right now of what He has done. We ourselves start to have sickness or disease when we want to carry the worries and burdens of the world in our body.

> 'Come to me all of you who are tired from the heavy burden you have been forced to carry. I will give you rest. Accept my teaching. Learn from me. I am gentle and humble in spirit. And you will be able to get some rest. Yes, the teaching that I ask you to accept is easy. The load I give you to carry is light.' (Matthew 11:28-30, ERV).

Every new day has its own problems, issues and burdens. Offer them unto Jesus, and let Him offer His load for you to carry, which is light. Each day of the month of October, and every day, rise up and call on the Father's name, Jehovah Rophe, our Almighty Father is our Healer. Because Jesus lives our Father's name, in Jesus' name offer every concern, worry and health issue to Jesus and receive His light to shine healing in your life.

October 1

~ *The 'faith of a wife'* ~

> *These older women must train the younger women to love their husbands and their children, to live wisely and be pure, to work in their homes, to do good, and to be submissive to their husbands. Then they will not bring shame on the word of God* (Titus 2:4-5, NLT).

A good wife is a gift from the Lord. A wife's faith can save a foolish husband from going down the wrong path. Abigail had great faith as a wife and spared her husband from his foolish acts. As long as the wife hears and hears the Word of God, her faith is built up. Faith comes from hearing and hearing the Word. This is how she grows in wisdom and become wise. Even the faith of a wife can bring a husband to life (see Hebrews 11:35).

> *His name was Nabal and his wife's name was Abigail. She was an intelligent and beautiful woman, but her husband was surly and mean in his dealings—he was a Calebite (1 Samuel 25:3, NIV).*

Abigail's husband's name was Nabal, which means foolish (see 1 Samuel 25:25). We actually become and live our name, and that is exactly what Abigail's husband was—a foolish man. Abigail was a wise wife who always covered up for her foolish husband.

My husband's name is Thomas, and he lives his name—a person of doubts. He will want to see everything before he believes it. When I remind him of God's faithfulness, he says, 'Oh well, seeing is believing.' When we were first married, he would do that most times. I got so annoyed, because even after many instances of God's invisible hand showing up to us visibly, he'd still want to see everything before he believed it. I remember saying to God, 'I can't believe you allowed me to marry this man who is so full of doubts, even after you do so many things for us right under his eyes.' Instantly, God spoke into my heart through the Holy Spirit and said, 'Yes, I gave him to you so his doubts will make your faith double up more stronger. You will grow more in your faith to make up for his doubts.' After hearing that, I have never questioned his doubts, I just show him doubled faith. We complement each other so well. Even though he is slowly coming out of being doubtful, he still sometimes brings up his doubts. I am so grateful as I can show him more faith whenever he doubts.

There are some things in life that we don't need to pray to remove, we just have to grow stronger to conquer it. Instead of praying for Thomas to stop doubting, I simply use it as a motivator to grow more strongly in my faith. Some sickness or disease can be part of us and is genetic, so instead of God removing it, you can grow stronger and conquer it every time it wants to show up. That is what makes you stronger—that you can do all things through Christ who strengthens you.

Jesus lived our Father's name, Jehovah Rophe, our Almighty Father is our Healer. We are here to hear and hear the Word of God to get more faith to be strong and conquer any sickness or disease. The 'faith of a wife' is the faith to accept the situations or battles life gives you and become wiser, stronger and conquer it.

One time I was in another country and asked my husband to come. This is what he said to me over the phone, 'Well, if you want me to come, you have to ask God to buy my plane ticket.' I didn't want to challenge him, knowing Thomas the doubter. So I just said, 'Sure, I will ask God for your plane ticket.' Within 24 hours he sent me a message saying God did give him the exact ticket money to come to me. He was walking in a warehouse and a dirty sock with $400 was lying in front of his feet. The ticket fare for the date I asked him to come was $400.

Every day, hear and hear the Word so you can grow your faith muscle and exercise it effectively in conquering sickness or disease over your life. Even if your sickness is still there, the Word that you hear strengthens you to carry on life in the midst of your pain.

October 2

~ The 'faith of a good mother' ~

Then Jesus said to her, 'Woman, you have great faith! Your request is granted.' And her daughter was healed at that moment (Matthew 15:28, NIV).

The Canaanite mother approached Jesus to have mercy on her and heal her demon-possessed daughter. Jesus didn't pay any attention to her, nor did the disciples. It actually depends here on how much faith you have, for that will move Jesus to work. Without faith it is impossible to please God. Jesus told her He didn't come for Canaanites, putting it in parable with children and dogs. The faith of this mother was a faith of the character of dogs. Even though Jesus was not paying attention to heal her daughter, she didn't stop bothering Him. She knew that He was the Master, and even though masters mistreat their dogs, the dogs are always loyal to their master and wait upon them. When Jesus treated her like a dog, she told Jesus even the rubbish you throw to the dogs is good enough for me. Jesus told her what great faith she had, and at that moment, the daughter was healed. It was her faith that pleased Jesus to allow healing to take place.

A mother's faith is like the character of a dog—they will continue to beg for mercy, forgiveness and healing, no matter how badly they are treated. Their faithfulness and loyalty throughout a situation is their great faith in receiving their healing. Jesus lived our Father's name, Jehovah Rophe, our Almighty Father is our Healer. He is our Master, and masters reward their servants for their loyalty. When we approach Jesus with the 'faith of a mother' with that character of a dog, we are showing our loyalty that Jesus is our Master and whatever He gives we will still make it through. We will receive our healing simply because we know who the Master is. A crumb received from Jesus can heal us completely, more than a feast from what the world can give.

> *'First let the children eat all they want,' he told her, 'for it is not right to take the children's bread and toss it to the dogs.''Lord,' she replied, 'even the dogs under the table eat the children's crumbs.' (Mark 7:27-28, NIV).*

Every day, let's live our Father's name, Jehovah Rophe, our Almighty Father is our Healer, by living the faith of a mother who also possesses that 'character of a dog' and start receiving our divine healing.

October 3

~ Christ-like character faith ~

> *If you then, though you are evil, know how to give good gifts to your children, how much more will your Father in heaven give the Holy Spirit to those who ask him! (Luke 11:13, NIV).*

God's name is His character and that is His gift to us. Jesus is a gift to us. He lived the Father's name. The Spirit of the Father, Holy Spirit, is the Spirit of truth, because everything about the Father and the Son is true. God was showing me how gifts, or when something has someone's name on it, it belongs to that person. He showed me especially how He has gifts for us with our names. He showed something for me, which I won't mention now, as it was for me. Instead of my name, it had some kind of characters that my character has to grow to be like, so my name can be on that gift. I have to live up to the characters in order to claim that thing which is mine. I can say I receive it in Jesus' name, but to do so I have to have Christ-like character, living the lifestyle of Jesus. In the past,

God would visit His chosen ones and give them a new name and the reason why they got a new name. He did that to Abraham, Jacob and Sarah. It was all a new beginning for them as that name always comes with specific characters and blessings or a new role upon their lives. It's just like when one becomes a dad, the name father is given to them because they have a new role or responsibility in their lives.

> ... to another faith by the same Spirit, to another gifts of healing by that one Spirit (1 Corinthians 12:9, (NIV).

Jesus lived the Father's name, Jehovah Rophe, our Almighty Father is our Healer. That is the gift of the Father. There are nine gifts of the Spirit and one of them is healing. When we keep on living and having the faith of receiving healing, we are growing our character to have our name on the gift of healing and we receive it. This is when we can also use this gift of healing to heal others around us. Some healings are always there, but we don't realise it as we think healing is about getting the sick well. Your encouraging words can also heal someone who wants to end their life, or give them hope to find the purpose of their life again.

Every day, live the Father's name, which is our gift so we can grow in the love of the Father and be Christ-like and receive those spiritual blessings of gifts.

October 4

~ The 'faith of a beggar' ~

> Jesus said to him (the blind beggar), 'Receive your sight; your faith has healed you.' (Luke 18:42,NIV).

Beggars have a desperate faith and will never keep silent from begging for a living. The blind beggar cried out for Jesus to heal him, and he cried even louder for Jesus when he was asked to remain silent. Jesus told him, 'Your faith has made you well.'

Beggars live by asking only for free gifts, a position they take to make their living. Even when they get it they will still ask and ask. On the way to prayers, a beggar reached out to Peter and begged. Peter healed the beggar, instead of giving what he thought was important (silver or gold). They gave him Jesus.

> *Then Peter said, 'Silver or gold I do not have, but what I do have I give you. In the name of Jesus Christ of Nazareth, walk.' Taking him by the right hand, he helped him up, and instantly the man's feet and ankles became strong. He jumped to his feet and began to walk. Then he went with them into the temple courts, walking and jumping, and praising God (Acts 3:6-8, NIV).*

To receive our healing we have to take that position of a beggar and constantly ask until we receive. Ask and you will receive. Jesus lived our Father's name, Jehovah Rophe, our Almighty Father is our Healer. He was healing all that asked for healing. Families brought their sick loved ones to Jesus and they were completely healed. Living the 'faith of a beggar' we can ask until we get our healing. A beggar is always looking with hope to receive what they ask for. This is the kind of faith we must have—to beg with hope that we will receive what we have asked of the Father.

Every day, let's take that position of the 'faith of a beggar' and ask for healing until we receive it. Like those blind beggars Jesus and Peter healed, cry out for healing, and cry louder if the enemy wants to silence you. Whatever your illness, take your position of the 'faith of a beggar' and receive your healing, be it cancer beggar, deaf and mute beggar or whatever disease beggar you want to approach your

Father with. He is Jehovah Rophe, that is His name. Jesus lived that name and conquered all curse-related activities. Power and authority have been given to the name of Jesus. In Jesus' name, we too can live and receive our healing.

October 5

~ Declaring your faith with action ~

You are of God, little children, and have overcome them, because He who is in you is greater than he who is in the world (1 John 4:4, NKJV).

One evening, October 5, 2021, the vacuum cleaner was in the kitchen area. After using it, we left it there, thinking we were going to use it again, but we didn't and it was left there. I realised I had to clear the area and removed it to make some space. As I did so, I heard the Holy Spirit say: You see, if you are praying to receive something, make space for it and clear out whatever is in the way. Make space to receive it. You can pray for what you want and declare the promises of God in His Word, but faith without action is dead. You have to do what needs to be done and action that faith to bring it alive.

If you want healing, declare healing upon your life and don't act sick, tell yourself to be stronger than your sickness. I remember one time I was feeling a little sick and was praying to get well. I didn't receive my healing, but I heard the Holy Spirit telling me, 'Greater is He that is in you than anything.' I started focusing on how great Jesus was in me, greater than the sickness, that even though the sickness was there I was feeling stronger.

I can do all things through Christ who strengthens me (Philippians 4:13, NKJV).

Jesus lived our Father's name, Jehovah Rophe, our Almighty Father is our Healer. By His stripes we are healed. In Jesus we are already healed. All we have to do is focus our faith to be healed in Jesus' name. We are stronger in Christ and can do all things in Christ who strengthens us. And this is where our healing flows out.

October 6

~ *The 'faith of the blind'* ~

Then Jesus placed his hands on the man's eyes again, and his eyes were opened. His sight was completely restored, and he could see everything clearly (Mark 8:25, NLT).

What God has made for us no eyes have seen. When we have that faith of the blind, even though we do not see, we will keep on believing because we are walking by faith and not by sight.

In the seen world, Abraham was too old to have a son, but with the 'faith of the blind' he saw the son that was promised to him. He kept seeing it by faith until he saw it by sight. Even though you do not see your healing, keep having the 'faith of the blind' that you will see your healing until you receive your sight to see healing taking place. The process of receiving your healing is a journey of building your faith muscles and characters.

A good dad lives his life like Elisha; he has the 'faith of the blind'. Elisha didn't see it, but he had faith that he was going to. He connected his physical eyes to look by faith and not by sight. Elisha even prayed to God to open the eyes of his servant so he could see what he was seeing (see 2 Kings 6:17-20).

Jesus came and lived our Father's name, Jehovah Rophe, our Almighty Father is our Healer. He came to make the blind see. We are blind and cannot see the healing that is taking place in us. Once our eyes are open and we are able to see Jesus, then we will see that we are healed and restored by Him. That peace and joy that comes from seeing Jesus when He reveals Himself to us brings healing. You may have an incurable pain or disease, but when Jesus opens your eyes to see Him in that, you feel that joy, peace, comfort and strength to live with hope. That is healing.

This is my personal experience: Towards the end of the month of May, 2022, I was treated at our public hospital. In the process of taking my blood, the doctors must have not cleaned the surface of my skin properly, so a bacteria went into the needle and into my bloodstream. I ended up with a very swollen and painful infected arm. For over a week, I was still in so much pain and hospitalised. I knew God allowed this to happen because I am always watchful in my prayers. That night, while in pain, I was beginning to get upset as I was praying for Jesus to heal me. Instantly, my eyes began to see Jesus on the cross and being crucified. Then I heard the sound of the nails going through his hands and feet. The sound was so real and loud that I was in tears for the pain Jesus went through, and not what I was going through. You see, Jesus didn't heal me, instead He opened my eyes to see the pain He went through and this gave me the comfort and strength to go through mine too.

> *For I'm going to do a brand-new thing. See, I have already begun! Don't you see it? I will make a road through the wilderness of the world for my people to go home, and create rivers for them in the desert! (Isaiah 43:19, TLB).*

Each and every day, let's have this 'faith of the blind' and keep seeing our healing until we sight it in our seen world. What God is preparing for us no eyes have seen. Since we have not seen it, we just trust God that He is working on it, and we just have to have this 'faith of the blind' until we see it in the seen realm.

October 7

~ Living in the 'faith of faithfulness' ~

Then Jesus said to her, 'Woman, you have great faith! Your request is granted.' And her daughter was healed at that moment (Matthew 15:28, NIV).

October 7, 2021, I was chatting with a friend who lives in my suburb. She is that person who loves to live where the beach is, but hardly goes to the beach to enjoy it. She had plans to move and relocate to another place, but because she loves the beach she never made that decision. She never enjoys the beach literally, but just the thought of being surrounded by the presence of the beach makes her feel good. After talking with her, this is what I heard the Holy Spirit say: You see, many people don't go to God as that loving Father and experience His presence and spend time with Him, but just seeing godly stuff on social media or being aware of the goodness of God makes them feel good. That moment you walk into the presence of God and experience Him yourself as a Father full of love, you will find your heart, soul and whole being mended and freshened up. You are going to be left broken in His presence and come out as a whole, restored person, knowing who your Father is and why He loves you and keeps loving and being faithful to you.

Jesus lived our loving Father's name, Jehovah Rophe, our Almighty Father is our Healer. With the 'faith of faithfulness' we can receive our healing when we go faithfully to our loving Father in Jesus' name for healing. Jesus shows this kind of faith in the parable of the widow who constantly and faithfully went to the unrighteous judge to grant the desire of her heart (see Luke 18:1-8). If the unrighteous Judge can grant her wish, just imagine what our righteous loving Father who is the good judge can do.

There is more goodness where you can find healing for your body, soul and spirit if you faithfully seek the presence of your loving Father in His Word, and in prayer every day, and not just by the thought of 'God is good and it's all good'. Enjoy what Jesus provided for you in His powerful name. There is healing in Jesus' name.

This is the prayer of a good dad as he seeks healing for himself and his house:

> *Heal me, Lord, and I will be healed; save me and I will be saved, for you are the one I praise (Jeremiah 17:14, NIV).*

October 8

~ Praying and walking in the 'faith of joy' ~

> *He sent out his word and healed them; he rescued them from the grave. Let them give thanks to the Lord for his unfailing love and his wonderful deeds for mankind (Psalm 107: 20-21, NIV).*

Joy heals us from sorrows and pain. A good dad walks and prays in the 'faith of joy'! Joy brings restoration to our soul. He sits daily in the counsel of His Father's Word, which brings joy and delight to him. He walks with joy on the current waves of his storms and pains; this is how he heals himself. Because he is always releasing joy, the pain cannot hold a position in his life. He celebrates the gift of everything life gives him by living and walking in the 'faith of joy' with prayers of thanksgiving because it is the will of the Father.

Jesus lived our Father's name, Jehovah Rophe, our Almighty Father is our Healer. He walked with the 'faith of joy' and saw the joy to come from the pain and suffering that He would go through. We are healed from His stripes and it is His joy to see us healed.

> *Rejoice always, pray without ceasing, give thanks in all circumstances; for this is the will of God in Christ Jesus for you (1 Thessalonians 5:16-18, ESV).*

Every day, we are to pray with thanksgiving to walk and live in the 'faith of joy', celebrating the abundant life we have in Christ. Even in our pains and suffering we are to walk in joy. Not only did Jesus suffer more pain than us, but the greatest joy of sharing His glory is waiting for us when we share His sufferings.

October 9

~ *The 'faith of a friend'* ~

> *Greater love has no one than this: to lay down one's life for one's friends. You are my friends if you do what I command. I no longer call you servants, because a servant does not know his master's business. Instead, I have called you friends, for everything that I learned from my Father I have made known to you (John 15:13-15, NIV).*

A friend can do anything for a friend. When trust is built, a friendship goes to another level where secrets are revealed to each other. The Holy Spirit is given to us as a friend. He reveals the secrets of the kingdom of God to us and He tells us only what He hears from the Father. I remember asking the Lord for many things I needed. Instead of giving me what I wanted, I would hear the Holy Spirit telling me what to do to get it. God was giving me wisdom through His Spirit to do what needed to be done to get it. The Holy Spirit talked to me as a friend would talk to a friend, advising them of what to do.

Friends will always find a way, even if there seems to be no way. 'The faith of the friends' is that kind of faith that you will do something to open a way for your friend, even when you see no way. When the room was completely full and the friends of the crippled man couldn't take him to Jesus, they opened the roof and went through it. Jesus, seeing the faith of his friends, healed the crippled man instantly. Keep doing what you are doing for your friends, even if you are struggling through many challenges. Jesus can see everything you are doing through His Spirit. The good news is He is now in the Spirit and can see everything, everywhere and every time we do something in faith to be healed.

> *Friendship with God is reserved for those who reverence him. With them alone he shares the secrets of his promises (Psalm 25:14, TLB).*

Jesus lived the Father's name, Jehovah Rophe, our Almighty Father is our Healer, and He laid down His life as a friend would do. He wants us to have that relationship as friends so we can share the secrets of the kingdom of God and live healthily and happily. When we have this 'faith of a friend' and see Jesus as a friend, we will grow closer to the Holy Spirit and see Him as a friend and trust without doubt that He will heal us.

October 10

~ *Living the 'faith of a teenager'* ~

Don't let anyone look down on you because you are young, but set an example for the believers in speech, in conduct, in love, in faith and in purity (1 Timothy 4:12, NIV).

October 10, 2021. Sometimes you just talk away and have conversations, and from that you hear the Holy Spirit taking part in what you say by teaching you something in your heart. Knowing Tom had other things to do but sacrificed himself so he could be with me and the kids and do things for us, I told him, 'Coming next week, you can be free from doing all these things you are doing with us.' After I said this, I began to hear the Holy Spirit as He opened my eyes to see the word 'FREE'. When you are free from something you are 'set free from doing it'. You won't be doing that particular thing. You are no longer attached to it.

Because our Father in heaven loves us so much, He sent Jesus to set us free from this world and the things of this world. We are 'FREE' not to do any worldly things, but we have the free will to choose whether to take part in what the world does or the Word of God says, to set us free from what the world says.

When we are not free from something bad we become a slave to it. When we are free from something bad we are living right in the righteousness of God. Be slaves of righteousness (see Romans 6:18). This is one of the ways of receiving your healing. You heal yourself and come out free from something not of good value that will rob your time and energy.

Use the 'faith of a teenager' and heal yourself and receive more healing and blessings to come into your life. This 'faith of a teenager' is to live a faithful life, to be obedient to our Father in heaven and be set free from anything that is not of the Father. The harvest of it is to receive more wisdom, knowledge and understanding and be more successful in life. Every one of us needs that faith of a teenager.

The teenage Daniel used this faith. He chose to keep himself free from taking part in the food the king offered. God Blessed him so much with more knowledge and wisdom (see Daniel 1:20). This is the 'faith of a teenager' to be free from the expectation of the world. All we know is Daniel and his teenage friends became advisers to King Nebuchadnezzar. David, as a teenager, lived the 'faith of a teenager'. He chose to be obedient to his father's word and mind the sheep in the pasture, and was free from doing the unnecessary things the other young boys would do. This is the kind of faith lifestyle to live in, to be obedient to our Father in heaven and be 'free from anything that is not of the Father'. And so, when he brought the food for his brothers and wanted to defeat the giant, his brothers just saw him as that little teenage brother. Long story short, with the 'faith of a teenager' he slayed the giant and was anointed by prophet Samuel to be king. Because God looks at the heart, not appearance.

The seventeen-year-old Joseph lived the 'faith of a teenager' and was always obedient to his father. His father loved him so much that his brothers grew resentful towards him and sold him as a slave. They gave a false report to their father that he was killed by a wild animal. We know with his 'faith of a teenager' he was able to live an obedient life to God and became the prime minister of Egypt.

And even our very own sinless God in flesh lived the 'faith of a teenager'. The last time He was seen He was twelve years old, lost and found in the temple. From there He entered His teenage years, about which nothing is found in the bible. The bible clearly says He remained obedient to His parents and to God, and found favour in God and grew in wisdom (see Luke 2:51). He lived the 'faith of a teenager' throughout His teenage and adult life. He was obedient to the Father by even choosing to hang on the cross for our sins. He is the very wisdom of God. For what He did we are FREE, totally free from the world. This is what the power of the 'faith of a teenager' can do. Be obedient to the Father's Word and be free from the devil's lies of this world.

> *How can a young person stay on the path of purity? By living according to your word (Psalm 119:9, NIV).*

October 11

~ Living and walking in the 'faith of patience' ~

And so after waiting patiently, Abraham received what was promised (Hebrews 6:15, NIV).

Like Abraham, a good dad waits patiently for his loving Father in heaven. He knows He will always do what He says He will do. To receive His healing, he patiently and faithfully waits in the Word and in prayer; he is walking in the fruit of patience and faithfulness. Patience and faithfulness are two fruits of the Holy Spirit that need to back each other up for character development. It's the 'faith of being patient' that while waiting to be healed, he becomes stronger in his faith and stronger than his illness. Sometimes we may not receive our healing, but we become stronger than our illness.

I remember one time I was feeling a bit dizzy with a migraine. I prayed for an instant healing, but all I heard was the Lord saying, 'You are stronger than that migraine.' It was then I realised the migraine was still there, but I was coping with it. I became strong and was raised to a higher standard to be able to do things without the migraine being an issue. It's just like people who have disabilities. Their disability is there, but they have adapted and become stronger than it, and are able to do everyday things, just like people without disabilities.

But he was wounded for our transgressions; he was crushed for our iniquities; upon him was the chastisement that brought us peace, and with his stripes we are healed (Isaiah 53:5, ESV).

We are already healed by the stripes of Jesus. All we have to do is know we can do all things through Christ who strengthens us, and be stronger than our illness. Every day, we live our Father's name, Jehovah Rophe, our Almighty Father is our Healer. Jesus lived our Father's name, and in His name, and by His stripes and wounds we are healed and made stronger. We have to have that faith of patience in the healing Word of God's Love. Our Father loves us and doesn't want to see us in pain. He will be there for us always.

October 12

~ *Living and walking in the 'faith of kindness'* ~

Love is kind (1 Corinthians 13:4, NIV).

Kill someone with kindness and heal them. God designed us to find happiness in being kind, and this is why we are 'mankind'. Man is kind, God is love. This is our connection and relationship to our loving Father in heaven. We are to be always kind to show our Father is love. LOVE HEALS.

When someone is hurt, the kind words spoken heal them. When Jesus was healing the sinners He was kind to them in words. He didn't blame them or their parents for their sins (see John 9). Instead, He said this happens so the glory of the Father can be shown. Everything is for the glory of the Father. The illness, pains, sickness, whatsoever is for God to be glorified because He wants to be in there with you and go through it with you.

Faith comes by hearing and hearing the Word. Action that faith by being kind. If you are hurting, speak kindness to yourself and receive your inner healing. Say all the kind and good things your Father in heaven says of you. Talk to yourself in the voice of the Father. A sick person, or dying plant or animal, blooms to life again when kindness is applied in caring for them. The love energy of kindness they receive strengthens them to be well again.

Jesus, the love of God, lived the 'faith of kindness'. He was the faith of kindness. Love is kindness. He lived our Father's name, Jehovah Rophe, our Almighty Father is our Healer. The greatness of the Father's love flowed out from the kindness Jesus gave to the world by forgiving those who crucified Him.

This is the prayer of a good dad:

> *...for your love and kindness are better to me than life itself. How I praise you! (Psalm 63:3, TLB).*

Every day, live the Father's name, Jehovah Rophe, and use the 'faith of kindness' and heal yourself completely. You can only heal others when you are healed and completely free yourself. An act of kindness heals. Kindness is the force and source of power from love.

October 13

~ Praying and walking in the 'faith of peace' ~

'I have seen their ways, but I will heal them; I will guide them and restore comfort to Israel's mourners, creating praise on their lips. Peace, peace, to those far and near,' says the Lord, 'And I will heal them.' (Isaiah 57:18-19, NIV).

October 10, 2021, I was eating a cup of spicy noodles. My two-and-a-half-year-old wanted it, but I explained to him it was spicy and told him no. He kept insisting, so I gave it to him. As soon as he tasted it he gave this look of hating it. The spicy part of it had really burnt his mouth.

This is what the Holy Spirit taught me: God says NO to many things we want in life, but we keep asking and wanting those things. Then when he allows us to taste it, we see and realise how burnt out we become in it. There are many children who are raised by Christian parents but they want to taste the world, and so they slip out to check and try out the stuff of the world. However, the fear and the love of the Lord that these children were raised in will always bring them back to God. The story of the prodigal son illustrates this well (see Luke 15:11-32).

One of the reasons God says NO to some of the things we want is because they are things the enemy will easily have access to in order to destroy us if we are not matured and rooted strongly in the Word. Just as much as I wanted my two-year-old to have the spicy noodles, I couldn't allow him to have it because he is not big and strong enough to handle the spiciest part of it which will burn his mouth.

At the right time, God allowed Jesus to come into the World and destroy the work of Satan. Jesus lived our loving Father's name in heaven, Jehovah Rophe, our Almighty Father is our Healer. The devil has easy access to our old rebellious self, and this is where he wants to destroy and kill us. Jesus came and made peace with this old self. He healed that old self with peace. He gave us peace so our hearts will not be troubled in this chaotic, unstable world. It's the peace of Jesus that will always keep us calm so we are healed in Jesus' name. The doctor's report can say you have an incurable sickness, but the peace of Jesus that the Holy Spirit produces in you will heal you by calming you. Your loving Father is your healer.

> *... by abolishing the law of commandments expressed in ordinances, that he might create in himself one new man in place of the two, so making peace (Ephesians 2:15, ESV).*

Every day is a new day to remind our old self to live in peace with the new life in Christ. The peace of healing we get is knowing that our body can fail us with health issues, but Jesus will never fail us. He will always get this body of ours that fails us and complete it to Himself as the head of our body. Psalm 73:26 says it all:

> *My health fails; my spirits droop, yet God remains! He is the strength of my heart; he is mine forever!*

October 14

~ *The 'faith of a widow'* ~

> *For some time he refused. But finally he said to himself, 'Even though I don't fear God or care what people think, yet because this widow keeps bothering me, I will see that she gets justice, so that she won't eventually come and attack me!' (Luke 18:4-5, NIV).*

The morning of October 10, 2021, I was writing my manuscript on the powerful healing name of Jesus. While I was doing my normal routine, my heart was seeking the Lord to show me how one can get an instant healing, and for another. It is a process.

This is what the Holy Spirit opened my eyes to see. It was just amazing: I saw a tree with its fruits, fresh and ready to be consumed immediately. Then I saw a person taking the fruit and eating it instantly. Later, I saw an image of someone preparing a meal to cook it. After preparing everything, they opened the oven to place the food in there—the prepared ingredients had taken a while to be put together before being placed in the oven. The fresh fruit taken and eaten right away is like the person who receives instant healing. As soon as the Word of healing is spoken to them, they are healed. The person who prays over them is connected to the fresh spring living water of healing. Healing is available for the moment. That also depends on the faith of the person receiving the healing, and whether they want to be healed or not. And if they have no doubts, they are healed instantly.

For another person, the Word declared over them is a process of healing. It is to build up their faith to that level of healing. While they are in the process of healing, God gives them the strength to cope with their illness. They go through the process of getting prepared to receive the healing, like the food waiting in the oven, ready and going through the process of cooking. If they can remain in the Word, then they go through many directions where the Lord will instruct them to stop some bad habit of their lifestyle of eating so they can come out being healed. For healing to take place, your sins must be forgiven first, and you have to believe you are healed. You are already healed, but your healing goes through a process where there are some issues that you need to deal with for the healing to be manifested. Faith comes by hearing and hearing the Word, so if you lack faith you have to hear and hear the Word that you are healed.

This is where we apply the 'faith of a widow' (see Luke 18:1-8). The widow was seeking the unrighteous judge until she received her request. The unrighteous judge was just fed up with her constant crying to him and granted her request. If the unrighteous judge can do that, then our loving Father full of love will give us our desire to be healed if we constantly cry out to him for healing and don't give up. In the process of crying out we are remaining in Him by constantly seeking Him, and this is where we believe we are going to be healed.

If you remain in me and my words remain in you, ask whatever you wish, and it will be done for you (John15:7, NIV).

In the name of Jesus, who lived our Father's name, Jehovah Rophe, our Almighty Father is our Healer, we are healed. As long as we believe in Jesus' mighty powerful name, and use it with our faith, we will receive our healing, whether it be instant healing or process healing. Our loving Father is so full of love for us He will always see us through this process.

October 15

~ *The 'faith of self-control'* ~

Don't sin by letting anger control you. Think about it overnight and remain silent (Psalm 4:4, NLT).

When you practice and live a life of self-control, you discipline and heal your body from becoming angry and upset. It's those kind of reactions that stress out our body and cells and make them worn out. This is also how some illness can be formed. When you want to vomit you feel the disgusting urge of it coming out from within you, and often you have no control over it. You just run off to a place where it is easy to release it all out so you feel better. When you want to release your anger, the urge of it also starts travelling from within you—then you release it all out. The volume and tone of your voice plays a major role in taking your message to the receiver. Your vomit contains some substances that you took into you but your body doesn't agree with and throws it out again.

Your anger arises also because your eyes and ears don't like what your mind processed from what you took in. Releasing the anger on someone is like throwing out your vomit on them. Because you are feeling bad you release that bad onto someone. Most times we do it on our loved ones, especially our spouses, parents or children. It does really hurt them, but because they love us the way we are, they put up with us and live with it. This is why Jesus said for us to have a quiet and gentle heart so we can calm down the anger when it is processed. Don't allow that anger to possess you when it is processing. Live the faith life of self-control.

> *In your anger do not sin. Do not let the sun go down while*
> *you are still angry, and do not give the devil a foothold*
> *(Ephesians 4:26-27, NIV).*

The devil gets a foothold on us when we hold on to anger. This is how he does his work through us, by putting unclean spirit within us that makes us feel unclean and unwell.

Jesus lived the Father's name, Jehovah Rophe, our Almighty Father is our Healer. He lived a gentle and quiet life. This is the life to live to cure any anger or upsetting moods that want to possess us. Once the anger possesses us, unknown little sicknesses or illness start playing up with our bodies. Every little thing also starts to trigger us to be more upset or angry. With the 'faith of self-control' we control and discipline our self to remain quiet and be gentle towards situations that can anger us.

October 16

~ God heals you by restoring your loss ~

God, your God will restore everything you lost (Deuteronomy 30:3, MSG).

September 29, 2020, I was almost eight weeks pregnant and went for a scan for the heartbeat. I remember lying on the bed as the heartbeat was about to be detected, and the sonographer told me there was no heartbeat. I didn't want to believe her words. I knew, being faithful to God, He would never let me down. I have always trusted God. I have seen my mustard seed of faith move many mountains in my life. Being able to clearly hear the Holy Spirit speaking to me on a daily basis, I knew there would be a heartbeat. And I was so sure, that after two weeks I determined I would go back for a second check, knowing it would be there, because God was already preparing me to write this book, *Jehovah God-like Mind is a Good Father-Like Character*, to write about the twelve most common names of Him.

His name is His character and He is always at work according to His name. For example, Jehovah Jireh, our Almighty Father is our Provider. This is the work He does for us—always and faithfully providing. I reminded God that His name is Jehovah Shammah, our Almighty Father who is there, and right then I knew He was there, He was with me. That's His name and He was there at work, making sure the heartbeat would be there.

After two weeks, another heartbeat check was done—still no heartbeat. The report was sent to my doctor. Oh well, I still believed in God that He is Jehovah Shammah, that is His name, He is there. The heartbeat was there, I told them, and I would only believe there was no heartbeat by an internal check in the womb. The internal check was done, a more advanced one. Long story short, I was referred to have the dead foetus removed. The lowest moment of my life. Too many questions—how could a loving Father whom I trusted so much allow something like this to happen to me, especially when every day I watch my life and please Him in everything I do?

Because of the connection I have established with the Holy Spirit through my time spent daily in Word and prayer, I could hear His voice as clear as crystal. This is something I am so blessed with, for the comfort and strength He provided was so amazing. This is the Word He gave me that I will never forget and that kept me strong: You will have a story to write about this. Do not be upset about what has happened. The miscarriage, pain and suffering you went through is making you stronger to prepare to receive in double portion blessings of the next baby you will be given for this loss. The pain and lowest moment of that time was in November, 2020. The missing heartbeat was discovered at the end of September. In October I was doing all the follow-up and check-ups, and in November I was on medication to remove the dead foetus.

The morning of September 29, 2021, exactly a year after the sonographer told me there was no heartbeat, Blessed (he was two years and seven months old then) declared the heartbeat of a baby in my womb. He excitedly laughed and touched my tummy, then shouted, 'There is a baby in Mummy's tummy!' I laughed so hard, thinking how crazy this child is. He kept repeating it and grabbing my tummy, then ran to his dad who was on the phone and screamed at him, 'A baby is in Mummy's tummy and wants you to see it.' Then he spoke the same words into the phone. My six-year-old came and pulled him away, saying, 'You are not supposed to tell anyone on the phone. It's our secret.'

Our loving Father is Jehovah Shalom, our Almighty Father is our Peace. In the midst of my storm, where I was totally lost and in pain, there was peace. He is His name. He is Jehovah Rophe. He healed me with peace. The morning of October 16, 2021, was my birthday, so I decided to get the pregnancy test to confirm if Blessed's prophesy was true. It was—I was positive. The joy of loving someone whom I have never seen, my unborn baby, must also be that kind of joy I must have to love God whom I cannot see.

October 17

~ *The 'faith of goodness'* ~

> *… how God anointed Jesus of Nazareth with the Holy Spirit and power, and how he went around doing good and healing all who were under the power of the devil, because God was with him (Acts 10:38, NIV).*

Though He was God in flesh, He was living the Father's name and this is one of the reasons why He said, 'Do not call me good, only God is good.' He was speaking from a position of humbleness. In another way, our Almighty Awesome Father has used the Son to walk and live on earth. Jesus was saying our Father is so good. He was teaching us that our goodness comes from our good Father. Jesus lived our Father's name, Jehovah Rophe, our Almighty Father is our Healer, and was carrying out His healing ministry in showing the goodness of the Father, not Him as the Son. He was even questioned on performing healing on the Sabbath day, and all

He said was, 'Why are you upset that I am doing something good?' We can heal evil around us with the 'faith of goodness'.

Never get tired of doing good, for the good we do we will also reap. The acts of goodness we do stop evilness from increasing. Evilness steals the joy and peace of us, because there is no more love. By being good we give joy and peace, and that is healing to the soul being.

> *'Why do you call me good?' Jesus answered. 'No one is good—except God alone.' (Mark 10:18, NIV).*

Every day, we are to live the Father's name, Jehovah Rophe, our Almighty Father is our Healer, in healing evil around us with the 'faith of goodness'. When we have the 'faith of goodness' and keep doing good, we overcome evil, even if we do not see the result. The good we give will always return back to us.

October 18

~ *'The 'faith of gentleness'* ~

A gentle answer turns away wrath, but a harsh word stirs up anger (Proverbs 15:1, NIV).

Gently live your life in producing the fruit of the Spirit. Gentleness brings healing to your life. When you are gentle with your body, you take good care of it by giving what is good for it. You treat your body kindly and show love to your body. It's not selfish, rather, you're treating your body well so it grows and ages in good health. You are nurturing it with love. Everything grows better with love.

The hurting Samaritan man found on the roadside was taken in and gently taken care of and he recovered. We are all like hurting sheep who have gone astray, but our Shepherd, Jesus, so gently takes good care of us and brings us closer to Him and heals us. He lived our Father in heaven's name, Jehovah Rophe, our Almighty Father is our Healer. The faith and lifestyle of living a gentle and humble life can heal us. Jesus has a quiet and gentle heart and this is the heart He transplants into our hearts when we receive Him into our hearts.

Every day, let's renew our mind to live the 'faith of gentleness' and gently take care of our body that houses the Holy Spirit. Let's also maintain our new, clean heart to be gentle and quiet.

> *Take my yoke upon you and learn from me, for I am gentle and humble in heart, and you will find rest for your souls (Matthew 11:29, NIV).*

If you find yourself or loved ones sick, take care of them gently. Give love through gentleness. God is love, and gentleness that flows out from love heals. Gentleness is a fruit of love from the Holy Spirit. (see Galatians 5:22-23).

October 19

~ Healing in the blood of Jesus ~

> *They triumphed over him by the blood of the Lamb and by the word of their testimony; they did not love their lives so much as to shrink from death (Revelation 12:11, NIV).*

Blessed always wants to come into the bathroom while I'm having a shower. He tries to open the door, sometimes getting his little stool to stand on so he can open it. When I hear him doing this I normally yell from inside the bathroom for him to go away. Since he is growing and understanding some little things, he is stopping a little from disturbing me so much. He will wait now while I finish in the bathroom, my place of having a little peace time. If I want to pray without disturbance I go into the bathroom. Other sorts of prayers I don't mind saying wherever I am, but if it is a prayer that I want to rip off and bind Satan devil and target him aggressively, I normally make a quick escape into the bathroom.

The morning of October 19, 2021, I went into the bathroom but didn't close the door properly, leaving it open a bit. While I was there, pulling down the strongholds of the devil and praying, cursing and binding him, I heard Blessed opening the door and making his way in. In the middle of this prayer battle, I yelled at him also to not come in. He left, but what the Holy Spirit taught me left me in awe: You see, I was praying and rebuking the devil, and Blessed just showed me that the devil too can have access because I left some doors of my life open for him. There I was, trying to fight against the devil and demolish him because I saw his attack upon something to which he had access. This would never have happened if I had never given him access. Likewise, Blessed was able to come in because I didn't close the door properly. If I don't watch my life properly, the devil will be able to come in and do what he plans—steal, kill and destroy.

Never say words like 'I am not feeling well' or 'I am experiencing pains in my body' when you need healing in your life. Those very words we use will be used by the devil to torment us to feel unwell. The devil uses our own words to get access into our life and do what we said ourselves.

We are healed by the power of the blood of Jesus. Cover every door of your life with the blood of Jesus so the devil will not have access. He comes to steal, kill and destroy, but when He sees the blood upon you he knows that whatever work he wants to do in you is defeated and destroyed by the blood. When you have the mark of the blood upon your life, the devil will not access your life, he will pass by. Jesus lived our Father's name, Jehovah Rophe, our Almighty Father is our Healer. He healed us through the work of the cross by the pouring of His pure, sinless blood. He has given us the power to use His blood to defeat the enemy and to heal us. His blood is multipurpose: It can do everything, from healing us to defeating the enemy and keeping us safe.

October 20

~ *The 'faith of the deaf'* ~

However, as it is written: What no eye has seen, what no ear has heard, and what no human mind has conceived— the things God has prepared for those who love him (1 Corinthians 2:9, NIV).

What God has prepared for us no eyes have seen nor have ears heard. No ears have heard is the 'faith of the deaf'. When you don't hear the results of what you want, apply the faith of the deaf that your ears will hear it. Elijah was one of the prophets, famous for his great faith. He didn't beat around in doubts. What he declared and spoke he did without doubts. Elijah declared the rain was going to come, even when he didn't hear the sound of it coming. He had to speak what he couldn't hear until he heard it—now that is the 'faith of the deaf'! Keep speaking, healing and declaring it until you hear healing taking place in your life, like Elijah who didn't hear the rain but believed it was coming, then he heard it.

We may not hear the healing messages from our doctors, but we have the 'faith of the deaf' that our healing is coming upon us. We are healed in Jesus' name, whom the Father has given power, because it is Jesus who lives the name of the Father, Jehovah Rophe, our Almighty Father is our Healer.

Jesus healed the deaf man in a such a hard way. He had to transfer His DNA into the man. DNA was in His saliva—this is where He used His spit. Jesus healed him and said, 'Be opened,' (see Mark 7:31-37). When our minds are open, 'the faith of the deaf' is activated—we are hearing what we want and desire before we see it.

> *He sent out his word and healed them, and delivered them from their destruction (Psalm 107:20, ESV).*

Also, this 'faith of the deaf' is where you live by faith and not by sight, and so you will not hear what negative people are saying because you are deaf with hearing in the physical and hear only by faith.

Every day, we are to live our Father's name, Jehovah Rophe, in Jesus' name and apply the 'faith of the deaf', and keep hearing and hearing that we are healed in Jesus until we see healing. Faith comes by hearing and hearing the Word. God sent His Word and He Healed us. Jesus is the Word who God has sent to heal us. Walk by faith and not by sight.

October 21

~ *The 'faith of a commander'* ~

> *And he called the twelve together and gave them power and authority over all demons and to cure diseases (Luke 9:1, ESV).*

Jesus has given us the authority to use His name and be a commander to His commands. His new command is to love the Lord God and to love others the way we would love ourselves. We rule and reign in that position of authority.

October 21, 2021, I was in my first trimester of pregnancy. I couldn't feel any of the early pregnancy symptoms I'd felt with previous pregnancies, but I knew the baby was inside of me, even though I couldn't see her. I loved the thought of her life in me and was already in love with her. The Holy Spirit opened my eyes to see how we have to love our heavenly Father whom we can't see: You see, just like how I love my child, who is right where she is supposed to be, God is right where He is supposed to be to do His work in our life. His name is His character. He is Jehovah Rophe, our Almighty Father is our Healer. When we love Him, we love the work He is doing in our life.

For the love of his son who was unwell, the commander came to find Jesus to heal his son. He knew the power of his position, what a commander is capable of doing, and what it is like to be under an authority. And so he told Jesus, just say the word and my son will be healed. I am a commander and I just give orders and my servants respond to my command.

Jesus told him how great his faith was (see Luke 7:7-10). You see, we have to just use the Word who is Jesus and command that sickness to leave. That's our position of authority. The 'faith of a commander'. Some sicknesses are caused by the devil's strong hold upon us, and when he sees that we are taking our position of authority and command him to leave, he will leave instantly.

> *But say the word, and my servant will be healed*
> *(Luke 7:7, NIV).*

Every day, we are to live our Father's name, Jehovah Rophe, in Jesus' name, and take our position of authority and command every sickness or disease to leave us and flee.

October 22

~ *The 'faith of a mustard seed'* ~

... if you have faith as small as a mustard seed, you can say to this mountain, 'Move from here to there,' and it will move. Nothing will be impossible for you (Matthew 17:20, NIV).

One morning, October 22, 2021, I was in my first trimester and thinking of my pregnancy and how high the risk of miscarriage is, especially in the first trimester. The Holy Spirit opened my eyes to see how a small seed can begin its life in an unseen dark place, and can be vulnerable. It's like the faith of a mustard seed. With the faith of a mustard seed, nothing is impossible—the big mountains in our life can even be moved. Faith comes from hearing and hearing the Word, and even with that mustard seed of faith, a life is made in the Word. Just like the life I carried within me would grow and grow until matured and ready to come out from me to live, so it is with our mustard seed of faith. The more we nurture and speak the Word of God with our mustard seed of faith, it will eventually bring life to our situations. I would see my baby by giving birth to her. We too will give birth to healing and blessings, even with the mustard seed of faith.

Healing, restoration and deliverance will take place when we use our 'mustard seed of faith'! Jesus lived our Father's name, Jehovah Rophe, our Almighty Father is our Healer. The seed of woman, He came to crush the head of the enemy (see Genesis 3:15). The power and authority He used to crush the head of the enemy is now given to us. We are His seed. With the power and authority He has given to us, we are able to move mountains and crush down our enemies with our mustard seed of faith. We just have to faithfully remain in the Word and action the fruit of righteousness for our mustard seed of faith to be more effective. The prayer of a righteous person is effective (see James 5:16).

October 23

~ *Praying and walking in the 'faith of love'* ~

> *... if my people, who are called by my name, will humble themselves and pray and seek my face and turn from their wicked ways, then I will hear from heaven, and I will forgive their sin and will heal their land*
> *(2 Chronicles 7:14, NIV).*

A good dad prays with the 'faith of love' and receives his healing. We cannot see God, but we can see the love of God through the love given to us by our loved ones. Faith without action is dead. To be healed, we have to action love and release forgiveness if we have unforgiveness. Where there is forgiveness, there is healing. Unforgiveness leads to many negative disorders that build our characters and cause sickness and disease. A clean, caring heart and a clear, loving mind creates a healthy glowing body.

A good dad doesn't play the game of blaming. As the leader and head of the family, he takes responsibility and solves the problem. In the garden of Eden, the first man blamed the woman and God. Adam told God, 'It's the woman whom you gave me made me disobey and I ate the forbidden fruit.' The woman then blamed the serpent (see Genesis 3:11-13). But God is our loving Father, full of mercy and love. He took the blame and responsibility. Jesus lived our Father's name, our Almighty Father is our Healer. Jesus took upon himself the guilt, blame and responsibility, and healed us from what sin will do to us.

> *Above all, love each other deeply, because love covers over a multitude of sins (1 Peter 4:8, NIV).*

For the love of our Father to flow freely in us, from Him to us, there has to be forgiveness. By faith, God gave His only Son, who gave us love and forgiveness. The 'faith of love' brings forgiveness and we are healed from within. We can heal others when we are healed first.

Our Father had faith and believed in us that we will love Him. He sent Jesus to action His love for us. We have received the love of our Father in Christ to love Him with all our heart, soul and strength. He loved us even when we were rebellious and in sin (see Romans 5:8), and we love because He first loved us (see 1 John 4:19). Our Father's love forgives, restores and heals. Jesus demonstrated that love on the cross.

Every day is a new day to live our Father's name and provide healing to ourselves and others by walking in the 'faith of love' and forgiving where we need to forgive. This is how we heal ourselves from hatred and unforgiveness, which when left can cause pains and aches in our body.

October 24

~ Faith of an 'expecting mother in labour' ~

> *Just as a pregnant woman writhes and cries out in pain as she gives birth, so were we in your presence, Lord (Isaiah 26:17, NLT).*

An expecting mother who is about to birth a child will be in pain and feel so many uncomfortable hurts or pains in her body. December 24, 2022, my tooth was aching so much. It had started two to three weeks earlier, but had become much worse over the previous two days. I prayed over it and the pain slowed down, but it would come again every now and then. I knew I was about to birth some great things within me, one of which was to publish this book, to bring it to life. That meant I had to live with the pain and be stronger than the pain. I couldn't even visit a dentist because it was a holiday season and most were already closed and would not resume after the new year. You see, I was stuck in a pain which I had to live with. This was not the first time I battled this. In 2020, when I was about to birth the devotional book *Holy Ghost-like mind is a Good Mother-like Character*, I went through the same experience.

> *During the meal Jesus took some bread in his hands. He blessed the bread and broke it. Then he gave it to his disciples and said, "Take this and eat it. This is my body."*
> *(Matthew 26:26, CEV).*

You see, many times we have to go through the same pain time and again because we are giving birth again. AGAIN, it's *a gain – no pain, no gain,* as you have heard. Jesus lived our Father's name, Jehovah Rophe, our Almighty Father is our Healer. He went through the pain. His flesh was broken so we could be healed. Before He died, He showed how He was to be broken in pain by breaking the bread as a symbol of His broken flesh. He gave it to all His followers, and as His followers now, we have received His broken flesh. The one pain He went through is being broken for us, in portions to go through, and give birth and bring alive the many potentials and greatness buried inside of us. Even Jesus said, 'You will do great things and even more greater than what I have done' (see John 14:12).

> *It will be like a woman suffering the pains of labor. When her child is born, her anguish gives way to joy because she has brought a new baby into the world*
> *(John 16:21, NLT).*

We are created for our Father's glory to live His name, Jehovah Rophe, with the 'faith of an expecting mother in labour', and heal our pain by going with the flow of the pain, knowing we are about to bring to life and birth great things we have conceived. Just like the joy and new strength the expecting mother receives after birthing her baby, we too will receive the joy and become stronger after going through the pain and giving birth to new achievements.

October 25

~ Heal your mind in the Word of God and have the mind of Christ ~

Do not conform to the pattern of this world, but be transformed by the renewing of your mind. Then you will be able to test and approve what God's will is—his good, pleasing and perfect will (Romans 12:2, NIV).

December 25, 2022, we were having a little picnic in our backyard. We have some queen ants around and normally try to be careful not to step into their territory. We took some red cushions from indoors to lie on. After eating and having a good time, I decided to clean up and take the things back into the house. But then I thought, *I must make sure to check the cushions properly in case some of the ants are attached and I take them into the house with me.*

Instantly, I heard the Holy Spirit teaching me this: This is what you must also do with thoughts entering your mind. Assess them and check that no thoughts that conform to the standards of this world remain in your mind.

Hear this: Thoughts are knowledge of information that we are aware of because we are alive. They are like rushing waters that flow into our minds. We can't control their movements into our mind, but we can control and check these thoughts and decide whether to allow them to remain in our mind and flow down into our hearts. Every second our mind is processing these thoughts of knowledge. Just as I wanted to make sure to check the cushions carefully before taking them into the house, we too must check our thoughts carefully before we allow them to remain in our mind and be part of our daily actions.

Because of our genetic, natural flesh birth, we have full access and rights to the tree of the knowledge of good and evil. Jesus lived our Father's name, Jehovah Rophe, our Lord God is our Healer. His flesh was broken and crushed to bring healing and restoration to us so we can have the mind of Christ (see 1 Corinthians 2:16) to have right thoughts of knowledge which can bring healing to our mind. When our mind is healed, our body and spirit is healed. We feed our flesh and spirit with the right things.

Most times, we think it's only our body that needs healing and we forget about our mind. When we have a sound, clear and clean mind that thinks good and right thoughts, we live a life of righteousness. The right thoughts in our mind lead us in doing the right things; this is living in the righteousness of Christ. Because of Jesus, we now can have access to the tree of life.

> *Then the angel showed me the river of the water of life, bright as crystal, flowing from the throne of God and of the Lamb through the middle of the street of the city; also, on either side of the river, the tree of life with its twelve kinds of fruit, yielding its fruit each month. The leaves of the tree were for the healing of the nations (Revelation 22:1-2, ESV).*

Every day, be born again with the birth of the new day, so you can enter and see the kingdom of God that gives you access and rights to the tree of life to heal your mind.

October 26

~ The 'faith of a daughter' - taking that daughter position ~

> *But Jesus said, 'Someone touched me; I know that power has gone out from me' (Luke 8:46, NIV).*

Every daughter believes in their father and that he can do anything for them. Even the strongest big man comes down to his knees and plays with his little daughter. My seven-year-old daughter believes everything her dad tells her and loves her father so much that he does anything to make her happy. He even plays with her and her toys, but most of all, he plays her favourite game of hide and seek. If a human father who is not perfect in love can do this, just imagine how our loving Father in heaven would shower us in His perfect love that has no flaws.

> *Then the woman, seeing that she could not go unnoticed, came trembling and fell at his feet. In the presence of all the people, she told why she had touched him and how she had been instantly healed. Then he said to her, 'Daughter, your faith has healed you. Go in peace.' (Luke 8:47-48, NIV).*

The bleeding woman took her faith position of a daughter. *If I can only touch his cloak, then I would be healed,* she thought. In the midst of a crowd of people her touch was so familiar to Jesus and power went out from Him. When a daughter touches his dad, she can make him weak, so he will do anything for her. Jesus asked,

'Who touched me?' It was a different touch as power flowed out from Him. Jesus said it right there, 'Daughter, your faith has healed you.' This is the 'faith of a daughter'.

Each and every day, take the 'faith of a daughter' and touch your Father—reach out to Him for healing and receive your healing. Daughters move their fathers. As a dad, you know how your daughters move your heart. Do the same to your Father in heaven.

October 27

~ God sent His Word who has become flesh to heal our flesh ~

He sent out his word and healed them, and delivered them from their destruction (Psalm 107:20, ESV).

It was a beautiful, sunshine-filled spring morning, October 5, 2021. Tom and the kids had left our car on the other side of the beach and walked. Tom said to leave them on the park and they'd walk back to the car. The Lord was trying to release a message to me. From time to time, I can easily pick it when He is about to do that. He makes me focus my attention on something around me. Sometimes it will be through walking or doing house chores. Feeling that signal, I told Tom no, I would walk back to get the car. As I walked, the Holy Spirit began to show me a bottle of clean water and said: If you put even a little bit of dirty water into it, the clean water bottle will become dirty. But then He showed me that the water can still remain clean if it continues to receive into it clean water. The clean water can empty out the dirty water that was put into it.

You see, we lived in a sick fallen world and will continue to see and hear evil around us. We can't stop this things of this world to enter our mind to pollute it, but if we continue to receive into us the Word of God, we will be made clean. And if we abide in Christ in His Word, fresh clean springs of living water will continue to flow out from us and remove all the uncleanliness and dirt. Jesus said you are clean because of the Word. The Word of God is healing and will heal you. Let nothing of this world bring you fear, because the Word of God will always heal you as long as you abide in it.

> *You are already clean because of the word I have spoken to you (John 15:3, NIV).*

There was healing in the spring water when an angel put healing power in and stirred the water up. When we keep praying and believing for healing, we create the form of healing in our flesh until it shows in our body. We create our healing from stirring the word of healing from within us. But for that to happen, we have to store within us the Word of healing from God's Word, because that will determine our faith level to receive that healing.

> *Whoever believes in me, as Scripture has said, rivers of living water will flow from within them (John 7:38, NIV).*

Jesus lived our Father's name, Jehovah Rophe, our Almighty Father, our Healer. He is the Word of God, whom God, Himself sent to heal, the Word who has become flesh so our flesh can now receive the Word of healing and be healed and set free from any sickness or disease.

Every day, we are to live our Father's name, Jehovah Rophe, and abide in Jesus, the Word of God who heals. We are to stir up the Word of healing and let healing flow out from us to those who need it.

October 28

~ Having faith in your belief brings healing ~

I will give you back your health again and heal your wounds (Jeremiah 30:17, TLB).

One cold winter's night, June 3, 2021, I was chatting with a friend and she told me how her one-and-a-half year-old was sick and vomiting a lot. I prayed over the child and said, 'You are healed in Jesus' name.' I then told the mum to buy Coke for her, as the gas in the Coke is good for the stomach. She responded, 'Oh, true?' I told her I do that for my kids and they get better. She was just afraid to give Coke to her baby. I later received a message from her that the baby was fine and quit vomiting after drinking the Coke. It was faith with action applied—after praying, we actioned our faith by giving Coke to the little one.

Why do we trust doctors whom we don't know about the type of medicine they give or recommend for us to drink? We have faith in them and believe their role as doctors, and that the medicine prescribed will make us well. It's just like how I believe gas from Coke is good for vomiting, and my friend placed that belief with me and it worked. We action that faith when we take into us the medication they give, and this is where healing takes place in our body. If you are on some medication, pray with faith and take your medication and this can bring healing to your body.

A good dad knows His Father in heaven is rich in loving kindness and wants healing for His children in all areas of life. He sits and stores the Word of the Father in his heart for his healing and his house. The Father has already sent His Word who is Jesus, the Word who has become flesh. A good dad remains in the Word and stirs up the healing within him to flow through him and out towards his household and all who need it.

> *He sent out his word and healed them; he rescued them from the grave (Psalm 107:20, NIV).*

Jesus lived our Father's name, Jehovah Rophe, our Lord God is our Healer. He had no education or background of a physician, yet He healed all kinds of sickness and disease. He is the Word who the Father sent so we can be healed.

Every day, remain in the Word that our Father sent for healing. That is faith. Then action that faith and walk in obedience with what the Father says in His Word. If there is a food that you believe is not good for your body to eat, then respond and obey what your body is saying and action it. The right food is medicine to our body and soul.

October 29

~ *The 'faith of a newborn baby'* ~

> *Be like newborn babies, crying out for spiritual milk that will help you grow into salvation (1 Peter 2:2, The Voice).*

One beautiful morning, August 14, 2022, I was feeding my newborn baby. As I was looking at her and thinking how she would only cry to get my attention to attend to her needs, the Holy Spirit taught me this: The faith of a newborn baby is what we also need to apply to get God to heal us instantly. Just like how a newborn baby cries to get the attention of a parent to calm them and give them what they need, we too need to cry to our Father in heaven until He attends to our needs of healing.

Jesus came and lived our Father's name, Jehovah Rophe, our Lord God is our Healer. He healed the blind man who constantly cried out to Him. The more we cry out to our Father in Jesus' name for healing, we will receive it. Since Jesus lived our Father's name, whatever we ask of the Father in Jesus' name will be given to us.

Do not give in to voices of the enemy to silence you from taking the position of the faith of a newborn baby—continue crying until you are heard. Keep crying until Jesus attends to you. There were even voices trying to stop that blind man, but he continued crying until Jesus attended to him and healed him (See Luke 18:35-43 for full story).

Every day, we are to wake up, and like a newborn baby, desire the spiritual milk of God's Word. And with our faith of a newborn baby, cry unto God to attend to our needs for the day, to heal us where we need healing and to prepare us to heal others who come our way.

October 30

~ Healed from brokenness ~

I prayed to you, Lord God, and you healed me
(Psalm 30:2, CEV).

One morning, February 15, 2021, I was thinking of seeing a dentist I know about my teeth. I thought *since I know the dentist, I don't really like the idea of seeing him because he will know what kind of bad teeth I have*. I was given a voucher from the government hospital to see a private dentist and he was the one on the list of the suburb I lived in. This is what I heard the Holy Spirit say: Many times you need help, but you don't reach out because you don't want people you know to know about the struggles you go through. Many want to come and know God and have a relationship with Him, but they procrastinate, saying, 'Oh, when my life is good I will start going to church, pray and read my Bible. At the moment, I am so messed up. Let me just sort myself out first.' But this is not what God wants from us. He wants us to come to Him when we need Him. He made you and me and He knows how to fix us right now, the way we are. Jehovah Rophe is His name, the Healer, and He will heal you in the state or condition you are in right now. How can He heal you when you don't have any brokenness for Him to heal?

A good dad goes to His Father in heaven and seeks Him to heal him in his broken state, not when he is fine. If he wants to be a good father figure to his household, he has to go with all the mess he has been piling up in his house so His Father, Jehovah Rophe, the Healer, can heal his conditions.

Jesus lived our Father's name. He ate and drank with the sinners and spoke with compassion to the broken people so He could heal them. Jesus said it was not the healthy who needed the doctor, but the sick. Our Father has given the name of Jesus the authority to heal every sickness and disease.

> *While Jesus was having dinner at Matthew's house, many tax collectors and sinners came and ate with him and his disciples. When the Pharisees saw this, they asked his disciples, 'Why does your teacher eat with tax collectors and sinners?' On hearing this, Jesus said, 'It is not the healthy who need a doctor, but the sick.' (Matthew 9:10-12, NIV).*

Every new day is another opportunity to use the power in the name of Jesus to declare healing upon our body so it can house the Holy Spirit perfectly. We need to go to our Father in heaven as a sinner, in need of His mercy and grace to sustain, restore and heal our ageing bodies. This body of ours is accessible to sin and needs the healing of God constantly.

October 31

~ *Rise up in the Word and declare words of healing upon you* ~

If the Spirit of him who raised Jesus from the dead dwells in you, he who raised Christ Jesus from the dead will also give life to your mortal bodies through his Spirit who dwells in you (Romans 8:11, ESV).

On the morning of February 10, 2021, I woke up with body aches, a sore throat and even a head cold that gave me migraines. As usual, I had a hard copy of my devotional book, *Holy Ghost-like mind is a Good Mother-like Character*. Reading through the last bit of February 10 in the book, it said:

Let me quote! Rise and shine with your new day by raising yourself up in the Word of God!

This was all I needed to hear, so I started raising myself up in the Word of God by declaring and quoting scriptures that said 'I am healed'. Within an hour I was feeling so much better! Tom didn't believe it, as I was so knocked down with the flu, yet in the next hour I was up and well and shining.

A good dad raises himself and his house to God to heal and remove any threats of sickness that are about to manifest. Being the head of his house, he connects his body to Christ, who is the head of his body. He declares scriptures of healing and makes His Word of healing to become flesh into his flesh. Just like how one vaccinates themselves to stay protected from viruses, he vaccinates his flesh with the Word who has become flesh.

> *He himself bore our sins in his body on the tree, that we might die to sin and live to righteousness. By his wounds you have been healed (1 Peter 2:24, ESV).*

Jesus Christ, the Word of God who became flesh, has lived our Father's name, Jehovah Rophe, our Lord God, our Healer. We are healed in Jesus' name to remain in that name of Jesus to heal ourselves and others. Every day, declare healing in the name of Jesus and vaccinate the Word of healing from the Word of God who has become flesh into your flesh and your household.

NOVEMBER

Jehovah Rohi! I AM Your Shepherd!

Jehovah God-like Mind is a Good Father-like Character

OUR LORD GOD IS OUR SHEPHERD.

~ The Shepherd is coming soon to take His sheep to the place He prepared for them ~

Therefore you also must be ready, for the Son of Man is coming at an hour you do not expect (Matthew 24:44, ESV).

December 9, 2021, I arranged to meet up with a woman who offered to sell me some things. She was to bring them to me herself. While I was preparing myself to be ready to meet her, this is what I heard the Holy Spirit say: We also are to be prepared while waiting for Christ to come and meet us. It's going to be a surprise as we do not know the hour of any day. It's either we go meet Him by transiting out of earth through death, or He comes as a surprise on the clouds.

The heroes of faith who are the clouds of witnesses and cheer for us have finished the race of faith and are waiting for Christ (see Hebrews 12:1). They are the dead in Christ who will rise up first when Christ appears on the clouds. The clouds of witnesses are ready to meet our Master when He comes on the clouds.

Jesus walked and lived on earth our Father's name, Jehovah Rohi, our Almighty Father is our Shepherd. He came not only for us to follow Him and hear His voice of direction to be on the path of life, but to be prepared and be ready all the time to meet Him. When we know how to hear His voice through the Holy Spirit, we will be committed to walking in righteousness every day. This is how we will be prepared each day and ready to meet up with Him. Hear this: I was prepared and ready to meet this lady when she came to my place because I had the money to offer to her for what she was to sell to me. This is the same with us, as we too have to be prepared to meet with Jesus to offer to Him a life of righteousness when He comes, because that is the eternal life in Him.

Each day of the month of November, and every day, we have to live our Father's name, Jehovah Rohi, our Almighty Father is our Shepherd, and be the voice of righteousness to lead others on the path of righteousness that leads to eternal life.

November 1

~ Becoming a son to lead the Father's sheep ~

For to us a child is born, to us a son is given
(Isaiah 9:6, NIV).

November 1, 2021, I was trying to get the juice blender to make some fresh juice. The blender is high up in the cupboard and I normally stand on a stool to reach it. The stool was where I was, but I didn't look properly and didn't see it. All I was thinking about was my two-year-old putting it somewhere, because he is the only one who moves it around. I checked around the house, knowing he must have taken it with him to stand on it. After some attempts to find it, I came back and noticed it right where I was.

The Holy Spirit opened my ears to hear this: Right where we are is where God plants us, but because our eyes are not opened to see, we go here and there until we learn something and our eyes begin to open to see it. All the promises of God are yes and amen in Christ, but we have to be matured in Christ for our eyes to be open to see it.

A child has to be mature to inherit a family's inheritance. To us a child is born and a son is given. When we are born again we become the child of God. When we walk and live in the love of God and are matured, we become a son. We become matured like Christ. For God so LOVES the world that He GAVE His SON. We too must LOVE like our Father to be a son. When we become a son we are matured to inherit, our Father's inheritance, and to shepherd others.

Jesus came and lived our Father's name, Jehovah Rohi, our Almighty Father is our Shepherd. He came to carry, guide and lead us so we can see where He is leading us in life. He is leading us to the path of green pastures of the abundant eternal life. I have seen a little picture here as well. My little two-year-old then, would carry this little stool with him to stand on it to get what he wanted. Jesus is our Shepherd and is carrying us around just so we can be strong and stand for Him and get what we want, instead of being misled and going astray. The more we are in the Word, even when we go astray we will always hear our Shepherd's voice and get back onto the path that leads to life.

This is the prayer of a good dad:

> *Let me live that I may praise you, and may your laws sustain me. I have strayed like a lost sheep. Seek your servant, for I have not forgotten your commands (Psalm 119:175-176, NIV).*

Every day, in Jesus' name, we are to live our Father's name, Jehovah Rohi, our Almighty Father is our Shepherd. Jesus lived our Father's name and it is now for us to live that name to carry, guide and lead our house in the path of abundant life in Christ.

November 2

~ Our Good Shepherd leads His sheep not into temptation but delivers and saves them from the evil one ~

But when you are tempted, he will also provide a way out so that you can endure it (1 Corinthians 10:13, NIV).

A good dad is a good shepherd to his household, and so he stays connected to his heavenly Father in Word and prayer. The *Lord's Prayer* is part of his everyday prayer because he desires for His Father to lead him not into temptation but deliver him from the evil one. To avoid getting into temptation, he renews his mind upon Psalm 101:3, 'I will set nothing wicked before my eyes' (Psalm 101:3 NKJV).

Our Father in heaven is called Jehovah Rohi, our Lord God is our Shepherd. Jesus lived our Father's name by being our good Shepherd, He left the ninety-nine sheep who remained in His righteousness to look for that one lost sheep to lead back to the Father. The other ninety-nine were well fed and had shelter already. He was concerned about that one lost sheep who was stolen to be killed and destroyed by the enemy, the devil, trapped in lies, blind with no sight to return home, cold, hungry and without shelter. Jesus was led into temptation by the tempter, devil Satan, yet He never sinned. He was delivered by declaring the Word of our Father.

God's Word can turn temptation into triumph when we use it to escape our temptation. Every day, live the Father's name in Jesus' name and be that shepherd to lead others away from the temptations of this world.

November 3

~ *Our Good Shepherd carries us through the seasons of pain into the season of eternal joy* ~

Because the Lord is my Shepherd, I have everything I need! He lets me rest in the meadow grass and leads me beside the quiet streams. He gives me new strength. He helps me do what honours him the most. Even when walking through the dark valley of death I will not be afraid, for you are close beside me, guarding, guiding all the way (Psalm 23:1-4, TLB).

The date of my appointment, November 3, 2020, I was waiting at the hospital to go in for an operation to remove my dead foetus, at around seven weeks gestation, because there was no heartbeat. My heavenly Father surely remembered me. While waiting for the doctors to call me in and thinking of how I was waiting for my time to come, this is what I heard the Holy Spirit say: How you wait on time is how you should wait on God. This is how you should seek God. You keep seeing the clock to see the time—keep seeking God that you are waiting on Him. He is the time. Jesus told the Samaritan woman a time is coming, and the time is here. He is the time and He is here.

Yet a time is coming and has now come when the true worshippers will worship the Father in the Spirit and in truth, for they are the kind of worshippers the Father seeks (John 4:23, NIV).

Our loving Father's name is Jehovah Rohi, our Almighty Father is our Shepherd. Jesus lived our Father's name and became our Shepherd. He is our Shepherd and we shall never be in want. All the time, and every time, he leads and provides for us. We just have to seek Him, look up to Him and wait on Him because He is our shepherd.

November 3, 2021, exactly a year after I was in the hospital to remove a dead foetus from my womb because there was no heartbeat from seven weeks gestation, I was at the hospital once more. Only this time, I was there to confirm that there was a heartbeat at seven weeks. Jesus Christ is the Shepherd who carries us through the seasons of pain into the season of joy.

November 4

~ Feed your mind with the Word of God so your heart can store that Word ~

Above all else, guard your heart, for everything you do flows from it (Proverbs 4:23, NIV).

Your mind, where your soul is with your will and emotions, must guide your heart and protect it. What goes into the mind goes down into the heart, then flows out. As a man thinketh, so is he (see Proverbs 23:7). Just like how you take your meal and it goes into your stomach to be used to give your body strength, the Word of God is the food for the soul. It goes into the mind, then into your heart where your spirit is, to give strength to the spirit. Man cannot live by bread alone, but by every word that comes out of God's mouth (see Matthew 4:4).

A good dad uses the fruit of the Spirit, 'self-control' to control his mind. He lets his mind guide his heart, because everything flows out from the heart. He is whatever he thinks he is, because from the mind it goes into the heart and flows back to the mind. From where it comes, it returns back.

> *For though we walk in the flesh, we are not waging war according to the flesh. For the weapons of our warfare are not of the flesh but have divine power to destroy strongholds. We destroy arguments and every lofty opinion raised against the knowledge of God, and take every thought captive to obey Christ (2 Corinthians 10:3-5, ESV).*

A good dad focuses on having the mind of Christ by holding every thought and making it captive to obey Christ. Like Jesus Christ who obeyed the Father and submitted to Him until death on the cross, he also controls his thoughts to submit and obey Christ so his flesh can die daily to the standards of this world.

Jesus lived our Father's name, Jehovah Rohi, our Lord God, our Shepherd. He is our Shepherd who leads and feeds us in the righteousness of the Father. Because of all He did, we are now able to feed on Him and have the mind of Christ.

Every day, we are called by our Father to live His name, Jehovah Rohi, and look for that one lost sheep to bring home to the ninety-nine sheep who are in the righteousness of Christ.

November 5

~ Living the faith life of a sheep ~

> *The Lord is my shepherd; I have all that I need (Psalm 23:1, NLT).*

A good dad lives a 'faith life of a sheep'. A sheep knows that as long as their shepherd is there, everything is going to be alright. They know the love they receive from their master. A good dad has the 'faith of a sheep', always gentle and quiet with a listening ear to His Master, Jesus. He knows his loving Father is His Shepherd. His name is Jehovah Rohi, our Almighty Father is our Shepherd. He sent His only Son to come down to earth and show us the love of a shepherd. Through the dark valley of life where a pack of wolves awaits, a good dad stays calm and at peace. He knows His Father, the Shepherd, is there watching, guiding, protecting and leading him through. Every day he finds rest in the green pasture of His Shepherd's Word and his soul is restored with delights.

> *He lets me rest in green meadows; he leads me beside peaceful streams. He renews my strength. He guides me along right paths, bringing honour to his name. Even when I walk through the darkest valley, I will not be afraid, for you are close beside me. Your rod and your staff protect and comfort me (Psalm 23:2-4, NLT).*

Jesus is our Good Shepherd. He fought the battle of death and conquered it. He did the Father proud by not only putting His life at risk, but He laid down His life for us, so we can also inherit the life of being a shepherd and live our Father's name, Jehovah Rohi. He left the luxury of heaven just to come and rescue that one lost sheep trapped in the misery of the world.

Every day is a new day to live our Father's name, Jehovah Rohi, and look for lost sheep to feed, clothe, or to keep them company and show our Father's love.

November 6

~ Our Shepherd calls us by our name and we know His voice ~

> *Praise be to the God and Father of our Lord Jesus Christ! In his great mercy he has given us new birth into a living hope through the resurrection of Jesus Christ from the dead (1 Peter 1:3, NIV).*

One rainy Saturday morning, November 27, 2021, I just felt so much better with no pregnancy moods. When you are pregnant and you don't feel pregnancy sicknesses or symptoms, you just start feeling worried, especially if you are in your first trimester. You wonder if everything is okay. I mean, I am supposed to feel all the symptoms to give me the assurance that I am pregnant. This is what I heard the Holy Spirit say: You are thinking all this because you are carrying a life within you, and so you are concerned whether that life is alive or not. The same too, when you receive Jesus. You are carrying a new life inside of you which you have to be mindful of, and you must renew your mind to have the mind of Christ (see 1 Corinthians 2:16). You are supposed to be full of joy and peace because you are aware that Jesus lives in you through the Holy Spirit, and the Holy Spirit produces His fruit of joy and peace.

When I was pregnant, I carried a life inside of me which caused my hormones to create and release pregnancy symptoms. When I have the Life of Jesus inside of me and when Jesus is alive, I have His Holy Spirit producing and releasing His fruit of righteousness. It's up to me to release and produce this fruit of righteousness or not.

Jesus lived our Father's name, Jehovah Rohi, our Almighty Father is our Shepherd. He came into this world and laid down His life so we can be born again into the life He has laid down for us. We can make Him alive in us by producing the fruit of the Holy Spirit in us so people around us can see that Jesus is alive and is living in us, or we can continue to be like a lost sheep without a shepherd. The eternal life of the Shepherd, Jesus is there to guide us so we are no_longer a lost sheep—we are called by our name to follow our Shepherd.

The birth of every new day is a reminder that we carry the life of Jesus in us and we are to give birth to His life in producing the fruit of His Spirit in us.

November 7

~ The Word of God is instructions to live and use our life ~

I will instruct you and teach you in the way you should go; I will counsel you with my eye upon you (Psalm 32:8, ESV).

December 8, 2021, was presentation day at my six-year-old's school. My daughter, who was in year one, received an award and brought her present to me, a box of coloured pencils. After she unwrapped it she wanted me to open it for her. The box was a bit big. I went ahead to open it, but it was not like the other small boxes that are easy to open. I thought I knew how to open it and never took time to read the instructions, so ended up doing the wrong thing. The Holy Spirit taught me an important lesson in this: It is the same with God's Word, the instructions of how we use our life, but we don't read the instructions of how to apply it in our life. Because it is our life, we think we know how to live it the way we want. Then we end up doing the wrong thing, like making wrong decisions on important issues of life.

Jesus came and lived our Father's name, Jehovah Rohi, our Almighty Father is our Shepherd. He leads us with His gentle and calming voice that is full of love through the Holy Spirit within us. His Word is what we need to take into us. It is the instructions of how to live and use our life. The Holy Spirit goes over the Word and brings it to life, and this is how we know what the Word is saying of things concerning our life.

Each and every day we are to abide and remain in the Word so we can live our Father's name, Jehovah Rohi, in Jesus' name. Because we know the truth and remain in the truth, we are to lead as a shepherd and be the voice of instruction for the voiceless.

November 8

~ Be faithful to your commitment ~

And may your hearts be fully committed to the Lord our God, to live by his decrees and obey his commands, as at this time (1 Kings 8:61, NIV).

Every Monday morning from 5:30 am, I normally join with other beautiful praying women of God. I normally set my alarm for 5 am so I can prepare myself before prayer session begins. One morning, November 8, 2021, I woke up and instantly a voice flew into my mind suggesting I should go back to sleep, because while sleeping my little finger had gotten twisted and it hurt a bit. Another voice instantly said: It's not your finger that is going to pray. You have made a commitment to pray every Monday morning and you have to rise up and pray. When you make a commitment to your job to work and earn a salary, you faithfully wake up, dress up and show up. You do that because you do not want to lose your job and have no source of income to sustain you. When you make a commitment to pray for your families, your country and your friends, you have to wake up, dress up and show up. You do not want the enemy to come around and find you exposed easily for him to attack you. After logging into my laptop for the prayers, the Holy Spirit revealed to me that it was not only me the enemy was trying to stop from praying, but the others as well. So I made it known to everyone how the devil must have attacked them in different ways, and almost everyone confirmed it.

They devoted themselves to the apostles' teaching and to fellowship, to the breaking of bread and to prayer (Acts 2:42, NIV).

You see, Jesus came and lived the Father's name, Jehovah Rohi, our Almighty Father is our Shepherd. The hour of the night He was to be handed over to die for us, He was praying. The Shepherd who was going to lay down His life for His sheep was praying to be comforted and strengthened. He was praying for the will of the Father. And the will of the Father was for Him to lay down His life. However, His disciples were sleeping while He was praying. He rebuked them to at least stay for an hour to pray.

We are to live our Father's name, Jehovah Rohi, and be the shepherd to carry our loved ones in prayer so the will of the Father can be done in their life. This is our commitment we have to fulfil for our loved ones. Love is faithful, and we have to be that faithful shepherd by carrying them closer to God in prayer. Every day commit the plans of all your commitment to the Lord and He will make it successful (see Proverbs 16:3).

November 9

~ Have compassion on someone's struggle and not comparison ~

The Pharisee stood by himself and prayed: 'God, I thank you that I am not like other people—robbers, evildoers, adulterers—or even like this tax collector. I fast twice a week and give a tenth of all I get.' (Luke 18:11-12, NIV).

I came across a discussion of some of the things people were grateful on social media, and they were mentioning how they were so grateful to have a roof over their heads while many are homeless, food to eat while others have none and a job, while someone just lost their job and many others are looking for a job. As I was thinking over what they were grateful for, the Holy Spirit opened my eyes and taught me how to pray and be grateful: Don't be grateful in comparison to someone else's struggles. Do not say, 'Thank you, Lord, I have a home to live in while many don't have homes.' You should be praying for them to have also what you are being grateful for. It's like the Pharisee who looked down on the taxpayer's humble prayer and started thanking the Lord he was not like that taxpayer man, that he fasted twice a week and faithfully gave to the Lord (see Luke 18:9-14).

This is one way of prideful living that the devil uses to get people to be grateful. Our Father in heaven is so full of love and compassion and doesn't want any of us go through any suffering. It's the choices and decisions we make in our lives that put us on the path of our destiny. Whether we are rich or poor, whether we have or don't have, we are all made in His likeness to give Him glory in whatever we do—and that's what matters to our Father.

> *Live together in peace with each other. Don't be proud, but be willing to be friends with people who are not important to others. Don't think of yourself as smarter than everyone else (Romans 12:16, ERV).*

A good dad doesn't teach his children to look at other people's suffering to compare themselves and feel how they are doing okay. He teaches his children compassion, mercy and to always be kind, because we don't know why someone lives the way they do until we walk in their shoes. He teaches them about the purpose and individual calling God has for them and to live that calling.

Jesus lived our loving Father in heaven's name, Jehovah Rohi, our Almighty Father is our Shepherd. He is the only way, the truth and the life. He laid down His life for us, His sheep, so we can enter into that path of life and walk in it to the eternal life of destiny. This is what we should be grateful for in life and live our Father's name,

Jehovah Rohi, in Jesus' name, so we can lead others to the path of life, instead of thinking how good we are in comparison to them.

Every day is a new day, calling to us to keep being that shepherd in practising the nine fruit of the Holy Spirit so the lost sheep can see the fruit of righteousness in us and follow us.

November 10

~ *Our characters must live the standards of God's position in our life* ~

> *Whatever you do, work at it with all your heart,*
> *as working for the Lord, not for human masters*
> *(Colossians 3:23, NIV).*

One Saturday, November 21, 2021, I was watching a television show of people taking holidays in holiday homes. The lady talking was an expert on judging holiday homes and her name and the title of her job appeared on her image as she was talking. Based on her title and position, she was judging and giving rating of the holiday homes, then explaining more about why each got that rating and what they could have done to improve their holiday homes more to get better ratings. As I was watching, the Holy Spirit opened my eyes to see who God is: His name is His position and title, and what He does is show us He is love. Jesus came and lived His names to show us His love. This is what this book is written about. He is Jehovah Rohi, our Almighty Father is our Shepherd. His love towards us is shown through what a Good Shepherd does for His sheep. His love never fails us, but is faithful in loving us while waiting patiently for us to return to Him.

You see, the lady in the show was doing her job because that is what she was trained and experienced in doing. She knew what she was doing. So it is with our loving Father. He is always at His work of being a Good Shepherd, and in all things He is working for our good, as that Good Shepherd. Jesus lived our Father's name, Jehovah Rohi, and laid down His life to finish the work the Father assigned Him to do.

> *...that at the name of Jesus every knee should bow,*
> *in heaven and on earth and under the earth,*
> *(Philippians 2:10, NIV).*

Every new day is another opportunity to do our work to the glory of our loving Father. In whatever work we do, we are to live our Father's name, in Jesus' name, by the power of the Holy Spirit.

November 11

~ Our Shepherd carries us in peace ~

> *The Lord is my shepherd; I shall not want. He makes me*
> *lie down in green pastures. He leads me beside still waters.*
> *He restores my soul. He leads me in paths of righteousness*
> *for his name's sake (Psalm 23:1-3, ESV).*

One early morning, November 11, 2021, I was woken up by my two-and-a-half-year-old at around 5:45 am. He asked me to wake up with him and not go to sleep. As we sat on the big brown recliner chair, the Lord began to show me the back door of our house and said: You see, the door is locked, meaning that only someone from inside can open the door and go outside. The person outside cannot come inside unless they have the key or the one inside opens the door for them. The same truth applies to the way we want to live in peace. Jesus gave us peace from inside of us through the Holy Spirit whom we house, not as the world gives.

Our peace is from the inside, not outside. The thief comes to steal, kill and destroy, and if we allow, or open up ourselves to allow him to come in and steal our peace, then he will. Just like the door of my house, I saw that our mind is like the door that opens up into our heart. If we allow our mind to receive disturbances, chaotic and depressing news of the world, then it can enter our heart and disturb our peace.

> *You keep him in perfect peace whose mind is stayed on you, because he trusts in you (Isaiah 26:3, ESV).*

Jesus is our Good Shepherd, Jehovah Rohi. He lived our Father's name in this world by saving our lives. He peacefully laid down His own life without fighting back, and He rose again by the resurrecting power of the Holy Spirit. When we believe in the power of His death and resurrection and receive Him into our heart, we carry His Spirit in us. The Holy Spirit produces His fruit of peace, and so we carry peace when we carry in us the Holy Spirit.

Every new day is another great opportunity to live our Father's name, Jehovah Rohi, and be that shepherd like Jesus to carry and lead lost sheep in peace to show them the love of the Father. Living in peace is the character of our Father. His character is His name. He is love, joy and peace and His Spirit lives in us and produces the peace inside us. Let's not allow the devil, the thief, to steal that peace.

November 12

~ *The Shepherd carries us in His love* ~

> *He tends his flock like a shepherd: He gathers the lambs in his arms and carries them close to his heart; he gently leads those that have young (Isaiah 40:11, NIV).*

Love is one of the nine fruit of the Holy Spirit. It is actually the fruit of Love that the nine fruit of the Holy Spirit flow out from. Note that this is the reason why Galatians 5:22-23 says 'FRUIT' of the Spirit and not 'FRUITS', as it is singular. Love is a person. God is love. 1 Corinthians 13 describes love, and it is the character of God that Jesus lived which is the fruit of the Holy Spirit. Jesus is the Seed of God who died and was resurrected by the power of the Holy Spirit. The fruit from the seed of Jesus is love, joy, peace, goodness, kindness, patience, faithfulness, gentleness and self-control. It is the power of love from the fruit of the Holy Spirit who resurrected Jesus from life, because nothing can separate us from God's love, not even death (see Romans 8:38-39).

Jesus lived the Father's name, Jehovah Rohi, our Almighty Father is our Shepherd. As a Shepherd who cares and carries His lost wounded sheep and attends to them with love, Jesus carried us in His love. Nothing can separate us from His love towards us, not even death, and this is why death couldn't hold Him. Darkness cannot exist in the presence of light. Death cannot exist in life. Jesus is the Life and death cannot exist in Him. He has risen and is leading us in His love as our Good Shepherd towards the abundant path of eternal life.

Every day is a new day and a new opportunity to live our Father's name, Jehovah Rohi, in Jesus' name. Jesus laid down His life as our Good Shepherd. We are to lay our life down and serve as a good shepherd and lead others in the life Jesus is leading us in.

November 13

~ Abide in Jesus and never live an abandoned life away from the truth ~

Yes, I am the Vine; you are the branches. Whoever lives in me and I in him shall produce a large crop of fruit. For apart from me you can't do a thing (John 15:5, TLB).

November 13, 2021, we were driving and saw a house going for auction. An abandoned house with nothing done on it for some years, it looked to have been abandoned for thirty years or so. Out of curiosity, we joined the interested buyers and explored the house. It was in a disgusting state. Thick roots and brown yucky stuff grew all over the house. I felt so sick that we left immediately. After a while, the images of that abandoned house came rushing into my mind and all I could see was the filth in it. Then the Holy Spirit began to open my eyes to see what happens to the body of Christ when we abandon it and don't allow the Word of God to live in us: When we receive into us the Word of God, it attracts the Holy Spirit to breathe life into the Word and bring it alive, and we become alive in Christ as the body of Christ. When someone doesn't spend time in Word and prayer, they abandon the place where the Holy Spirit is to live, therefore the place becomes disgusting as it creates a good habitat for the enemy to reside and carry out his horrible, disgusting and evil plans through them.

> *The thief's purpose is to steal, kill and destroy. My purpose is to give life in all its fullness (John 10:10, TLB).*

Jesus came and lived our Father's name, Jehovah Rohi, our Almighty Father is our Shepherd. We are His body which has been abandoned. He came to find us, His lost sheep, and saved us from the enemy who stole us and is trying to destroy us. He wants His Holy Spirit to live in us so we are not abandoned again and exposed as a place the enemy can easily move into and do what he wishes to do.

Every new day is another opportunity given to us to spend time in Word and prayer so we do not abandon the place where the Holy Spirit is to live in us. We are to live our Father's name, Jehovah Rohi, in Jesus' name, to be a shepherd by feeding more and storing in us the Word so we can feed and lead any lost sheep we see.

November 14

~ Enjoy the life of Christ while you are alive in your flesh ~

Money cannot be trusted, but God takes care of us richly. He gives us everything to enjoy (1 Timothy 6:17, ERV).

November 14, 2021, I was thinking of our home, where we were residing but did not own. Knowing one day we would move out from there because we were renting it, I started trying to enjoy everything that place could offer. I was only focusing on the good things it offered and enjoying them. I heard the Holy Spirit say: The same truth applies to us while we are here living on earth. We are to enjoy the goodness of being alive in our flesh and enjoy it while we live in it. A day will come when we will exit from earth and leave our flesh and go to our place of rest to wait for our Messiah. Jesus came on earth to give us a life of abundance so we can enjoy life while we are waiting for Him on earth. He brought His heavenly life of abundance and sowed it into this world we live in, so we too can sow this abundant life here on earth and reap a harvest of eternal life crowned with glory in heaven.

Jesus lived our Father's name, Jehovah Rohi, our Almighty Father is our Shepherd. He laid down His life of abundance for us so we can live in His life. A shepherd can lay down his life to protect his sheep from its enemies, and this is what Jesus did. He laid down His life to protect us from the enemy who had trapped us so he could destroy us.

I am the good shepherd. The good shepherd lays down his life for the sheep (John 10:11, ESV).

Every new day is another new opportunity to sow the life of abundance and enjoy it by living our Father's name, Jehovah Rohi, in Jesus' name, to the glory of the Father. We are now the shepherd to lead the lost sheep to find their life of abundance.

November 15

~ Reveal the goodness of God to others and you will be remembered for what you have done ~

Then those who feared the Lord spoke to one another, and the Lord listened and heard them; so a book of remembrance was written before Him for those who fear the Lord and who meditate on His name (Malachi 3:16, NKJV).

The Holy Spirit really teaches us how to pray and helps us to do so. Quite often, when I approach God on His throne and say, 'Remember me, your servant,' and present my request to Him to grant it, I see my request granted and prayers being answered. I didn't know that every time we do something good for God in talking about His love and doing His goodness, a remembrance book is created for us by God. This was something the Holy Spirit directed me to do. I later discovered it and relate it well to my life.

When God remembers us through our remembrance book, he grants us our request. It's not that God forgets us, but when He remembers us it means that He is going to release the blessings we are praying for. It's like someone remembers you for the good things you did for them, and in return wants to do something good for you.

Then God remembered Rachel; he listened to her and enabled her to conceive (Genesis 30:22, NIV).

Jesus is our Shepherd, the Good Shepherd who teaches us all about the loving kindness of the goodness of the Father so we can walk in His Love. He lived and actioned a life of love so we can remember everything of the Father He showed. Jehovah Rohi, our Almighty Father is our Shepherd. A book of remembrance is created for us when we live our Father's name, Jehovah Rohi, in Jesus' name, and be that shepherd who gently shows and leads others in the path of the fear of the Lord and His righteousness. We can then know that as long as we approach God on His throne to remember us, He will remember us.

Every day, live the Father's name, Jehovah Rohi, our Almighty Father is our Shepherd, and talk about the righteousness of God and live in the fear of God. Your good deeds will be written in your book of remembrance, so never get tired of doing good.

November 16

~ Speak your words with love in its season and season them with grace and kindness ~

Let your conversation be gracious as well as sensible, for then you will have the right answer for everyone (Colossians 4:6, TLB).

One evening, November 16, 2021, I asked Tom to cook dinner. It was a beef steak, which I cook using a lot of seasoning and it turns out delicious. He didn't use any of my spices as he was not sure which ones to use and was worried he'd use the wrong one. He cooked it so plain that it was not something we could enjoy, not the nice meal it was supposed to be. As I sat and tasted the dinner, the Holy Spirit opened my eyes to see how our words too have an effect on the other person, depending on how we season them with God's love and grace.

You see, the meat was plain and not seasoned, and tasted so dull that I couldn't enjoy it. When we walk in the nine fruit of the Holy Spirit and are led by the Spirit, we have nine flavours of love in us, which are the nine fruit of righteousness that we can season, add flavour and use in someone's life in the right way.

> *… speaking to one another with psalms, hymns, and songs from the Spirit. Sing and make music from your heart to the Lord (Ephesians 5:19, NIV).*

Jesus came and lived our Father's name, Jehovah Rohi, our Almighty Father is our Shepherd. He came and led us out of this world so we won't live and behave like we belong to this world. Rather, we are to live the fullness of His love, with words of psalms, hymns and spiritual songs to each other.

Every new day is a new day of opportunity to live our Father's name, Jehovah Rohi, to lead others the way our Chief Shepherd, Jesus, showed us, and that is to lead through His Spirit that lives in us. Always be led by the Holy Spirit.

November 17

> *~ Put on the image of Christ and see the power of the Holy Spirit come alive ~*

> *I am the light of the world. Whoever follows me will not walk in darkness, but will have the light of life (John 8:12, ESV).*

November 17, 2021, I woke up and the Holy Spirit pointed out to me the bedside lamp light. It was connected to the main power point, however, it also had its own button right on it to which you can use to switch it on or off, as long as the power is on. The Holy Spirit opened my eyes to see how His resurrecting power works in us—it is one of the amazing things, which I could see through the demonstration of the bed side lamp: The power of the Holy Spirit is inside of us and is alive and on. Jesus is alive in us through the Holy Spirit, the power of God who resurrected and gave life to Jesus to LIGHT up LIFE inside us. When I put the bedside lamp on, it comes on. If I want to set the power of the Holy Spirit in me to be effective, I have to put on the new image of Christ, the life of Christ that the Holy Spirit resurrected.

Jesus lived our Father's name, Jehovah Rohi, our Almighty Father is our Shepherd. He lived the life of a Good Shepherd and showed light to the lost sheep to follow Him. As the light of the world, He opened the eyes of the sheep so they could see and follow Him in the path of an abundant life. He laid down His life for the sheep and was resurrected by the power of the Holy Spirit.

> *And when you were baptized, it was the same as being buried with Christ. Then you were raised to life because you had faith in the power of God, who raised Christ from death (Colossians 2:12, CEV).*

Through the work of death, burial and the resurrection of Jesus Christ, we now have the power of the Holy Spirit flowing in us. We are now to live our Father's name, Jehovah Rohi, in Jesus' name, by putting on the new life of Jesus and being the light to the lost blind sheep in the world. We are the ones who will lead them to the path of abundant life.

Every new day is a new opportunity to put on the image of Christ, which is the light for people to see the power of the Holy Spirit that is at work within us.

November 18

~ The Holy Spirit is our inner alarm that warns us of danger ahead ~

When the Spirit of truth comes, he will guide you into all the truth, for he will not speak on his own authority, but whatever he hears he will speak, and he will declare to you the things that are to come (John 16:13, ESV).

November 20, 2021, I remember Tom's words—he gave me warning instructions to take precautions to not lock myself out of the house, because the lock on the door was playing up. Taking in his warnings, I was able to save myself from being locked out. The Holy Spirit opened my eyes to see how He also gives us warnings for the traps the enemy has for us, so we don't go down that path to where the trap is. We cause disasters in our own life when we don't pay attention to the danger alarms that the Holy Spirit raises. Just like how when we go down a dangerous, narrow road and we see signs of caution appearing so we can drive with extra care, the Holy Spirit also raises signs in our life to show us the danger of what lies ahead.

The steps of good men are directed by the Lord. He delights in each step they take. If they fall, it isn't fatal, for the Lord holds them with his hand (Psalm 37:23-24, TLB).

Jesus came and lived our Father's name, Jehovah Rohi, our Almighty Father is our Shepherd. He shepherds our life and carries us along the path that is full of goodness and not danger. He is the Good Shepherd. Even when we go through the shadow of darkness where there is danger, His presence leading us keeps us safe on the right path.

Every new day we are to spend time in Word and prayer so we can see what precautions to take in life. The Word of God not only has precautions to warn us of dangers, but words to comfort and strengthen us if sudden storms of life hit us along the way.

November 19

~ Like fish designed to live in water, we too are designed to live and move in God ~

*For in him we live and move and have our being
(Acts 17:28, NIV).*

I had been doing a lot of driving around, November 19, 2021, I acknowledged Jesus with His name Emmanuel, God with us. I asked Him to drive and I would drive through Him. I realised that I found a whole new level of joy and strength just by asking Him to drive.

A little while ago, I was looking at a leaf. Red in colour, it was so transparent I could see clearly all the veins running across it. The Holy Spirit opened my eyes to see, and taught me how we too have all our movements in God: The veins in the leaf is us and our connections to all the movements we make which exist in God. We live and move in Him. When we live more in His Word and spend time in prayer daily, He becomes great and we become less. This is when the enemy sees us as a threat to his kingdom of darkness, because our every move can destroy his plan.

Jesus came and lived our loving Father in heaven's name, Jehovah Rohi, our Almighty Father is our Shepherd. He saved us and took us out from a falling and cursed world and led us on green pastures of life to live and move in Him, just like a shepherd leading his sheep to a place of abundance, peace and security. That was what Jesus did for us. He even willingly laid down His dear life for us so we can rise up in His new life and lead others on that path.

We are to follow our Master Shepherd and live our Father's name and bring the lost sheep to come and live in Jesus. The lost sheep need to know the Shepherd is standing and knocking at the door of their hearts to come and live in them so they can move and have their being in Him.

November 20

~ The very hands of the Good Shepherd that hold the universe hold us ~

Jesus knew that the Father had put all things under his power, and that he had come from God and was returning to God (John 13:3, NIV).

November 20, 2021, the Lord showed me a water fountain holding all the water as it flowed through the fountain, in and out. This is what the Lord said: This is how I hold the universe in my palms. I am aware of everything that is happening in the universe I created. Every happening in your life happens because I allow it. Everything that comes to you comes through me to you when you are in me. We are in the palms of the hands that hold the universe. The universe is smaller than our Almighty Father's hands.

See, I have written your name on the palms of my hands (Isaiah 49:16, NLT).

Jesus came and lived our Father's name, Jehovah Rohi, our Almighty Father is our Shepherd. He came and lived like a shepherd to hold us closer to Him. He laid down His life for us not only to lead us, but to live inside us and lead us from inside through the Holy Spirit. Like the water fountain that goes back to where it flows out, Jesus too came and lived our Father's name and finished the work and returned back to the Father, from where He came.

> *He will feed his flock like a shepherd. He will carry the lambs in his arms, holding them close to his heart. He will gently lead the mother sheep with their young (Isaiah 40:11, NLT).*

Every day, we must remember where we come from, and that with each passing day we are one step closer to returning back.

November 21

~ Live a patient and faithful life as you go through the test of time ~

Truthful words stand the test of time, but lies are soon exposed (Proverbs 12:19, NLT).

November 21, 2021 I was thinking of how God showed up in my dream with what I had desired in my heart to have, and said, 'Everything you wanted I have given you.' I woke up and the Holy Spirit had to explain everything to me while I was trying to figure it out. This particular thing that I wanted so much would be mine after several years. You see, it's already mine, but I have to go through the time test of character building to be patient and faithful to possess it, for it to belong to me.

Jacob had to work for Laban for fourteen years for both Leah and Rachael. It's the time test for characters. The first seven years he worked for Laban, Jacob was cheated. Jacob only reaped what he sowed, when after cheating on his brother and stealing his birthright, Laban cheated on him and instead of giving Rachael, he gave Leah. Jacob had to work for another seven years again to be given Rachael. Whatever we have longed for and desire is ours. We have to start sowing the seed and name those desires as our harvest. The moment we sow, the harvest of our desire is about to show up, but we have to go through a time period to remain patient and faithful to receive it.

Our loving Father is a Good Shepherd, His name is Jehovah Rohi, but for His name to be shown to us, He had to sow the seed of Jesus coming and living the name Jehovah Rohi. Jesus lived as the Good Shepherd, He too had to go through the test of time—birth, childhood, teenagerhood and finally at thirty, He began His ministry to show us the Father's love. He lived love in all His actions. Our Father in heaven harvested the seed when Jesus laid down His life as the Good Shepherd and rose again so we can live in His new, resurrected life. Jesus is the seed the Father sowed into the world so we can enjoy the harvest, which is the nine fruit of the Holy Spirit. This is also why Jesus had to go back to the Father, so the Holy Spirit can come live in us to produce His fruit.

Each day we are going through the test of time. We have to sow the seeds of what our heart desires and go through the test of time of character building to reap the harvest at the right appointed time. There is a time for everything, and God made everything beautiful in its time (see Ecclesiastes 3:1,11).

November 22

~ Born again—cut yourself from fleshly desires ~

So I say, walk by the Spirit, and you will not gratify the desires of the flesh (Galatians 5:16, NIV).

One morning, towards the end of October 2021, the Lord opened my eyes to see how He asked me to lose connection or cut off certain things in my life that my flesh was so attached to. The reason being so I am not focused on it, as distractions of my flesh keep my spirit not in the realm of the Spirit and the courts of heaven. For example, if I am focused on worldly things, how I can I be focused and living in the realms of the Spirit, the courts of heaven where God sits on His throne and rules by making righteous decisions. I too have to dress in the full amour of God, with the breastplate of the righteousness of God that will keep me standing upright in righteousness in His sight.

> *For you died, and your life is now hidden with Christ in God (Colossians 3:3, NIV).*

The Holy Spirit showed me a baby being birthed, coming out of her mother, then cut from the mother through the umbilical cord that had fed her when she was in the mother's womb. Now born and in the world, the baby had to lose connection to what she used to be. So it is with us. We are now born again in spirit in the kingdom of God, and therefore must cut loose all fleshly connections of desire in our previous life. When Jesus said to be born again, it is to enter the kingdom of God and live in the kingdom of God, in another realm, in the courts of heaven, the place where God lives with His people. You have become one of His people too.

> *Jesus replied, 'Very truly I tell you, no one can see the kingdom of God unless they are born again.' (John 3:3, NIV).*

Jesus lived our Father's name, Jehovah Rohi, our Almighty Father is our Shepherd. He came and lived our Father's name and saved the lost sheep from being trapped by the enemy. He destroyed the work of the enemy so we can now be saved by believing and having faith in what He has done for us. Because of all He has done, we can be born again into the kingdom of God and live with our loving Father.

Every day we have to be grateful that we rule and reign with Christ in the heavenly courts of our Father where He makes the righteous decisions of our life.

November 23

~ Live and work in the light ~

In the beginning, God created the heavens and the earth. Now the earth was formless and empty, darkness was over the surface of the deep, and the Spirit of God was hovering over the waters. And God said, 'Let there be light,' and there was light (Genesis 1:1-3, NIV).

On the night of November 23, 2021, the lights were on and I was reading. This is what I hear the Holy Spirit say: You cannot work or do anything in the dark; there has to be light so you can see well to work. Even before God does His work He has to create light. This is where He created everything, through Jesus and work. His names are who He is and He is at work all the time by what His name says. Jesus came and lived the Father's name.

The Lord formed me in the beginning, before he created anything else. From ages past, I am. I existed before the earth began (Proverbs 8:22-23, TLB).

Our Father already had the great plan that Jesus was going to live His name. Before you and I were born, we were already created in

Christ Jesus, then we were born. God created everything in Jesus, because Jesus was going to come and be the light and lived our Father's name, where we can live and work. Jehovah Rohi, our Almighty Father is our Shepherd, is one of the twelve common names of the Father that Jesus lived. He is the Good Shepherd who came and gave sight to the blind sheep and led them into the path of light so they are able to see and live.

Every new dawn of day we arise and are able to see and do whatever we want to do. We are able to live and work because of the new day of light. Because of what the Good Shepherd, Jesus, has done, we are able rise up in His new life and see the new perspective of life. We are no longer blind and in the dark.

November 24

~ Getting fed right from the Shepherd's mouth ~

Please receive the law and instruction from His mouth and establish His words in your heart and keep them (Job 22:22 AMP).

November 24, 2021, a dear friend sent me a scripture from Job 22:22, and reminded me of a vision I'd had about four years earlier, in 2017.

In my vision, I saw a long table with different layers of shelves. The long table was right in front of the throne of God. There were different sizes of babies coming to the table to be fed in those shelves. Babies who could only sit were feeding on the food at the first shelf. Others were crawling over to the shelves where they could reach up and be fed, while others were taking their first steps and some could walk over to the shelves. Depending also on their height, they would reach out for food on the shelves. On the top shelf, which was the same height as the throne of God, I saw fresh food and God Himself feeding the ones who were able to reach that top shelf.

This is what the Holy Spirit opened my eyes to see and ears to hear: Every one of us feeds from God differently, depending on our level. Some are newborn babies who feed on spiritual milk, and then they grow, feeding on different levels of food. The top shelf, where God was doing the feeding, are the ones who received fresh revelation or food straight from God's mouth. These are the ones who are upright with God and connect with Him daily, and so the shelf where they are fed is right where the throne of God is. They receive the word of the moment straight from God.

> *Suppose one of you has a hundred sheep and loses one of them. Doesn't he leave the ninety-nine in the open country and go after the lost sheep until he finds it? And when he finds it, he joyfully puts it on his shoulders and goes home. Then he calls his friends and neighbours together and says, 'Rejoice with me; I have found my lost sheep.' (Luke 15:4-6, NIV).*

Jesus came and lived our Father's name, Jehovah Rohi, our Almighty Father is our Shepherd. He left the ninety-nine sheep to find the lost one to feed. The ninety-nine are the righteous who have access and know how to get fed in the Word. The one that is lost is the one Jesus was concerned about finding and feeding. The heavens rejoice when that one sheep is found, because the Shepherd has found one of His lost valued possessions.

Every day, sit still and know that He is God. Get yourself fed in the Word so you can grow to be in a position where you can meet God right where you are and receive fresh revelations.

November 25

~ God not only risked His position in flesh, but made the great sacrifice to send Jesus to die for us ~

Since we, God's children, are human beings—made of flesh and blood—he became flesh and blood too by being born in human form; for only as a human being could he die, and in dying break the power of the devil who had the power of death (Hebrews 2:14, TLB).

October 31, 2021, I was thinking of stepping out of my comfort zone and doing some things where there had to be some risk taken and sacrifices made. This is what I heard the Holy Spirit say: You see, your Father in heaven also had to take the risk and sacrifice His only Son to come and live on earth. The risk He took was that if Satan deceived Him and He sold His birthright to Him, Lucifer would become God in flesh.

In 2017, early one morning, at 2am, I remember clearly, I was praying and decided to ask Jesus a question. I was talking to Him like someone who was just sitting next to me. I said, 'Jesus, when Satan asked you to worship him, and said he would give you the world and the splendour of it, you didn't succumb. You came to save the world and you could have just taken that offer from Lucifer, but you decided to face the pain of dying and going through all that humiliation.' I was emotional, with tears in my eyes just remembering the sacrifices He made. Instantly, the atmosphere of the room changed. I felt His presence sitting next to me, except that I couldn't see Him. All I could hear was His voice speaking in my heart. He said, 'If I had not taken the cross but had worshipped him, I would have given him my position as the Son of God, while I would have taken his position as the ruler of this world. I came to destroy His work as the ruler of this world, and the only way to do that was through death. Also, for me to receive the resurrected eternal life from the Holy Spirit and give that to you, I had to die for you so the resurrecting power of the Holy Spirit could bring me back to life. This is how I destroyed his work. I now give you that life, to rule and reign with me. You have authority over this world.'

This encounter happened four years ago, but is as fresh as new and I remember every moment of it vividly as I write.

Jesus lived our Father's name, Jehovah Rohi, our Almighty Father is our Shepherd. Shepherds sacrifice their lives for their sheep to be with them all the time, and they risk their lives to save their sheep from the enemies. Jesus did that. He not only laid down His life for us, His sheep, but He risked His life, and lived His life in this evil world full of His enemies. For this, the Father has given power to His name, no other name but only at the name of Jesus, every knee shall bow.

> *Greater love has no one than this: to lay down one's life for one's friends (John 15:13, NIV).*

Every day, we are to be grateful to Jesus and love Him more for the risk and sacrifice He went through to give us an eternal life of abundance and save us from death. We have to show our love to live our Father's name too, Jehovah Rohi, and reach out for the lost sheep that the enemy is trapping in this world. We are now the Father's shepherd.

November 26

~ Operate from and for the kingdom of God by leading the lost sheep to the kingdom of God ~

> *Flesh gives birth to flesh, but the Spirit gives birth to spirit (John 3:6, NIV).*

One Saturday morning, November 26, 2021. I was in my first trimester of pregnancy, with morning sickness and uneasy and uncomfortable moods draining the life out of me. As I was going through all this, I heard the Holy Spirit say: You see, you operate in two realms, the physical and the spiritual. It is in the spiritual realm, the kingdom of God, that you are born again. Operate from the spiritual realm if you are not feeling well in your physical realm. The moment I heard that, I felt a whole new strength entering me and I started to focus on the things of the spiritual realm, which is of the kingdom of God. I started sharing the word of God in social media to friends. I was using myself to operate in the things of the Spirit more.

You see, when we are not feeling well in our physical body, the enemy tries to make us lose focus on doing anything for the Lord. The devil is a liar. Let that sick body be sick and talk about Jesus, and you'll be amazed at how much strength you have in doing that in a body that is sick. Remember, we may be fading in our physical body, but we are renewed in the Spirit.

> *So we do not lose heart. Though our outer self is wasting away, our inner self is being renewed day by day (2 Corinthians 4:16 ESV).*

Jehovah Rohi is His name, our Almighty Father is our Shepherd. Jesus lived our Father's name. He came to find and feed the lost sheep. He was committed to doing this. Even when there were obstacles in many of His physical contacts with people, that never stopped Him from operating from and for the kingdom of God. Jesus said, 'The kingdom of God is coming and it is here.' The resurrected life of Jesus, by the power of the Holy Spirit, is the kingdom of God for us to live and operate from. The life we are born again into.

Each and every day, operate from the kingdom of God, even when your physical world is not treating you well. Live the Father's name, Jehovah Rohi, and keep feeding His lost sheep, whether it be the ninety-nine righteous saints or the one lost sinner.

November 27

~ Our Good Shepherd knows our identity of who we are in Him and He calls us by our names ~

I will bow down toward Your holy temple and give thanks to Your name for Your mercy and Your truth; For You have made Your word great according to all Your name (Psalm 138:2, NASB).

One morning, November 27, 2021, I was praising and thanking God and just being grateful for the place I was living at. I mentioned the house number and the name of the street the house resides in because that is my place of identity, where people can find me in that particular suburb. The Holy Spirit opened my eyes to see this: Revelation 13, the number 666 is actually the name of a person. We all know who that person is. Our loving Father in heaven also has a number which is actually His name, Jesus lived our Father's name, His twelve names that He is most known by. One of them is Jehovah Rohi, our Almighty Father is our Shepherd. Jesus lived His life as a Good Shepherd. He laid down His life for us so He can now be that Good Shepherd to lead us from both outside and from within us as we house Him through the Holy Spirit.

Every day, we are to live our Father's name, Jehovah Rohi, in Jesus' name, and be that Shepherd to lead the lost sheep to produce the fruit of the Holy Spirit. To produce the nine fruit of the Holy Spirit is to show our identity. The number nine is the number of the

Holy Spirit. It was nine in the morning when the Holy Spirit came down from the Father (see Acts 2:15). And the name of the nine fruit which are LOVE, JOY, PEACE. PATIENCE, KINDNESS, GOODNESS, GENTLENESS, FAITHFULNESS and SELF-CONTROL, are the characters of Christ. This is our identity to live the Christ-like life. So is the number twelve, for it is the number of the Father and His twelve names are His position and character to which Jesus lived. Our heavenly Father has described everything that belongs to Him comes in the number of twelve. Power and authority has been given to Jesus because He has lived the name of the Father and brought victory to His name.

November 28

~ *Our Father engraves us in His hands which hold the universe in balance* ~

The Lord called me before my birth. From within the womb he called me by my name (Isaiah 49:1, TLB).

You may look at sheep and see them as all the same, but not the Shepherd of your life. He knows your name and calls you His very own. To be a good dad to his children, a good dad personally understands and loves his child/ren the way they are. Every character, feature and taste of his child/ren is special. He names, calls and believes in them. To him all his child/ren are different and special in their unique ways. He asks His Father in heaven to lead him as the shepherd so he can be that good shepherd to his flock.

He is Jehovah Rohi, our Lord God, our Shepherd. He not only knows our name and calls us, He has engraved it on the palms of His hand (see Isaiah 49:16) and with that very hand leads us towards the green pasture of abundance as our Good Shepherd.

> *I am the good shepherd; I know my sheep and my sheep know me—just as the Father knows me and I know the Father—and I lay down my life for the sheep (John 10:14-15, NIV).*

Jesus lived our Father's name. He is our Good Shepherd who calls us by our very name and leads us. He even leaves the other ninety-nine just to come and look for you to lead you back to the Father.

November 29

~ The voice of our Shepherd is gentle and doesn't cause us to fear life ~

> *The gatekeeper opens the gate for him, and the sheep listen to his voice. He calls his own sheep by name and leads them out. When he has brought out all his own, he goes on ahead of them, and his sheep follow him because they know his voice (John 10:3-4, NIV).*

September 29, 2021, I washed the knife and put it away on the dish rack. I could see the knife in a vision as if it was a sword. It was flashing in the empty air, swinging itself to and fro. This is what I heard the Holy Spirit teaching me about the Sword of the Spirit: You see, when you use the Word of God to the enemy, it flashes on him like this. It is the truth. It keeps him away from you because he can't deceive you. He can't come near you. When you keep hearing and hearing the Word of God, you become so familiar with God's Voice. An unborn baby inside the mother knows the voice of the mother, even though the baby has not seen the mother. The baby has to feed through the mother to survive and hear her voice. The mother's voice is familiar to the baby. This is how God is through His Spirit. He lives in us and we have to feed on His Word so we can hear His voice more.

Jesus came and lived our Father's name, Jehovah Rohi, our Almighty Father is our Shepherd. He is the good shepherd who feeds His sheep and we will know His voice as long as we follow Him and feed from Him. His voice is not to frighten or give us fear, but to give us boldness, courage and strength to face the challenges of life. If you hear any voices that weaken or cause fear in your life, it is the voice of the enemy, so shut it out quickly. The Holy Spirit inside of us is not a spirit of fear.

> *I, the Lord, am your God, Who brought you up from the land of Egypt; Open your mouth wide and I will fill it*
> *(Psalm 81:10, NASB).*

Every day, make sure to feed on the Word of God, the truth, so you will become familiar with God's Word and be that shepherd to bring lost sheep back to the Father.

November 30

~ Let God use and feed you so you can feed the lost sheep ~

> *In the same way, I tell you, there is rejoicing in the presence of the angels of God over one sinner who repents*
> *(Luke 15:10, NIV).*

November 26, 2021, I was tidying my food spices/flavours in the kitchen and pushed to the back the ones I don't regularly cook with. Out in front, I put the ones I use daily. The last rows of spices became the front rows of spices. The others that I put right at the back were the ones I use only occasionally. This is what I heard the Holy Spirit say: The kingdom of God is like this. There are shareholders and investors of the kingdom of God. Those who share and keep the message of the Word of God daily are the front commanders of God that He uses every day. Others that do not do much are just at the back, and whenever they feel like doing it on special occasions they come forward, like your spices that you put at the back and use only on certain occasions.

I am writing this encounter here because I want to encourage each and every one of us to be the front commanders of God whom He can use daily. Encouraging someone with the Word of God or sharing on social media a scripture means a lot to the kingdom of God. As a shareholder and investor of God's kingdom, we have to share His love. You will be surprised when you get to heaven and Jesus brings strangers to you and tells you, because of you, he/she made it to heaven.

> *Those who are wise will shine like the brightness of the heavens, and those who lead many to righteousness, like the stars for ever and ever (Daniel 12:3, NIV).*

As the shepherd of God, we are to feed the lost sheep every day. We need to be always in front of our sheep and be fed and used by God to feed the lost sheep. Just like how I put the spices that I use every day in front, God too can put us in front to go out and look for that one sheep that has gone astray and bring it back to Him. This brings joy to the heavens.

DECEMBER

Jehovah Shalom! I AM Your Peace!

Mizraiim Lapa-Pethe

OUR LORD GOD IS OUR PEACE.

~ Our Good Father remembers every good thing we do ~

So a book of remembrance was written before Him for those who fear the Lord and who meditate on His name (Malachi 3:16, NKJV).

One lunch hour, December 6, 2021, I was looking at my bookshelves in the house and thought *anyone will put books in their bookshelves, books of what they like. You cannot just get any books and put them there. You would love to have your favourite author with their book where it's just handy for you to reach out and read it.* This is what I heard the Holy Spirit say about the remembrance book that God has created and has for us: It's not that He forgets, but it's for our records, for us to ask God to remember us for the good things we have sown so we can reap the harvest. This is the book where everything we do for God is written. When we go before Him, seated on His throne, we are to seek Him to remember us by our books, our records. When our book is open, what is ours is released to us.

I always like to keep a book of my own to link up to my remembrance book in the courts of heaven. So what I would write is all my plans of life and the desires, my dreams of what I want to achieve in life. I make sure that the date is written each time, and also any scriptures, the truth from God's Word that supports my dreams. By doing that, I have seen how God moves in my life and gives me exactly what I have put down in my book.

> *For to us a child is born, to us a son is given, and the government will be on his shoulders. And he will be called Wonderful Counsellor, Mighty God, Everlasting Father, Prince of Peace (Isaiah 9:6, NIV).*

Jesus came and lived our Father's name, Jehovah Shalom, our Almighty Father is our Peace. He was the peace of God. Everything written of Him by the prophets was what He lived. A virgin would give birth to our Saviour who would be our Prince of Peace (see Matthew 1:23).

Every day, and each day of the month of December, write your story and link it to what God has written about you. You are the author of your life, in the peaceful life that Jesus has given, not as the world has given.

December 1

~ Maintain your body, the temple of the Holy Spirit, with peace ~

> *So whether you eat or drink or whatever you do, do it all for the glory of God (1 Corinthians 10:31, NIV).*

I took up a challenge in doing the ten-day Daniel fasting of vegetables and water. The morning of December 1, 2021, I was waiting on the Lord to speak to me regarding the fasting we'd ended. As I waited upon the Lord, He showed me how a house needs a great deal of maintenance after being constantly used. The house needs a lot of fixing and work to be done in the inside, the same as how we did the fasting of vegetables and water. Our body too needs some work and maintenance from the constant work it does. It is the house of the Spirit of God and God has to do some work in us to make it the way He wants it to be. Most food we eat can be unclean and bad for our health. The ten-day fasting was a time where God was working to maintain our bodies to be healthy and clean. It is good from time to time to commit to the Daniel fasting for ten or twenty-one days, so God can work in our body to make it healthy and clean for His Spirit to live in.

Jesus came and lived our Father's name, Jehovah Shalom, our Almighty Father is our Peace. He gave us His peace where we can walk, live and eat in peace in the midst of all the world's fears around us. We have to use our body to worship God whenever we eat or drink. Everything we do must be to glorify God.

> *When you enter a house, first say, 'Peace to this house.'*
> *(Luke 10:5, NIV).*

Every new day is a gift wrapped up for us to open. We may like some surprises and not others, but as long as we live our Father's name, Jehovah Shalom, in Jesus' name for our Father's glory, there will always be peace in our house. We house the Father's Spirit, who produces peace in His house, and that peace will also be in our house where we will enjoy love, joy and peace of family bond.

December 2

~ *Taste the goodness of peace* ~

> *Taste and see that the Lord is good; blessed is the one who takes refuge in him (Psalm 34:8, NIV).*

One evening, December 4, 2021, I thought I bought chocolate milk for my kids, but instead it was coffee milk. I poured it out and gave it to them and my almost seven-year-old said, 'This tastes like coffee.' I said, 'So you know the taste of coffee—have you been drinking coffee without my knowing?' All these questions came pouring out. The Holy Spirit began to open my eyes to truly understand what Psalm 34:8 means: Taste and see that the Lord is good. You will only know the taste of something when you truly try it out and experience how good or bad that thing is. Other people's good experience with God will never give you answers to whether God is a good God.

Jesus came and lived our Father's name in heaven, Jehovah Shalom, our Almighty Father is our Peace. He came and lived in the world we live in, experiencing everything we go through, but He never sinned. He has tasted the kind of life we live and He offers to us the peace of the Father, not as the world gives, so we can taste and see the goodness of our Father and how He loves us so much and wants us to live in peace. Jesus said, my peace I give you. Jesus is the peace from God who was given to the world. The enemy was not at peace when He was born. The enemy doesn't like peace and comes to steal our peace. Never allow the enemy to steal your peace. When he does, your joy will be gone too.

Every day is another new day to live our Father's name, Jehovah Shalom, in Jesus' name, and taste the goodness of God. We need that goodness to conquer any evil that arises in this day.

December 3

~ Humble yourself and live a life of peace ~

The Lord gives strength to his people; the Lord blesses his people with peace (Psalm 29:11, NIV).

Driving for school drop off, December 3, 2021, I was thanking God for His goodness and kindness. I was in awe of what

He gave me; it was exactly what I longed to have. I was so excited by the goodness of God and the kindness He had shown me that I wanted to announce it on social media, thinking how everyone on my contact friends list would be congratulating and praising this news. This is what the Holy Spirit put into my heart to teach me humility: What your Father in heaven gave you is for you to receive it and live in humbleness. You are to humble yourself, because you didn't get these things by your own strength. What He gave you is nothing compared with what He still has in store for you. He owns the fields and everything in the field. Out of nothing, He creates something. Our Father owns everything, and what He gave us is nothing compared to what more He can pour into our life through His glorious riches in Christ Jesus. The enemy, Satan Lucifer is the father of a prideful life and he can use that to make us become prideful. 2 Kings 20:12-19 speaks of how Hezekiah was showing off with pride what he had in his palace and The Lord had to send the prophet Isaiah with a word for him.

> *"The word of the Lord you have spoken is good," Hezekiah replied. For he thought, 'Will there not be peace and security in my lifetime?' (2 Kings 20:19, NIV)*

Jesus left all He has in heaven and came to live our Father's name, Jehovah Shalom, our Almighty Father is our Peace. He lived a life of humbleness. He wants us to live in His Word that gives peace, not in the wealth and lust of the world that will drain our joy and peace.

> *For you know the grace of our Lord Jesus Christ, that though he was rich, yet for your sake he became poor, so that you through his poverty might become rich (2 Corinthians 8:9, NIV).*

Jesus became poor so we can become rich, but we have to seek His kingdom first and all these things will be given to us. The wealth from our Father's kingdom gives us joy and peace. It's not like the wealth from the world that leaves us restless and makes it hard to fall asleep every night, thinking of every bad thing happening in the world that will affect the wealth we are building.

Every day is another new day to live a humble life so we can live our Father's name, Jehovah Shalom, in Jesus' name. Living a peaceful life and enjoying everything the Lord has given us to enjoy should be the life we aim to build in the presence of God.

December 4

~ Live in peace ~

The Spirit of the Lord will rest on him—the Spirit of wisdom and of understanding, the Spirit of counsel and of might, the Spirit of the knowledge and fear of the Lord—and he will delight in the fear of the Lord (Isaiah 11:2-3, NIV).

One morning, December 4, 2021, I was trying to teach my children how to do some house chores and a little simple cooking with my eldest, so they can do it and I can relax and rest a bit more. The Holy Spirit began to open my eyes to see how Jesus came to live our heavenly Father's name, Jehovah Shalom, our Almighty Father is our Peace: He gave us peace and taught us to live in love by living in peace. Once we have learnt through the life lessons to truly live in peace, He can rest in us. His work is complete in teaching peace. On the sixth day, our Father finished His work of creation, and so He rested on the seventh day. When Jesus finished the Father's work He cried out and said, 'It is finished,' and He rested. He finished the work of restoring peace to our old self with the new self in Him (see Ephesians 2:15).

> *In peace I will lie down and sleep, for you alone, Lord, make me dwell in safety (Psalm 4:8, NIV).*

You see, I too can rest when I teach my children to do the kind of work I want them to do and they can skilfully do it. So it is with our Father's Spirit. He can rest in us when we can naturally and skilfully live our Father's name, Jehovah Shalom, and produce the fruit of peace.

Every new day is another new opportunity to live our Father's name, Jehovah Shalom, and rest peacefully in the complete finished work of the cross.

December 5

~ Faith heroes live a peaceful life ~

> *Peace I leave with you; my peace I give you (John 14:27, NIV).*

All the heroes of faith have challenges and they took a leap of faith in those challenges. It's the peace from God's Word that goes with them and gives them the security, strength and courage to accomplish the call in their life. A good father lives a life of a faith hero.

Like David, he faces the giants of his life that disturb the peace of his nations. In whatever little way, he uses his mustard seed of faith to bring down the giant.

Like Abraham, he moves out of his comfort place to go to the unknown if God directs. He does it because that kind of faith Abraham took was for his family. A good dad does it for his family.

Like Elijah, who faced the prophets of Baal, he is able to hold his faith up for the truth of God's Word and face the false teachers.

Like Moses, he will carry out God's calling, even if he lacks the resources. There is always a pharaoh he has to face who is keeping his loved ones trapped.

Like Joshua, a good dad is strong and has the courage to conquer new lands with instructions from the Lord.

Like Daniel, he will always stand up for righteousness. He is not afraid to be thrown into the lion's den because the perfect love of His Father in heaven drives out any fears.

Like Jesus, a good dad lives His Father in heaven's name, Jehovah Shalom, our Almighty Father is our Peace. When he moves, he is moving in the peace Jesus gave. To live in peace, everything that moves with and lives with him must be at peace.

Every day, wake up and live like the heroes of faith and walk and move in peace. As long as you are in Christ you are one of the heroes of faith walking on earth.

December 6

~ Your feet should always walk in peace ~

On your feet wear the Good News of peace to help you stand strong (Ephesians 6:15, NCV).

November 25, 2021, I was thinking of how often I tell my kids, especially Blessed, to wear footwear to protect their feet. The Lord reminded me of how His Word protects us. Peace especially is for our feet. You see, my kids need to wear footwear so they don't hurt their feet when they stumble into something in their way. We too need to wear peace in our feet and stand on it so we do not stumble in our faith. When we begin to love God's Word, we spend more time with Him and do what the Word says and this increases our peace. God's presence is full of peace.

> *Great peace have those who love your law, and nothing can make them stumble (Psalm 119:165, NIV).*

Jesus lived our Father's name, Jehovah Shalom, our Almighty Father is our Peace. He is the 'Prince of Peace.' Our Father in heaven loves us so much and gave Jesus to us in this world. Jesus loves us so much that He gave us peace through the Holy Spirit. He is the Word and His great peace comes from the love we grow in His Word and not from the love of the world.

Every new day is made with love for us to live our Father's name, Jehovah Shalom. We have to spend time in the Word to have this great peace, so great that nothing in this world can disturb our peace in Christ Jesus.

December 7

~ We have been set free to walk and live in peace ~

> *I will walk in freedom, for I have devoted myself to your commandments (Psalm 119:45, NLT).*

April 25, 2021, was a beautiful Sunday morning, the last day of the forty-day prayer journey we took to give respect to the first Prime Minister of Papua New Guinea (PNG) who served his life very well to the nation. I asked the Lord to give me a Word to end this prayer journey.

I went to church that morning for a wonderful Anzac service where we celebrated the lives of the heroes who served Australia to defend freedom and peace. As I was looking at the front pulpit and thinking how nicely it was set up, and the sound system, the Holy Spirit gave me the word to end the forty-day journey: You see, there are some people who set up beautifully the front stage so you can come and enjoy the church service, with a lovely gifted music team. You don't have to do anything. It has been done already and you just came and enjoyed what was done. It was the same with the Grand Chief, Sir Michael Somare. He has done everything already in bringing PNG into freedom by gaining independence, and so everyone born in PNG can live in freedom and peace. It's the same with Anzac Day—today, you remembered the lives of those who served Australia and laid down their lives so everyone born in Australia can enjoy the freedom of living in peace. And it is the same with the Son of God. He laid down His life so everyone who is born again in the kingdom of God can live in freedom and in peace. Jesus strongly stressed it Himself that He has given us peace to live in this world and be an overcomer.

Praise the Lord, whether we live in PNG, Australia or any part of the world. Jesus said, 'I come to serve and not to be served.' He laid down His life so everyone in this world we all live in who is born again can have freedom and live in peace.

So the message is this: Every day is the day that the Lord has made already for us to rejoice and be glad in it. The day has already been made new for us to enjoy that brand new 24 hours. We have a battle to face every day, but Jesus has given us peace to walk in victory and freedom.

December 8

~ Live happily, ever in peace with everyone ~

… but rejoice that your names are written in heaven (Luke 10:20, ESV).

November 15, 2021, I was thinking of a place that I always wanted to go and live in. Then it hit me hard that I was going to go and live in that place. Even though I didn't live there yet, I knew I was going to go soon and the joy and delight overflowed in me. The Holy Spirit opened my eyes to see the joy I was supposed to be experiencing now, knowing that very soon the Master will return to take me to heaven, should I not die and He returns.

Jesus came and lived our Father's name, Jehovah Shalom, our Almighty Father is our Peace. The peace He gave us before He left is for us to live in and be grateful and joyful, because it is not something the world can give, but is something that is of heavenly nature. We have to live in peace with everyone happily, knowing that very soon we will exit earth for heaven, and heaven is all about peace and joy.

For the kingdom of God is not a matter of eating and drinking but of righteousness and peace and joy in the Holy Spirit (Romans 14:17, ESV).

We have to welcome each day joyfully and live our Father's name, Jehovah Shalom, in Jesus' name, to the glory of the Father. Each new day is one day closer to exiting earth for heaven.

December 9

~ Peace and joy attracts each other ~

When the righteous are in authority, the people rejoice
(Proverbs 29:2, KJV).

When the righteous are in authority and rule peacefully, the people rejoice. Any dad can perform his role as a father and have authority over his family, but a good dad rules in peace. This is how his house is full of joy. The love he has for His Father in heaven gives him the joy to know more about Him in His Word. He prays until peace overflows in him.

Peace is one of the fruit of the Holy Spirit which gives you joy when you are able to produce it from within you. When you are at peace, you are in your own place of happiness, a place of prosperity. Joy is also a fruit of the Holy Spirit. When you are rejoicing, you think of no problems, troubles or worries of this world. Jesus lived our Father's name, Jehovah Shalom, our Almighty Father is our Peace. He showed the Father's love through His death that brought peace, and His resurrection gave us joy. That was what love can do. It brings forth peace and joy.

The thief comes only to steal and kill and destroy.
I came that they may have life and have it abundantly
(John 10:10, ESV).

We are now to live in authority over our day, every day, in showing the love of the Father by living our Father's name, Jehovah Shalom, and die to our old self so we can live a peaceful life and rise up in the new life of Christ that is full of joy. A life of abundance.

December 10

~ Kindness draws a peaceful atmosphere ~

Do not be overcome by evil, but overcome evil with good (Romans 12:21, ESV).

A good dad actions his faith with kindness to draw a peaceful environment so his family doesn't stumble in their path. He not only spends time finding his joy and peace in the Word of His Father in heaven, but he actions it in kindness. His aim and goal is to make Psalm 119:165 become his flesh.

Those who love your laws have great peace of heart and mind and do not stumble (Psalm 119:165, TLB).

His love is to live in the Word of God, and whatever he does must not destroy his relationship with His Father in heaven. The more we feed our spirit with the Word of God, the more the Spirit of God begins to work His perfect love over us and His love overflows, which causes us to desire and love His Word more, and so we do not get offended by the things of this world.

And may the Lord make your love for one another and for all people grow and overflow, just as our love for you overflows (1 Thessalonians 3:12, NLT).

Jesus lived our Father's name, Jehovah Shalom, our Almighty Father is our Peace. He is the Word who has become flesh. He was so kind and good to everyone in meeting their needs. He was kind with the right Words and it brought peace. God created the first man by working on the ground. Jesus created peace in writing on the ground when everyone was trying to stone the woman caught in the adulterous act (see John 8:1-11).

As manKIND we are to live each and every day with kindness. This is how we live in peace. We are to be kind to each other to bring peace to our surroundings. You live in peace with everyone when you action kindness to them. Peace and kindness are the fruit of love from the Holy Spirit. When you are kind to yourself you are at peace with yourself, and you can be at peace with others as well.

December 11

~ The blood of Jesus is security and peace ~

And so, dear brothers and sisters, we can boldly enter heaven's Most Holy Place because of the blood of Jesus (Hebrews 10:19, NLT).

To enter a special place, we need an access pass or some kind of password. Tom is a builder, and some of his wealthy clients live in millionaire's estates where the gates are remotely controlled with passwords. This is security. They want to live in peace. Sometimes on weekends, he takes us, the families, to go to the site to hang out with his clients while he finishes off what he needs to do. Every time we drive to those clients he gets out of the car, walks up to the gate, enters a password and the gate opens to give us access.

It is the same with the courts of God. We are to enter His gates with thanksgiving for the blood of Jesus, confessing that the blood of Jesus has set us free from sin so we can enter boldly into the presence and throne of God and lay down our requests. The access password into the courts of heaven is the 'blood of Jesus'. When we confess with our mouth that we are being bought with the blood of Jesus, we have access into the Holy Place of God. In the past, it was the blood sacrifice of the animals that the holy priest used to enter the holy place once a year. We are so blessed to have lived in the times where God sacrificed the living blood of His one and only Son so we can use it ANYTIME, ALL THE TIME and EVERY TIME we want to enter our Father's court room.

Jesus lived our Father's name, Jehovah Shalom, our Almighty Father is our Peace. Our Father loves us so much He wants us to return to Him and have a peaceful relationship with Him. The blood of Jesus restored that relationship and gave us access to live in the dwelling place of the Father, where there is peace. We can now freely enter the courts of God and decree the blood of Jesus that declares peace, and silence the accuser all the time when he wants to accuse us.

Like King David, this is the prayer of a good dad:

> *Better is one day in your courts than a thousand elsewhere;*
> *I would rather be a doorkeeper in the house of my God*
> *than dwell in the tents of the wicked (Psalm 84:10, NIV).*

Now with the blood of Jesus we can have access EVERY DAY to the courts of God. My encouragement to us all is *let's all make the most of the blood of Jesus and have access into the Holy Place of God every day.* This is the dwelling place of the almighty, where we can be safe (see Psalm 91). The blood of Jesus is our security and peace. The blood of Jesus is our birthright of the new holy life to live in the courts of God where there is peace.

December 12

~ The blood of Jesus not only silences the accuser, but declares peace as well ~

… and through him to reconcile to himself all things, whether things on earth or things in heaven, by making peace through his blood, shed on the cross (Colossians 1:20, NIV).

God is our loving Father, but when we approach Him in prayer on His throne we must remember His position as the righteous judge and approach Him in that manner. The reason is that the accuser, Satan devil, is there and he is accusing us of all those sins, some of which we may not be aware of, such as generational sin from our ancestors. This is why sometimes when we are praying hard to God for something, we hear whispers that give us doubts. This is the voice of Satan accusing us. And this is why we have to remember to approach our Father through the access of the blood of Jesus into His throne as the Judge, and silence Satan from accusing us (see Revelation 12:11).

Sometimes when my kids make a lot of noise, I silence them so there can be peace. This is also what the blood of Jesus does when we ask Him to silence the accuser. The blood of Jesus has paid the price to bring peace. There is life in the blood. When we ask the blood of Jesus to speak on our behalf, the blood silences the accuser and there is peace. It also reminds Satan that he is defeated and the blood cleanses us of our sin so Satan can't accuse us before the righteous Judge.

For the life of a creature is in the blood, and I have given it to you to make atonement for yourselves on the altar; it is the blood that makes atonement for one's life (Leviticus 17:11, NIV).

Every day, in Jesus' name, live the Father's name, Jehovah Shalom, our Almighty Father is our Peace. Jesus lived our Father's name and brought peace to us with His blood. We are now to live the Father's name and let the blood of Jesus speak for us to bring peace into every situation we will face.

December 13

~ *Peace is a person—He is Jesus, the 'Prince Of Peace'* ~

I have told you all this so that you may have peace in me. Here on earth you will have many trials and sorrows. But take heart, because I have overcome the world (John 16:33, NLT).

You have become victorious in life when nothing can offend you. To have peace is to have victory and joy. Have peace in your storms, in your sick bed and in every moment of life. As the psalmist says, 'Great peace have they who love your law and nothing can offend them,' (see Psalm 119:165). You house the living peace in you, the Holy Spirit. Living things grow and move. Peace is not just a living thing—it is a living LIFE—the new life in Jesus Christ.

I pray that God, the source of hope, will fill you completely with joy and peace because you trust in him. Then you will overflow with confident hope through the power of the Holy Spirit (Romans 15:13, NLT).

Jesus came and lived our Father's name, Jehovah Shalom, our Almighty Father is our Peace. Jesus is our Prince of Peace. His name is Emmanuel, God with us. Peace is a person, and He is Jesus. Peace is with us. When the peace of God comforts you in pain, you will feel the presence of someone and that is Jesus. The peace that the world gives will not give you rest, but the peace that the Word of God gives will give you rest and comfort.

Every day, live the Father's name, Jehovah Shalom, in Jesus' name. Find your peace in that day and happily go out and enjoy what the day has in store for you.

December 14

~ *Get vaccinated in the Word and be immune to sin* ~

> *I have said these things to you, that in me you may have peace. In the world you will have tribulation. But take heart; I have overcome the world (John 16:33, ESV).*

October 14, 2021, the Holy Spirit was opening my eyes to see how His vaccines work to make us immune to sin. His vaccine is to make us stronger to the next trial and suffering that awaits us. It's part of the journey of life that when we go through a test or trial we come out stronger, then we enter the next hard trial awaiting us, and so on and on. We are vaccinated in the Word to go through trials and tests to build our character in the nine fruit of the Holy Spirit. The vaccine of God is His faithful Word that stands forever and exists to build our character to be Christ-like. The Word we have hidden in our hearts will not make us sin (see Psalm 119:11).

This is the prayer of a good dad:

> *With all my heart I try to obey you. Don't let me break your commands. I have taken your words to heart so I would not sin against you (Psalm 119:10-11, NCV).*

In all our pains or storms we go through we need peace. Peace is our victory over any battles of our life. The blood of Jesus is our vaccine to every foreign sickness in our body. By His blood we have been cleansed from sin and healed from every sickness and disease.

> *… and through him to reconcile to himself all things, whether things on earth or things in heaven, by making peace through his blood, shed on the cross (Colossians 1:20, NIV).*

Jesus lived our Father's name Jehovah Shalom, our Almighty Father is our Peace. The pouring of His blood was to restore peace. His ever presence gives us peace. Before He left for the Father, He gave us peace, His peace is not like the one we find in the world. It's a special kind of peace that your feet will remain in, and it stops you from stumbling or falling when you walk through the shadow of death. Jesus is the peace and He was able to walk through death and make peace.

Every day, we are to keep our feet perfectly fit in peace and not come out of it, even though this fallen world continues to fall and shakes us. We are here to live our Father's name, Jehovah Shalom, in Jesus' name, to the glory of the Father. The vaccine from the Word will give us peace and keep us stable, victorious and stronger through every test, trial and suffering.

December 15

~ Write your own story of peace and live in it ~

> *But Jesus bent down and started to write on the ground with his finger (John 8:6, NIV).*

October 13, 2021, I was looking at a pen lying next to my devotional book and thought *I have to move this pen away, because if Blessed sees it, he might scribble on the book.* He'd never done that to my books, but I had seen him doing it to his sister's. This is what the Holy Spirit opened my eyes to teach me: You see, we have the hand print of our Father. He wrote a story for us, but the enemy comes to write over it and ruin it. The story of the woman caught in an adulterous act sounds so similar. God had a purpose for her and wrote a beautiful story for her, but the enemy possessed her and started writing her story. He scribbled on her and did what he wanted to do. She no longer lived the way she was originally scripted to, but started listening to the lies of the devil and lived an immoral life until she was caught in the act and dragged into the public to be seen.

Jesus came to give us life to live in peace. He lived the Father's name, Jehovah Shalom, our Almighty Father is our Peace. When there was roaring from the crowds for the woman to be stoned to death, Jesus wrote on the ground a new story for the woman, a new beginning of living in peace. He looked up on the crowd and asked if anyone who had never sinned would be the first to throw a stone on her. There was peace. Everyone left, starting from the elder. Jesus was the only one who was worthy enough to stone that woman, because He had never sinned, but He forgave her.

> *"Do not judge, and you will not be judged. Do not condemn, and you will not be condemned. Forgive, and you will be forgiven (Luke 6:37, NIV).*

We are to live our Father's name, Jehovah Shalom, our Almighty Father is our Peace. When someone is found guilty or is in the wrong position, we must reach out in forgiveness and make peace, because only Jesus is worthy and He has forgiven us all. We are all sinners and have fallen short of the glory of the Father.

Every day, live your own story of peace and never allow the devil to use his pen to scribble over you with his chaotic stories of lies from this evil world.

December 16

~ Live in the peace Jesus leaves with you ~

Peace I leave with you; my peace I give you
(John 14:27, NIV).

One beautiful spring night, October 18, 2021, I was in my early trimester of pregnancy. The Lord showed me how I was carrying a life in me, and how we too carry a life in us when we receive Jesus into us. All being well, it would normally take nine months for my baby Christos to become a full image of us and for us to see her, and so it is with the life in Christ. It will take of us to be fully walking and matured in the nine fruit of the Holy Spirit for Christ to become fully developed in us so people can see Christ in us.

You see, because I had my baby Christos in me, I was so aware of what I was doing and the activities I got myself involved in. I didn't want to do anything to terminate the life forming in its early development within me. When we carry the life of Jesus around, we also have to be cautious of every activity we get ourselves involved in. It is peace that the life of Jesus has to live in. We have to walk and live in peace. The food that Jesus would live daily is the Word that comes from the mouth of our Father. This is the food that we have to feed on daily so Christ can become big and we become less.

Don't worry about anything, but pray about everything.
With thankful hearts offer up your prayers and requests
to God. Then, because you belong to Christ Jesus, God

> *will bless you with peace that no one can completely understand. And this peace will control the way you think and feel (Philippians 4:6-7, CEV).*

Jesus lived our Father's name, Jehovah Shalom, our Almighty Father is our Peace. Every Word that comes out of our Father is love, to make us live in peace whether we have what we want or not. Jesus lived and made peace through the suffering He went through so we can live a life of peace. This is the life He gave us and this is the life we carry within us.

December 17

~ Wait patiently in peace in the quest of life as you wait upon the Lord ~

> *Wait for the Lord; be strong and take heart and wait for the Lord (Psalm 27:14, NIV).*

October 11, 2021, I was at the post office to post some books. I had the addresses, but not the phone numbers of the recipients I was going to post my books to. I stopped to message my costumers for their numbers, but they never got back to me. *That's fine,* I thought, *I will just go ahead and see if I can post without providing their number.* Because I'd paid the postage already, I just had to go ahead of the line and get served, but then I thought *no, I will wait on the queue because I need some time to hear from them.*

This is what I heard the Holy Spirit say on waiting upon The Lord: You see, when you are waiting on the Lord to receive from Him, take your time in enjoying what you have while waiting. Earth is your waiting place to be called to go to heaven. Just like I was waiting in the queue and didn't want to rush because I needed some outstanding information, also wait and do not rush in life, for you will always get what you are waiting for.

A life of peace while waiting patiently and faithfully is the life Jesus wants us to live, and that's why He gave us peace to live in it in this world. He has gone back to the Father, but He lived the name of the Father, Jehovah Shalom, our Almighty Father is our Peace. He is peace and He gave us the name of the Father, and wants us to also live our loving Father's name.

Each and every day, as we wait in the queue line of life, let's live the life of peace while waiting for our names to be called to enter life through death. When we die, we will enter peacefully into our resting place while waiting for our Prince of Peace, Jesus, to peacefully take us home. While we are alive, let's practice living peacefully.

December 18

~ Trusting God's Word for peace ~

Agree with God, and be at peace; thereby good will come to you. Receive instruction from his mouth, and lay up his words in your heart (Job 22:21-22, ESV).

Many times, I find Tom just agrees with me because he wants peace in the moment. Many wives would agree with me on this, that they can talk about things they are interested in with enthusiasm, only to discover their husband is not interested, but will just agree because they know this will keep their wives at peace.

A good dad is obedient to His Father in heaven, and agrees with every word that comes out of His Father's mouth. God's Word will keep him at peace because he knows His Father, and knows

He always does what He says He will do. He has developed a trust upon the Father's love. He knows that the more you spend time with someone, the more you know about their nature or character. As he spends more time in Word and prayer with the Father, he comes to know how trustworthy our Father in heaven is. He can depend entirely on Him without giving up, because the time he has spent with the Father has built his faith muscles to be strong and renewed. He has faith to place his hope in God.

The more his situations get chaotic, the more he trusts the Father's peace to drown his chaotic situations. Peace like a river, trust like a mountain, with the love of an ocean—this is his place of happiness and joy of how he views his Almighty Father. The trust he has for the Father's love, joy and peace is like a mountain—unmovable and unshakeable.

> *Those who trust in the Lord are like Mount Zion, which cannot be shaken but endures forever (Psalm 125:1, NIV).*

No problems and worries can shake away his faith. His mind is regularly renewed in the peace of God.

> *You will keep in perfect peace those whose minds are steadfast, because they trust in you. Trust in the LORD forever, for the LORD, the LORD himself, is the Rock eternal (Isaiah 26:3-4, NIV).*

God keeps us in perfect peace through His perfect love, the Holy Spirit. The more we put our trust in God, the more we perfectly feel at peace with the peace from the Holy Spirit. We have the mind of Christ (see 1 Corinthians 2:16), and we have the mind of peace. Jesus has lived our Father's name, Jehovah Shalom, our Almighty Father is our Peace, so we can now live His name by the fruit of peace that the Holy Spirit produces in us.

December 19

~ A heart of peace walks in peace ~

The Spirit of the Lord God is upon me, because the Lord has anointed me to bring good news to the poor; he has sent me to bind up the brokenhearted, to proclaim liberty to the captives, and the opening of the prison to those who are bound (Isaiah 61:1, ESV).

One morning, October 8, 2021, after I finished making fresh juice I cleaned the juice machine. As I removed all the parts and washed it, I noticed how the machine looked all broken into different pieces. The Holy Spirit opened my eyes to see how when we too are broken, it is a time where our loving Father can easily clean and wash us up. As it is written clearly, the brokenhearted are close to God. David was a man after God's heart, because he was broken all the time for all the sins he committed. Even though he walked closely with God, he showed how imperfect he was by falling into sin many times and going back to God with a broken heart of repentance.

Like David, this is the prayer of a good dad:

Have mercy on me, O God, according to your unfailing love; according to your great compassion blot out my transgressions. Wash away all my iniquity and cleanse me from my sin. For I know my transgressions, and my sin is always before me. Against you, you only, have I sinned and done what is evil in your sight; so you are right in your verdict and justified when you judge. Surely I was sinful at birth, sinful from the time my mother conceived me. Yet you desired faithfulness even in the womb; you taught me wisdom in that secret place. Cleanse me

> *with hyssop, and I will be clean; wash me, and I will be whiter than snow. Let me hear joy and gladness; let the bones you have crushed rejoice. Hide your face from my sins and blot out all my iniquity. Create in me a pure heart, O God, and renew a steadfast spirit within me. Do not cast me from your presence or take your Holy Spirit from me. Restore to me the joy of your salvation and grant me a willing spirit, to sustain me (Psalm 51:1-12, NIV).*

You see, I took the fruit machine apart, making it look all broken into pieces to clean them, and then put them back together so it would be ready to serve its purpose. So it is with our Father. When we go to Him in brokenness, He takes all our pieces, washes us clean and sets us apart to be holy for His purpose. Jesus lived our Father's name, Jehovah Shalom, our Almighty Father is our Peace. He is the peace of God. The Prince of Peace. He was broken for our sins to bring peace into our life. He made peace with our old selfish 'Me it is' life (see Ephesians 2:15).

Our brokenness is now healed in the peaceful nature of Christ life that the Holy Spirit produces in us. Every day, the Holy Spirit is setting us apart to be holy and ready to serve our purpose. One of our purposes is to walk in peace. This is where our feet connect to our heart, a heart of peace that walks in peace.

December 20

~ There is eternal peace when we connect back to our Father's love ~

> *For I am sure that neither death nor life, nor angels nor rulers, nor things present nor things to come, nor powers,*

nor height nor depth, nor anything else in all creation, will be able to separate us from the love of God in Christ Jesus our Lord (Romans 8:38-39, ESV).

One beautiful night, October 10, 2021, the Holy Spirit showed me through a gift box I had how beautiful the love of the Father is, and that nothing can separate us from that love—not even demons, angels, life or death, future, present or any power. No one and nothing. I was looking at this beautiful gift, a pretty notebook designed beautifully with its cards. I thought to myself, and told my family, *look at these cards with the address notebook. It's so lovely I just don't want to use it. If I use the cards and give them away, I will be left only with the notebook. They are meant to be together to show-off their beauty.*

This is when the Holy Spirit opened my eyes to see the Father's love: Jesus gave you the most beautiful gift of His perfect abundant life. His life is designed to connect to you to make your life beautiful and worth living. You have the notebook, beautifully designed with its package of cards. Separating it by using up all the cards won't show the complete beauty of its connection to the notebook. So it is with you. You are designed to connect to the Love of God, Jesus, and complete His love. Life without Jesus is meaningless and incomplete. You can't live without God's love. When you connect into God's love and complete His love, nothing will separate you from God's love. Just like how you see the beautiful picture of the gift box that contains the cards and its notebook, God sees a complete, beautiful image of His love completing you. He even showed us by raising up Jesus from death through the power of His Spirit, because not even death will separate us from His love.

No one has ever seen God; but if we love one another, God lives in us and his love is made complete in us (1 John 4:12, NIV).

One of the beautiful gifts Jesus gave us is His peace. Not the peace that the world has given, but the peace that His Word gives. That peace we receive for loving Him, the Word who has become flesh (see John 1:14). It's this peace that bonds us in His love.

Jesus lived our Father's name, Jehovah Shalom, our Almighty Father is our Peace. Every day, we are to live the name of our Father, Jehovah Shalom, and walk in peace from His love. Nothing can ever separate us from the love of the Father that we walk in every day, and nothing can even separate our loved ones from us if we bring them with us to walk this journey of life in the Father's love.

December 21

~ A life of abundance is a life full of peace ~

Have your roots planted deep in Christ. Grow in Him. Get your strength from Him. Let Him make you strong in the faith as you have been taught. Your life should be full of thanks to Him (Colossians 2:7, NLV).

October 6, 2021, I was eating a cup of spicy noodles. My two-and-half-year-old then, wanted it, but because it was spicy, I explained that to him and told him no. But he kept insisting, so I gave it to him. As soon as he tasted it he gave this look of hating it. The spicy part of it had really burnt his mouth.

This is what the Holy Spirit taught me: God says no to many things we want in life, but we keep asking and wanting those things. Then when he allows us to taste it, we see and realise how burnt-out we become in it. There are many children raised by Christian parents, but they want to taste the world and so they slip out to try out the stuff of the world. However, the fear and Love of the

Lord that these children were raised in will always bring them back to God. The story of the prodigal son illustrates this well (see Luke 15:11-32). One of the reasons God says NO to some of the things we want is because they are things the enemy will easily access to destroy us if we are not rooted strongly in the Word. Just as much as I wanted my two-year-old to have the spicy noodles, I couldn't allow him to because he was not big and strong enough to handle the spiciest part of it that would burn his mouth.

At the right time, God allowed Jesus to come into the World and destroy the work of Satan. Jesus lived our loving Father's name, Jehovah Shalom, our Almighty Father is our Peace. The devil has easy access to our old rebellious self, and this is how he can easily destroy us. Jesus came and made peace with this old self. He healed that old self with peace. He gave us peace so our hearts will not be troubled in this chaotic, unstable world. It's the peace of Jesus that will always keep us calm so that we are healed in Jesus' name. The doctor's report can say you have an incurable sickness, but the peace of Jesus that the Holy Spirit produces in you will calm you, because you know that your loving Father is your healer.

Every day is a new day to remind our old self to live in peace with the new life in Christ. When we walk in peace, we not only live our Father's name, but we are walking in His love and living the life of abundance.

December 22

~ When goodness conquers evilness, peace is restored ~

If anyone, then, knows the good they ought to do and doesn't do it, it is sin for them (James 4:17, NIV).

Procrastinating is a bad habit. On the morning of October 8, 2021, I was trying to juice some celery I'd left in a bowl. Now, that celery had been outside there for a week. I kept saying I would juice it the next day, but when the next day and the next day came, I never did anything, until I realised my procrastinating would cause the celery to go bad. This is what the Holy Spirit taught me: You see, when you continually postpone doing something good in your life, nothing good happens in your life. If there is something good in your mind that you think of doing, and if you are able to do it, then go ahead and do it.

> *Be very careful, then, how you live—not as unwise but as wise, making the most of every opportunity, because the days are evil (Ephesians 5:15-16, NIV).*

In this world where evil surrounds us, we cannot procrastinate goodness, because evilness is rising all the time. It may be a small, simple act of goodness, but it has a big effect towards the evil kingdom. Jesus lived our Father's name, Jehovah Shalom, our Almighty Father is our Peace. He defeated and destroyed the work of evilness once and for all with His precious blood. His blood brings peace and is the good news to save us all from sin and evilness. We are trapped in our evil desires, but now we can be set free because Jesus has made peace with our selfish, rebellious life to live in peace with the abundance of the goodness found in our new life.

Every new day brings new opportunities to do that good thing and decrease the work of evil. When goodness increases, evil decreases and peace is present.

December 23

~ The peace of God gives us strength to make it through this world ~

In peace I will lie down and sleep, for you alone, Lord, make me dwell in safety (Psalm 4:8, NIV).

July 22, 2021, as I was trying to fall asleep, I realised how tired I felt. When I was just about to doze off to sleep, I heard the Holy Spirit say: This is how you are supposed to feel towards unrighteous and ungodly things of this world. You should be feeling so tired and be at peace and rest towards it. This was what Jesus came for—to create peace with your old self that was born into this world.

A good dad is the strength for his house because he rests his old self and puts it to peace every time it tries to take its position of the rebellious 'it is me' life. He uses his strength in the Word and does all things through Christ, who strengthens him to create peace.

> *'Do not be afraid, you who are highly esteemed,' he said. 'Peace! Be strong now; be strong.' When he spoke to me, I was strengthened and said, 'Speak, my lord, since you have given me strength.' (Daniel 10:19, NIV).*

Jesus lived our Father's name, Jehovah Shalom, our Almighty Father is our Peace. He was the peace of the Father, the Prince of Peace. Emmanuel is His name. God with us, Peace with us. Jesus told us, 'Peace I leave with you.' The peace is now produced by the Holy Spirit who lives in us.

Every day is another day to rise up and live our Father's name, and put to rest and make peace with our old self nature that wants to be alive and rebellious.

December 24

~ *Fit your feet with peace before you walk* ~

> *Let the peace of Christ rule in your hearts, since as members of one body you were called to peace. And be thankful (Colossians 3:15, NIV).*

Before someone dies, they give out their blessings to their loved ones. Before Jesus died, He released His blessings to His disciples by washing their feet. He blessed them with PEACE. He was the Prince of Peace, the Peacemaker from God. Blessed are the peacemakers, for they will be called children of God (see Matthew 5:9). He made peace for His disciples and told them to do it to others. He gave us the Holy Spirit to continue His ministry of making peace. Peace is one of the fruit of the Holy Spirit that we have to produce in this chaotic world where we live in. Why did Jesus choose our feet for peace? You see, when we are angry we rush off with our feet to let our frustrations out on whoever angers us. The whole idea is for our feet to walk in peace and not in a hurry to make war. Ephesians 6:15 tells us to fit our feet with the gospel of peace when we put on the amour of God.

A good dad learns and follows everything from his loving Father in heaven. He is slow in anger. He may get angry, but there is patience in his anger, and so he is slow to anger and is able to make peace in every situation that could cause his anger to rise. Jehovah Shalom, our Lord God, our Peace is the name of our Father in which Jesus lived. We too, as children of God, are to live our Father's name, Jehovah Shalom, and be peacemakers.

Every day is a new day to produce the fruit of the Holy Spirit, peace. Being productive in the making of peace is what we are called to do as a child of Jehovah.

December 25

~ Put to peace your old life every time it rises to have its own way ~

There is a way that appears to be right, but in the end it leads to death (Proverbs 14:12, NIV).

March 10, 2021, I was driving a rental car with Victorian licence plates in New South Wales (NSW) when I drove the wrong way into a 'one way' lane and nearly got bumped by a car coming through the other way. We didn't do the right thing—the other car did. The driver, looking at our plate number, realised it was from another state and smiled. So instead of being angry towards us, she was friendly, understanding we were new in the area because of the plate number of the car. This is what the Holy Spirit taught me: The kingdom of God is like this. Jesus is the only way to the Father. When you come out of this world to go into the WORD who is Jesus, you become new. The old you lifestyle will keep coming out of you, trying to go back the way you left but are not supposed to enter. Going towards the only way in Christ with your new life is the way you are supposed to be. You will bump and clash with yourself when you allow the 'old you' to come out and live, because your 'old you' will want to go back to where it used to be.

You see, it's like the rental car from another state that I drove the wrong way. When your 'old me' life wants to keep being alive and move with your new life, you will bump into each other. Your new life in Christ goes through the only way to the Father, and when your old self-centred life of this world rises up too and tries to move and live, it faces against the way your new life is travelling, causing a collision.

A good dad will always make peace from his new life in the Prince of Peace, Jesus Christ, to his old self-centred lifestyle. Whenever his 'old me' wants to come and live, he puts him to rest in peace and rises up in the new life of Christ and continues to move towards the Father, in Jesus, who is the only way. Our Father in heaven has a name that He wants us to live and move in every day. He is Jehovah Shalom, our Lord God is our Peace. Jesus lived our Father's name; He is our Prince of Peace. Jesus' name is the only name that gives us access to receiving everything the Father has in store for us. Our name is called for peace, to move and live in peace as children of God.

> *Let the peace of Christ rule in your hearts, since as members of one body you were called to peace. And be thankful (Colossians 3:15, NIV).*

See every birth of your new day as the day Jesus was born for you. The birth of Jesus is the birthday of Love, where all creations of nature were at peace and heaven was rejoicing. Peace and Joy celebrate the arrival of Love. Every day, we are to be born again in love and celebrate in peace and joy, and let go of our old rebellious life.

December 26

~ Peace is an inside job by the Holy Spirit ~

> *Grace, mercy, and peace will be with us, from God the Father and from Jesus Christ the Father's Son, in truth and love (2 John 1:3, ESV).*

A good dad has a good relationship with His Father in heaven, so whenever he needs a solution to a problem he goes within, not outside, to solve that problem. Like David, he prays, 'Create in me a new heart, O God, and renew a steadfast spirit within me,' (see Psalm 51:10). Real change is an inside job. Once the inside job is done, the outside problem will be fixed.

You might alter things for a day or two with money and systems, but the heart is what matters, and always will be the matter of the heart. Peace reigns when the heart is at rest in the matters of God. A good dad's goal is for peace, who is Jesus, to reign in his heart, and so he makes sure the Word in His HEART becomes his STRENGTH in his flesh by renewing his mind, his SOUL and WILL in the Word. This is how he shows he loves his loving Father in heaven with all his heart, soul and strength.

> *And let the peace of Christ rule in your hearts, to which indeed you were called in one body. And be thankful (Colossians 3:15, ESV).*

Jesus, Prince of Peace, rules and reigns with the Father and we rule with Him also. He lives the Father's name, Jehovah Shalom, our Lord God, our Peace. Jesus loves the Father as much as the Father loves Him too. Jesus has given us His peace through the Holy Spirit who is inside us. Peace is an inside job by the Holy Spirit who produces it.

> *My covenant was with him, a covenant of life and peace, and I gave them to him; this called for reverence and he revered me and stood in awe of my name. True instruction was in his mouth and nothing false was found on his lips. He walked with me in peace and uprightness, and turned many from sin (Malachi 2:5-6, NIV).*

Rule and reign with the Prince of Peace, Jesus, in your new day and live in peace with everyone.

December 27

~ The devil is looking for opportunities to steal your peace with Jesus ~

> *The Lord gives perfect peace to those whose faith is firm (Isaiah 26:3, CEV).*

One morning, March 31, 2021, the Holy Spirit pointed out to me where often I would pass certain people, strangers, people I don't know, and start thinking all kinds of unkind thoughts towards them, mainly because of the way they dress, especially when they are dressed in almost nudity. This is actually the work of the enemy who wants to steal the peace of Christ. Peace is the presence of Jesus, and this is what the devil doesn't want. He doesn't want to see you move around in the presence of Jesus. You see, we are to live a quiet life of minding our own business, and not look on how other people live their lives.

> *First of all, I ask that you pray for all people. Ask God to bless them and give them what they need. And give thanks. You should pray for rulers and for all who have authority. Pray for these leaders so that we can live quiet and peaceful lives—lives full of devotion to God and respect for him. This is good and pleases God our Savior (1 Timothy 2:1-3, ERV).*

A good dad knows that Peace is a present thing and it is the presence of Jesus. Peace is a person. Jesus is peace. Jesus lived the Father's name, Jehovah Shalom, our Lord God is our Peace, and became peace. Whatever he does, a good dad ensures that he safely guides his peace with the Word of God, and before he displays his anger, he ensures that peace is with him before he says or does anything.

> *Following after the Holy Spirit leads to life and peace, but following after the old nature leads to death (Romans 8:6, TLB).*

Jesus is now the present peace through the Holy Spirit who resurrected His life. The devil tries hard to stop us from taking the Word into us, because once we receive into us the Word he cannot take it from us. The Word is Jesus, and He can't take Jesus from us.

Each day, live the Father's name, Jehovah Shalom, in Jesus' name and make it as peaceful as ever.

December 28

~ Keep peace with you through every life challenge ~

As pressure and stress bear down on me, I find joy in your commands (Psalm 119:143, NLT).

One night, March 31, 2021, Angelilly was telling me she felt so itchy when I rubbed a special myrrh oil treatment over her boil and blister. I told her that was a good sign, as it showed the oil was working on her skin. This is what the Holy Spirit taught me: The kingdom of God is like this. When the Word of God is working in you to build up your character to become Christ-like, you will go through many situations and life challenges. This is so the Word of God working in you can become flesh. You see, the oil will make the flesh of Angelilly be restored, so is the Word of God working within you—it will bring you back to your original nature that God designed you to be.

A good dad works on his relationship with His Father in heaven to restore himself back to the original design he was made for. He sits in the Word and in prayer to build himself in the characters of Christ. Regardless of facing challenges or whatever stirring of storms in life, he has the peace of Christ in the Word. To be like His Father in heaven and live His name, Jehovah Shalom, he has to remain in peace and be calm and peaceful in all the storms of life. He knows the truth—that you're either in a trial right now, just coming out of one, or heading towards the next one. And so, he has to keep peace handy within him all the time.

Jesus came and lived our Father's name, Jehovah Shalom, our Lord God is our Peace. He is our peacemaker, and in His name He has blessed us to be peacemakers to live our Father's name, Jehovah Shalom. Live your day in peace with each other and make peace in any situation and life challenges that want to put you down.

December 29

~ As peacemakers, always walk to create peace where you set your foot ~

...and do your best to live at peace with everyone (Romans 12:18, CEV).

March 17, 2021, I drove home and saw someone parking right in front of my driveway. Anger made its way through me before I could think properly. I thought *I am going to go in the house and get a pen and paper and stick it on his/her car to tell him/her not to park on people's driveways.* I parked quickly and rushed on with my 'two legs' to do what I planned to do. This is what the Holy Spirit taught me: You were praying to sow righteousness, the fruit of righteousness of the Holy Spirit. This is now the right time for you to sow patience and self-control. I stopped instantly, repented and thanked the Lord, and the Lord said, 'You see, you now reap peace. Peace is what you will reap instantly. And this is how you build your characters in Christ.'

The Holy Spirit reminded me of Jesus washing the feet of His disciples. He washed their feet to walk in peace. It's our feet that carry us to rush off and do something when we are angry. In my case, I was angry and rushing off with my feet to get a pen and paper.

A good dad sows the fruit of righteousness from the Holy Spirit in his everyday life for everyone he is in contact with. For him to do it well, he remains connected to His Father in heaven every day. He cannot lose His Father-child relationship with His Father if he wants to be a good dad to his children, and so he remains connected in Word and prayer to the Father every day. The peace he inherited from His Father in the Holy Spirit is what he sows into any situation that wants to steal his peace.

> *Now that I, your Lord and Teacher, have washed your feet, you also should wash one another's feet. I have set you an example that you should do as I have done for you (John 13:14-15, NIV).*

As we rise up in the morning, we must make sure our heart connects peace to our feet to walk on, and joy to our hands to give cheerfully the fruit of the Holy Spirit to those who are in need.

December 30

~ Sow peace to reap peace ~

> *Peace I leave with you; my peace I give you. I do not give to you as the world gives. Do not let your hearts be troubled and do not be afraid (John 14:27, NIV).*

A good dad knows that in order to be rich and wealthy with His Father's riches, he has to be in a right position of giving. He will only move His Father's hand with giving. God loves the world and demonstrated the power of sowing into this world by giving His only Son so He can receive many sons. A good dad sows peace and joy into his household so he can reap peace and joy from his household. Everyone wants to be rich and wealthy so they can be at peace and full of joy and enjoy their wealth. A good dad sows joy and peace by demonstrating his love to his family.

As the body of Christ, what part of our body we use in doing good is how our Father will move towards us with blessings. When we cheerfully give with our hands, our Father too, cheerfully moves His hands with blessings into our hands. The hands of the Father are so big that our little hands cannot contain the measure of what we receive from Him. The blessing we receive from what we gave will overflow in us (see Luke 6:38). If we sow peace, we reap an overflow of peace. We can also sow finance towards the work of the Lord and reap overflowing finances. What we sow, that we will reap.

Our Father in heaven, Jehovah Shalom, our Lord God, our Peace, sows into this world His only Prince of Peace, His Son, Jesus, so our old rebellious self can be at peace with our new Christ-like life. Jesus lived our Father's name, Jehovah Shalom, and left that peace with us and returned to our Father in heaven. Our Father sowed peace and He reaped peace in the finished work of the cross.

> *... by setting aside in his flesh the law with its commands and regulations. His purpose was to create in himself one new humanity out of the two, thus making peace (Ephesians 2:15, NIV).*

Make peace from your new peaceful life in Christ to your old self-centred life every time it arises with its negative vibes towards things around you.

December 31

~ Rest in the eternal peace of the Word in this temporary world ~

In peace I will both lie down and sleep; for you alone, O Lord, make me dwell in safety (Psalm 4:8, ESV).

November 11, 2022, around midday, after putting my five-month-old baby to sleep, I sat down to do some work on the laptop. Blessed, my three-year-old, came to me and said, 'Mum, I made noise, but Christos didn't wake up.' It was the last thing I wanted to hear, because I wanted Christos to sleep so I could do some work. This is what the Lord opened my eyes to see: Blessed made noise, but Christos was still sleeping peacefully. This is what we too should do. Even when there are disturbing voices around, we should be resting peacefully in Christ. Jesus said, 'I gave you peace not as the world gives.' Even though we are in the world, we must be at peace, because we are resting in the peace Christ gave. Jesus was telling us that only His peace can keep our mind and heart calm in this chaotic world where evil is rising up all the time.

Jesus lived our Father's name, Jehovah Shalom, our Almighty Father is our peace. He is the way, the truth and life to give us a life full of peace in this world of fear. Blessed made noise but Christos didn't wake up. There will always be a voice that makes noise to purposely disturb your peace, don't wake up to it. Rest peacefully in the love of the Father that Jesus gave to you in the peace He provided. Like Jesus, we have to sleep through our storm.

> *Suddenly a furious storm came up on the lake, so that the waves swept over the boat. But Jesus was sleeping (Matthew 8:24, NIV).*

Every day, there will always be a storm coming our way. Rise up and live the Father's name, Jehovah Shalom, in Jesus' name. And rest in the peace that Jesus gave through the Holy Spirit within you.